BUT WHERE IS LOVE?

BUT WHERE IS LOVE?

A NOVEL BY

ABBE LANE

A DOVE BOOK

WARNER BOOKS

A Time Warner Company

Warner Books, Inc., 1271 Avenue of the Americas, New York, NY 10020

 A Time Warner Company

Printed in the United States of America
First Printing: February 1993
10 9 8 7 6 5 4 3 2 1

LIBRARY OF CONGRESS CATALOGING-IN-PUBLICATION DATA

Lane, Abbe.
    But where is love? / Abbe Lane.
      p.   cm.
    ISBN 0-446-51598-1
    I. Title.
PS3562.A4837B87   1993
813'.54—dc20   92-50176
                                                          CIP

Book design by Giorgetta Bell McRee

I am deeply grateful to my publisher and editor Nanscy Neiman for her encouragement and support. Her unfailing belief in me carried me through difficult times. I respect her wisdom and treasure our friendship.

Heartfelt thanks to Michael Viner for introducing me to my dear Nanscy.

BUT WHERE IS LOVE?

PROLOGUE

Julie sat huddled on the bed, trying to sort out her life. She hadn't eaten or slept in the last thirty-six hours, but she ignored the alarms sounded by her body. She was desperate.

"Oh, God," she cried. "Please help me. Show me what to do."

Only moments ago she'd actually thought of ending it all, actually thought about how easy it would be to find freedom . . . freedom from guilt, responsibility, frustration, pain . . . by a simple step over the railing of the balcony outside her bedroom. She tensed in anguish. She wasn't a coward to take that way out. And she couldn't bear the thought of what such an act would do to her parents.

Our poor baby, they would cry. Why didn't she turn to us?

And Paco. Paco, the cause of so much of this pain. The cause of this crisis. He would be shocked, perhaps even really hurt and sad, but in a short time he would be over it and replace her. That was his style.

The newspapers would have a field day with the story. The press would speculate, invent, titillating readers, then dropping the story the second a hotter one came along.

She felt boxed in, alone with no one to turn to, as she had been for these last ten years, as she had been last night when this latest crisis came to full boil.

It was their closing in Pittsburgh, and they'd just finished the first of their two nightly shows. They were destined for Vegas after their next stop on the tour, Chicago.

The moment Julie had shut the door of her dreary dressing room against backstage visitors and the rest of the cast, she'd begun to weep. She couldn't shake off her feelings of depression and fear. And she was terrified that Paco would barge in any second. He was pushing her too hard, too cruelly. Dear God, what would happen if she lost control?

She didn't have long to ponder the question for, as she feared, Paco banged open the door. He was in a nasty mood, and Julie shuddered.

"What are you doing in that robe, for Christ's sake? Get dressed. I'm hungry and we don't have much time."

Without a word Julie snatched the street clothes she'd laid out before the show and fled into the bathroom. Full of dread at being with Paco, she frantically tried to think of what she could do to protect herself. If they weren't alone together . . .

"I'm going to ask Lita and Ramon to join us," she called out. Before Paco could protest she quickly rapped on the wall separating their dressing rooms. "Hey, kids, want to grab a bite to eat now?"

"Sure," Lita sang out.

"You'd better hurry your amigos next door," Paco snarled. He grabbed his coat and strode out the back exit into the parking lot.

Paco didn't want Julie to have any friends, especially male friends, but Ramon and Lita were a good dance team, and he put up with their affection for his wife for the good of his show. His irritability and temper had worsened over the last few years to the point that he terrorized his musicians and performers. And all of them felt protective of Julie because they knew she bore the brunt of it. Paco's possessiveness and jealousy of his gorgeous and talented young wife went beyond all bounds, frightening and angering everyone who cared about Julie.

Now Julie rushed, not daring to provoke her husband, who obviously was spoiling for a fight. When she joined him outside, he was gunning the motor of their Rolls-Royce. Lita and Ramon were not far behind her, and after they slid into the backseat, Paco turned and in his sarcastic manner asked, "Are you two here to keep my dear wife company or just tagging along for your usual free meal?"

Lita glanced nervously at her husband, whose fists were tightly clenched. Paco had been goading them unbearably these last few weeks, and she was concerned that Ramon's hard won control over his temper might snap.

"We don't need your free meal, Paco," Ramon said angrily. "If it weren't for Julie, we wouldn't be here." Ramon's eyes were blazing.

Julie flinched. Ordinarily Ramon was respectful and wouldn't even have dreamed of speaking to Paco that way.

Tires squealing, Paco barreled onto the highway. "Well, Julie," he said, "it looks as if your friends would like to work for someone else, eh? I think that can be arranged." He floored the accelerator and, over Julie's pleas to slow down, continued to drive fast and recklessly.

Paco's antagonism toward everyone, including the couple in the backseat, had been growing for months. "Dammit," he cursed. "I'm sick of having these two around all the time." He took his eyes off the road and glared at Julie. "They've been putting ideas in your head and don't think I don't know it."

Just then they reached the restaurant and Paco slammed on the brakes. He got out and yanked open the back door. "Get the hell out," he yelled at Lita and Ramon. As Julie moved around the car to follow her friends who were racing up the steps of the restaurant, Paco clutched her arm.

"Don't you dare go near those bums," he screamed as he jerked her roughly to him. "That cheap dancer probably wants to screw you. I can see that he's got the hots for you."

Julie pulled herself free and ran to Lita, who was waiting while Ramon called a cab. Ignoring anyone who might be listening or watching, Paco reached for Julie, pulling her inside the restaurant, then toward an empty booth.

"Let those bastards go and you sit down here."

Julie glanced around nervously, praying that no one would pay attention to him. "What's wrong with you? Why are you in such a vile mood and saying such horrible things?"

"Because, my dear, you are too stupid to realize what they're up to. But they can't fool me!"

"They haven't done a damn thing. They've been good friends to me and they help me to deal with my loneliness."

This remark only infuriated Paco more. "Why the hell should you be lonely? You've got me. No, Julie. I know what's been going through your head. For years you've been dreaming about some young macho stud who would take you away from me. But forget it. That's not going to happen."

With this remark he grabbed her mouth with the fingers of his large hand and squeezed her lips so hard that tears poured from her eyes.

When he finally let go, she felt hot pains in her mouth and cheeks, but the humiliation was almost worse, and she lowered her head in shame. Finished with his call, Ramon glanced over to where they were sitting, and, when he saw the marks on Julie's face, he exploded. Lita tried unsuccessfully to restrain him. He ran over to the booth and pulled Paco to his feet, pushing him against the wall.

"You dirty old bastard, what have you done to her?"

People who had been listening to Paco sensed there might be trouble and got up from their tables. The manager, who had been summoned by one of the waiters, rushed out from the back to see what was wrong.

"Ramon," Julie pleaded. "Stop it. Don't hit him. He isn't worth it. You'll go to jail."

Ramon stood there for a moment, clenching Paco's jacket, itching to hit him. Then, heeding Julie's pleas, he released Paco and shoved him toward the door. By now a crowd had gathered.

Realizing that he was no physical match for Ramon, Paco anxiously pushed his way through the crowd and ran outside to safety. When Julie reached the street tears were streaming down her face and her body was trembling. *Why had she asked Ramon and Lita to join her in the first place?*

Touching her face, she could feel her mouth starting to swell. *How the hell am I going to do another show?* she wondered, panic setting in.

Paco ran down the steps and was into the car before Ramon could reach him. Taking off quickly, he left Julie, Lita, and Ramon standing in front of the restaurant.

As they waited for the taxi to arrive, Ramon remarked angrily, "Julie, I don't know why you continue to put up with him. Someone should teach that bastard a lesson. How I wish it could be me."

A few minutes later, the three of them piled into the cab and arrived back at the club just in time to prepare for the second show.

As Julie entered the back door, she prayed that Paco would not be in the dressing room. Sharing a room with him was bad enough in good times . . . Lita and Ramon quickly ducked into their dressing room, hoping to avoid another scene. If they could just keep out of Paco's way before the show, then it would be easy for them to pack up while he was still onstage and leave unnoticed.

Julie opened the door tentatively and peeked inside. Luck was with her. The room was empty. *Thank God for that,* she thought. Now she could compose herself and, she hoped, fix her face. But she wasn't prepared for what she saw in the mirror. The imprint of Paco's fingers were turning to bruises that were so dark and so red she knew that no amount of makeup would cover them completely. Desperately, she tried to make herself presentable, when suddenly the door opened and Paco stormed in.

Leaning over her menacingly, he threatened, "If I ever see you talking to those *hijos de putas* again, I'll fix them so they'll never dance. You know I've got friends in Las Vegas who can handle scum like them."

Julie whirled around to face him. "Paco, shut up and leave me alone. Instead of threatening people, why don't you take a good look at my face and tell me how in God's name I'm going to do the next show?"

"Why didn't you think of that before you got me angry," he shouted.

"It takes very little to set you off, Paco, and if you must know, I'm sick and tired of your moods. Furthermore," she added, her voice rising, "I'm tired of work, I'm tired of traveling, and most of all, I'm tired of you!"

Furious that she would answer him that way, Paco began to pound the walls and scream at her in Spanish. Ordinarily that would have frightened Julie into submission. But not tonight. The commotion in their dressing room had to have been heard by everyone, because Paco's brother, Luis, came rushing into the room.

"*Madre de Dios*, what are you two doing? You have a show in fifteen minutes!"

Paco turned to his brother, fury emblazoned on his face. "Then tell her to get ready. And she'd better do a good show. I may want to play here again."

If Julie hadn't been so distraught she would have laughed in his face. *Play here again*, Julie thought. *The whole club probably knows about this by now, especially the owner, who already has a poor opinion about show people. All Paco thinks about is the next time. It's just like him not to give a damn about me or our serious problems. His only concern is how he can protect the almighty buck.*

Turning to Luis, she said angrily, "Tell him to get the hell out of here so I can get ready. And keep him away from me till I get onstage."

Julie practically pushed them out the door. Quickly, she slipped out of her street clothes and into her evening gown. As she stood in the wings waiting to go on, she prayed for strength to get through this night.

Julie gave the acting performance of her life that evening. Somehow she managed to get through her songs and dances, for during those numbers she had no physical contact with Paco. But when the time came for her to join Paco in a corny duet that he insisted she participate in, she almost buckled under the strain. Smiling at her tenderly, Paco encircled her waist with his arm as they stood in front of the micro-phone. Acting as if they were the happiest couple in the world, he proceeded with his standard patter that only a few members of the audience found amusing.

"Here we are, my friends," he said laughingly. "Beauty and the beast. And I'll bet you don't know which one is the beast."

Julie squirmed under his touch, but being thoroughly professional, she just smiled wanly and waited for him to continue.

Noticing her silence, he said, "My beautiful wife seems a little quiet this evening. I guess we both ate too much between shows. Right, *querida?*"

"Oh no, Paco," Julie answered quickly. "It's just that you were so amusing during dinner that my face hurts from laughing."

Paco immediately stiffened at the sarcasm and hidden meaning he sensed in her voice. Signaling to the band, he led her into their song. When it was finally over, they exited quickly without saying a word.

Not until they were in the car on their way back to New York City could Julie finally settle down. She had finished the show and done what was expected of her. It hadn't been easy but it was over. But still ahead of her were seven hours of confinement in the car with Paco.

How much longer can I keep this up? Julie questioned as they drove along in silence. *I'm so weary, not only from performing, but from all the arguments that we have day in and day out. When is this all going to end?*

The sound of Paco's voice startled her back to reality—Paco's real-ity.

"I think you should add a couple of Italian songs in Chicago, Julie. There are a lot of Italians there and they'll love it."

Julie didn't answer him. She was still too angry and hurt by his unprovoked cruelty to want to speak to him.

"Julie, I'm talking to you. Shall we put in 'Arrivederci, Roma'?"

"I don't care what you do. Just leave me alone."

Paco mumbled something in Spanish, but Julie ignored him. Turning her head, she gazed out the window. The sky was pitch black and the monotony of the highway was making her sleepy, but she forced herself to stay awake. Her cheeks still ached and her throat was bone dry. She would have loved to stop for a cup of coffee, but she didn't want to ask. She preferred not to give Paco an opportunity to engage her in conversation. She could sense that he was back in his "I don't know why you're upset. I just want to take good care of you" moods.

He knows damn well why I'm upset, she thought furiously, reliving the scene before the second show. *He's so damn smug because he thinks that I'll never find the courage to leave him. But one day he'll wake up and find me gone.*

New York City was alive with the usual early morning crowds hurrying to work as Julie and Paco approached their apartment. The rain had stopped during the night and the streets had that fresh-washed look that concealed the dirt and grime ever present in a big city. Julie had not slept at all during the trip home and had barely spoken. But Paco had ignored her silence and rattled on about their next engage- ment and future tours. He was exhilarated by the thought of how much money he was going to make. When they pulled up to their apartment building on Park Avenue, the doorman unloaded the car, and by the time they reached their bedroom, it was nearly ten A.M. Julie headed straight to bed. By now, she was so exhausted she could barely walk. All she wanted was to climb between the cool sheets, wrap them around her tired body, and sleep. But before she could undress, Paco called to her from the other room.

"Julie, Luis is on his way over. You'd better get the suitcases you want ready so they can be picked up for the airport."

She shook her head wearily. "Paco," she called, "can't he wait until I've slept a couple of hours? I'm so tired I can't move."

"No, he can't wait and you know it. The bags have to go on ahead with the bus!"

Seething with anger, Julie dragged her suitcase to the bed. *Always an order, always a deadline,* she thought. *Why can't they let me rest first and get the bags later? I'm not a machine.*

"Did you hear me, Julie?"

"Yes, dammit. I heard you."

Before tackling her suitcases, Julie glanced around the room at the pretty objects she had collected through her years of traveling and thought sadly, *What's the use in having all these beautiful things when I'm never home long enough to enjoy them?* She picked up one of her life-size dolls that was sitting on the chair. Her mother had laughed when Julie bought them at F.A.O. Schwarz.

"Aren't you a little too old to be playing with dolls, Julie dear?" her mom had asked.

Julie was ashamed to tell her that she wanted them because they reminded her of real babies—babies she would probably never have as long as she was married to Paco.

She opened the valises and started sorting out the clothes she would take to Chicago. When she had finished, even though she was dead tired, she decided to take a hot bath to cleanse herself. She undressed quickly and turned on the hot water, pouring her favorite bath oil into the tub. Just as she was about to step into the tub to submerge her aching body in the inviting water, Paco came in. The moment he saw her naked body a familiar look came into his eyes.

"*Mi amor, que ¡linda estás!*"

Paco turned off the water and roughly pulled her to him. "You have the most beautiful body in the world."

Julie tried to extricate herself from his grasp, but he was holding her too tightly.

"Come, my angel. Make Paco happy."

Revulsion gripped her as she futilely pushed at his arms, trying to get him to release her.

"Let me go, damn you. I'm not feeling well. I'm exhausted. I want to take a bath and go to bed."

But Paco was too aroused to pay any attention to her pleas. Pulling her into the bedroom he flung her down on the bed and started for her, his face flushed with desire. Julie tried to fight him off, but he held her captive.

If he forces me to make love to him, I swear I will kill him, Julie thought. *I don't care what happens to me, but I will kill him.*

Just then the front door slammed and Julie could hear Luis calling from the living room.

"*Hola, Paco, ¿dónde estás?*"

There was a moment's hesitation on Paco's face as he looked down at Julie's inviting body. But deciding that this could wait for later, he reluctantly tied his robe and left the room.

As soon as he was gone, Julie jumped up and grabbed her bathrobe. She'd be damned sure not to let him see her naked again. Slamming the suitcases shut, she hastily shoved them out the door.

"Luis, the bags are outside. I'm going to sleep now, so please don't call me."

She was tempted to lock the door but knew all too well that if Paco wanted to get in, he would only pound on it until she opened it, or he'd break it down. By now, she was too tired and upset to care about a bath so, she crawled into bed and almost immediately fell into a deep sleep.

After what seemed like only a few minutes, Julie could feel someone shaking her shoulder.

"Wake up Julie, it's time to get dressed."

At first she thought she was still dreaming but the shaking grew stronger.

"Wake up now or we'll miss the plane."

Oh no, it can't be time already, she thought. Opening her eyes, she saw Paco leaning over her.

"Julie, get up. We have to leave."

"But, I just went to bed a few minutes ago."

"No, you didn't. You've been asleep almost three hours."

"Oh well," she said sarcastically. "That's different. At least I had a good long rest."

Ignoring her sarcasm, Paco turned and left the room. Julie stretched her arms and legs, hoping to feel some energy returning, but instead of feeling refreshed, the few hours of sleep had made her even more tired. Turning over, she closed her eyes and started to drift off. *Just five minutes more*, she promised herself, *and then I'll get up.*

A few seconds later Paco entered the room, but this time Luis was with him.

"Julie, we can't wait any longer. It's getting late."

She tried to lift her head off the pillow but found that she was unable to and sank back wearily on the bed. "Paco, I can't move. Don't you understand? I'm exhausted. I need more sleep. I can't get on a plane right now. I'd collapse."

Julie could feel herself bordering on hysteria. She wanted to lash out and hit him, hit herself, anyone. Paco took a step back and studied her face. He had seen Julie nervous and tired many times before, but never like this. He must have noticed something strange in her eyes because, for the first time in many years, he relented, turned to Luis, and asked, "Is there a later plane she can make?"

"I think so, Paco. Let me check the airlines."

As Luis left the room, Paco turned back and looked at Julie, who was staring at him with tears streaming down her cheeks.

"We'll see if you can take a later plane, Julie. You can rehearse when you arrive."

She nodded. Anything would be better than leaving now. She prayed that Paco and Luis would leave the apartment quickly and get on that plane without her. She desperately needed time—time to rest and time to think. Moments later, Luis returned with her new travel schedule.

"Julie, you can take an eight o'clock plane tonight and still make an eleven o'clock rehearsal at the hotel."

Paco waved his hand to Luis to go ahead and make the reservation. He wasn't too pleased that Julie wouldn't be accompanying him, for he never wanted her out of his sight. Not even for a few hours. *But maybe*, he thought, *the additional rest will quiet her down.*

"Now, Julie," Paco said with unusual solicitousness. "You be a good girl and rest. I'll call you when I arrive in Chicago. I will also arrange for Luis to pick you up later and take you to the airport."

With that, he bent over to kiss her on the lips, but Julie turned her head just in time so that his kiss landed on her cheek.

"Adiós, Julie."

Julie could not believe they were really gone until she heard the front door slam. It was only then that she dared breathe a sigh of relief. She realized that it would be only a matter of time before Luis came to fetch her and that once she was on that plane to Chicago it would be all over. Since their marriage had begun to deteriorate, Julie had never been able to summon up the courage to leave Paco, and suddenly she knew that if she couldn't change her life, then she didn't want to live anymore.

I have no personal happiness, she thought, *and I can't even find joy in entertaining anymore. So, what's left for me?* Julie was too confused to come up with any answers. But one thing had become very clear. If she did find strength to leave him, she would have to do it when he was far away. Based on her experiences with him through the years, and the most recent, horrible episode in Spain, she couldn't risk any more confrontations with a madman, and that's what he had become. *But where would I go?* she wondered in despair. *He has control over all our money, and my family is so dependent on me. Will I have to start all over again?*

She would have to search her soul and find out whether she had the courage to go on living. Only then could she make her decision. She began to think back over the years to when she had first met Paco and she wondered, *What direction would my life have taken if I had never met Paco Castell?*

CHAPTER
1

Julie Ann Lehman made her entrance into the world with all the drama one would expect of a future star. She was born by cesarean section in the Brooklyn Maternity Hospital on a cold and snowy day in December 1935. Doctors had warned Sam Lehman that the baby might not survive due to severe complications after a fall Rose had suffered late in her pregnancy. But they hadn't counted on the mother's and daughter's determination and strength. So despite a grueling twenty-four hours of labor and surgery, Julie Ann Lehman surprised the doctors and staff and became known in the hospital as the Miracle Baby. They say all babies are beautiful, and perhaps to their parents and relatives they are. But Julie was truly an extraordinary baby. Because of the cesarean delivery she had none of the redness and marks that sometimes mar a newborn's face, and throughout her early childhood she would hear her mother boast about what a special and perfectly formed baby she was. Even at that tender age, it was a good feeling, and throughout her life, Julie would try to set goals for herself that would indeed set her apart and make her special.

Rose and Sam doted on their beautiful baby and, in doing so, unintentionally neglected their older son, Marshall. It must have been devastating to a nine-year-old boy to have been usurped by a gurgling brown-eyed baby sister. But whatever Marshall's feelings may have been, he couldn't help but fall under Julie's spell. He never blamed her for his parents' neglect. He adored his little sister and protected her.

Sam Lehman was in the garment business in the City, and his hours were long and hard. With all the traveling back and forth from Brooklyn, he didn't have much time to spend with his beloved daughter, and after consulting with Rose, he decided to move his family into Manhattan. Rose was ecstatic.

"Oh, Sam, I'm so happy. We can get a better apartment, and maybe have more room for Julie."

Julie was only three years old and didn't need more room, but Rose knew that Sam would do anything for Julie, and she figured that was a good excuse to get a larger place. The apartment they lived in was small, with only one bedroom for Sam, Rose, and the baby. Marshall slept in an alcove off the dining room. Though not consulted, Marshall was all in favor of moving to a bigger apartment in hopes of getting his own room. With strict instructions from Sam not to look for anything beyond their means, Rose began to search for an apartment in Manhattan. The only problem she faced in moving away from Brooklyn was her family. Leaving her mother, Esther, and her sisters was going to be very painful for Rose. She was the eldest, and although all the sisters were married, they had depended on Rose ever since their father, Aaron, had died of pneumonia when the girls were very young. That left Esther Goldman a widow at thirty-two, and fourteen-year-old Rose was forced to quit school and look for work to support her family. She didn't have a trade and, not having the proper education, was unable to find any kind of secretarial work. But she was bright and good with her hands. She could sew beautifully and had been making clothes for herself and her sisters for quite a while. She also was very beautiful and gutsy. This combination gave her the courage to strike out to new territory, and she finally landed an apprentice job in a ladies dress store in Brooklyn. With her meager earnings, and with whatever her sisters could contribute, the family managed to survive. By the time Rose was sixteen, she had blossomed into an incredibly beautiful young woman. With her auburn hair, enormous dark eyes, and shapely body, she attracted attention wherever she went. Her friends constantly told her she looked just like a movie star. Nothing could have pleased her more, for that was all she dreamed about. Rose's mother would carry on whenever she found out that her daughter was wasting money at the movie house.

"What are you bothering with all that *narishkeit*, that foolishness? What are you expecting to be? A big Hollywood movie star?"

"No, Ma. It's not foolishness. I just like to look at the clothes they wear. It gives me ideas for patterns I can make for the store."

This wasn't entirely the truth. Rose wanted desperately to be up there on the screen right along with Dolores Del Rio and Clara Bow, but she knew that could never happen. She was stuck in Brooklyn and would never get out. So instead she dreamed and fantasized how one day maybe she would have a beautiful little girl who would grow up and become a famous star.

When Sam Lehman first saw Rose Goldman he couldn't believe his eyes. She was unlike any of the girls he had dated. She had a very provocative air and was pretty enough to be a movie star. A mutual friend had arranged a double date, but unfortunately Sam was stuck with the other girl. Sam could see that Rose was more interested in him than the guy she was with, so toward the end of the evening Sam managed to get Rose alone long enough to ask her for a date.

"Rose, I hope you don't mind my being so forward, but I would love to see you again."

Rose was thrilled that this handsome young man was attracted to her. She quickly gave him the address of Miss Irene, the place where she was employed, and told Sam it would be better if he met her after work. Though she wouldn't admit it, she was ashamed to let him see her meager circumstances. The apartment was shabby and the three girls had to sleep in one bed. Her mother slept in a pull-down bed in the "living room," and no matter how hard they tried, the place never seemed clean. Sam happily pocketed her address and promised to pick her up after work the very next day.

Unable to sleep that night, Sam could barely wait until he finished work the next day in anticipation of seeing Rose. He couldn't stop thinking about her engaging smile and her dark flashing eyes. They had gazed up at him with a look that was part innocence and part vixen. She had awakened an emotion in him that he had never experienced before. That evening Sam stood outside of the shop with a tiny bouquet of flowers and enormous anticipation. When Rose emerged from the shop, he quickly drew her aside.

"Rose, these are for you. I hope you like them." His eyes drank in her beauty, which seemed even more radiant than the night before.

"Oh, Sam, they're lovely. Thank you. I don't get flowers very often."

Her lack of guile was quite disarming to Sam, and he felt terribly drawn to her. "Where would you like to go, Rose? There's a nice little restaurant a few blocks from here."

Rose hesitated for a few moments, uncertain whether to tell him that she ate only kosher food. She liked this handsome and kind young man so much, and didn't want to say or do anything to discourage him.

As if reading her thoughts he said, "The place I had in mind is a dairy restaurant. You see, Rose, my mother keeps a kosher house and all of us observe the tradition."

Rose smiled up at him and told him that she too came from an Orthodox family. Taking her tiny hand in his, Sam walked down the street, but his feet never touched the ground.

From that day in August of 1924 until they were married, Sam Lehman and Rose Goldman spent every possible moment together. Sam courted her with flowers and candy and waited every evening for her outside of the store where she worked. His kindness and love not only captured Rose's heart but won her family over as well. Esther Goldman was delighted that her sixteen-year-old daughter had found such a good man. She only wished her Aaron were alive to see it. After meeting Rose, Sam decided not to continue with his career in accounting. This angered his parents considerably. He told them he preferred to strike out on his own in the garment business, and even though he didn't know very much about the trade, he had a flair for design and felt he could learn the business quickly. When Sam informed his parents he intended to marry Rose, they weren't too happy with his choice of a wife. Rose's background was not what they had hoped for from their oldest son's future wife. Sam's mother, Hannah, was especially vocal in her feelings.

"Sam, I don't know what's gotten into you. You could have your choice of girls from good homes, whose fathers are comfortable, and you have to pick this girl. Think what you're doing."

Sam's father was more understanding, but firm.

"Sam, I realize that she is a sweet girl and as pretty as a picture, but you're only nineteen years old—a baby. Don't you think you should wait awhile?"

Feeling about Rose the way he did, there was nothing they could say or do that would persuade Sam to give her up. So at the end of the year Sam and Rose were married.

By the time Marshall was born in April of 1926, Sam and Rose were both doing better than either of their families had expected. Rose had continued to work at her job during her pregnancy. She was eventually made assistant to the designer and, with her raise in salary, was able to save a little money for the baby's arrival and still help her mother and sisters. Sam was working for a small, but successful, manufacturer of ladies dresses. He was rapidly learning different aspects of the business, and his employers were pleased with him.

Their adorable little boy, Marshall, was a good baby, and though they loved him, because of their jobs they couldn't spend as much time with him as they would have liked. Esther Goldman was delighted to take care of her first grandchild while Rose was at work. She pampered him and often spoke to him in Yiddish while fixing his dinner.

"*Ess, kindela.* Eat, my child. Mama will be home soon."

Though Rose was concerned her mother would spoil the baby, she also knew she adored the child, and after all she had no alternative due to their limited finances.

For the next few years Sam made small strides in his job, but much to Rose's discontent, they were still living in the same modest apartment that they had moved into when they were married. After Marshall's fourth birthday, Rose gave up her job, finding it too difficult both to work and keep up with an energetic child. She had miscarried twice after Marshall's birth and felt that the physical stress had contributed to the miscarriages. Wanting another child so desperately, especially a little girl, Rose decided to devote herself to her home and family, even though the loss of her income created a financial strain. Frustrated by their circumstances, Rose began to harp on Sam to go to his bosses and get more money.

"Sam," Rose would complain, "why don't you tell them that unless you get a raise you're through! You've been with that firm for five years, and look where we are, still living in this dump."

Sam would look at his beautiful wife and try to explain to her as patiently as he could. "Rose baby, listen. There's a depression. People are on bread lines. They're starving. I'm lucky to have this job. Do you think that with things the way they are they're going to give me a raise? We'll be lucky if I don't get fired."

Rose knew everything that Sam had told her was true. With their husbands unemployed, her sisters were now working in the same place where Rose had worked before meeting Sam and were making barely enough to feed themselves and their mother. Without the few dollars that Rose slipped them every month, they couldn't have paid their rent.

"Yes, Sam, I know you're right. It's just that you're such a timid man when it comes to such things. I don't want them to take advantage of you."

When Rose finally became pregnant in April of 1935, times had changed for the better and the country was beginning to emerge from the turmoil of the previous years. The New Deal under President Roosevelt seemed to be effective, and optimism for the future was felt everywhere, especially in the Lehman household, where Rose happily awaited the birth of their baby. When Julie arrived, Sam and Rose were overjoyed with their adorable little girl. Rose made all of the baby's clothes and, being very superstitious, tied a red ribbon on her carriage to keep away the "evil eye."

Julie developed quickly, and by the time she was three, she was an energetic and precocious toddler, adored by her parents and brother. When Rose found an affordable apartment on Riverside Drive in Manhattan, the family quickly settled into their new home. Rose was thrilled to be living in Manhattan and began to make plans for the future. Sam on the other hand was content just to return home every evening to his beautiful wife and children.

CHAPTER
2

"J ulie Ann, don't you dare get that dress wrinkled. We're going to Grandma Hannah's and I want you to look pretty."

Julie had no intention of wrinkling her beautiful dress even if it meant standing up straight and still all day. She was only five years old, but she knew better than to upset her mother, especially when they were going to visit relatives. She wasn't afraid of a spanking, at least not on Sunday when her daddy was home. She just hated to do anything to displease her mother. After all, didn't her mother make her pretty clothes and little hats to go with them? When Rose and Julie walked on Fifth Avenue on Saturdays, Rose would look at all the beautiful children's clothes in the department stores and copy the ones she liked best for Julie. The only problem was that she didn't like Julie getting them dirty or wrinkled. Sometimes Julie wished she could have clothes just for rolling around in her grandma's garden and having fun. But Rose would have none of that.

Straightening Julie's already perfect skirt and rearranging her daughter's auburn curls under her bonnet, Rose reminded her, "You are 'different' young lady and just you remember that!"

Julie didn't understand why she was different. True, she was bright and good in school, but so were a lot of girls. Yes, people were always saying how pretty she was, but when she looked in the mirror, she didn't see anything special. Then why was she "different"? Maybe it was her love of music and the fact that she liked to perform. Her proud parents delighted in telling anyone who would listen, "Our Julie sang before she talked."

It was an exaggeration, of course, but Julie was musical and could sing and memorize lyrics after hearing a song once or twice. Rose was thrilled that her little girl was blessed with the talent she never had. She promised herself that it would not be wasted.

As she brushed her daughter's hair, she instructed her. "One day, Julie, you are going to grow up and become a famous star. You will marry a rich man and have beautiful clothes and fabulous jewels. All the things that I've never had."

It was hard for the little girl to understand what her mother meant by "all the things I've never had." They had a nice apartment, a shiny blue car, and although her mother didn't have a lot of jewelry, she did have pretty clothes and lots of sparkling crystal bottles of perfume on her dressing table. That seemed like an awful lot to Julie.

Her mother, however, was not satisfied with the way her life had turned out. Although Sam made a decent living, he was still unable to own his own business. He had tried several times to raise the capital to start his own company, but even his own family rejected his pleas for financial assistance. Rose would complain about his lack of ambition at the drop of a hat.

"Sam, for God's sake, do something or you'll wind up an old man still working for someone else!"

Sam would smile tolerantly and urge her to be patient. "Rose, be a good girl and let me read my paper. We'll be all right."

Sam was happy with his life. He had a good job and a devoted wife, even though there were many times when Rose's frustrations would prompt her to lash out at him and fights would ensue. Having a good son and a beautiful, loving daughter, who was his pride and joy, more than compensated for these occasional difficulties with Rose. Often, if Julie was nearby, he would pick her up and sit her on his lap.

"Who is Daddy's little girl?" he would ask.

And, Julie would always answer, "I am, Daddy."

And, for Sam, that was enough to make his life complete.

When the Lehmans had moved to Manhattan from Brooklyn, it had been in hopes of getting a larger apartment. But it didn't turn out that way. True, the neighborhood was nicer—a more impressive address for Rose. But the rooms were barely larger than their old apartment. Marshall never did get his own bedroom and continued to sleep in what was really the dining room alcove. Julie slept in her parents' bedroom in what was known as a "youth bed," and they all shared one tiny bathroom. Rose had kept most of the furniture from their old place, but by scrimping and saving, she managed to save a little each month to buy new things.

Julie loved school, was an excellent student, and because of her good behavior and sweet nature, was loved by all her teachers. After school, instead of running off with the other kids to play, she would go directly home to do her homework. Sometimes Marshall would be there, and she liked watching him lie on the floor reading or doing his homework. Julie loved to talk to her big brother and ask him questions about high school. But, at fourteen, he was totally preoccupied with girls and unfortunately rarely around long enough to be any kind of companion.

Julie's favorite times were when Rose was cooking dinner and the kitchen was warm and cozy, filled with the aroma of Julie's favorite dishes simmering on the stove. It was then that she would have her mother's complete attention. Cuddling her favorite doll, she would lean her curly head on Rose's hand and ask her mother questions about what it was like when she was a little girl. She was especially fascinated about stories concerning her Grandma Esther, Rose's mother. Julie never tired of hearing of how, as a young girl in Russia, Esther had met Rose's father, Aaron, who came from Germany, and how he had fallen in love with the beautiful girl with the long blond hair that, when left untied, cascaded down to her waist. Rose would then tell her daughter about her own childhood. Wiping her hands on her apron, her dark eyes gleaming as she remembered the past, Rose would sit beside Julie as she reminisced.

"You should have seen what a pretty girl I was. All the fellows were crazy about me, but I only had eyes for your father."

This was not said out of vanity but rather as a lesson to her little girl. Over and over again, Rose would remind her daughter, "Don't be like me. If you have looks you can get someplace in this world. You can be sure of that. And, if you have talent too, then, my beautiful Julie, you can become a star."

This was Rose's credo, and she not only believed it—she eventually made Julie believe it too.

CHAPTER 3

By the time Julie was nine, the war in Europe was raging, and despite her parents' pleas, Marshall enlisted in the air force. Even though her big brother had gradually stopped being a full-time presence in her life, she still missed him desperately. Rose was desolate, consumed with fear that her teenage son would be thousands of miles away, fighting in a war that had already claimed many thousands of lives. But she also harbored deep guilt that she and Sam had not given Marshall the attention he deserved when he was a boy. She vowed that when he returned, she would do everything in her power to make it up to him.

Sam was equally concerned about his son but tried not to show his emotions in front of Rose. Putting his arms around his wife, he tried to comfort her. "Don't worry, sweetheart. He'll come home safe and sound. You'll see."

For the first time in Julie's life she was not the center of her parents' attention, and she was only too glad to relinquish the spotlight. The telephone that had rung constantly when Marshall was home was strangely silent. Julie, who had graduated from the youth bed in her parents' bedroom years ago, had shared part of the dining alcove with her brother. Her father had put up a makeshift divider in the children's "room" for privacy, but now with Marshall away, she became the sole occupant. Julie now had a little more space but still no privacy because you had to pass through that alcove in order to get to the kitchen.

When Marshall was sent to an air force base in England, Rose carried on like a banshee. "Oh my God, if something happens to him I'll kill myself."

Sam was frantic about what would happen to Rose if they lost their son. Every morning before leaving for work, he would remind Julie, "Baby, if a telegram comes, don't give it to Mommy. Call me at the office and I'll come right home."

Julie was terrified of this responsibility and also of her mother's fragile emotional condition. She hoped that her mother's dedication in taking her to dancing lessons and their plans for Julie's career would serve as a diversion. Saturdays were Julie's favorite day of the week, because that's when she and her mother went to the movies. After the movie and stage show at Radio City Music Hall or the Roxy, they would have an ice cream soda and, as a special treat for Julie, take a ride on the huge double-decker Fifth Avenue bus. Even though it was out of the way, Julie loved to ride upstairs in the open air and look at all the beautiful shops that lined Fifth Avenue. She and Rose would talk endlessly about their hopes and dreams for the future. Julie fanta-sized seeing herself up there on the screen singing and dancing, and the minute she got home, she would borrow something of her mother's, put on makeup, and pretend to be the glamorous star she had seen on the screen.

"Julie," Rose would ask laughingly as she watched her daughter pose in front of the mirror. "Who are you today? Judy Garland or Lana Turner?"

Flinging her red hair over her youthful face and copying the flirta-tious look she had studied that afternoon, Julie would answer, "Mom, can't you see? I'm Rita Hayworth."

Julie's tap dancing lessons on Saturdays would begin at nine and finish at eleven. Before starting class, the children loved to play while their mothers compared notes in the hallway.

"Rose, have you heard they're having auditions for 'The Children's Hour' radio show Monday at four?"

Rose's friend Fanny, who also had a child in Julie's class, was a reliable source of information. She knew everything that was happening in show business and was a stage mother in every sense of the word. Not caring about the competition because her daughter couldn't sing and Julie could, she generously passed along the news.

"Oh, Fanny, thanks. I wonder if I could get Julie in?"

"Sure you can. Just go over to Station WHN and leave your name. Oh, and be sure to have some music with you."

That afternoon, instead of going to the movies as they did every Saturday, Rose took Julie to the music store and picked out a song for her to sing for the audition.

On Monday, on the way over to the station, Rose coached Julie on what to say. "Julie, just tell them how much you like the program, and how you listen to it every Sunday. I'll handle the rest."

When it was Julie's turn to sing, Rose, holding her daughter's hand, walked over to the piano player and handed him the music. "Excuse me, but can you play 'Bei Mir Bist Du Schön'?"

"Lady, I not only can play it, I wrote it," a bemused Saul Chaplin replied. He looked up at the attractive woman standing by the piano and smiled at her patiently. Having dealt with child actors and their ambitious mothers many times before, nothing fazed him.

Julie impressed the producers with her voice and was chosen as a substitute to fill in whenever one of the regulars on the show was unable to work. This small taste of show business encouraged Rose and made her even more determined that Julie continue her musical studies.

Unfortunately, the dancing and singing lessons came to an abrupt halt when Julie suddenly became ill. Her illness had crept up insidiously, and what was first thought to be simply a lingering virus turned out to be rheumatic fever. Julie had no idea how serious her illness was, but Rose and Sam were devastated. After Julie went to bed, they would talk long into the night about their problem. Sam Lehman, who had never approved of Julie's strenuous schedule, pointed an accusing finger at Rose.

"How could she possibly have *not* gotten sick with all the schlepping around that you subjected her to? Regular school, plus all that other crap that she needs like a hole in the head. What did you expect?"

Rose turned on her husband, furious that he would attack her so unfairly. "The doctor said that her lessons had nothing to do with it. It's a virus that she could have picked up anywhere. I'm miserable enough, with my angel so sick, without you blaming me."

Turning away from him, Rose began to cry—tears for her daughter and tears for all the dreams she and Julie had shared together and now might never be realized. The doctor demanded that Julie have complete bed rest, and the months she would spend bedridden became the unhappiest time of her young life. When she was forced to move back into her parents bedroom because it was quieter there, Julie felt trapped and desolate.

As the weeks dragged on, Julie's dolls, her books, and the radio became her only companions. Rose spent as much time as she could with Julie, but caring for Sam and running the household also demanded her attention, so Julie was left alone a great deal of the time. She loved listening to her favorite shows on the radio. At least that gave her some contact with show business—a business she so much wanted to be a part of one day. At night, to pass the time while waiting for Sam to come home, Rose would tell Julie about Sam's parents. His family were wealthy German Jews who had lived in great luxury before the war.

"Julie," Rose explained, "your Daddy's family was very aristocratic. Grandpa Max was in the jewelry business and when he married Grandma Hannah they lived in a beautiful home in the prettiest section of Berlin."

Although Julie was interested in hearing about her grandparents, it was the stories about her mother's aunt in Russia that really fascinated her. Her Great Aunt Olga had been a famous opera singer who became very celebrated, not only for her voice, but also for her great beauty.

"Yes, my *kindela*," Rose would say, stroking Julie's hair. "You definitely take after my side of the family."

Time passed very slowly for Julie. Other than an occasional visit from members of the family, she was alone most of the time. When the bedroom window was open, she could hear her friends playing in the street below. How she longed to be there with them. They sounded so happy and carefree. Before her illness, Julie's days had always been filled with activities—school, lessons, and those wonderful Saturdays that she spent with her mother at the movies. All that was gone now and the isolation became intolerable. She prayed every night that soon she would be well. But the months seemed to stretch on endlessly.

From his base in England, Marshall completed thirty-five bombing missions over Germany, but, because of wounds he received on his last mission, he was sent to a hospital back in the States. Rose was grateful that his injuries were not serious but apprehensive that once he was well, he would be transferred to the Pacific theater of operations. At night she would often cry.

"Sam, what's happened to us? My poor baby Julie is so sick and now my Marshall. Why is God punishing us?"

Julie tried to console her mother and reassure her that she was getting better every day and that Marshall would soon be home. "Mommy, everything's going to be the same as it was, you'll see."

When, after months of confinement, the doctor gave his consent for her to resume school, Julie was ecstatic. She had missed so much she was afraid she'd never catch up. But, with the help of her teachers and extra tutoring, she was able to advance to the next grade. Just when things began to look brighter, the Lehman family was confronted with a new and terrifying crisis.

Shortly after Julie was finally discharged from her doctor's care, as she was returning home from an errand she had run for her mother, she suddenly lost all feeling in her left arm. The milk that she was carrying so carefully crashed to the ground and her arm began to shake uncontrollably. Julie ran home panic-stricken.

"Mom, come quick," she cried. "Something's happened to my arm."

By the time Rose ran in from the kitchen, Julie had collapsed on the floor and was unable to control the movement in her left leg. The numbness she had felt had spread to the left side of her body accompanied by an uncontrollable twitching movement. Screaming frantically, Rose ran to her neighbor for help. Banging on the door, she yelled, "Sylvia, come quick. Something's happened to Julie."

The two women ran back to the apartment. Sylvia grabbed Julie and held her in her arms while Rose rushed to the telephone. By the time she reached Sam, she was hysterical. "Sam, come right home. Something's happened to the baby."

Sam hurried home and Julie was rushed to the hospital. After tests were made, Julie was diagnosed as having chorea's syndrome, commonly known as Saint Vitus's dance, a disease that attacks the nervous system and very often follows rheumatic fever. Sam and Rose reeled under the news of this very serious and debilitating illness. Julie was inconsolable.

"No, no, it can't be," she cried out. "All those months in bed and now this." Julie smashed her fist into her pillow, wanting to lash out at someone, anyone, in her frustration. All her dreams of becoming a famous star, of seeing her name in lights, were suddenly shattered when the doctor told them the news. Once again, she was forced to go back to her parents' room, back to bed, and what was worse, back to her loneliness.

"Dr. Braverman," Julie pleaded during one of his weekly visits. "Please tell me how long I'll have to stay in bed?"

The doctor, who had already treated her for rheumatic fever, which had kept her immobilized for all those months, looked down compassionately at his patient's young, sweet face.

"Julie dear, I can't give you any answers right now. Your recovery depends on how good a patient you are and how good a doctor I am."

An overwhelming sadness consumed Julie. Nobody would tell her the truth. The doctor, her parents, all they ever said was, "Be patient." But how could she be patient when there were so many questions left unanswered? Would she ever fully recover? And if she did, would she ever be the same? She was bewildered and frightened by the whispering she heard in the next room and the worried glances she saw on her parents' faces when they thought she wasn't looking. Whenever she moved, her parents reminded her of the doctor's strict orders to remain motionless and avoid any kind of excitement. Her father even had to carry her to the bathroom.

If I'm this sick, she thought, *how will I ever be strong enough to dance and sing?*

Praying that this almost intolerable confinement would cure her, Julie obeyed her doctor and submitted to endless blood tests and neurological examinations with barely a whimper. She found great release by writing in a diary that her father had bought her, and though she had no real activity to record, it still felt good to be able to write down her thoughts and dreams. For dreams were all she had.

September 5th

Dear Diary,

Grandma Esther came by today and brought me a sweater she crocheted for me. It's too small, but I told her it was perfect. My teacher brought me some work, but I don't feel strong enough to do it now. Maybe after supper.

September 11th

Dear Diary,

Nothing much happened today, but I am expecting to get my period any day now. Maxine Rosenfeld came by yesterday and she got hers, so I guess I'll brush up on a few facts on that subject. Should I speak to Mom?

P.S. I think my bust is growing. I hope so.

The first thing that Sam Lehman did upon returning home each evening was to rush in and greet his bedridden daughter. He often brought her little presents to help cheer her up. This particular evening, one she never would forget, her father came into the room and smiled at her as he placed his gift on the dresser near her bed.

"Oh, daddy, a record player," Julie exclaimed gleefully. "I've wanted one so much and you got it. Thank you, thank you."

The sparkle in his daughter's eyes, the first he had seen in months, was thanks enough.

"That's not all, sweetheart. I've brought you some records too—the ones you said you liked listening to on the radio."

Sam placed the records on the bed near Julie and was thrilled to see the look of joy on her face. Quickly she found the one that was her favorite and asked her father to play it for her. Sam had thought her request rather strange at the time, but his daughter had already developed strong musical tastes. Her choice was "Besame Mucho" and the orchestra, Paco Castell's.

Julie leaned back on her pillow and, as she listened, imagined herself up there onstage, dressed in a beautiful gown, singing with the band. She was transported into another world, and for the first time in a long long while, she felt happy.

While Julie was struggling to get well, three thousand miles away the famous bandleader Paco Castell was having one of his glamorous parties at his home in Beverly Hills. It was the kind of party that always attracted every motion picture star and starlet in the business. Paco had just divorced his vocalist-wife Lola Caldero and was having a great time squiring Rita Hayworth and Ava Gardner around town. They were in between husbands and loved to dance. Though dazzled by their beauty, Paco was even more interested in being seen with them in order to further his career and image. Paco was not considered a handsome man. Certainly not in a town that boasted screen idols like Robert Taylor and Tyrone Power. But women did find him attractive, especially when he was up on the bandstand performing. He dressed well and expensively and knew how to seduce women with his Latin charm. Having brought Latin American music to the attention of the North American public, he had become singularly responsible for popularizing it. After achieving huge success in nightclubs, he eventually attracted the attention of Metro-Goldwyn-Mayer and was signed to a long-term contract during which he made several successful musicals. Paco was now not only a famous bandleader, but a movie star as well. He often used to reflect on how different his life-style was now, compared to his humble beginnings in Spain and later on in Mexico, where he had been a struggling violinist. His family had been very poor and had sacrificed a great deal so that Paco could pursue his dreams of becoming a concert artist. He never forgot those lean years and loved to entertain his friends with stories about his past.

"You know L.B.," Paco confided one evening at a party in Hollywood, "I was a poor boy, too, just like you, and now look at the two of us."

He was one of the privileged few allowed to address the famous Louis B. Mayer that intimately. But Mayer found Paco and his accent amusing and, being a good business man, liked the money Paco's films were raking in at the box office. He and Paco shared an insatiable appetite for the opposite sex. But while the studio head tried to keep his philandering secret, Paco flaunted his in order to further his image as a great Latin lover. On and off the set, he had a habit of slicking back his hair and, when eyeing a pretty girl, boasting, "I may not be as good-looking as those matinee idols, but I sure know how to please the ladies."

Since his divorce, Paco had been searching for a new vocalist to replace Lola. One night he came across a voluptuous young girl singing in a little club on Olvera Street in Los Angeles. Her name was Lupita Del Barrio, and when Paco offered her a job, she was thrilled that she had been noticed by the great Paco Castell. As was his custom, he promised her a career in films. It wasn't long before she became his new "discovery," and as he had done in the past, he molded her in the image he had created with all his other singers, the Latin Spitfire.

By the time Julie was well enough to resume school, the war in Europe had ended and Marshall finally returned home. Though his physical wounds had healed, his emotional state rendered him unsuitable for further combat and he was discharged.

In the months that followed her recovery, Julie noticed a big change in her parents. Her father became more withdrawn, and it troubled Julie to see him looking so sad. Rose, who at first rejoiced in having her son home, also changed. The strain of the war and Julie's illnesses had taken their toll, and Rose had begun to lament that "her life was over."

"Oh, Julie," Rose would confide, "your father is stuck in a rut. He hasn't had a raise in years and we'll never have enough money to go anywhere or do anything."

The only consolation Julie could offer her mother was to remind her that she was still a young woman and had a lot to live for. But Rose's unhappiness continued. When she would hear that one of her friends had received a mink coat, she would carry on.

"Can you imagine? That fat slob who can't even boil water gets a mink coat and what do I get?"

Julie understood her mother's frustration, as did Sam, but neither one was able to do anything about it. What had started out as little quarrels over finances soon turned into bitter fights. Julie was caught in the middle and was frightened that her mother would pack up one day and leave—a threat she had made often. Julie was too young to realize that her mother would sooner have died than leave her "baby"—that it was just a tactic she used in order to motivate her husband to do something more with his life. Julie was now more determined than ever to resume her lessons and become successful. Whenever she spied her mother's sad face, she would try to reassure her.

"Don't worry, Mom. One day I will buy you the most beautiful fur coat in the world and then I'll send you and Dad on a trip to Europe on the *Queen Mary*. You'll have everything you've ever wanted. I promise you that!"

"I believe you, baby. I know you can do it. You have to. You're my only chance."

CHAPTER
4

The attractive, dark-haired secretary looked at the young girl sitting across from her and summoned her to her desk.

"Miss Lehman, I'm afraid Mr. Abbott cannot see you without an appointment. Why don't you leave your picture and résumé and we'll call you."

Julie didn't really think she had a chance of getting in to meet the famous George Abbott, but her singing teacher Esther Lieber had read the script of the upcoming Abbott show and was convinced that Julie was ready for Broadway.

While riding down in the elevator, Julie was lost in her thoughts and unaware of the stares she was receiving from two young men. At thirteen she had developed from a skinny and awkward young girl into what promised to be a beautiful woman. Her shiny coppery tresses framed her oval face. She had inherited her father's almond-shaped light brown eyes and her mother's pale golden skin. Even at this tender age, she had the rounded curves and shapely breasts that, in a very few years, would prove irresistible to men. What made her even more appealing was her innocence and lack of vanity. Not that she was a fool. Julie knew she was pretty. She had been reminded of that ever since she could remember. But she intended to be more than just another pretty face. She wanted the world to know that she also had talent.

On the way back home, Julie studied the casting sheet that she picked up at the newsstand and wondered, *How will I ever get into a show? Besides having no experience, I'm only thirteen and you have to be at least sixteen to be able to get a job in a musical.*

When Julie arrived home, she could see that her mother was agitated. "Julie, I've been waiting on pins and needles. Why didn't you call me? How did the audition go?"

Julie threw off the beige coat that had once belonged to her mother and sank down dejectedly on the living room couch. "I didn't get to see him, Mom. Mrs. Lieber's letter wasn't enough. I need an appointment."

"Well, tell her to get you one. You wasted a whole day and missed school."

Julie heaved a deep sigh and once again began explaining her predicament. "Mom, we should be grateful to Mrs. Lieber. She's done so much for us. She's giving me singing lessons free because she believes in me. I can't ask her to also be my agent."

That night, after her parents had gone to sleep, Julie decided that she would cut classes the next day and return to Mr. Abbott's office. She diskliked lying to her mother. It was something she rarely did, but she wanted to avoid a scene. It would be even worse if her father ever found out. Besides being dead set against a theatrical career, he was inflexible when it came to her studies. Julie feared a verbal scolding from him more than a slap from her mother.

Before Julie reached George Abbott's office, she tried to decide on what strategy she would employ in order to get in to see the famous producer. When she walked back into his office, Julie jumped in before the secretary Miss Rollins had a chance to speak.

"Miss Rollins, I know I don't have an appointment, but can I sit here anyway just in case he can see me?"

Something about the way Julie spoke and the fierce determination in her eyes touched Miss Rollins, and she decided to try and help.

"Listen, my dear. I can't promise anything, but why don't you just sit down and wait, and we'll see."

Julie waited patiently most of the day, not even daring to leave to grab a bite of lunch. If she wasn't home by four, her mother would surely know she had not been in school. But it was too late to worry about that now. At three o'clock, the office, which had been crowded all day, was practically empty. Suddenly a tall white-haired man stepped out of a room. Julie's heart started beating rapidly as he approached her.

"Now, young lady, are you the girl my good friend Esther Lieber told me about?"

Julie, usually not at a loss for words, could barely speak. "Ah, yes, sir. I think so," she stammered. "I mean I am the girl, Mr. Abbott."

"My secretary tells me you've been sitting here for two days, Miss . . . what is your name again?"

"Julie Lehman, sir."

"Oh yes, Julie. Well, why don't you come into my office and let's see what we can find for you."

Julie couldn't believe this was happening to her. *I must be dreaming,* she thought. *I wish Mom was here to see this.* Glancing gratefully over to Miss Rollins, who was smiling at her, Julie followed him back into his office. Motioning for her to sit down opposite him, George Abbott settled his long and elegant body into his chair and studied the young girl seated before him.

"Now tell me, Julie, what kind of experience have you had?"

Julie had expected to be asked that question, but nevertheless she was still unprepared with an answer.

"Well, Mr. Abbott, I've appeared in a lot of school plays and have done some modeling, and when I was a little girl I sang on radio."

Realizing that the things she mentioned were hardly the necessary credentials for a part in a major broadway show, Julie hastened to add, "Mr. Abbott, although I haven't appeared on Broadway or even done summer stock, Mrs. Lieber feels I'm ready."

As she spoke, George Abbott's eyes never left Julie's face. He was more interested in observing her poise and style than in hearing about what he already knew would be her limited experience.

"How old are you, Julie?"

"Sixteen," Julie lied.

A broad smile brightened his face. "I see," he said, pausing for a moment. "Well, my dear," he continued, pulling out a script, "I would like you to read this for me. Study it for a while. Take your time. It's the part of Carol. Pages fifty-one through fifty-six. I'm going next door for a while. Call me when you're ready."

Julie took the script, and when he left the room, all the self-confidence she had tried to exude, vanished.

Oh my God, I can't do it. I'm not prepared.

Never dreaming that she would be considered for anything more than a minor singing role, she had no idea where to begin. She read the pages silently over and over again. Her mouth had gone dry and she could feel that the back of her hair was wet with perspiration. Afraid of taking too long, she opened the door and said she was ready. Abbott came back into the room, and with him cueing her, she began to read. When she finished, she was afraid to look up at him.

"Thank you, Julie. I know that must have been difficult for you. Even experienced actors hate to read cold."

Grateful that he had not dismissed her after what she knew to be a poor reading, she handed him back the script.

Leaning back in his chair, George Abbott studied her. "Julie, now I want you to tell me the truth. How old are you really?"

In a voice that was practically a whisper, she answered, "Almost fourteen, Mr. Abbott."

"I thought so. But I must say you are an extraordinarily poised young girl for your age."

Rising from his chair, he came around his desk and cupped her chin in his hand. "Julie, I want you to take this script home and memorize the same pages. Then I would like to hear you sing. My secretary will contact you as to where and when, but it probably will be sometime next week."

Later that evening, when recounting the day's events to her parents, Julie tried not to omit one single thing that had happened to her that day. She had left his office on cloud nine, rushing over to Esther's studio to thank her and tell her the good news. Her teacher was delighted but not entirely surprised that Julie had made an impression. She cautioned her pupil not to get her hopes up too high. There would be lots of competition from girls with far more experience, and the chances of landing a major role would be slim. Nevertheless, Esther encouraged her and promised to help her all she could.

That night Rose was convinced Julie had it made, but Sam wisely counseled her, "Don't be disappointed, sweetheart, if you don't get the part. The fact that a man as famous as George Abbott liked you well enough to see you again is a great honor."

Julie listened intently to her father's advice and she knew that what he said made sense. But no amount of logic could extinguish the bright flame of ambition that burned fiercely inside of her. Somehow she knew that no matter how inconsequential the role, no matter how many others she had to beat out, she would be in that show.

When the telephone call finally came from the Abbott office, Julie was prepared and had her songs selected. Now all she needed was something to wear. Rose agreed that Julie's girlish dresses were inappropriate. If Julie was going to try and pass herself off as an older girl, she would need something different. Since finances were always a problem in the Lehman household, Rose was in a quandary.

"Julie, we can't afford a new dress, and even if we could, there's no time."

"Oh, Mom," Julie pleaded, "all I have are my school sweaters and skirts. I'll look like a kid next to those other girls. Please try and think of something."

Rose went to the closet and started rummaging through her clothes frantically. The audition was set for noon the next day. What could she improvise that might work? Reaching to the very back of the closet that housed not only her clothes, but Sam's and Julie's as well, Rose found an old dress of hers that did not look too matronly and pulled it out.

"Julie, come here and take a look at this. Aren't the colors pretty? Would you like to try it on?"

Julie quickly got out of her clothes and slipped on the dress. Running over to the mirror, she was thrilled at her reflection. She looked like a young lady even with her hair in a ponytail. The dress was turquoise and black with a tiny peplum and a sweetheart neckline. It was perfect.

Throwing her arms around her mother, she hugged her. "Oh, Mom, you're an angel. It's perfect. Can I wear it, please?"

Rose sat down on the bed and stared at her daughter pensively. "Julie, if your father sees you in this outfit he'll kill me. You know how he feels about you wearing lipstick and grown-up clothes. He'll have a fit!"

Julie grabbed her mother's hands and knelt before her. "Mom, don't worry. He'll be gone by the time I leave the house and I'll change before he gets home."

Looking at her daughter's face and her beseeching eyes, Rose had no choice but to give in. "All right, you can wear it. But first let me fit it on you. It's too big, and if you're going to wear it, I want it to look right."

The next day, standing in the wings of the theater in her mother's dress and high-heel shoes, Julie felt more confident. When the stage manager finally called out her name, Julie walked out to the middle of the stage and waited for instructions. She had been there for several hours waiting for her turn to sing and had watched girl after girl begin a song, only to be interrupted by someone in the audience who said, "Thank you very much. We'll let you know."

Only a handful of girls had made it past sixteen bars of music, and those few were now standing on the side of the stage, awaiting the outcome.

"Julie, are you ready?" a voice out there asked.

The theater was pitch black—the only light coming from a large lamp hanging down in the middle of the stage. She had no idea whether the voice belonged to George Abbott. The tone was gentle, yet commanding.

"Yes, sir, I'm ready." And with a nod to the pianist, she began, "I've got music in my heart. It makes me feel like singing the whole night through."

Her interpretation today wasn't Judy Garland. It was Ethel Merman—hands outstretched, feet apart, belting out a song. After a few more bars of music, that same voice bellowed out, "Thank you, Julie. That will be all."

Julie's heart sank right down into her mother's too-tight shoes. *Oh God*, she thought. *They didn't like me.*

Turning dejectedly away from the pianist, she started to leave the stage. But before she could get very far, the stage manager came up and tapped her on the shoulder.

"Mr. Abbott will be up here in a minute and would like to speak to you."

Not daring to hope that she still had a chance, Julie joined the tiny group of other hopefuls who were waiting for his decision. Minutes later, Julie watched as the famous producer bounded up the steps leading from the audience and approached them.

His presence was overwhelming and everyone held their breath as they waited for his decision. "Young ladies, I want to thank you for coming here today. You all have lovely voices, but unfortunately we only can use one girl for this part."

Turning to a pretty young blond with ivory skin and pale blue eyes, he motioned for her to come forward. Leaning over, Abbott gave her a kiss on the cheek. "Annabel, congratulations. I'm happy we will be working together again. I think you'll be wonderful in the show."

Julie looked at the girl who had won the coveted role and her first reaction was one of intense disappointment. But then Julie began to rationalize that although she hadn't gotten the part, she had come this far and had lost out to a girl that George Abbott already knew and had worked with before. *I can't let this get me down*, she thought. *I'll just have to keep on trying.* As Julie turned to leave, Abbott stopped her.

"And where do you think you're going, young lady?"

Julie looked up in surprise. "Well, Mr. Abbott, I thought as long as you've found someone I would go home."

"Nonsense. Don't you want to be in my show?"

Julie was flustered by his question. "Of course I do, sir, but I don't understand what you mean?"

"Well, what I mean is you're too young and inexperienced to play such an important role, but I would like you to understudy Annabel and be in the chorus."

Julie stood there, frozen to the spot, not knowing whether to laugh or cry with happiness. She wanted to throw her arms around this kind and gentle man and kiss him. But instead, she could only thank him for his kindness and belief in her talent.

All the way home Julie planned on how she would break the news to her parents. When she opened the front door and saw her father and mother standing there, their faces reflecting their anticipation and anxiety, her carefully planned words flew out of her mouth. Excitedly, she blurted out, "Mom, Dad, it's happened. I got the job. I'm on my way."

CHAPTER
5

Julie's demanding work schedule in the George Abbott show forced her to leave the High School of Music and Art during her freshman year and enroll in Professional Children's School. Sam was furious.

Sitting in their living room, he slammed down the evening paper and lashed out at Rose. "With her grades and intelligence, she could become a teacher and have a wonderful career."

"She'll have a better career in show business and make more money," Rose responded angrily. "Can't you understand that she doesn't want to be a teacher? She wants to be on the stage."

"That's because you've drilled that into her head ever since she was able to talk. You want her to be what *you* always dreamed about being—a movie star."

"And, what's wrong with that?" Rose answered furiously.

Sam had touched on the truth, and hearing it only evoked greater resentment.

"Do you want her to end up a housewife like me—worrying each month about how she's going to make ends meet?"

Sam turned away from his wife and left the room. He loved Rose and he was fearful that if he stayed there much longer, they would have a serious argument and he might say something he would later regret.

The arguments were endless, not only over Julie's future, but over the same old subject—money. With each passing day, Rose seemed to grow more dissatisfied with her life, and no matter how hard she prodded Sam, he still refused to change jobs or go back to his parents for financial help. What made matters even worse was the glamorous life-style that Rose was exposed to now that Julie was in the theater. Her envy only served to fuel her anger. However, her anger was never directed at Julie, who was enjoying the first taste of a glorious new life.

Tired of Rose's endless complaints, Sam decided to try to augment his income by taking the summer off, when business was slow anyway, and renting the coffee shop and drugstore concession in a hotel in the Catskill mountains. The money needed to rent the space and buy supplies would just about deplete their savings, but if things went well, they could more than double their investment. Rose was all for it, even though it would mean hard work. She also figured that it would be good for Julie to get out into the country now that the play was closing on May first. There were no new shows being planned for the summer, and by fall they would all be back in New York.

Julie wasn't too keen about leaving the City and her singing lessons, but it was useless to argue with her parents once their minds were made up.

Just before the Memorial Day weekend, the Lehmans arrived at the Brooklawn Hotel, the Jewel of the Catskills, so the brochure read, and began to get the store ready to open. The work was hard and the hours long. Julie would have loved to explore the hotel and grounds, but she had very little time to herself, as she was expected to tend the soda fountain and cash register. Although the stately hotel and grounds were beautiful, Julie couldn't take advantage of any of the activities—not only because of the demands of her job, but also, as she quickly learned, because strict hotel rules forbade employees from using the facilities.

On their first evening there, Julie suffered a humiliating experience—one that she would never forget. After a long day in the coffee shop, stacking food and supplies, the family showered and went into the dining room for dinner. Unable to locate the maître d', they sat down at the first available table near the entrance. Already seated were two other couples and a teenage boy of about sixteen. Julie looked around at the huge dining room that must have accommodated at least five hundred people and whispered to her mother, "Mom, you were right. This place is incredible."

Before her mother could reply, a heavyset man with a red splotchy face appeared from out of nowhere at their table.

Glaring down at them as if they were insects, he shouted, "Just what do you think you're doing here? You're help. You're not supposed to sit with paying guests. Get up and follow me." Turning, he motioned for them to follow him.

Rose's face turned beet red. Dropping her napkin on the table she fumbled for her purse. Julie was mortified. She felt that every person in the dining room must be staring at them.

Her father rose and said, "Come on, Rose, Julie. Let's go."

Her faced flushed with embarrassment, Julie marched with her parents to the back of the dining room and sat down behind a partitioned area marked Employees. Her parents said nothing, but Julie could sense their humiliation. The other employees at the table chatted away happily and gorged themselves on the huge dinner. But Julie and Rose barely ate. The whole episode had ruined their appetites. When they returned to their quarters, Sam went back to the store to check on last-minute details while Julie and her mother prepared for bed. As Julie undressed, she expressed her disappointment in her father's submissive behavior.

"Dad should have said something to that jerk," she told her mother. "That man treated us like dirt. He could have at least told us to move quietly instead of humiliating us in front of the entire room."

Her mother shook her head in resignation as she tried to make her daughter understand. "Julie, sit down here on the bed and let me explain something to you. If your father didn't speak up it's because he probably figures what's the use? You have to accept the fact that we're here for only one reason—to make some extra money. That's all that matters."

Julie shook her head, finding it hard to accept her mother's logic. She didn't like being looked down upon and being treated rudely. That night, after her parents were asleep in the next room, Julie vowed to herself that no matter how hard she had to work, one day she would be important and successful enough to ensure that she would always be treated with respect.

The activities the Brooklawn had to offer were numerous, and most of the guests were up early to utilize the facilities. As Julie stood behind the counter making sodas and washing dishes, she could hear through the screen door the voices of young people laughing as they made their way to the tennis courts and swimming pool. There were many kids her own age vacationing there with their parents, and she would have loved to have been able to join in the fun. But beside the restrictions imposed by the management, her father and mother would not allow her to leave the store and shirk her responsibilities.

"We need you, Julie," her father explained. "Marshall's working and we can't afford to hire anyone else and by having you here, it helps free your mother to cook."

Sometimes Julie would skip lunch in the dining room and slip down unnoticed to the lake for a quick swim and an hour of leisure. It was usually deserted at that time of day, except for the lifeguard, and Julie could soak up the sun and relax for a short time before returning to the store.

One afternoon as she stretched out on the sundeck in her white shorts and halter top, the lifeguard, who had been watching her for days, struck up a conversation. He told her that his family was from Long Island and he was working during the summer to help put himself through college and eventually business school. Julie thought Marvin Jacobs was the best-looking boy she had ever seen. He had dark wavy hair and beautiful blue eyes that were framed by thick black lashes. His muscular body had turned the color of burnished gold from spending so many hours in the sun. Julie enjoyed the time they spent together because Marvin was smart and had a good sense of humor. Several weeks later, as Julie emerged from a swim, Marvin approached her.

"Julie, how about coming to the movie with me tonight?"

Julie looked at him with uncertainty, not knowing what to say. Her father's rules about dating had always been very explicit. "No dates until you're fifteen."

Maybe, she hoped, *he might relent tonight. After all, it isn't really a date.* Everyone would be going into the social hall after dinner to see the movie—even her parents, since the store would be closed. *Anyway,* she thought, *it was worth a try.*

"Marvin, I'd love to go but I have to ask my father's permission."

"Sure, Julie, I understand. If you can make it, just meet me at the entrance at nine o'clock. I'll save us some seats."

Running back across the magnificent lawn that separated the huge lake from the main buildings, Julie literally flew into the store. Her father was busy making out a list of supplies and her mother was nowhere in sight. Approaching him timidly she said, "Dad, can I speak with you for a minute?"

Sam finished what he was writing and placed it on the counter. "Okay, Julie, I'm finished. What is it, baby?"

Breathlessly recounting her conversation with the young man, she asked if it would be okay if she went to the movie with Marvin. Hoping to convince him, Julie added, "You've see him around, Dad. He comes in often for sodas. He's a nice Jewish boy and he just started college."

"I'm sure he's nice, Julie, but I still feel you're too young. You know my rules about dating at this age, and I don't wish to discuss it any further. Now, I'd like you to help out for a while. Your mother is back at the bungalow resting."

With that, he returned to what he was doing, leaving Julie standing there perplexed. *It's not fair*, she thought as she stepped behind the counter and donned an apron. *It's only a movie, not a real date*. At that moment she felt a deep resentment toward her father. All the other girls her age were having fun, and as usual, she was being treated like a child.

Julie stopped her trips down to the lake and Marvin must have sensed her parents' objections, because he no longer came to the store.

The only ray of sunshine for Julie, in an otherwise dismal summer, was the Friday night amateur show, in which she sang. Alone up there onstage, singing the songs that were always so effective when she auditioned, Julie felt not only accepted, but special. The audience applauded enthusiastically, impressed by her voice and poise. And Julie glowed with their approval. She would have loved the opportunity to perform on Saturday night, which was when they used the important entertainers. But that night was reserved for headliners. Julie was thrilled that she got to see Sinatra, Martin and Lewis, and several other top names. She would sit in the back of the Casino and intently study their performances, trying to absorb all she could about show-manship.

Occasionally, a star would arrive earlier in the week and, on Friday night, drop in to watch the young kids perform. One evening, after the show, Julie was stopped as she was leaving the Casino by the guest star for that week.

"Kid, wait a second. I just saw the show and I think you've got a lot of talent and, what's more important, a lot of moxie. You're gonna make it."

Coming from a great star like Milton Berle who was the top-rated television entertainer of 1949, Julie was overcome with emotion. "Oh thank you so much, Mr. Berle. You don't know what this means to me. But I'm not an amateur you know," she hastily added. "I just closed in George Abbott's show."

"Really, how about that. What part did you play?"

"Well, I was only in the chorus, but I also understudied the second lead. Unfortunately, she never got sick so I never got the chance to go on."

Berle laughed when he heard this, and Julie couldn't understand why until she realized what she had said. She could feel herself blushing.

"Oh, Mr. Berle, I didn't mean that the way it sounded. I didn't want her to get sick or anything like that. But I do wish I could have played the role just one night."

"That's okay, kid, I know what you mean. Just be patient. You'll get your shot. Uncle Miltie knows talent when he sees it."

The summer wore on tediously, and just when Julie thought she could never make another ice cream soda or banana split, it was Labor Day and time to leave. Even though she would miss the Friday night shows, Julie was relieved. She was terribly anxious to get back home, resume her lessons, and once more concentrate on what she wanted more than anything else in the world—a career.

CHAPTER
6

After the Lehmans returned to New York, Julie desperately tried to find work, but without success. Esther Lieber arranged as many auditions as she could, but Julie's age and inexperience were still a handicap. Her one Broadway credit was inconsequential when she found herself pitted against girls who were not only older but also had already been in several plays. Esther decided that the only way to get Julie out of the chorus and into speaking parts was to engage a drama coach. Her next step was to call upon her good friend and colleague Claudia Bettes. Claudia, a former actress herself, had trained many successful Broadway actors. Some of her students had done so well under her tutelage that they had gone on to Hollywood and important film careers.

Reaching her by phone one afternoon after Julie had completed her lesson, Esther came right to the point. "Claudia, I have a very talented young pupil who has been studying with me for quite some time. I'd like you to meet her."

Julie, who had been waiting nervously outside Esther's studio, was ecstatic when she heard that Claudia would see her. But Esther cautioned her not to get her hopes up. "Claudia takes on very few pupils, my dear. Let's hope that you will be one of them."

When Julie came home that night and discussed the conversation with her mother, Rose was more than a little apprehensive. "Julie, just where are we going to get the money for a drama teacher? No, it's out of the question. We can't afford it."

"Mom, please listen to me. Unless I have some training, I'll never get ahead. I could work much more if I wasn't limited to just jobs in the chorus. I could even do straight plays."

Rose looked at her daughter's anxious young face and sighed. "I don't know where we're going to find the money, but go, *Mamale*, go and see this teacher and see how much she charges. Then we'll talk."

The next afternoon, Julie set out by foot for Claudia's apartment on West-Seventy-second Street. She needed time to think of what she was going to say and how she was going to convince Claudia to accept her as a pupil. Looking up at the sky, Julie began to walk faster. It had rained constantly during the night, and although it had let up some-what during the early morning hours, the sky once again looked threat-ening. Julie stopped for a moment and looked through her purse. *Darn it*, she thought. *I don't have enough for a taxi. I should have taken an umbrella*. Buttoning her coat, Julie hurried on. Suddenly, the rain began to fall, at first gently, and then with greater intensity. Julie began to dart under the canopies of the big apartment buildings for shelter. By the time she reached the address she was searching for, she was soaked through. The doorman announced that she was expected, and Julie took the elevator up to the apartment. When she reached the floor, Julie caught a quick glimpse of herself in the mirror and let out a groan of despair.

"My God," she muttered to herself. "I look like a drowned rat." Shaking out her hair as much as possible and removing her wet coat, Julie rang the bell. The door was opened by a petite, dark-haired woman who appeared to be in her early forties. She was wearing an elegant black dress with white collar and cuffs and her smile was warm and friendly.

"Oh my, you poor dear," she said as she ushered Julie into the library. "Let me take your coat. You must be soaked. Couldn't you find a taxi?"

Julie handed over her wet things as she glanced around the room. "No, Miss Bettes. The rain started suddenly and all the taxis were taken."

"Well, come here and sit down by me. Would you like some tea or coffee to warm you up?"

"I'd love some tea," Julie answered gratefully, "if it wouldn't be too much trouble."

"No trouble at all."

Claudia picked up the phone and pressed a button. Seconds later, a maid came into the room.

"Helga, please bring a pot of tea with lemon and some honey."

Julie smiled at her. "Miss Bettes, how did you know I like honey?"

"Well, my dear, Esther told me you are a singer, and all the singers I know take honey for their throats."

As Julie slowly sipped the hot tea, warming her chilled body, Claudia took a chair opposite her.

"Esther has told me how talented you are and that you would like to study with me. Is that right?"

"Yes, Miss Bettes. I would love to."

"Well, I *am* very busy, and ordinarily I do not take on new students, especially if they are not currently working. But Esther has raved so much about you, I would like to hear you read so that I can judge how much work you would need."

Picking up a script titled *The Royal Family*, Claudia asked Julie to read the part of Penelope. When she had finished, Julie watched Claudia's face for a reaction.

"My dear, it's obvious that you have natural ability, but you do need proper training in order to develop into an actress. I don't have much time available, but because Esther has such belief in you, I would be happy to take you on as a pupil."

Julie was thrilled that this accomplished teacher, who was so much in demand, would coach her. But before she could commit herself, Julie told her, "Miss Bettes, I'll have to discuss it with my parents. I don't know if they can afford it."

That night, as Julie and Rose sat in the kitchen Julie pleaded. "Mom, ten dollars a lesson is half of what she normally charges. She wants to see me twice a week. I know it's a lot, but the sooner I get started, the sooner I'll get a job."

Rose agreed that it was important for Julie's future, but even with the money that they had made that summer, they still couldn't afford it. There were car payments to be made, food and clothing, and as she reminded Julie, they were still paying off doctor bills.

Julie didn't want to add to her parents burden, and with a heavy heart, she realized that for the time being, she would have to pass up this great opportunity. Explaining this the next day to her beloved friend and teacher, Esther, Julie tearfully thanked her for all the trouble she had gone to in arranging the meeting.

Esther motioned for Julie to come and sit next to her, and patting her hand, the gentle, gray-haired woman comforted her. "I've grown to care for you as if you were my own daughter, Julie dear. I can't let this happen. If you're going to fulfill all my hopes and expectations for you, I'll have to find some way of convincing Claudia to take you on, money or no money. When you get a show, you can repay her. Now, dry your eyes while I make a call."

Handing Julie her lace handkerchief, Esther went into her study and picked up the phone. When she was alone, Julie looked around the studio where she had spent so many hours and began to think. *How happy I've been these past years in this room, with Esther seated behind the piano, smiling proudly at me when I'm good and frowning when I hit a clinker. It's been like a dream.* Oh please, please, she whispered to herself, *let me keep my dreams.*

Minutes later, Esther returned and noticing her pupil's face wrought with anxiety, she quickly gave her the news that Julie prayed she would hear.

"Relax my dear, you start on Tuesday."

Julie threw her arms around her dear friend and champion and hugged her with delight. "Oh, Esther, I'm so lucky to have found you. I promise that one day I'll make you proud of me."

When the day arrived for her first lesson with Claudia, Julie was nervous and apprehensive. Singing came so naturally to her that she never gave it any thought. But acting was different. She had felt self-conscious when she first auditioned for Claudia, and even though Claudia had accepted her as a pupil, Julie was still uncertain about her capabilities as an actress.

Like Esther, Claudia's studio was part of her apartment, and it was decorated beautifully. Besides the hundreds of books and manuscripts lining the overcrowded shelves, there were framed photographs of all her famous students. In the center of the room were comfortable sofas covered in a beautiful chintz. The whole atmosphere was cozy and inviting.

Claudia selected several different plays for Julie to study and told her the parts she wanted memorized. Julie's speaking voice, thanks to Esther Lieber and her years of training, was well modulated and needed very little work. What Claudia hoped was to teach Julie stage technique and also prepare her for a possible future in films.

"Gestures that seem perfectly natural on the stage," Claudia explained, "can be too broad for films. The camera has a tendency to make movements with your hands or any part of your body seem exaggerated. But before we get into film technique, let's first begin with your interpretation and understanding of the part."

Claudia, who had been so instrumental in preparing actors for both stage and film, had her own theory about coaching.

"I want to help you understand the characters you will portray, but I don't want you to copy me or anyone else. Your talent as a singer will be of great help to you as an actress. Remember, every time you sing a song you are telling a story and creating a different mood. That, my dear, is acting. I also know you are intelligent, and that, too, is an asset. Understanding that you have to sublimate your own personality and act and react as the character you are portraying would, helps to make a good actress. And now," she said, placing a script in Julie's hand, "let's begin."

While Julie made slow, but steady, progress with Claudia, her life at home had not improved—perhaps it even worsened. She was almost fifteen now, but her father still imposed severe restrictions on any dating. Julie couldn't understand what harm there was in an occasional date. After the many months she had spent confined to her bed, without the companionship of kids her own age, she yearned for the freedom that other girls had. But her father was unrelenting.

Julie tried to avoid confrontations with her father because it not only angered him but also caused arguments between him and her mother, and that was something she couldn't bear. Rose had been unable to convince him to ease up on Julie, and because of this Rose became even more angry with Sam.

Unhappy with the situation at home, and without any real friends, Julie focused all her attention and energies on her career. She continued her schoolwork, her singing and dramatic lessons, and showed up at all the auditions. She was determined to break through, and this time, if she got the opportunity, she would be prepared.

CHAPTER 7

Hundreds of people at the Waldorf-Astoria danced enthusiastically to the exciting Latin rhythms as Paco Castell and his orchestra helped welcome in 1950. Life had been good to him in many respects. At fifty he was at the peak of his career and was acclaimed on two continents. But his marriage to his third wife, Laura, was shaky, and if she had her way wouldn't last much longer. His first two attempts at matrimony to Latin women had been brief and tempestuous and his many romances in between, volatile. This marriage and eventual divorce could prove to be not only painful but very costly.

He had first seen Laura two years earlier on the set of one of his films, and her beauty immediately caught his attention. Her green eyes, tall and sensuous body, and platinum blond hair were a startling contrast to his former wives and girlfriends, and he knew instantly that he had to have her.

Laura, he quickly discovered, had very expensive tastes and knew how to use her sex and beauty to get what she wanted. Though young, she was hardly unsophisticated, having been the mistress of two eminently successful men. When Paco became aware of her past, he turned insanely jealous and began to watch her constantly. One evening, during an appearance at the Coconut Grove in Los Angeles, Paco noticed Laura undulating to the music with a young man on the dance floor. Jumping off the stage, he flew into an uncontrollable rage.

Pulling her away from her startled escort, Paco warned, "Laura, goddammit, stop your flirting. I'm not one of your stupid *gringo* boy-friends who will sit around watching you make a fool of me."

Laura looked at him for a moment, her green eyes gleaming with amusement. "Paco, you're just being a jealous fool. I can't help it if men find me attractive."

Grabbing her by the wrist, Paco pulled her off the dance floor and told her to sit at their table until he returned. Laura glared at him furiously, trying to control her temper. Ordinarily she would have walked out right then and there and broken off their relationship, but she was a shrewd and calculating woman. She knew that Paco was not only famous, but a man of considerable wealth, and she didn't want to risk losing him. Thinking it over, she decided to behave, at least until she became Señora Castell.

Once they were married, Laura quickly reverted to her old ways. In spite of Paco's repeated warnings, she resumed her flirtations and her excessive spending. Both activities soon became serious bones of contention between them.

Each month, as he reviewed the bills, Paco became more and more agitated at her extravagances. "Laura, for God's sake, how many new dresses and shoes do you need? These bills are outrageous."

"Oh, Paco," she would murmur as she wound her arms around his neck and caressed his face. "Don't be so stingy. You want your Laura to look beautiful don't you?"

Laura knew exactly how to stroke his ego and flatter him. But most of all, she knew how to satisfy his sexual appetite. In bed she was an experienced courtesan who knew how to use sex in order to get her own way.

Paco's new bride was unhappy with his modest home, and after considerable wheedling, she finally persuaded him to sell his attractive hacienda in Beverly Hills and buy a beautiful mansion in Bel Air. Knowing Laura's penchant for spending money, Paco warned her to exercise restraint in furnishing it. Even though he was making a fortune in nightclubs and motion pictures, Paco was still reluctant to spend it. Laura immediately hired a well-known decorator to assist her, and when Paco complained, she convinced him he was being unreasonable.

"You're a big star. And you should live like one."

Once the house was completed, Laura resumed her pursuit of jewels and furs, which further infuriated Paco. When he tried to curtail her spending, she lashed out at him.

"You're a cheap bastard and I'm sick of putting up with you. There are plenty of men around who would gladly buy me anything I wanted."

Paco realized that he had made a serious mistake. As much as he still physically desired her, he began to see her for what she really was, and he knew that their marriage was doomed.

A few days later when the excitement of New Year's Eve had died down, Paco thought about this as he sat in his hotel room at the Waldorf. He began to contemplate how he could extricate himself from an unhappy marriage without having it cost him a fortune.

Across town, Julie Lehman and her mother were just leaving a theater where one of Paco's movies was playing. It was a wintry afternoon, the kind of day most New Yorkers prefer to stay indoors. But not Julie and Rose. These Saturdays had become almost a ritual. When they reached the street, they decided to have some hot chocolate at Schrafft's, one of Julie's favorite spots. It had started to snow as they left the theater, and as they trudged through the streets they buttoned their coats tightly around their necks to protect themselves from the cold. Once they were settled in their cozy booth, Julie began reviewing the movie they had just seen.

"Mom, did you notice that beautiful girl that walked down the stairs and started singing with the orchestra? She was fabulous. I think that Paco Castell's music is just the best in the world. Anyone could sing to those rhythms."

Rose took a sip of her drink and nodded. "Yes, Julie, he's good, but I'd rather watch Van Johnson."

But Julie was undaunted. Her face was flushed with excitement as she continued. "Oh, Mom, couldn't you just feel that music? It was so thrilling."

"I know, Julie, you've told me a hundred times."

Rose knew that if she would have permitted it, Julie could have stayed and seen the picture over again. But Rose was anxious to get home. By the time they left the restaurant, it was starting to get dark, and a lot of snow had already accumulated on the ground. People were rushing through the streets, their heads bent low to avoid the snow. Rose grabbed Julie's arm and pulled her toward the bus stop. But Julie had one more request.

"Mom, it's not too far from here. Could we go past the Waldorf-Astoria just one more time? Please? I love to look in the lobby."

Rose wasn't surprised, as this was another one of Julie's fantasies—to appear at that famous hotel. "Julie, it's snowing and getting late. This is not the kind of weather to go walking."

Rose looked at Julie's crestfallen face and relented. "All right, Julie," Rose said resignedly. "But just a few minutes. It's getting cold and your father will be home soon and expect his dinner."

When they reached the front of the hotel, which was on Park Avenue, Julie let out of a squeal of delight. "Mom, what a coincidence. Look who's appearing here? Paco Castell!"

Julie grabbed her mother's arm and pulled her through the revolving doors. Running up the steps with Julie to the lobby, Rose could barely catch her breath.

"Slow down," Rose panted. "I'm not as young as you."

Julie looked around, dazzled by the splendor—the marble floors, the velvet couches, the bronze doors that led to the Empire Room, where Paco Castell was appearing. It all had an air of elegance that Julie yearned to be a part of. Running over to her mother, she took her hands and held them tightly.

"Mom, I just know it. I can feel it in my bones. One day I'm going to be starring here."

Rose smiled patiently and nodded her head. "Yes, sweetheart, I know you will. But now let's hurry. We have to get home."

By the time they reached the bus, the streets were practically deserted. The snow was falling so heavily now that most people had already sought refuge in their homes or nearby restaurants. Julie didn't mind the weather. She loved the snow, especially when it was like this—clean and white. Helping her mother up on the bus, Julie began to settle down, but her eyes were still glowing from excitement and the cold. She continued to chatter happily about the future and how famous she was going to be. Rose listened for a while but soon became distracted. She shouldn't have let Julie talk her into staying out so late. She hated for Sam to come home to an empty apartment. Fortunately, the snow had delayed him and they arrived home first.

When Sam walked through the front door that evening, Julie ran to her father and gave him a big kiss. Her exuberance filled the air.

"Dad, we had such a good time today. First, we went to a movie at the Roxy and then to Schrafft's. Then we walked over to the Waldorf-Astoria. Oh, Dad, it was wonderful. That hotel is so elegant. And what do you think? Paco Castell and his orchestra are appearing there. Remember when I was sick and you brought me his records? I've loved his music ever since. I can't wait until I'm old enough to sing there."

Julie's eyes sparkled with the excitement of youth and ambition, and although Sam was happy for her, he was fearful. He didn't want his daughter to be hurt, and in the profession she had chosen for herself, there was every possibility she would be if she didn't make it to the top. *After all*, he reasoned to himself, *how many of them do?*

"Baby, I'm glad you and Mom had a good day. But now be a good girl and get me my slippers. I want to read the paper before dinner."

Julie did as she was asked, but she was disappointed that her father didn't share her enthusiasm. *Never mind*, she consoled herself as she opened up her movie magazines and began to dream. *One day, he'll see.*

CHAPTER
8

During the month of August, the blistering pavements of the streets of New York could penetrate right through your shoes, especially if you were out all day long looking for work. As Julie made the endless rounds, she soon began to realize that in order to find a job on Broadway she would first have to find an agent. But when she approached them, most of the successful theatrical agents gave her the same story: "Come back, kid, when you've had more experience. We don't handle newcomers."

The smaller agencies, which might have been interested in Julie, just didn't have the "juice" to push an unknown. Another disturbing factor, and one that bothered Julie a great deal, was the fact that often the junior agent, usually a young man in his early twenties, would try to date her.

"Look, beautiful," some smart aleck jerk would crack, "you gotta be seen around town so people will notice you. Lemme take you to the Copa tonight. Frank's opening there."

Julie was getting used to guys making passes at her, and so far, she had managed to discourage them without being nasty. But it wasn't all that easy. Over the past months, Julie had blossomed from just a pretty girl into a beautiful young woman, and even at the tender age of fifteen, she exuded a sensuality that men found hard to ignore. Perhaps if her father had been less rigid and possessive and had allowed her the freedom other girls her age enjoyed, Julie would have been better prepared to deal with the opposite sex. But that had not been the case, and Julie soon began to realize that she would have to learn how to handle not only herself, but men.

As the weeks wore on, frustrated and unable to get representation, Julie began to rely totally on Claudia and Esther, and occasionally leads from other actors, for news of auditions.

It was during a quick lunch break at Hanson's Drugstore, the famous meeting spot for actors, writers, and comics, that Julie first heard about the new Mike Todd show.

Sitting at the crowded counter with the casting paper propped up in front of her, Julie searched for open auditions. Suddenly, she felt someone tug at her sleeve.

Turning around, Julie saw Lou Mandel, one of the "regulars" who frequented Hanson's.

"Hey, kid, did ya hear that Beverly Michaels left the Todd Show for Hollywood? There's a spot open now, but ya better hurry. They're already in rehearsal."

Lou, a struggling comedy writer who knew everything that was going on around town, was attracted to Julie but always acted like a gentleman, because he knew she was only a kid.

"Gee, thanks, Lou," Julie said, a smile brightening her face. "Do you know where they're rehearsing?"

"At the Winter Garden. But, honey, you'd better move it. I just told the same thing to two other girls."

Julie paid her check and sped out the door like a comet. When she reached the stage door, she was dismayed to find scores of other girls ahead of her. After waiting nearly an hour, Julie finally found herself inside the theater. Looking around, she instantly recognized a gray-haired man standing in the wings holding a call sheet. Leaving her spot in line, Julie walked over and tapped him on the shoulder. "Mr. Harris, do you remember me? I'm Julie Lehman. I was in the Abbott show."

"Oh yes, Julie, of course. How are you?"

"I'm fine, thank you, but I've been looking for work. Are you the stage manager here?"

"Yes, I am. I've been on vacation since our show closed, but now I'm back in harness again."

"Well, Mr. Harris," Julie asked, peeking out to the stage where a girl was singing, "do you think I could get an audition for the Beverly Michaels part? I heard she left the show."

"Well," he answered, scratching his head, "I'll tell you, hon, there are a couple of girls that Mike Todd has already seen and he likes a lot." Noticing Julie's crestfallen expression, he added, "But why don't you get your music and be back here tomorrow at ten. I'll see to it that you get on." Julie gave him a quick hug of thanks and immediately rushed home to tell her mother. Rose was thrilled but decided to wait for the outcome before mentioning anything to Sam.

The next morning, with her mother's help, Julie selected a pink angora sweater with short sleeves that fit her rounded curves like a glove. With it, she chose a slim black skirt and black high-heel shoes. Instead of pinning her hair up in an attempt to look older, Julie brushed it vigorously and let the soft waves cascade around her face. With a good luck kiss from her mother and her music tightly clutched in her hand, Julie set out for the Winter Garden Theater and Mike Todd. Because the show was already two weeks into rehearsal, there wasn't the mob scene that usually accompanies a "cattle call," as the agents so appropriately named auditions. Bobby Harris, who had been with George Abbott for years and was now working with Todd, was waiting at the piano when she arrived.

"Julie, take these pages and look them over for a few minutes. Mr. Todd wants to hear you sing and then read when you're ready."

Julie took the pages and sat down in a corner where some other girls eyed her cautiously. After a short while, when Julie was satisfied that she remembered Claudia's training and advice on how to handle a cold reading, she motioned to him she was ready.

Walking to center stage, Julie glanced out into the audience. She could hear some whispering, but she couldn't make out where the voices were coming from. As soon as her accompanist was seated at the piano, Julie began to sing. After she had finished, the silence was deafening. Uncertain whether or not she should continue, Julie asked, "Would you like me to read now?"

A loud, gruff voice boomed back at her, "Wait a second. How old are you, kid?"

Julie was taken aback, unprepared for that question. Hesitating for a moment, she answered, "Seventeen, sir."

A chuckle could be heard in the theater and then a command. "Okay, kid, let's hear you read."

Trying not to glance at the pages in her hand too often, Julie read the part of Corrine, the sexy show girl. When she finished, a short and stocky man jumped up onstage and came up to her. Chewing on a huge cigar, he studied her closely. "Listen, sweetheart, I know you're not seventeen and you know you're not seventeen, so let's cut the crap, right?" Taking the cigar out of his mouth, he yelled to Bobby, "Get your ass over here."

The stage manager hurried over. "Yes, Mr. Todd?"

"Take Julie . . . what's your name again, kid?"

"Julie Lehman."

"Right. Julie Lehman." Pausing for a second as he reflected on it, he said, "Lousy stage name, kid. You should change it. Bobby, take her over to Madame Varinska's and get her fitted for the part of Corrine. You got an agent, kid?"

"No, sir," Julie answered tremulously.

"Okay, no big deal. Standard actor's contract, seventy-five a week, half for rehearsal. We open in New Haven September twentieth." Turning, he walked down the steps and into the audience.

Julie did not even have time to thank him, as he disappeared too quickly. *But it's just like in the movies. The gruff, tough producer and the young frightened chorus girl. Only this is for real and not make-believe.*

The next few weeks were a combination of happiness and anxiety. Everyone who believed in her talent was delighted that Julie would finally be getting a chance to show her ability. Even though her role was small, it could, in the words of the stage manager, "be a standout." Her real problem was not with the show, but with her father. Rose, of course, was ecstatic, already visualizing Julie in Hollywood. Sam, on the other hand, was not at all thrilled. But he knew how much this opportunity meant to Julie and therefore he tried to be supportive. Of course this new show meant that once again there would be an upheaval in their lives, and he didn't like it. Rose would have to accompany Julie for the out-of-town tryouts, and that would leave him alone and without his family. Rose was irritated by Sam's attitude, not fully understanding his thinking. But Sam felt he had reason for concern. He was fully aware that every day Julie was blossoming more and more into a woman, and a sensual one at that. As a father, he also worried how naive his "innocent baby" was and how, without his guidance, she might be led astray. In light of this, Sam was ambivalent about giving his blessing, and yet, he could not find it in his heart to stand in her way. He was torn between what he felt was right for his daughter and her blinding ambition. But with Rose already supporting Julie's dreams, he had no alternative but to give her his consent.

CHAPTER
9

As the train pulled into the station in New Haven, Julie's body tingled with anticipation and excitement. The past few weeks of rehearsal had been strenuous but very rewarding. Unlike the George Abbott show, where Julie played a high school cheerleader, she was now portraying a sexy femme fatale, and the men in the cast took notice of her. Mike Todd had immediately taken Julie under his wing and treated her like a daughter. "Keep your distance," he had warned the actors. "She's just a kid. So, hands off."

Even if he hadn't been their boss, no one in the cast would have dared to cross a man like Todd. He was tough, and they knew it. In keeping with his reputation as a flamboyant producer, Todd had gathered together some of New York's most beautiful women to make up the cast and had spent a fortune costuming them. Julie felt reasonably secure when it came to her talent, but when confronted with competition from older and much more glamorous women, she was horribly insecure. At night, after a long day's rehearsal, Julie would often voice these insecurities to her mother.

"Mom, they'll never notice me when I'm out there with those gorgeous girls. They're so tall and have big bosoms. Next to them I look like a kid."

Rose guessed that her daughter's fears were probably unfounded. "Listen to me, Julie. Mike Todd wouldn't have given you a part, especially one that calls for you to play a sexy show girl, if he didn't think you could handle it. Those *shiksas* have been around a lot and you're a new and fresh young face. Besides that, you have talent. So stop your worrying."

Julie had to laugh when her mother spoke like that. To Rose, everyone who had blond hair, blue eyes, and wasn't from New York was a *shiksa*, or, as Julie translated when people didn't understand, not Jewish. Rose seemed to forget that practically all of Sam's family were blond and blue-eyed and that Julie herself had been born with light hair.

To overcome her insecurities, Julie worked extra hard not just to perfect her role but at her studies as well. It was extremely difficult for Julie to juggle her schoolwork and rehearsals, but inasmuch as she was in her last year at Professional Children's School and a good student, her teachers reassured her she would graduate on time.

Each day when Julie arrived at the rehearsal hall, which was located over a Jewish dairy restaurant on the Lower East Side, she felt an increasing sense of excitement. Just being around the other actors, writers, and the director gave her a feeling of belonging. In her previous show, she had been much younger and only in the chorus. Now, however, she was a "principal" in a production that was already being touted as the musical of the season.

Before leaving town, Rose tried hard to find someone to come in to take care of the house and Sam in her absence. She eventually found a part-time woman to do the cleaning, but she was concerned about the meals. Sam tried to reassure her, telling her not to worry.

"Listen, Rose, I'll be fine. During the week I'll grab a bite downtown after work, and on Sunday I'll go to my mother's. So there's no problem."

"Your mother?" Rose asked as she wrung her hands in despair. "You know how you hate her cooking. You'll get sick eating that food. She's never made a decent meal in her life. You've said so yourself a million times."

"Rose, calm down. Don't worry about my food. I'll eat. Just take care of yourself and my baby. That's all I care about."

Rose compulsively cleaned their already immaculate apartment as she prepared for their departure. She too was excited about the trip, even though she had been to New Haven and Boston before during the George Abbott tryouts. But this time it was different. Julie would be making more money, and her name, however small, would be featured in the program. Rose couldn't understand why, but she had a strong feeling that this new step in Julie's career would be a turning point in their lives.

Leaving the train station that morning, the entire cast was bused over to the hotel where they would be staying for the next few weeks and given their rehearsal calls. That night, when Mike Todd arrived with his entourage, the cast was already seated onstage, ready for the orchestra run-through. Todd's presence in the theater made a huge difference in their attitude. Suddenly everyone was on their toes. The girls quickly began touching up their makeup, hoping to impress the boss, and the guys stopped kidding around. Even though Todd was friendly most of the time, they also knew that he was the kind of man who would not tolerate anything less than total professionalism.

After rehearsing for eight weeks with only a piano as accompaniment, it was a thrill when Julie heard her song with full orchestra. After running through their numbers several times, the cast was dismissed until morning, and they wearily made their way back to the hotel. But Julie's energy level was so high that when she and Rose went to bed that night, she couldn't fall asleep.

"Mom," Julie whispered softly, "are you asleep?"

"What is it Julie? I'm tired."

Climbing out of her bed, she sat down next to her mother and hugged her knees to her chest. "I'm sorry, Mom. It's just that I'm so excited. I know this show is going to be a big success and I can't wait until opening night."

Lifting herself up slightly, Rose looked at her daughter's enthusiastic face. "Yes, darling, I feel it too. I just know that great things are going to happen once they see what you can do."

Julie kissed her mother good night and went back to her bed to dream about the future.

The weeks that followed were a glorious time in Julie's life. As was expected, the show received good notices in New Haven and, after some revisions and more rehearsal, even greater ones in Boston. Julie was singled out in both cities by critics who called her "a fresh and talented new face who shows great promise."

Rose called Sam as frequently as possible, and only when he assured her that he hadn't been poisoned yet by his mother's cooking could she, without guilt, continue to give Julie her full attention.

On their last night in Boston, Mike Todd assembled the cast onstage right after the performance. He emphasized that even though the critics had been kind to them on the road, the cast couldn't afford to get sloppy and complacent. Chewing on his ever present cigar, he paced back and forth like an expectant father, explaining what he wanted from them once they got to New York.

"Kids, the next few days when we begin previews are going to be the toughest you've ever spent. I want you to get to the theater early each day for rehearsals and I expect a great performance each night. By the time we open on Friday, this will be the tightest and best goddamn show in New York or my name ain't Mike Todd! And," he added, "if it's not a smash hit, remember, you'll all be out on your asses looking for a job!" With his words still ringing in her ears, Julie returned to New York, her father, and the awesome responsibility that lay ahead—opening night.

Sam was terribly relieved to have his wife and daughter back home safely, and hoped that things would now be getting back to normal. He hadn't wanted to upset Rose while she was on the road, but he had suffered terrible loneliness during their absence.

When opening night finally did arrive, Julie sat in her dressing room surrounded by fifteen other girls who shared the space with her and tried to steady her nerves. The stage manager had just called half-hour, and suddenly the room that had been alive with noisy chatter, fell silent as the girls began finishing up their makeup in preparation for the big night ahead of them.

Julie had been ready for more than an hour. Her father had dropped her off and returned home for dinner and to change before returning with Rose to the theater. Her parents had bought seats for themselves, and Marshall and his new bride and were planning to meet Julie backstage after the show. Julie picked up her mirror for the hundredth time and studied her reflection. *Is my makeup on right? Am I wearing enough mascara?* Nervously she began to brush her hair over and over again.

The cast had been there since nine o'clock that morning and had completed their last run-through at two o'clock. By the time Julie removed her makeup and had returned home, there was barely enough time to rush back to the theater. Now she was sorry her mother had insisted she eat something because she felt sick to her stomach.

Placing her mirror back on the dresser, she tried to remember what Esther and Claudia had told her. "Breathe deeply and relax. Keep your mind focused on what you have to do and try not to let anything distract you."

That wasn't easy when you were dressing in a room with fifteen other girls. Most of them were experienced and had already appeared in many Broadway shows. Maybe to them, this was just another job with good pay but not to Julie. This was her first real opportunity, and she was determined to make the most of it.

"Fifteen minutes," a voice boomed out over the loudspeaker. "On-stage everyone."

Fifteen minutes, Julie thought. *Well, this is it. Please, God, don't let me disappoint my family and teachers, who believe in me.*

Her hands wet with fear, Julie walked over to the rack where all the costumes were hanging and slipped into her opening gown. She picked up the fan that was one of her props and, with a last quick glance at herself in the mirror, went out the door and into the wings. Peeking out through the curtain, Julie's heart started to beat rapidly. Seated in the audience were some of the most important people in show business—producers, directors, and actors—a truly star-studded opening night. As the overture began, Julie took a deep breath. Suddenly, the nerves were gone. She was ready.

Hours later, the private dining room upstairs at Sardi's restaurant was lined with wall-to-wall bodies. The chorus kids were standing around with drinks in their hands, chatting happily, for the show had gone well. But the bit players and stars waited anxiously at their tables for the reviews. Everyone was watching the door, expecting Mike Todd and his beautiful movie star wife to arrive at any moment. But more important, they were all waiting for the newspapers. In less than an hour, their fate and the fate of the show would be decided by seven men.

Too excited to engage in conversation, Julie stood near the door, next to her parents. In her mind she was reliving the past few hours, and although she had been very nervous, she was certain she had done her best. Rose was just about to ask her one more time when she thought Todd would arrive, when suddenly there was a commotion outside the door. Photographers piled into the already crowded room, and immediately behind them, smiling broadly, were the energetic and ebullient producer with his fur-draped wife.

"Mike, Joan, look over here, smile," a photographer shouted. "Put your arm around her, Mike. That's it. Wait, let me get a few more."

Everyone in the room was anxious to congratulate Mike Todd and at the same time hear his comments on their performance. But they would have to wait, for at that moment, Bill Doll, the company's press agent, arrived with the papers.

"Smash hit for Mike Todd," raved the *New York Post*.

"Todd has assembled a bevy of beauties for his lavish production," wrote the critic of the *Herald Tribune*.

The other newspapers were equally generous, with the exception of the *New York Times*, which did not consider the show another *Oklahoma* or *Carousel*, but nevertheless predicted that it would probably have a good run.

Each time a new review was read, thunderous applause sounded in the room. The stars and other actors were happy and relieved that they had been well received, while the kids in the chorus were thrilled to know their jobs were secure.

Julie's name had been briefly mentioned in two of the newspapers and although they had not called her a new Ethel Merman, the fact that she had been noticed in a very tiny role was, in itself, gratifying.

As the noise and commotion started to die down, Julie prepared to leave when, suddenly, Todd and Bill Doll approached her and drew her aside.

"Julie," her boss said, "you did me proud. You've got real talent, and this show is gonna do you a lot of good. I've told Bill to set up some interviews with newspapers and TV. The publicity will not only help you but the show as well. Now go home with your folks and get a good night's sleep. You've got a big day ahead of you tomorrow."

What Mike Todd had prophesied for Julie on opening night turned out to be true. In the months that followed, Julie Lehman's name appeared regularly in Earl Wilson's column. Even Dorothy Kilgallen, who was not known to favor newcomers with space in her widely read column, mentioned that "a beautiful and very young redhead is worth watching in the new Mike Todd show."

Julie couldn't believe her eyes when she read the newspapers. *Imagine*, she thought, *Dorothy Kilgallen singled me out of all those beautiful women*. Realizing that on any given night there might be columnists and other important people in the audience, Julie made every performance count. Not that she wouldn't have anyway. She was already too much of a professional ever to let down.

In contrast to all the attention Julie was receiving, family life at home continued in its usual mundane fashion. The only difference in their routine was Sam's appearance at the stage door most nights to take Julie home. He was very concerned, not only about his daughter's traveling home alone late at night, but also about the "stage door Johnnies" who constantly hung around the theater. The other girls in the show were much older and far more experienced, and because Julie's appearance belied her youth, Sam was determined that nothing happen to his young and innocent daughter.

As the months went by, Julie began to think of her future. The show had settled into a comfortable run, and although her performances and publicity appearances kept her very busy, she still was not satisfied. Having been noticed and admired was not enough. She was now anxious to move on to stardom. Even Rose couldn't understand her daughter's restlessness.

"For God's sake, Julie. You're making seventy-five dollars a week. You're in a hit show and you're receiving a lot of attention. What more do you want?"

"Mom," Julie answered impatiently, "you don't understand. It's only a small part. I'm not onstage that long. If I wait until the show closes, I'll be out there looking for work with all the other kids. I want to move up now."

As fate would have it, Julie's future was already being planned and, once set in place, her destiny sealed.

CHAPTER 10

W ake up, Julie. It's Mr. Doll's office on the phone."

Julie stretched her weary body, looked over at her clock, and pulled the covers back over her head.

"Julie, hurry up," Rose called. "They said it's important."

"All right," Julie answered sleepily. "I'm coming." *What in God's name can they want?* she grumbled to herself as she reached for her robe. *It's only nine o'clock and I'm dead tired.*

Taking the phone from her mother's hand, Julie spoke briefly to the head of the publicity department and hung up the receiver. Instead of going back to bed, Julie went into the kitchen and poured herself some orange juice. The morning sun was streaming into the room as she sank into a chair and watched her mother, busy at the sink washing some vegetables.

"So, what was so important that they had to get you out of bed?"

Julie yawned, still not fully awake, and repeated the conversation. "The 'Vincent Lopez Show' has a television spot available for a girl singer tonight, and Bill Doll wants me to get down there for rehearsals by one o'clock. It's just one song, but they say he has a big following. Besides that, the publicity will be great."

"Oh, Julie," Rose cried out enthusiastically, turning off the water. "That's wonderful. I must call your father right away, and the neighbors, and Marshall, of course. Let's see, who else?" Suddenly, Rose stopped as another thought crossed her mind. "Julie, what in the world are you going to wear? They probably expect an evening gown, and you don't have one."

Julie laughed. "Mom, the world could be coming to an end and the only thing you'd worry about was what was I going to wear."

"That's because the way you look is important, Julie. Especially on television."

"I know, Mom, and I agree, but please don't get so excited. It's important, but it's not the 'Ed Sullivan Show.' "

"I know that, sweetheart, but it's your first singing appearance on television, and I want you to come across great."

Julie embraced her mother, giving her a hug. "I'll do my best, Mom, and thank you for always encouraging me. I love you."

"I love you too, baby. Now, go and take your shower or you'll be late."

Julie headed for the bathroom, but before closing the door, she turned. "Mom, I forgot to tell you. You'll never guess who the guest star is tonight. Paco Castell."

Julie arrived at Channel 5 a little before one and was ushered into the studio where the "Vincent Lopez Show" was rehearsing. Julie took a seat and watched as the other guests went through their numbers. When her turn came, Julie sang her song through twice—once for the orchestra and once for the cameras. Satisfied with her performance, the director excused her and told her to report to the makeup and hair departments.

Julie was just finishing some last-minute touches in her dressing room when the floor manager knocked on her door. "Miss Lehman, the producer would like you to go to the greenroom when you're ready. We have half an hour before show time."

Julie quickly slipped into the emerald green evening gown the wardrobe department had provided for her and, with a final glance in the mirror, went to join the other performers already seated. Julie looked around for Paco Castell, but he was nowhere to be seen. Then she overheard the stage manager say that the famous bandleader would arrive just in time for the show. Julie felt disappointed because she had hoped to meet him before she went on. After her appearance, she would have to change quickly, then dash madly back to the Winter

Garden in order to make the curtain in time. Taking a chair near the television monitor, Julie waited with the others for the show to begin. Suddenly the door opened and a group of people walked into the room, chattering noisily in Spanish. Julie instantly recognized that the man in the center, wearing the blue pinstripe suit with the red carnation in his lapel, was Paco Castell. He looked exactly as she remembered him on the screen except, perhaps, a little shorter. She didn't realize that she was staring until all at once he turned to her and she came face-to-face with the man she had admired for so many years. Looking at him now up close, Julie was startled by his eyes. Unlike most Latin men, Paco Castell had the most intensely blue eyes she had ever seen. And those eyes were now staring at her with such interest that she could feel her face redden with embarrassment. Not knowing what to say, Julie stuck out her hand and, in a shy voice, introduced herself.

"Mr. Castell, my name is Julie Lehman, and I'm on the show tonight. I've always been a big fan of yours. In fact, I've seen all your movies." Suddenly embarrassed by her childish outburst, Julie began to blush uncontrollably. Paco's eyes gleamed at her with amusement and his mouth turned up into a smile.

"And what else do you do besides watch my movies and make all the young men fall in love with you?"

Julie began to stammer, as she was unaccustomed to having a man talk to her like that, especially a famous movie star. "Well, right now I have a small singing part in the Mike Todd show."

"I see," Paco said.

But before he could continue, the floor manager appeared and summoned Julie to accompany him to the studio. Julie politely excused herself and followed him down the hall. *Why did I act like such a gushing teenager?* Julie asked herself as she walked to the studio. *He must think I'm an idiot.*

After her number, Julie rushed down the hall to the dressing room. But before she could reach the door, Paco Castell came out of the greenroom and blocked her way. Standing there, his eyes devoured not only her face but her entire body. His physical presence became so overwhelming that Julie could feel her knees trembling.

In that still heavily accented voice, which had successfully charmed so many women, he said, "Julie, I just watched you on the screen and you looked beautiful. You also have a lovely voice. Tell me, do you know where Nola Studios is?"

"Oh yes, Mr. Castell. I've rehearsed there a few times."

"Well, my dear, could you be there at ten o'clock tomorrow morn-ing? I would like to hear you sing with my orchestra."

Julie's mind began to whirl feverishly. She had to get back to the theater quickly, and she didn't have time to think clearly. Could it possibly be that Paco Castell was offering her a job? If so, it was almost too incredible to believe.

Hesitating only a moment, she answered, "Yes, Mr. Castell. I'll be there."

On the way back to the theater, Julie was in a daze. *Why did I say yes*, she wondered. *I must be crazy.*

During intermission that evening, Julie called home to get her mother's reaction to her television appearance. Rose was ecstatic.

"Julie, you were wonderful. The whole neighborhood was watching. Marshall called, and your father saw the show in the restaurant across the street from the office. You should have heard him, Julie. He was so proud."

"Really, Mom?" Julie asked. "Oh, I'm so glad. I was a little nervous. I hope it didn't show."

"No, sweetheart," Rose assured her. "You looked beautiful and relaxed, just like you had been doing this a hundred times. By the way, did you get to meet that bandleader, Castell?"

Julie hesitated, not knowing whether to repeat Paco's conversation and offer to her mother right now, or wait until she got home. She decided to wait. It would be easier to explain in person than over the phone. "Yes, Mom, I met him. Look, I've got to run. I'll tell you everything tonight when I get home."

When Julie emerged from the theater that evening, several of the guys who hung around the stage door waiting for their girlfriends came up to her and congratulated her on her TV performance. Julie thanked them but didn't linger because she noticed her father's car parked at the curb. On the way home, Sam confirmed what her mother had already told her and reassured her that he was very proud. Julie didn't mention anything about her audition the next day because she wasn't quite sure how her father would react. Paco Castell's name had been in the newspapers a great deal lately because of his impending divorce, and she was certain her father would have grave reservations about her working for a man like him, if indeed she was lucky enough to get the job. *Anyway, why worry*, she thought. *He's always had Latin singers and very exotic girls. I'm certainly not that type. He was probably just being polite.*

But a tiny little voice inside her head kept telling her that Paco Castell's interest was very real and had little to do with her voice or whether or not she was Latin.

Later that night, when Sam was in bed, Julie and Rose sat huddled together like two school chums discussing a date while they plotted their course of action. After Julie took her aside and broke the news to her, Rose agreed to allow Julie to audition on one condition—that she stay away from the musicians.

"Bums, that's what they all are," Rose warned her. "And Castell is probably a bigger bum than all of them."

Julie tried to stifle her laughter. "Mom, not all musicians are bums. You know that the musicians in the show always act like perfect gentlemen."

"That's because they're legitimate musicians—not a bunch of *trom-beniks,* bums, running around all over the country playing in night-clubs." To try and reason with her mother when she was in this kind of mood was useless, so Julie promised to keep her distance, sing her songs, and call her the minute she got out of there.

The next morning Julie carefully chose what she would wear to Nola Studios. After trying on several different outfits, she decided on a simple but attractive form-fitting green wool dress, trimmed with gold buttons at the sleeve and neck. Rummaging through her mother's costume jewelry, she found a small pair of gold earrings that comple-mented her dress. Brushing her red hair until it shone like a newly minted copper penny, Julie then carefully applied her lipstick and a touch of mascara. Having inherited her mother's beautiful complexion, Julie didn't require any rouge. Satisfied that she looked her best, she kissed her mother good-bye and set off for Nola Studios.

As Julie walked through the door in Studio B, she could hear the familiar strains of "Besame Mucho" being played. *How wonderful it is,* she thought, *to be in the same room listening to this beautiful music, instead of hearing it on our old record player at home.* Julie waited at the back of the room until the music stopped, hoping that someone would notice that she was there. Moments later a very tall man who resembled Paco Castell came up to her and introduced himself.

"Excuse me, *señorita.* My name is Luis Castell. Are you Julie?"

"Yes, I am," Julie replied. "I'm here to audition for the orchestra."

"*Sí, como no,* of course, I'm Paco's brother. Please come with me. He is waiting."

Taking her arm, he led her to the bandstand, where Paco was

engaged in what seemed like a heated discussion in Spanish with one of the musicians. Unlike his elegant attire the evening before, this morning he was in shirt-sleeves with a silk handkerchief tied around his neck. The moment he spied Julie, he drew her to one side and looked at her admiringly.

"Well, my little one, you are here, and you look even more beautiful than I remembered you."

Julie looked around nervously, first at him and then at the musicians, who were watching her with knowing smiles on their faces. She felt embarrassed by Paco's familiarity and wished that she could just get on with the audition. There was something about the way he looked at her that made her feel very uncomfortable.

Sensing this, Paco immediately became more businesslike and asked if she had any music she would like to sing.

"Well, Mr. Castell, I've brought something from my show, if you'd like to hear it?"

"Don't you know anything in Spanish?"

"The only song I know is the one you were playing as I came in, 'Besame Mucho.' I learned it from your record."

"*Muy bien*, that's fine. Go over to the piano and Rafael will find your key. Then sing it for me please."

Julie did as she was asked, and minutes later she told him she was ready. As she began to sing, Julie tried to think back to the movies she had seen in order to emulate Paco's former vocalists. Swaying to the music, she prayed she wouldn't forget the Spanish lyrics.

By the time she had finished, her hands were ice cold, even though the room was quite warm. When Paco came over to her, Julie apologized for what she felt was an inadequate rendition of the song.

"Mr. Castell, I know that I wasn't at my very best, but I didn't realize that you would want me to sing in Spanish, and I only learned that song phonetically."

"Don't worry, lovely one. You did very nicely. Besides," he murmured moving closer to her, "when someone looks the way you do, who cares about the way they sing."

"Well I do, Mr. Castell," Julie answered, backing away. "I've been studying music all my life, and I want to be a success because of my talent, not because of my looks."

"My, my," Paco laughed, "a spitfire too. I like that. Now, who said you didn't have talent. My dear, I am a master showman. I have created more stars than anyone else in show business. I do not hire people to work for me who do not have potential. Remember that. All I meant, and forgive my bad English, is that you are very young and very beautiful, but with very little experience. But if I choose to, I, Paco Castell, can take the potential that I see in you and turn you into a star."

CHAPTER
11

Julie left Nola Studios in a daze, uncertain if what had happened was real, or just a dream. She had accepted the challenge of an audition with Paco Castell's orchestra never really believing that she had half a chance. Now she was returning home with the realization that he not only wanted her, but wanted her quickly—in fact, as soon as she could free herself from the show.

Slowly Julie walked up Broadway in the direction of the apartment. She was reluctant to go home before she had a chance to think things out. Facing her was a momentous decision, one that could probably affect her whole future.

As she crossed Fifty-seventh Street, Julie spied the Automat, one of her favorite eating spots when she was in a hurry and didn't have much money. Suddenly, Julie felt a pang of hunger. She had been too nervous to eat anything before she left that morning and she decided that she couldn't walk another block without some nourishment. After finishing a chicken pot pie, Julie lingered over her hot chocolate as she thought back to Paco's parting words. "Julie, I'm certain with my guidance you could have a very important career. But, you must give me your decision quickly. I have auditioned several other girls, and though I would prefer to have you, I cannot wait too long for your answer."

Although Paco had acted very professionally when he discussed his offer, Julie still had misgivings about his full intentions. Though inexperienced and unsophisticated, Julie's instincts warned her that if she accepted the job, a relationship with Paco Castell might be part and parcel of the deal. The thought of any kind of romantic involve-ment with him was unthinkable. She had not even been allowed to date young men her own age, and here was a man, practically as old as her father, who seemed smitten by her.

It appeared to be such an impossible situation that Julie wondered if she should just forget completely about it and continue in the Todd show. But the idea of singing with Paco's band and the possibility that she could achieve stardom much sooner with his help were so tempting that they soon began to overshadow her fears. As she started for home, Julie pondered her situation. *How will I convince my parents, especially Dad, that I can pursue my career goals without compromising my virtue?* The task ahead of her seemed almost impossible, and she realized it wouldn't be easy. *But*, she thought, *I must find a way.*

Julie was relieved to find the apartment empty when she opened the door. She needed more time to think and time to plan. Getting her mother's consent would be hard enough. But her father's . . . Julie shuddered at the thought.

Whenever her father picked her up at the theater, he would make a habit of pointing out the difference between his sweet "baby" and the other girls in the show. "Those women may be young, Julie, but already they look shopworn. That's not going to happen to you, sweet-heart. Not with your dad to look out for you."

Now Julie was faced with the dilemma of how to tell him that she wanted to join a band whose leader was a man well known as a womanizer. With a deep sigh, Julie went into her parents' bedroom, kicked off her shoes, and stretched out on her parents' bed. She looked around lovingly at the familiar surroundings. The double dresser that her mother had inherited from Grandma Esther and that Rose compul-sively polished every day to gleaming perfection. The large mirror hanging over the dresser where she had posed and played "make-believe" for so many years. Her eyes lingered on the now faded wallpa-per with the little pink roses that Julie had stared at for so many lonely months while confined to this very bed. All these bits and pieces of her childhood memories suddenly became very important to her, and for some strange reason, she felt frightened.

Suddenly, Julie heard the front door slam.

"Baby, are you home?"

Julie could hear packages being placed on the kitchen table and her mother's footsteps on the linoleum as she put away the groceries. "Julie, where are you? Come tell me what happened."

"I'm here, Mom, in the bedroom. I'll be right there."

Julie went over to the dresser and stared at her flushed reflection. *Try and act natural*, she told herself. *You mustn't let Mom suspect that this job has any strings attached to it. Besides, you're not even sure that's the case. Just tell her about the job, how much traveling is involved, and the many opportunities that Paco pointed out this morning. And above all, don't forget to mention the hundred dollars a week.*

Bracing herself, Julie walked down the hall. But before entering the kitchen she put a big smile on her face. "Hi, Mom. Do you need any help?"

Rose closed the cupboard door and turned to face Julie. "No, it's done. So, tell me. How did it go?" Before she could answer, Rose interrupted her. "I know, he said you're a very talented young girl but he's looking for another type, right?"

"Wrong, Mom," Julie answered. "I know it sounds unbelievable, but he wants me to give two weeks' notice and join the band in Hartford."

"What!" Rose yelled. "Is he crazy, just like that, leave a successful broadway show and travel alone with a bunch of musicians? What does he think—that we're out of our minds and that we would let our daughter, who has never even been away to camp in the summer, leave home alone?"

Rose was building up to such a frenzied pitch, Julie could barely hear her own voice as she tried to explain. "Mom, please, calm down. Listen. He says that you can come along on the road with me. We'd travel on the bus and stay together in the hotels and you could come to the ballrooms every night and watch the show. You'd be with me all the time and it would be fun."

"Fun. What are you talking about fun? Who would take care of your father? Do you expect me to leave him alone? No, no, it's out of the question."

Julie paused, searching frantically for something else that she could say that might help convince her mother.

"Listen, Mom. It won't be a long tour, and we wind up in California. Paco told me he's going to make a new movie and I would be in it."

This wasn't an invention of Julie's because this was one of the promises Paco had dangled as bait. What Julie was being evasive about was the length of the road tour. Paco had indicated that they would be gone for at least four months, which included a trip to South America. But that disclosure could come later, Julie decided, once she had succeeded in overcoming the first hurdle.

As soon as Rose heard that Hollywood and motion pictures were in the offing, her manner seemed to soften considerably.

"Well, that's a little different. Now he's talking. I'm sure you wouldn't want to schlep around the country just being a band singer. What about salary? What is he offering you?"

Julie swallowed deeply, hoping to free herself of the lump in her throat. She'd gotten this far. Now maybe the additional money she would be making would serve to further soften her mother.

"One hundred dollars a week clear, Mom. He'll take care of the hotels. All we would pay for is our food."

Rose, who up until now had been pacing the room like a caged animal, suddenly relaxed and sat down. Julie joined her at the kitchen table, and both mother and daughter clasped their hands together.

"Julie, *Mama sheyne*, think carefully. Is this what you really want?"

"Yes, Mom," Julie pleaded. "This could be my big chance."

Watching her daughter's intense young face and eyes burning with ambition, Rose was reminded of herself when she was that age. Instead of pursuing her dreams, Rose had compromised, opting for security. She loved Sam dearly, but she wanted her child to have a chance to make something more of her life.

Rising from where she was sitting, Rose came over and clasped her daughter's face to her bosom. "Don't worry, sweetheart," Rose assured her. "Somehow we'll have to convince your father to let us go."

Across town, Paco Castell sat in his lavish apartment at the Waldorf-Astoria and stared at the images on his television set. But he was oblivious to what was happening. His mind was still on Julie.

Dios mio, my God, he thought. *What am I getting myself into? She's so goddamn young and innocent.* Paco's divorce had been progressing very slowly because of Laura's extravagant demands, and if a new woman were to enter his life, especially one as young and beautiful as Julie, things could get messy.

Ay Paco, he thought. *Why can't you concentrate more on your music and less on your sexual appetite. You would be better off.*

Ever since he met Julie on the "Vincent Lopez Show," Paco had been unable to get her out of his thoughts. There had been so many beautiful women in his life who had literally thrown themselves at him, that he had never found it necessary to pursue anyone. But something about Julie was different. He was convinced that conquering this ambitious and beautiful young girl would be more difficult, and that would make the pursuit even more exciting. But first, he knew he would have to deal with her family.

When he'd offered her the job as vocalist with his band, he could see the exhilaration in her eyes, and it was quite apparent how anxious she was to accept. But she had declared her position instantly by telling him in no uncertain terms that she would never consider traveling without her mother. Obstacle number one. Then there was the matter of her age. She was not yet sixteen, and that was young even by Paco's standards. Obstacle number two. Finally, he seriously doubted her suitability for his orchestra. All his singers had been Latin, with the temperament and personality needed to interpret his music. Here was a redheaded Jewish girl whose training had been geared for the Broad-way stage and who did not even speak Spanish. Obstacle number three.

Paco's experience and logic told him that it was foolhardy even to consider her. But the memory of those sensuous lips and ripe body, still innocent and untouched by any man, were too enticing to be ignored, and he felt he had to have her—no matter the cost.

That evening, when Rose heard Sam's key in the door, she had already made up her mind on what she would say. "Sam, you're home early," Rose called from the kitchen. "Come in after you've washed up. Dinner's ready and Julie is home. Now remember," Rose warned her daughter, "let me do the talking. I know your father better than you, and if you say the wrong thing he'll just say no."

Sam Lehman walked into the kitchen, and after kissing his wife and daughter, he smiled as he sniffed the aroma of his favorite meal cooking on the stove—brisket of beef and potato pancakes.

Sitting down at the table, he poured some seltzer water into a glass and unfolded his newspaper. "So, my two girls, what have you been up to today?" Before either of them could answer, a thought suddenly occurred to him and he looked at his watch. "Julie, how come you haven't left for the theater yet? Won't you be late?"

"No, Daddy. I've still got half an hour before I have to go. I was hoping you would get here before I left."

"Well, the buyers in the showroom left early, so I rushed home. I don't get a chance to see you too much during the week. Whenever I pick you up after the show, we're both so tired we never even have a chance really to talk."

Julie started to speak, but Rose immediately interrupted her. Sitting down opposite him, she looked at her husband pleadingly. "Sam, listen. There's something that I want to discuss with you concerning Julie."

Sam put down his glass and looked at his wife and then back at his daughter, who was staring at him with frightened eyes. "It must be serious if I get brisket during the week."

"Sam," Rose urged, "listen to what I have to say and please don't form any conclusions until you've heard me out."

Rose then proceeded to tell him the whole story about the audition and the subsequent offer. Instead of reacting in the way they would have expected, Sam Lehman sat very still and listened. When Rose finished speaking, he quietly pushed his uneaten food aside and in a very calm voice reminded Julie that it was getting late.

"You had better leave for the theater, Julie." Turning to Rose, who had been expecting a furious outburst, he said, "Keep my dinner until later. I'm not hungry right now. I think I'll go into the living room. I need time to think."

Julie gathered up her purse and coat and followed her father into the room. Walking quietly over to where he was sitting, with the evening paper still unopened in his lap, Julie put her arms around her father and gave him a kiss.

"Daddy, I'm so sorry. I don't want to do anything to hurt you or Mom. Please, don't be angry with me. I love you so much."

Sam Lehman looked into Julie's amber eyes, seeing a mirror reflection of his own, and smiled sadly at his daughter's troubled face.

"Baby, I know you love me, and believe me, I'm not angry with you. I can't blame you for being ambitious. It's only natural, I guess. But all I want to do is protect you. I know what the world is like out there and you don't. You are the most trusting and obedient child a parent could ever ask for, and I don't want anyone to take advantage of you. That would kill me."

Watching his daughter's eyes fill with tears, Sam tried to comfort her. "Don't be upset, sweetheart. Go do your show. We'll talk later, when you get home." Taking some money from his wallet, Sam pressed it into Julie's hand. "Forgive me, sweetheart, if I don't pick you up tonight. I want to discuss this situation with your mother. After the show, ask the stage manager to find you a taxi."

The apartment was quiet when Julie returned home that night. All the lights had been turned off except for the little lamp in the hall that Rose left on during the night because she was afraid of the dark. Assuming that her parents were asleep, Julie tiptoed around quietly, removing her clothes and slipping on a robe so as not to disturb them. As she was about to climb into bed, her mother called out from the bedroom.

"Julie, we're awake. Come in."

Julie opened her parents' door and saw that they were both wide awake. Her father was sitting up in bed, while her mother sat in her favorite "sewing chair."

Patting the coverlet, her father spoke first. "Julie, baby, come sit down on the bed. Mom and I have been talking things over and we'd like you to know our feelings."

Fearing the worst, Julie sat down at the foot of the bed and tremulously waited to hear her parents' decision.

"First of all, I must tell you that I am disappointed and more than a little upset that you never told me beforehand about the audition. But I'll forgive you for that. Now, after giving this matter considerable thought, I want you to know that I am opposed to you going out on the road with a band, especially when the bandleader is Paco Castell, who has a bad reputation where women are concerned."

Oh no, Julie thought. *He's not going to let me go.*

"Julie, you're a child who has never been exposed to that kind of life. This man is much older, he has been married several times, and even with Mom traveling with you, I would not feel at all comfortable having you surrounded by a bunch of musicians."

Watching Julie's crestfallen face and large eyes that were about to brim over with tears, Sam continued quickly. "Julie, please don't cry. Mom has explained how much this means to you, and so, despite my reservations, I'll agree to let you go on one condition. Now listen to me, Julie, and listen carefully. This will only be a trial period. It is not permanent. Your mother has assured me that she will not let things get out of control. If she feels unhappy or if any difficulty arises while you are out of town, you will return home immediately. Do I make myself understood?"

Julie threw her arms around her father and hugged him. "Oh, Daddy, thank you. I promise that I'll do whatever Mom says."

Kissing her parents good night, Julie went back to what served as her bedroom and got into bed. But she was too excited to sleep. She still couldn't believe it. Her father was going to let her go. Julie couldn't imagine what her mother could possibly have said to convince him. But it didn't matter. What mattered was that she, Julie Lehman, was going to be the vocalist with Paco Castell's Orchestra and go to Hollywood and become famous. Hugging herself with delight, Julie turned over and closed her eyes. She wanted to get up bright and early. There was so much she had to do and so little time.

From that night on until the moment they got on the train for Hartford, things moved very quickly. Julie gave the show two weeks' notice and joyfully began to prepare for her new adventure. Mike Todd was in California when he heard she was leaving, and upon returning to New York he tried to persuade her not to make such a foolish mistake.

Calling her into his office one Saturday afternoon after the matinee, he tried to reason with her. "Julie, for Christ's sake," he bellowed, "that guy's a lecherous bum. Sure he's a big star, but you don't need him. You've got beauty and talent. You'd make it eventually, and on your own."

"Oh, Mr. Todd," Julie answered, touched by his concern, "I appreciate everything you've done for me, and please don't think I'm not grateful. But I'll be protected. My father would never permit me to go without my mother along as chaperone. Besides, Mr. Castell hasn't done anything to make me feel that he's interested in anything but a new singer."

"Bullshit, kid. He's got eyes. You're young, you're beautiful, and you're a good girl, which makes you even more desirable for a guy like Castell."

Realizing he wasn't reaching her, Todd tried a different approach. "Look, Julie. I'm very fond of you and I don't want to see you get hurt. If I thought that this guy was on the square I'd give you my blessing. But I think you're in for trouble."

As much as Julie respected Mike Todd, she just couldn't turn back now. And so, with the blind determination of youth and oblivious to the pitfalls that were being pointed out to her, Julie proceeded with her plan.

Rose, too, was busy. Once Sam consented, she quickly made arrangements for a part-time maid who would keep her house in order while she was away. Sam would have to fend for himself as far as food was concerned, although Rose's best friend, Marsha, a neighbor, promised to invite Sam over as frequently as possible to have dinner with the family.

Even though Rose was slightly apprehensive about all the traveling they would be doing, in a way this new opportunity would be an adventure for her as well as for Julie. Other than the tryout cities that she and Julie had stayed in before her shows had opened, Rose had never been out of New York. Some of the excitement that Julie was feeling eventually began to rub off on Rose, and she found herself actually looking forward to the trip.

When the day finally arrived for their departure, anyone looking at their faces would have thought there had been a death in the family. Even Marshall and his wife, whom Julie had not seen for some time, came to see them off. But everyone looked terribly somber.

Sensing the tension that existed, Marshall tried to lighten things up by teasing his sister. "Sarah, old girl, you're on your way."

Julie had to giggle at Sarah Heartburn, her brother's silly nickname for her—a takeoff on the famous actress Sarah Bernhardt.

"Oh, Marshall, you always make me laugh when you call me that."

Gently ruffling her hair, he fondly embraced his sister, feeling love and pride for her success and achievements. "Pretty soon now I'll be going to the movies to watch my kid sister up there on the screen."

Holding on tightly to her brother, she gave him a hug and kiss. "Thank you for believing in me," she whispered.

After kissing Sam dozens of times and reassuring him that they would both be fine, Julie and Rose boarded the train that would take them to the beginning of a new chapter in their lives. Leaving behind not only her family and friends, but her childhood as well, Julie sensed that nothing would ever be the same again.

CHAPTER 12

The air was brisk, with gusty March winds blowing dust and soot across the platform as a tired Julie and her mother arrived in Hartford. Gathering their suitcases from the train, Julie and Rose found a porter to help them find a taxi, and they proceeded to the hotel that Paco's brother, Luis, had arranged for them.

After they checked in, Julie looked around the room that had been assigned to them, and which would be their home for the next week. "It's a pretty room, isn't it, mom?" Julie asked, admiring the lace curtains and beautiful bedspread. "I'll bet this hotel was elegant when it was new."

Rose nodded her head, too busy unpacking to engage in idle chitchat. She was anxious to get settled before Julie was called for rehearsal. Just as Julie was about to pick up the phone to inform Luis that she had arrived, there was a knock on the door.

Straightening her wrinkled dress and glancing quickly in the mirror to make sure her hair was tidy, Julie went to the door and opened it. She found Paco Castell standing there with a wide grin on his face and a devilish look in his blue eyes.

"May I come in, Julie?" he asked. "I'd like to meet your mother."

As Julie stepped aside, Paco paraded grandly into the room and introduced himself. "*Buenos tardes, señora.* I'm Paco Castell and you must be Julie's mother."

Rose Lehman, who had never been up close to a bona fide movie star, was overwhelmed. Dropping the clothes she had been sorting out in the bureau drawers, she immediately came forward, a smile brightening her face.

"Yes, Mr. Castell. I'm Julie's mother, Rose. It's a pleasure meeting you. My daughter has always been a big fan of yours."

Embarrassed that she might have offended him, she quickly added. "And, by the way, so have I."

"*Muchas gracias, señora.* You are very kind. You have a very lovely daughter, and now, after meeting you, I can see where she gets her beauty. I hope you both are going to be very happy with our little family."

Julie, who had been standing by silently, watching Paco charm her mother, now spoke up. "Of course we will, Mr. Castell. Mom and I can't wait to meet everyone and get started."

"Well, my dear, you will soon have your chance. Tomorrow I would like you to be at the Schubert at ten o'clock to run over some material. The theater is just down the block from the hotel. I'm sure you won't have any trouble finding it." Turning once more to Rose, he said solicitously, "*Señora,* your daughter will have a lot to learn and very little time before her first performance. I would suggest that she get some rest. If you ladies are hungry, please order something from room service." Glancing at his watch, Paco added, "Now, it's getting late and I must leave. *Hasta mañana.*"

Until her meeting with Paco Castell, Rose had been quite negative in her feelings about him but now was somewhat taken by his charm and respectful manner. Resuming her unpacking, she began to think, *Well, Sam, so far so good. Let's see what tomorrow brings.*

The Schubert Theater, which once had been a legitimate theater for Broadway-bound plays, had been converted into an auditorium for variety shows. When Julie and Rose arrived in front of the theater, the marquee was being changed to announce the upcoming attraction. The posters were already in place in the two glass window boxes that flanked the box office. Julie ran over to them, anxiously searching for her name.

The Schubert Theater proudly presents
directly from the Waldorf-Astoria

PACO CASTELL AND HIS ORCHESTRA

FEATURING . . .

MIGUEL SANCHEZ AND HIS CANCIONES DE MEXICO

JOSÉ AND ESTELLA—DANCE TEAM EXTRAORDINARIO

RUBY GONZALEZ—FIERY LATIN BOMBSHELL

Besides a huge photograph of Paco, there were pictures of the other performers, including one of a beautiful dark-haired girl in a sexy gown, posing provocatively with maracas in her hands.

Julie was bewildered. Where was her name and picture? Surely there had been plenty of time since she first signed on as vocalist to include her in the billing. There must be some mistake.

Entering the darkened theater, Julie and Rose walked down the aisle to the stage, where the musicians were already gathered, tuning their instruments.

Motioning for her mother to be seated, Julie climbed the stairs up to the stage. Suddenly it seemed everyone stopped talking at once and began to stare at her. Feeling very uncomfortable in an environment totally alien to her, Julie anxiously looked around for a familiar face. Moments later, she saw Luis Castell entering from the wings and coming toward her with some music in his hands.

"Good morning, Julie. Did you have any trouble finding the the-ater?"

"No, Luis. It was easy." But she really was thinking, *The only trouble I had was finding my name on the billboard.*

Taking her arm, he led her over to the piano. "Rafael, I think you've already met Julie, our new vocalist. Here are some songs that Paco has selected. Find her key and run through them a few times. He'll be here shortly." And turning, he walked away.

Leaning over the pianist's shoulder, Julie looked at the music that she was expected to sing and panicked. "Rafael, all of these songs are in Spanish. Don't you have anything in English? Perhaps something from a Broadway show?"

"*Señorita*, I only play what the maestro gives me. Nothing more and nothing less."

Oh God, Julie thought. *What am I going to do? Maybe I can learn the lyrics phonetically in time for the show.*

As Rafael began to play, Julie thought the melody sounded vaguely familiar. Then she realized it was "Frenesí," one of Paco's famous hits. Julie started to hum the music, not daring to attempt the words in Spanish—not with the whole band looking at her. Halfway through, Julie started to sing the English lyrics, which she read off the sheet music. In a few minutes, some of the rhythm section joined in to help her, and all at once the music and sound of her voice blended into one.

Just as she was finishing the song, Paco appeared onstage. Unbeknownst to her, he had been watching Julie from the back of the theater while she was singing. Taking her hand, he walked to center stage and introduced her to the musicians. "*Caballeros,* I want you to meet our new vocalist, Julie Lehman, or, as she will be known for the time being, 'Ruby Gonzalez.' "

"Ruby Gonzalez," Julie gasped, startled by his announcement. "Who is she?"

"You, my dear. At least until we can find a new name for you."

"But, Mr. Castell," Julie said softly, "there's a picture of a girl out front with dark hair and *her* name is Ruby Gonzalez."

"*No importa,*" he answered. "She was my last singer and her real name wasn't Ruby Gonzalez either, just a stage name I invented. Now she's gone to Hollywood to make films, so it really doesn't matter. Besides," he added, "you need a new Latin image and a name to go with it. The advance publicity had already gone out for the tour with her name and picture featured, so it's too late to change now." Suddenly impatient with the conversation, Paco said abruptly, "Enough. Let's not discuss this anymore. It is time for you to rehearse and learn how to become Ruby Gonzalez."

Julie felt like she had been shot out of a cannon and had landed in never-never land. She dared not look at her mother, who was still seated in the audience. She knew she would be livid. And rightly so. Not having the courage to argue with him, she had stood meekly by and accepted his decision.

Paco tapped the music stand with his baton and called for attention. "All right, *muchachos*. I want you to play 'Frenesí' once again, and this time everyone join in."

Turning to Julie, he instructed her to sing into the microphone so he could hear her better. Tentatively at first, Julie started to sing. She was nervous and unaccustomed to singing into a microphone. On the Broadway stage, an artist was expected to be heard without amplification. After stopping a couple of times to correct notes and tempo, Paco finally seemed satisfied with what he heard and gave the band a fifteen-minute break.

Julie's hands were clammy with fear and nervousness. Instead of feeling secure because she already had the job, she was afraid that at any moment he would fire her. She couldn't understand what the musicians were saying, or Paco for that matter. He obviously preferred speaking to them in Spanish.

If I'm going to survive, Julie thought, *I'd better learn Spanish, and quickly.*

Taking advantage of no one being on the bandstand, Julie approached Paco hesitantly. "Mr. Castell, was that okay? Did you like the way I sang the song?"

"Yes, Julie," he responded. "It was fine. But we have to find some more material for you. You can't sing just one song. Furthermore," he added, "I would prefer it if you would learn how to sing in Spanish and move your body a little more to the music. You are too, how do you say it, too rigid. I want you to feel the rhythms and let your body move along with the beat."

He might as well have been speaking Chinese at that moment, for Julie didn't understand what he was saying.

When he hired me, she thought, *he knew that I wasn't Latin. How can I develop a style and learn a language in just two days?*

Bewildered, Julie pressed him to explain. "Mr. Castell, I don't understand. You never told me that I would have to become a Latin singer. I thought you liked me just the way I am."

Patting her cheek, he answered her. "Julie, *querida,* I do. But that doesn't mean that I cannot make you better. In a short time, I will transform you into a Latin spitfire. You will be so sexy, not even your mother will recognize you."

That's what I'm afraid of, Julie thought.

As the band wandered back to the bandstand, Paco handed Julie two more songs and told her to rehearse them with Rafael in the dressing room backstage. "There's a piano there, and when you're finished, we'll go over them with the orchestra."

Somehow Julie got through the rest of the morning, and by the time they broke for lunch, she was exhausted physically and emotionally. Still ahead of her was an inevitable confrontation with her mother, and she dreaded it.

Rose was waiting just where Julie had left her three hours earlier, and as she approached her mother, Julie could see sparks of anger flashing in her eyes. Before Julie could speak, Rose grabbed her arm and pulled her up the aisle.

"Ruby Gonzalez," she began to shout at the top of her voice. "Who the hell does he think he is? I've left your poor father all alone in New York so my daughter could make a name for herself—and now it's not even going to be your name. That's it. We're going home."

"Mom, please, keep quiet," Julie begged. "They'll hear you."

"What do I care if they hear me? I watched you stand there and let him walk all over you. Well, he won't do that to me."

Julie was so distraught she could barely see where they were going. When her mother finally stopped, she found herself standing in front of the theater. Pulling Julie over to the poster, Rose shouted at her furiously.

"Look, my brilliant daughter. Is that your picture or your name up there? What will I tell your father and all our relatives and friends? That Julie Lehman is all of a sudden this Ruby garbage? Listen to me, young lady. Either you speak to him or I will."

Julie was on the verge of tears. "Mom, please listen. I have so much to learn and so little time. Tomorrow night I have to get up on that stage and sing three songs I'm unfamiliar with, and two of them in Spanish. Please, I beg you. Wait until after the opening, and then we'll straighten it all out. No one knows me up here, so what difference does it make whose name I use?"

Rose shook her head angrily and started to walk down the street, but Julie ran after her. At first Rose refused to be mollified. But after much pleading on Julie's part, and assurances that the problem would be rectified as soon as possible, she grudgingly relented.

After grabbing a quick lunch at a nearby coffee shop, Julie and Rose returned to the theater. The other members of the show were now present, waiting to rehearse. Julie recognized them from their pic-tures—the dance team José and Estella, and sitting off in a corner, a very handsome olive-skinned young man, who, she figured, must be Miguel Sanchez.

As Julie sat waiting to be called, someone suddenly tapped her on the shoulder. Looking up she saw a tall, stately woman with light blond hair pulled tightly into a bun at the nape of her neck. She guessed her to be about her mother's age or a little older.

"How do you do, Julie. I'm Marion Morello, Mr. Castell's secretary."

Julie got up and extended her hand. "How do you do, Miss Morello. I'd like you to meet my mother, Rose Lehman."

"We're so happy to have you both with us," Marion said warmly. "If there's anything I can help you with, please call me." She started to leave, but abruptly turned back. "Oh, by the way, Paco would like to see what evening gown you're intending to wear tomorrow night."

Evening gown, oh my God, Julie thought. *How could I have been so stupid. He thinks I've got a gown and it never occurred to me that they wouldn't provide one. What am I going to do?*

Glancing helplessly at her mother, who had remained silent, Julie searched for an answer. "To tell you the truth, Miss Morello, I don't have an evening gown. I've never needed one because I've only worked on Broadway and have always had my costumes supplied by the producer."

"I see," Marion replied. Pausing for a moment as she reflected on this, she said, "Well, let me speak to Paco. We'll have to see what we can come up with. I'm afraid the stores up here won't have too much of a selection."

Excusing herself, she went in search of her employer while Julie sat down dejectedly and looked at her mother.

"Don't look at me like that, Julie. Even if we could afford it, which we can't, where in the world could we find a decent dress that fits you properly by tomorrow night?"

"I don't know, Mom, but I've got to wear something. I don't understand why they didn't tell me about this while we were still in New York."

"Because," Rose explained, "they thought you probably had evening gowns and were bringing them with you. Though only God knows why a girl your age would be expected to have clothes like that."

Julie sat there dejectedly, thinking, *God, what a day this has been. First, Ruby Gonzalez and now this.*

In a few minutes Marion returned, and beckoning for them to follow her, they quietly slipped out of the theater and into the street. Grabbing Julie with one hand and Rose with the other, Marion hustled them into a nearby taxi.

"Hurry, ladies. We're going shopping."

The next few hours were spent in a whirlwind of activity. The only decent gown they could find that did not make Julie look like a little girl wearing her mother's clothes was in a bridal shop. Settling on a pale green gown that looked more suitable for a high school prom than for a budding Latin temptress, Rose took it back to the hotel and tried to improvise some improvements. Marion promised them that in Boston, which was the band's next destination, they would find something more appropriate.

Julie fell into bed that night too tired to think. She had stayed backstage quite late working on the songs with Rafael while Rose had gone next door to get them sandwiches. Even though Rafael tried to reassure her that she had nothing to worry about, Julie was still apprehensive about opening night.

Just as she was about to fall asleep, the telephone rang. Julie couldn't imagine who could be calling them at this hour. They had already spoken to her father earlier in the evening, so it couldn't be him.

"Hello," Julie answered softly.

"How is my beautiful little Ruby?"

At first, Julie thought the person at the other end had made a mistake and asked for the wrong room. But then when she recognized Paco's voice, she knew he was speaking to her.

"Hello, Mr. Castell. Is anything wrong?"

"Wrong, what could be wrong?" he answered in a voice as smooth as silk. "I just wanted to tell you there is a beautiful moon and I am standing at the window looking at it and thinking of you."

Julie put her hand over the receiver, afraid that her mother might hear this intimate conversation.

"Oh, Mr. Castell, that's nice. I want to thank you for all your help."

"Mr. Castell. You sound so formal. You must call me Paco, or if you like, Paquito."

Embarrassed and afraid her mother might hear, Julie mustered, "Thank you for calling. I'll see you tomorrow."

Julie pulled the covers over her and tried to sleep, but it was useless. The intimate telephone call had unnerved her too much. If her mother had heard him, they would already be on a train back to New York.

"Who was it?" Rose asked sleepily from her bed.

"It was Paco Castell, Mom. But it was nothing important. He just wanted to see if we were okay."

Rose went back to sleep and Julie heaved a deep sigh of relief. She would have to find a way to deal with Paco and still keep her job. She knew that would not be easy.

The next evening, Paco's voice rang out over the microphone and into the crowded theater. "Ladies and gentlemen, I take great pride in presenting my new discovery—a young lady who I predict will one day be a big star. The beautiful and talented Miss Ruby Gonzalez."

When the music started it took Julie a moment to realize that she had just been introduced. Fighting back her nervousness, she walked out onstage in her green "bridesmaid" dress with tulle ruffles billowing out of the skirt and faced her first audience as "Ruby Gonzalez."

Somehow Julie managed to get through the show, but after her performance she had no idea as to whether she had sung well or not. She did recall receiving a fair amount of applause from the audience, but everything else was a blur.

When she returned to the dressing room she shared with Estella, the female half of the dance team, the dancer greeted her cheerfully.

"*Hola*, Julie. I watched the show from the wings and you were good."

"Thanks, Estella," Julie said as she began to unhook her gown. "One thing is for sure. I was pretty nervous."

"Oh, don't worry about that," Estella said as she twisted her long black hair into a braid. "Everyone is nervous when they first start out with the band. You'll get used to it."

Pausing for a moment, Estella looked at Julie, trying to choose her words carefully. "Julie, I'd like to give you some advice. You've got to get rid of that crappy dress you're wearing. It makes you look like a schoolgirl. It's not sexy enough for a Latin band."

Julie removed her gown and stared at it disgustedly. "I know, Estella, but it was the only thing we could find on such short notice."

Carefully placing the gown back on the hanger, Julie grabbed a robe and began to remove her makeup as she waited for her mother to come backstage.

All at once, she heard a gentle rapping at the door and Paco's voice outside. "Girls, are you dressed? Can I come in?"

Wrapping her robe tightly around her body, Julie opened the door. Paco walked in, and after greeting Estella in Spanish, he turned his attention to Julie. Estella quickly left the room, realizing that Paco wanted to be alone with Julie.

"Well, Julie, how do you feel after your first performance?"

"Alright I guess, Mr. Castell." Then seeing his eyes look at her questioningly, she corrected herself. "I mean, Paco."

"You did very well considering you had so little rehearsal and did not understand the meaning of the lyrics you sang. But the most important thing is the audience. They liked you, and you cannot fool the public. Remember that. With hard work on your part and some changes in your hair and wardrobe, you will soon be the Latin bomb-shell that my public expects."

Julie's hands flew up to her head the minute he mentioned her hair. *What did he have in mind,* she wondered? *Does he plan to change my hair as well as my name? Oh no,* Julie thought. *If Mom hears that she'll really kill me, or even worse, make me quit.*

Before she could question him further, her mother suddenly appeared in the doorway. "Hi, Mom. How did you like the show?"

Rose walked in and, after kissing her daughter, acknowledged Paco's presence. "Good evening, Mr. Castell. It was a very good show. I enjoyed it very much. But, to tell you the truth, I would have liked it even more if you had used my daughter's real name."

Julie glanced nervously over to Paco, hoping he wouldn't get angry at her mother's bluntness.

"*Señora,*" he answered, with the charm he was famous for oozing out of every pore in his body, "I can assure you that when my press agent has had enough time to change all the advance billing, and when we find a more suitable stage name for Julie, which I'm sure you will agree is most important, I will be happy to have her drop the name Ruby Gonzalez. Until then, I beg you, please be a little patient. It won't be for long."

Bowing his head, Paco started to leave the room, but when he reached the door he paused for a moment and turned. "Ladies, my brother, Luis, has arranged for a late dinner in the hotel dining room. I would be happy to have you join me."

As soon as he was gone, Julie started breathing normally again. She hadn't expected her mother to confront Paco so quickly and was surprised and delighted that his response had not further agitated her mother. Instead of discussing the matter any further, Rose started to place Julie's street clothes on the vacant chair. Julie grabbed her mother's hands, forcing her to stand still.

"Mom, for goodness' sake, say something. How was I?"

"I think you were very good tonight, Julie, and he knows it. I also think we'd better get busy and find a name for you. I want to be sure that by the time you reach Hollywood, Ruby Gonzalez will be gone and forgotten." Patting her daughter's cheek, she smiled and said, "Now get dressed and let's go have dinner."

Relief flooded over Julie's face when she realized that she had gotten past a major hurdle. From now on she would devote herself to learning Spanish and developing a more Latin style. But most important, she would try to find a way to discourage Paco's romantic overtures before they got out of hand.

CHAPTER 13

The tremendous roar of the bus as it thundered through the night toward their next destination, coupled with the uncomfortable seats, had made sleep out of the question for Julie. She had been tossing and turning for hours. Now she glanced over at her mother, who was curled up next to her, leaning on a pillow they had "borrowed" from the last hotel they had stayed in, but her eyes were closed. Directly in front of them, Julie could see that Paco was out like a light. Since joining the band, she never ceased to marvel at the way he could fall asleep at the drop of a hat. It was no wonder he was the only one who arrived at their destination rested. They had been on the road now for six weeks, playing mostly one-nighters, and after Boston, all of the other cities had become a blur. As Marion Morello had promised, Paco had provided the money for two new evening gowns, but Rose wasn't too thrilled with Marion and Julie's choices. She felt that they were too low cut and much too sophisticated for a girl Julie's age. But Marion, who had become a friend to both of them, patiently explained to Rose that Julie needed to look more glamorous, and Rose finally agreed. Julie heard her mother stir and adjust her position, but she made no sound, so Julie leaned her head back and tried to relax. But her mind kept reliving the past six weeks.

Since leaving Hartford, their lives had become a steady routine of work, travel, and rehearsals. Although it was a far cry from the glamorous life that Julie had anticipated, she wasn't discouraged. Paco had explained that one-nighters were always difficult, but necessary. It gave thousands of his fans an opportunity not only to see him in person, but to dance to his music. All of the famous bands did at least one tour like that a year—Dorsey, Benny Goodman, Harry James. The fun, Paco promised, would begin when they played nightclubs and big hotels. Julie was content, even though the work was grueling. She was making progress. She had begun to understand a little Spanish, although much of her vocabulary consisted of "dirty words" that the musicians delighted in teaching her when Paco wasn't around. But what encouraged her most of all was how fast she was adapting to the image that Paco expected of her and how rapidly she was broadening her repertoire of songs.

The ballrooms where they appeared were all pretty much the same— a vast open space with a bar stuck off in the corner and a huge bandstand surrounded by fake palm trees. Hanging from the ceiling was the ever present mirror ball, and when the spotlight hit it, it would send prisms of light all over the ballroom, creating a dazzling effect in an otherwise barren room.

The dance music would usually begin at eight and be over by midnight. The accepted routine was that Paco and the band would play forty-minute dance sets and then take a twenty-minute break for coffee, or, if the guys could sneak it without being seen, booze. Paco had very strict rules about drinking while they were working, so they had to be careful.

Julie and Miguel sat on opposite sides of the bandstand during the entire sets, and upon hearing their music, would get up and sing. Right from the beginning, Paco's instructions to them had been very explicit. "Sing the songs exactly the way we play them without any variations. We're playing dance music now, so save your vocal interpretations for the show."

Paco would present the show at ten o'clock, as the audience flocked around the bandstand. José and Estella would perform their interpretations of the rhumba and samba, twirling around with intricate steps that always brought enthusiastic applause from crowd. José was a short but very well built young man in his midtwenties, and his wife, Estella, though barely five feet tall, was beautifully proportioned. She had long jet black hair that she wore parted in the middle, and with her dark eyes and white skin, she looked like a porcelain doll. They had been with Paco for almost a year, but had been married only a few months.

After their act, Paco would present his new discovery, "Ruby Gonzalez," and if the public was surprised that this very young, red-haired girl did not at all resemble the picture outside, no one seemed to care. With her new sexy gowns and voluptuous body, Julie created her own kind of impact. By repeating the same songs each night, Julie had been able to perfect them to the point where she could finally relax and concentrate on her dancing ability. She carefully watched Estella's movements every show and had learned quickly how to inject a little of that Latin sensuality into her own performance. The "minishow" would close with Miguel Sanchez, who had been with Paco the longest. His repertoire included many of Paco's famous hits, and the audience loved him. Miguel was an extremely good-looking young man who was rather shy when not performing in front of an audience. He had a beautiful baritone voice that, with proper training, could have propelled him toward more serious music. But he was not ambitious or motivated enough to want anything more than what he had right now—a good job, plenty to eat, and the opportunity to accumulate just enough money to open one day a small business in his native Mexico.

At the end of the evening, while the band boy and musicians packed up the instruments, Julie and Estella would have to brave the stares of any lingering patrons in the ladies room while they removed their makeup and changed into street clothes. It was embarrassing not to have any privacy, but there was seldom any dressing room facilities, except for Paco. After consuming a greasy meal in an even greasier diner, they would board the bus again and move on to the next stop. With Paco paying for their very modest hotel accommodations, Rose had been able to send home the major portion of Julie's salary, and only this fact helped to quiet her constant grumbling.

Suddenly, as the bus came to a screeching halt, Julie was jolted back to the present. Looking out the window, she could see the lights from an oncoming train. Rose, who was now awake, stretched her aching body and asked Julie the time.

"It's two-thirty, Mom. The bus driver told me we should be in Detroit by seven in the morning."

"Good," Rose answered. "Then maybe we can check into a hotel and get some sleep. I'm exhausted." Motioning to Paco in front of them, Rose whispered, "I don't know how he does it. He's on the bandstand all night, eats all the junk in those bad restaurants, and never gets sick. He must be made out of iron."

Shaking her head in wonderment, she picked up her pillow, which had slipped to the floor, and curled up again, trying to find a comfort- able position. "Julie, baby," Rose urged. "Try and get some sleep. Otherwise, you'll be exhausted by the time we arrive."

Julie nodded, and for the next few hours dozed fitfully until they arrived in Detroit.

Their schedule continued at a hectic pace, and as the weeks passed, Julie found herself making steady progress. However, she now had other problems to contend with. Paco's obvious interest in her was not only making her uncomfortable, but also making her mother more suspicious with each passing day.

After the show one night, in a ballroom outside of Cleveland, Rose cornered her as she was leaving the bandstand.

"Julie, come over here," Rose commanded. When Julie reached her, Rose lashed out.

"Julie, I see the way he keeps looking at you while you're singing. He's devouring you with his eyes."

Julie tried to laugh it off, even though she knew it was the truth. "Mom, don't be silly. You're imagining things. It's just part of his performance. People expect it."

"Don't argue with me, Julie. I'm not a fool. He's got designs on you, and I don't like it. If I told your father my feelings, he'd have us both back in Manhattan on the next train."

Julie cringed, realizing that what her mother threatened was true. Her parents *could* pull her away at any moment. Julie tried to allay her mother's misgivings and promised her that she would be cautious. But Julie feared that the situation was not in her control.

As the tour progressed, Rose's growing antagonism for Paco, coupled with her acute dissatisfaction with the traveling and working condi- tions, began to make Julie's life a nightmare.

She now had reason to have genuine concern about Paco's behavior, because every chance he got, even on the bandstand, he would whisper familiar endearments and look for an opportunity to touch her.

Julie avoided being alone with him because she was afraid he might become amorous if the opportunity presented itself. One night in Akron, Ohio, she discovered that her fears were well-founded. During a band break, Julie found herself alone behind the bandstand waiting for the next set to begin. They had been playing to an especially enthusiastic audience that evening, and Julie needed a few minutes to catch her breath. Even though it was only May, the nights were getting hot and humid. Fanning herself with some sheet music that she had been studying, Julie rested wearily against the back of the bandstand. Suddenly, she felt someone's arms around her and turned quickly, about to scream, when she saw that it was Paco.

"Oh, my God," Julie gasped, clutching her chest. "You startled me."

Before she could say another word, Paco's arms reached out and grabbed her. Crushing her tightly against him, he leaned over and kissed her trembling lips. Julie tried to break away, but his strong arms would not release her from their grip. His kiss became steadily more insistent as his tongue tried to pry her lips apart. Julie jerked her head away sharply and, gasping for breath, asked him to release her. Paco saw the fright in her eyes, and reluctantly, he dropped his hands. But he did not move away. Even in the half-darkness, Julie could see the desire in his eyes, and her instinct was to flee.

"Ay, Julie, mi preciosa," Paco sighed, aroused by her nearness. "I've been wanting to do that since the first time I saw you. You are a temptress, and having you near me and not being able to touch you is driving me mad."

Julie's body began to tremble. She had never been kissed like that before, and the passion in Paco's kiss frightened her. She glanced around nervously to see if anyone had seen them, but they were alone.

"Paco, please," she pleaded. "You shouldn't have done that. You've been very kind to me and I like you very much, but I couldn't possibly be interested in you romantically. I'm not even sixteen. I've never dated anyone and you're a married man."

Paco smiled at her, undaunted by her objections. "Julie, if that's all that's bothering you, then don't worry. My divorce will be final soon, and as far as your age is concerned," he whispered, leaning closer, "girls in my country marry very young."

Julie stared at Paco, stunned by his words. Fortunately their conversation came to an abrupt halt as several of the musicians approached them on their way to the bandstand. Realizing that this would give her an opportunity to escape, Julie mumbled something about finding her mother and ran off in search of Rose and safety.

Searching for her mother, Julie's apprehension intensified as she walked through the throngs of people. Paco had not only kissed her in a way that had left her shaken, but also dropped an unexpected bomb in her lap by indicating that once his divorce was final, he might be interested in making her his wife. *My God,* Julie thought. *What am I going to do?*

Paco watched Julie dash off like a frightened little rabbit while he remained behind, trying to regain his composure. In a few minutes, he joined the musicians and told them to start the next set without him. He wanted time to think. Pushing his way through the crowds standing around the bandstand, Paco found his way to the office, which also served as a makeshift dressing room. Loosening his tie, he sat down in the only comfortable chair and began to think.

What am I getting myself into? She is nothing but a child encased in a woman's body, and that could mean trouble. To make matters worse, I'm convinced her mother suspects something because she never leaves us alone—not even for a minute. Somehow, I've got to get rid of the mother if I want to have the daughter. But how? Paco tried to think logically, but he couldn't. He was still too aroused by the memory of Julie's sweet and sensual lips, and the delicious feel of her firm young flesh. Savoring his thoughts, it took him a few minutes to realize that someone was knocking on the door.

"Paco, are you there?" Luis called. Hearing no answer, he knocked again, this time more firmly. "Paco, *contéstame,* are you there? The crowd is waiting for you."

Annoyed by the interruption, Paco got up and opened the door. "Come in, Luis. I was just getting a few minutes' rest."

His brother came right to the point. "Paco, there's something I'd like to discuss with you, now that we're alone. You know that I never have interfered in your private affairs. Even when I knew you were making a mistake in marrying Laura, I kept silent. I understand that you are a man with strong sexual desires, and I always respect your wishes. But this new fantasy that you have with Julie is very bad."

Irritated by his brother's words, Paco tried to interrupt him, but Luis pressed on. "Listen to me, my brother. Everyone is beginning to talk. The band sees how you look at her. Marion has already mentioned to me that the mother has been making remarks about going home. If that were not enough, you seem to have forgotten that technically you still are a married man."

Paco turned on his brother angrily. "*Basta,* Luis, that's enough. Do not tell me how to run my life. I don't give a shit about what they're saying. As for Julie's mother, she won't do anything. She wants her daughter to be a star even more than Julie wants it herself."

Softening his tone, Paco patted his brother on the shoulder. "Don't worry, Luis. I will take care of everything. Just leave Julie to me. You speak to my agents in New York tomorrow and tell them to finalize our dates for the South American tour. I want to leave the country as soon as possible. Now, go tell the musicians I will be there shortly."

The minute Luis closed the door, Paco picked up the telephone and asked the operator for his number in California. He hoped that Laura would be home. Once and for all he would have a showdown with her and maybe accomplish what his lawyers had been unable to—get her out of his house and out of his life.

On the fourth ring, Laura picked up the phone. Her voice sounded breathless and husky, a sound Paco was all too familiar with. It was the way she sounded when she was making love. The moment she heard Paco's voice, her tone hardened.

"Well, Paco, fancy hearing from you. I shouldn't be talking to you directly, you know. My lawyers wouldn't approve."

"Fuck your lawyers. We have to get this thing settled. I'm tired of paying bills and having you stall. I want my house back."

"Your house!" Laura screamed. "You selfish son of a bitch. Who says it's *your* house. You bought it when you married me. We do have community property in California, in case you didn't know. Half of this house is mine, and I'm not giving it up."

Paco's temper had reached a boiling point, and he wanted to lash back at her with all the fury he was feeling. But his instincts told him to control himself.

"Laura, you're not being reasonable. I've offered to pay your half of what the house is worth. You're a young, beautiful woman. You'll come away with a lot of money from the settlement. You could build a whole new life."

Laura realized that Paco was trying to soften her up, and she felt victorious. Now that she had him by the balls, she would try buttering him up. *Besides,* she thought as she looked at the naked young man lying at her side, *I don't want Nico to think that I'm a heartless bitch.* As if reading her thoughts, Nico reached over and began caressing the inside of her thighs, which made Laura giggle with pleasure.

"Well, Paco, that sounds a little more reasonable. Maybe we can work things out."

When Paco heard her laugh and the sensuous timbre of her voice he realized that she was not alone. Suddenly, his suppressed rage surfaced and he screamed, "You whore. You're not alone are you? There's somebody there."

Laura brushed Nico's hand away as she tried to regain control. "You jealous fool. There's nobody here. It's just your goddamn imagination."

But Paco knew better and refused to listen. "How dare you bring that scum home with you to sleep in *my* bed in *my* house," he screamed. "You're nothing but a cheap slut."

"Don't you dare scream at me, you stingy bastard. I'll do what I want, when I want. And, there's not a damn thing you can do about it. Besides," she added, "you can't prove a thing."

Paco slammed down the receiver and began to curse her under his breath. "*Puta más grande del mundo.* Whore, now you won't get a red cent."

But Paco knew deep down in his heart that he would have to pay and pay dearly if he wanted his freedom. And he did want his freedom, desperately. But he vowed to himself that no woman would ever again play him for a fool.

CHAPTER
14

As the weeks passed, Julie grew more confident, but the tensions continued to heighten between Paco and her mother. If it weren't for the fact that the Chicago engagement was approaching, Rose would have returned to New York with Julie in tow. But Rose was anxious, not only for Julie to be seen in a major city, but also for Paco's agents to become aware of her daughter's talent. She figured that once they saw Julie in the kind of showcase that Paco offered, they would sign her immediately, and that would put an end to Julie's relationship with Paco Castell.

When the troupe arrived in the Windy City early in July of 1951 to begin a two-week engagement at the Edgewater Beach Hotel, major events had been taking place all over the world. North Korean forces had broken through the 38th parallel and taken Seoul; the Rosenbergs had been sentenced to death for espionage; and Julie Lehman had finally found a new name.

Not willing to change her first name, she had searched for something suitable to go with Julie. During their long drives between cities, Julie would take out a pad and pencil and try different combinations, but nothing seemed to work. One evening, while glancing at the newspaper in a Chinese restaurant after the show, Julie happened to see an advertisement for *The African Queen*, which was playing in a local theater. Having always been a fan of Humphrey Bogart's wife, Lauren Bacall, Julie began to play around with the sound of Julie Lauren. The more she repeated it to herself, the more she liked it. Deciding she needed a second opinion, Julie tried it out on her mother.

"Mom, do you realize that in a week we'll be in Chicago?"

"Thank God," Rose answered. "At least we'll be staying in a decent hotel, and for two whole weeks. I can hardly wait."

"I know, Mom, it's great. But I sure don't want to appear there as Ruby Gonzalez."

"Of course you don't," Rose agreed, "but Paco doesn't like your last name. He doesn't think Lehman is theatrical enough. As a matter of fact, neither did Mike Todd."

"Well, what do you think of the name Julie Lauren?"

"Julie Lauren, Julie Lauren, Julie Lauren," Rose repeated several times. "I like it, and it would look great on a marquee."

"You're right, Mom," Julie answered. "Then, if it's okay with Paco, why don't we try it? I've been using someone else's identity long enough. I want to be myself."

As Rose and Julie strolled through the elegant lobby and grounds surrounding the Edgewater Beach Hotel, they were stunned by its beauty. They both compared it to the only other hotel of its kind that they had ever seen, the Waldorf-Astoria. But even that grand hotel couldn't compare with this splendor. There were beautiful paintings everywhere. A fountain with a marble statue sat right in the middle of the dining room, and above it, a huge crystal chandelier with prisms that sparkled like diamonds. But the most thrilling sight of all was the enormous swimming pool surrounded by cabanas with striped awnings. As Julie glanced at the people seated around the pool, her mind flashed back several years ago to the summer they had spent at the Brooklawn Hotel. She still had vivid memories of the rudeness and humiliation they had suffered. The vow she'd taken then still echoed in her thoughts—one day she would be important and successful enough to be treated with respect. She had worked hard since then to achieve her goals. She wasn't a star yet, but Julie was proud that her new name and photograph were prominently featured all over the hotel and in the newspapers and that she had the promise of an exciting future. Now her next objective was to impress Paco's agents, the powerful Music Corporation of America, or as it was commonly known in the business, MCA.

While Julie was busy readying herself for her Chicago debut, Paco was in his sumptuous suite in another part of the hotel, engaged in a heated discussion with his agent.

"For Christ's sake, Freddie. Stop beating around the bush," Paco complained. "Where is my new contract with MGM?"

"Calm down, Paco. You're getting your blood pressure all worked up for no reason. As my associates in California and I have tried to explain to you, we're working on it."

"Working on it," Paco fumed. "You've been giving me that crap for the past six months."

Freddie Barnett, one of MCA's brightest young talent agents, was trying not to lose his cool. He had been personally handling Paco Castell from the New York office for several months, and his instruc-tions from California had been very clear: "Keep him happy and out there working. He's one of our biggest money-makers, and we can't afford to lose him to William Morris or any of the other agencies."

Striding over to the bar to fix himself a drink, Freddie continued to try and reason with Paco, who was pacing the room and muttering to his brother in Spanish. "Paco, listen to me. The entire agency is working hard to get you a new motion picture contract. But the studios are cutting back on musicals. They're running scared about big budgets because of television."

Realizing that his words did not have a calming affect on Paco, he tried another tactic. "We just heard that RKO is very interested in making a musical with Rita Hayworth. If they can sign her, I'm sure we'll be able to make a deal for you. They know how much she likes you and would enjoy working with you again. So relax, and give us a little more time. We'll come up with something."

Freddie sank into the couch and watched Paco's face for a reaction. It was true that RKO was talking a deal with Hayworth, but, so far, no one had expressed any interest in Paco. Freddie figured that the agency would have to call in one of its "chits" in order to make a deal.

While Freddie had been talking, Paco was busy thinking. He knew that his leverage with MCA, or any other talent agency, was his earning power, which was still enormous. With fifty weeks a year of steady income from nightclubs and theaters, plus record royalties, which were considerable, he still held the trump card.

Joining his agent on the couch, Paco smiled disarmingly and deliv-ered his ultimatum. "Either get me a deal for at least three movies, or when my contract expires at the end of the year, I will find other representation." Motioning to Luis that he wished to speak to him in private, Paco excused himself and left the room.

Freddie sat there alone for several minutes and reflected on what Paco had told him. Moments later, he left the suite to join his associates. As he waited for the show to begin, Freddie plotted his next course of action. The minute he got back to New York he would call California. With all the big stars they represented, the agency would have to use their leverage to get Paco a movie deal. Otherwise, as Paco had threatened, he would "stick" it to them.

Julie arrived in her dressing room rather early that evening to prepare herself for the show. Rose helped her pile her luxurious red hair on top of her head, separating tiny curls that she let cascade down her forehead and frame her oval face. Estella, too, was very helpful in getting her ready for this special evening. Sitting in the dressing room they shared, she enhanced Julie's natural beauty with heavier accents of makeup, much more than Julie was used to wearing.

"Look, Julie," Estella pointed out, "put this bronze eyeshadow around your eyes. There, you see how it makes your eyes look more golden? Now a little more rouge and you'll be ready."

Estella stepped back to admire her handiwork, and even she was startled by Julie's beauty. Gone was the baby face. In its place was an exquisite young woman with flawless skin, almond-shaped eyes, and a voluptuous body that was likely to be envied by most women and desired by many men.

"God you look great, Julie," Estella said admiringly. Giving her friend a hug for good luck, she told her, "Now go get 'em."

When Julie stepped out onstage that night, everything that she had learned during the past few months magically came together. Wearing a white jersey gown that clung to her body like a second skin, she glowed in the spotlight that followed her every movement.

Julie's voice had a deep resonance that was especially effective in the ballads, and when she switched to the more rhythmic melodies, her body moved sensually to the music. The effect she made on the audience was dazzling. They loved her and she loved them. When she exited the stage after her performance, the applause was still ringing in her ears. Rose, who had been watching the show from the audience, was waiting for her backstage.

"Julie," she raved enthusiastically, "you were wonderful. The audience just ate you up. I hope those agents from MCA were there. Did you happen to notice where they were sitting?"

"No, Mom," Julie answered, lowering her voice to a whisper. "Let's go back to the dressing room. Paco will be coming off the stage soon."

As she walked along the corridor to her dressing room, Julie was euphoric over her apparent success. "Mom, it's the strangest thing. This was the first time I've felt really comfortable since I started with the band."

"Of course you felt comfortable," Rose agreed. "You were using your own name, or at least part of it. You're appearing in a fabulous hotel, instead of those lousy ballrooms, and you've had a chance to show your singing talent in a real show instead of sitting on a bandstand all night."

Julie and Rose entered the dressing room, expecting to find Estella, but the room was empty. As Rose cleared away some of the clutter the girls had created, Julie sat down and looked at herself in the mirror. As she smoothed her damp curls back in place her eyes were bright and her cheeks were still flushed with excitement.

Moments later, there was a gentle knocking on the door, and Julie went to open it. Standing there were three attractive, very well-dressed men in dark suits, sporting warm smiles on their faces.

"Excuse me, Miss Lauren," the man standing in the middle said apologetically as he extended his hand. "I hope you'll forgive our intrusion, but we wanted to congratulate you on your show. I'm Freddie Barnett and these are my associates, Norm Adler and Larry Fields. We're Paco's agents."

Julie quickly ushered them into the dressing room. "Oh, please come in. It's no intrusion. I was just going to change, but that can wait. I'm afraid there aren't enough chairs in here, or I'd ask you to sit down."

Aware that she had neglected to introduce her mother, Julie turned around. "Gentlemen, I would like you to meet my mother, Rose Lehman."

Freddie, who appeared to be the spokesman, greeted her. "Mrs. Lehman, your daughter was wonderful tonight, and she looked just beautiful out there. We think she is one of Paco's best discoveries and has a great career ahead of her."

Julie was about to thank him when all of a sudden the door flew open and Paco rushed in. He was still in his tuxedo and his face was flushed and wet with perspiration. "Well, my fine friends, so this is where you are. Going behind my back to steal away my young beauty."

Unsure as to whether he was serious or not, but unwilling to take a chance on offending such an important client, Freddie immediately became defensive. "Paco, we were waiting for you to come offstage," he explained. "We have to make a plane back to New York tonight, but we did want to congratulate you on the show. It was, as usual, just great."

"Oh," Paco answered sarcastically, "did you see all of it, or is it just my imagination that you left before it was over?"

"Well, Paco," one of the other agents, Norm, hastily explained, "we've seen Miguel before, and to be honest, we wanted to congratulate your new singer before we left. She's got a delightful style and great appeal."

Julie stood by silently, but Rose would have spoken up if Julie's eyes had not begged her not to interfere. Uncomfortable because of Paco's attitude, Freddie and the others hastily made their good-byes and left the room. When they were safely out of hearing range, Paco turned his attention to Julie.

"My dear, please do not let these agents turn your head. You did well tonight because I was there to support you and to create a showcase for you. But don't forget that I'm the star and the people out there tonight came here to see *me*. I also want you to understand that *anyone* I present would have an immediate built-in acceptance with the public. Without me, they would be just another act struggling to make a living."

Abruptly he left the room, leaving behind a bewildered Julie and a furious Rose. "What kind of garbage was that," Rose fumed. "Does he think they liked you just because he's there? That egotistical fool. They liked you because of you—and for no other reason."

Julie wasn't convinced that her mother was telling the truth. Perhaps Paco was right? Julie could suddenly feel her self-confidence slipping away and insecurity setting in.

Later that night, when Julie was asleep, Rose put in a call to Sam in New York. After reassuring him that everything was fine and they were both well, Rose began to describe, in great detail, Julie's success that evening. When she finished, she then began to ventilate her feelings about Paco.

"Sam, that guy has some ego. He thinks he's the world's biggest star. If you ask me, I think his best days are behind him."

"Rose, don't get so excited," Sam pleaded. "In two weeks you'll be home and we'll have time to discuss what we're going to do. Frankly, the way I feel now, I don't want to see you go off on the road again.

Honey, you don't know how lonesome it's been here without my two girls. Marshall has come by a few times, but you know how he is, off in his own world. The apartment is so empty without you. I hate to complain, but I don't know if I can stand this life much longer. I've tried my best to adjust, but I want my wife home with me where she belongs."

"Sam, please don't make things any harder. Do you think I like all this schlepping around the country with a bunch of musicians who don't even speak English? If it weren't for Marion, I would go crazy. At least I have someone to talk to while Julie's rehearsing or is onstage."

Suddenly her manner changed and in a voice brimming with pride, she continued. "Sam, everything we've been going through has been worth it. You should have seen her tonight. What joy you would have had watching her entertain."

"I will have even greater joy when the day comes that I see her walking down the aisle married to a nice Jewish boy."

"Sam, she has time for that after she's a star and has achieved her goals. But let's not talk about that now. It's late and you'd better get some sleep. Take care of yourself, dear. I'll call you in a few days and tell you when we'll be arriving."

After Rose hung up, she lay there in bed, thinking. *Our lives have been severely disrupted for the past few months and I'm worried about Sam. He's still a very good-looking man and he's all alone in a city teeming with women without any scruples. Although he's always been a faithful husband, how much longer can he remain that way if I continue on the road? My mother has always warned me that a man needs sex and lately he has been without it. Who knows what could happen?* The pull between her daughter's career and her life with Sam was driving Rose to despair. How could she stay and protect her daughter from the obvious danger that Paco represented and still be a good wife? All of these questions preyed on her mind and prevented her from sleeping. When she was too exhausted to wrestle with her problems any longer, she turned over and in the remaining few hours left to her, tried to sleep. *When we get home,* Rose thought as she began to drift off, *we'll sort it all out.*

The days that followed opening night in Chicago were so crammed with activity that Julie never did get a chance to use the hotel pool. During the day there were newspaper interviews penciled in between rehearsals. The Chicago critics had been more than kind in their praise of Julie's talent. The Chicago *Sun-Times* had called her, "a great new find for Paco Castell." The *Chicago Tribune* reported, "a new Latin sex symbol is gracing our fair city and her name is Julie Lauren."

Latin sex symbol, Julie thought, laughing, as she read it. *Well, that's the image Paco wants me to project, and I guess everyone is buying it.* Julie was thrilled by the accolades and saved every review and article to send home to her father. One night after the show, Paco informed the troupe that instead of going to Hollywood as planned after their four-week layover in New York, they would fill in with dates in the East in preparation for their South American tour. Julie was bitterly disappointed that their visit to Hollywood was postponed, but she consoled herself with the fact that South America would be not only thrilling, but also her first trip out of the country. Julie was almost certain that her mother had heard rumors about the upcoming South American trip, but since Rose never mentioned it, neither did Julie.

She wasn't sure she could convince her mother to go to South America, and even though she would be almost sixteen by the time they left, she was certainly way too young to go by herself. Furthermore, she was wary about being alone with Paco far away from the protection of her family.

Almost every night during their engagement in Chicago, Paco invited Julie and Rose to join him and his brother for a late supper after the show. He instructed room service to have dinner ready for them in his lavish suite, and he made sure that everything was perfect. In his silk dressing gown with a foulard tied casually around his neck, he looked every inch the Don Juan. Rose didn't protest this arrangement because there were no decent places open that time of night and, besides, as she rationalized to Julie, "He won't be alone with you and it sure saves us a lot of money."

While the rest of the troupe was wolfing down hamburgers in some joint on State Street, Julie and Rose were being introduced to delicacies such as vichyssoise (Rose called it lousy cold potato soup), caviar, beef Wellington, and cherries jubilee. Trying exotic foods were another part of Julie's learning process and she was a good student.

During the day, as they walked up Michigan Avenue between interviews or radio appearances, Paco would point out all the sights—the art galleries, elegant shops, and exclusive restaurants. Having decided on a new strategy, one that he was sure would charm both mother and daughter, he offered his services as a guide. When he behaved in this fashion, there was no one in the world more charming than Paco, and sometimes, after an especially enjoyable day, Rose would wonder if she hadn't been too hard on him.

"You know, Julie," Rose confided one night as they were preparing for bed, "I can see why he has such a reputation with women. He's very suave and sophisticated and he sure knows a lot of important people."

Rose was thinking back to the previous evening when he had taken them to the ultrachic Pump Room in the Ambassador East Hotel. It was their night off, and Paco had called them earlier in the day. "Julie, how would you and Rose like to dine with me tonight at the Pump Room? I think you would enjoy it, and I would love to show you off."

Julie immediately accepted because she was sure that when her mother heard what a glamorous place it was, she would agree. She was right, but Rose did have some reservations. "Julie, I'd like for us to go, but do you think we have clothes fancy enough for a place like that?"

Julie paused for a moment before answering. She hadn't thought of that. "Sure, Mom. You can wear your pretty black dress with the lace top and I can wear the green jersey dress you found for me in Detroit." With their wardrobe decided, they spent the rest of the day like two sisters, fussing over their hair and makeup in preparation for the big evening.

As they stood at the entrance of the elegantly furnished dining room, waiting to be seated, Julie and Rose kept on pinching each other to make sure they weren't dreaming. When the maître d' escorted them to their table, their entrance caused a small sensation, and Julie began to realize the enormity of Paco's fame. People stopped eating to look up when they saw him approach. Their table was one of the special booths reserved for celebrities, but when Julie slipped into her seat next to Paco, she suddenly felt terribly insecure. Looking around at the elegantly dressed women with their dazzling jewels, she felt like the young kid she was, and poorly attired. Her mother obviously did not have the same problem, because she was thrilled just looking around the room searching for celebrities.

Suddenly, Rose grabbed her hand. "Julie," her mother gasped. "Look over to your right. There's Joan Crawford."

Julie turned her head, and sure enough there she was, larger than life and quite striking. The dark-haired actress was wearing a black evening hat with a short veil and she looked as if she had just stepped out of *Mildred Pierce*.

"Paco," Julie whispered, "Joan Crawford is sitting in the next booth!"

Paco glanced over, and excusing himself, he went over to greet her. Julie and Rose sat transfixed at the sight of Paco embracing Joan Crawford. Paco sat down next to her, and for the next few minutes, they were engaged in deep conversation. After kissing her hand, he returned to the table and asked Rose's permission to dance with Julie.

"Sure, go right ahead. I'm enjoying myself just sitting here and watching."

Promising Rose the next dance, he carefully guided Julie toward the dance floor. As they passed Crawford's table, Paco stopped and introduced Julie to the famous star. Joan Crawford looked up and her enormous eyes widened at the sight of Julie. "Paco, my dear. Where have you been hiding this little beauty? Is she your new 'discovery'?"

Julie didn't like the way that sounded, but she said nothing.

"Joan, dear, this is my new vocalist, Julie Lauren, and I predict she is going to be a big star."

"Well, Paco, if anyone can do it, you can."

Turning her gaze once more to Julie she smiled and said sweetly, "Pay attention to whatever Paco says. He's a good teacher and," she added sarcastically, "I'm sure you'll learn fast." Embarrassed, Julie took Paco's arm as they moved toward the dance floor.

Other than a few steps that they had improvised together on the stage, this was the first time Julie had ever really danced with Paco. He was a superb dancer, and with his guidance, she glided across the floor with smoothness and grace, never missing a step. Her dance training had been in ballet and tap. All she knew about Latin dances was what she had picked up from José and Estella. But Paco was so expert that he made her look good. The band was playing a slow rhumba, and she could feel everyone's eyes on them. The inexpensive jersey dress that had seemed so inadequate only minutes before was unimportant now. The soft folds of jersey caressed her supple body, and Julie's instincts told her to keep her movements subtle and ladylike, which of course made her appear even more sensual.

When the music ended, Julie felt heady with excitement. She was aware of the admiring glances and so was Paco. Holding her tightly around the waist, he whispered in her ear, "My beautiful one, you have made me so proud. I am the envy of every man here. But I don't mind them staring as long as they look but don't touch."

When Paco returned to his hotel room that evening, the phone was ringing. Loosening his tie and dropping into a chair, he picked up the receiver.

"Hello, Paco," the voice on the other end greeted him. "This is Harold. I'm glad I caught you in." Harold Ross was Paco's California attorney and the man handling his divorce.

"Hello, my friend. What's happening out on the Coast?"

"Things are not going too well, Paco. We're having problems with Laura. She still refuses to vacate the house, and we have reason to believe she's moving out some of your paintings."

Infuriated at the news, Paco reacted violently. "Goddammit, Harold. How in the hell could you let that happen? That's why I'm paying you guys, to protect my interests."

"Paco, take it easy," Harold urged. "You know the laws about community property. If you want to keep the house, you'll have to buy out her interest and come to terms about alimony. As far as the paint-ings are concerned, as soon as we strike a deal with her, we'll advise her lawyers that she has to return them. Paco, I strongly advise you to give her what she wants. Dragging this out will only cost you more money in the end."

"Give her what she wants," Paco shouted. "That bitch has cost me a fortune already. It makes me sick to think of her enjoying my beautiful home, screwing around in bed with some gigolo while I'm paying the bills."

By now, Paco's temper was fully aroused and his lawyer hesitated before telling him the rest. "Paco, calm down and listen to me. Let me go ahead with an acceptable offer and terminate this whole mess. You'll get your house back, your paintings, and most of all, your freedom. Speaking of freedom, are you alone?"

"Of course I'm alone," he answered brusquely. "Why do you ask?"

"Because we've heard through the grapevine that you have a new girlfriend."

"Bullshit," Paco answered. "Who's been telling you that crap—my brother?"

"That's not important, Paco. But if it's true, you'd better be careful. If Laura found out that you were interested in someone else, she would use that to up her demands and drag this divorce out indefinitely. Take my advice and stay clear of other women until we have a settlement."

"All right," he answered angrily. "But make it soon."

Slamming down the receiver, Paco walked into his bedroom, still fuming over the conversation with his lawyer. Gone was the mellow

mood he had enjoyed during his evening with Julie. He was furious
that just when he was beginning to get somewhere with her, he would
have to exercise restraint because of that bitch, Laura. Throwing off
his clothes, he slipped on his robe and lay down on his bed. *Women,* he
thought, *they're all whores. You take them out of their humble existence,
pamper them, and what do you get? Misery. But not Julie, she's different.*
Recalling the feel of Julie in his arms, his body began to ache with
desire. *I can't wait too much longer,* he thought. *If the only way I can
have her is marriage, then so be it.*

CHAPTER
15

Sam stood at the gate, waiting impatiently for the airplane door to open. When it finally did, the first passengers to step out onto the steps were Rose and Julie. Seeing them standing there, their faces glowing in the brilliant sunshine, Sam thought his heart would burst with joy. Brushing by others who were also waiting to greet loved ones, he ran to the gate. Embracing them fiercely, they hugged and kissed one another, laughing and crying at the same time. Rose was the first to pull away, and she looked up appraisingly at her husband.

"Sam," she beamed. "You look great. A little thin maybe, but it's becoming."

"Well," he said, grinning and patting his stomach, "I have taken off some weight because I'm not eating as much. I guess I miss your cooking. Now, let me look at you." Standing back, he studied his wife and daughter. "You both look wonderful. Traveling and hard work seem to agree with you."

Julie held on tightly to her father's hand. He did look fit but a little older than she remembered. His eyes seemed tired, and there were creases in his forehead she hadn't noticed before.

"Daddy," she said, her throat tightening with emotion, "it's so good to see you. I've missed you so much."

"I've missed you too, baby, more than you know. Life hasn't been the same without you and Mom."

Embracing them once again, he picked up their makeup cases and led them to the baggage claim area. Behind them came the musicians. Sam kept glancing around to see if he could find Paco, but he was nowhere in sight.

"Julie, where's Paco Castell? Wasn't he on the plane?"

"No, Dad. As soon as we closed in Chicago, he and his brother flew out to California for a few days. It had something to do with his divorce."

Piling all their luggage into the Buick, they left La Guardia Airport and drove into the City, which was sizzling under a summer heat wave. On the way home, Julie and Rose tried to update Sam on all that had been happening. He listened patiently, especially to Julie, who was bursting with enthusiasm. But all he could focus on was that finally, after months of loneliness, he had his wife and child back home—he hoped for good.

When Julie entered the apartment on Riverside Drive, it seemed strangely unfamiliar. She couldn't understand why. Her eyes swept across the room, and she could see that all her things were exactly where she had left them—her books, her records. Nothing had changed. Then what was different? And then suddenly it struck her. It was *she* who was different. When she left home she had been a child who had lived a sheltered life and whose parents, especially her father, had influenced her every waking moment. Now, after months of traveling on the road, performing in front of thousands of people, meeting famous celebrities, Julie was a different person. Suddenly, she felt liberated. The butterfly had finally emerged from the cocoon and was now ready to try its wings.

For the next few days, Julie luxuriated in the freedom of not having to follow any schedule. She slept late, or as late as possible, considering that her tiny alcove had no door and her mother was an early riser. As Julie began sorting out her clothes, she tried to find space for her newly acquired stage wardrobe, but the closet she shared with her parents was already jammed. Rummaging for space through the tiny hall closet that served as a catchall for the family junk, she found toys she had played with as a little girl. It was difficult trying to decide what she could dispose of because each item brought back some memory of her childhood. Suddenly she came across an old battered doll that once had blond hair and a pretty dress and bonnet. Her Grandma Hannah had given it to her on her fourth birthday. Julie smiled as she remembered how she had dressed and undressed this favorite doll a hundred times, and how she had slept with it next to her pillow for years. Pulling it out of the box that Rose kept for storage, Julie clutched it tightly to her chest. For some inexplicable reason, her eyes started to fill with tears as she fondled her old "friend." Although she didn't completely understand her feelings, somehow she knew that she was saying good-bye to her childhood.

Since her return, Julie had been receiving daily telephone calls from Paco in California. Explaining them away to her parents, Julie tried to pretend that they were business calls related to the upcoming tour. Part of that was true. Paco was indeed pressing her for an answer about South America. But she didn't tell them that over the telephone he had also resumed his romantic overtures.

One afternoon, he reached her just as she was leaving the apartment. "Julie," he complained, "it's so lonesome here without you. What are you doing today?" Julie tried to change the conversation, but Paco refused to be detoured. "Are you going out on dates, Julie?" he inquired like a jealous lover. "Who are you seeing?"

Julie resented being questioned that way. She had never consciously given Paco any reason to feel so possessive. Furthermore, his attempts to woo her on the road had been futile. Now even though they were three thousand miles apart, he had resumed his pursuit. Julie felt a nagging anxiety that a showdown was inevitable, and she dreaded the thought.

Aware of her parents' joy in being reunited, Julie hesitated about approaching them regarding her future with the band. But time was growing short. In order to take advantage of the publicity the trip to South America could offer, she would be obliged to give Paco an answer, and soon.

Rose was so happy to be home she refused to think about anything but Sam. She shopped and cooked for him and tried to make up for her long absence. The only break in her busy schedule were her visits to her mother and sisters. Esther Goldman, Rose's mother, was beginning to show signs of deteriorating health, and Rose was terribly concerned. Her sisters were doing the best they could to help their widowed mother, but it was Rose, the eldest, to whom Esther had always turned.

One particularly hot and humid day, Rose decided to visit her mother, and as she trudged up the steps of the old apartment building in Brooklyn where she had grown up, she looked around. She couldn't help noticing how dilapidated everything had become. If only she could convince her mother to move in with one of them. But Esther was stubborn. Whenever the subject was brought up, she refused, pro-testing that she didn't want to be a burden to her children. Opening the door, which was always unlocked, Rose found her mother seated in the kitchen. Kissing her on the forehead she sat down and joined her for a cup of tea and a piece of cake.

The elderly woman leaned forward anxiously. "Rose, my kindela. Tell me about Julie. She is doing well?"

"Mama, you would be so proud of her. In the last few months she has blossomed into a beautiful young girl. And you should hear her sing—like a bird. She's going to be a big star."

Patting her daughter's hand, Esther smiled. "A big star, just like you wanted to be, remember?"

"Yes, Mama, I remember. But I didn't have what Julie has—talent and ambition. She won't allow herself to get sidetracked. She will succeed where I failed."

"Rose, Rose," Esther sighed wearily. "You haven't failed. You have a wonderful husband, who is a good provider and loves you very much, a devoted son, who has never given you any trouble. And you have Julie."

"I know, Mama, and believe me I am grateful. But I want much more for my daughter. I don't want her beauty and talent to be wasted. She deserves to have beautiful clothes and jewels, and a fine home where she can entertain like a queen. She's smart and talented. She can have a great career, and someday when she's ready, she can marry a rich man who will take care of her properly."

As Rose described Julie's sensational success on the tour, Esther's eyes never left her daughter's still lovely face. Rose's eyes gleamed with a fire that betrayed her feelings. Esther, in her wisdom, realized that her daughter was describing exactly the kind of life for Julie that Rose herself had yearned for but had been denied. Now that it was too late for her, she would see to it that Julie would have it all.

"Listen to me, Rifka," Esther answered, using Rose's Hebrew name, "don't push her too hard and too fast. Let her be a child a little longer, or God forbid, you may be sorry."

Kissing her mother's tired face, she tried to assure her that she would take her advice. But Esther was not convinced. Her Rose had tasted a different kind of world because of Julie, and whether she realized it or not, she would never be satisfied with her old life again.

As Rose prepared to leave, she looked around the shabby apartment with its faded furniture and drab walls and she was consumed with sadness. Her mother had never known comfort, let alone luxury. She had struggled alone to raise her children and give them good values. Now she was old, and it was too late to change things for her.

A huge wave of fear welled up inside of Rose as she envisioned the future. *Oh God,* she thought. *I don't want to end up like Mama, poor and alone. What if something happened to Sam? What would become of me?* Suddenly, she knew the answer: Julie. *Julie will never let me down. Things will always be all right as long as I have my Julie.*

Embracing her mother, Rose begged her, "Mama, please take care of yourself. I need you so much. We all do. One day you'll see. You'll be dancing at your granddaughter's wedding, and what's more," she said, breaking into a smile, "I'll make your dress."

"I'll do my best, Rifka, to live for that glorious day. Now go, my child. Sam will be home soon and you should be there."

With a heavy heart, Rose left the apartment, promising that she would return soon with Julie. As she boarded the train for the long trip back to Manhattan, she tried to sort out her responsibilities. *I can't go away again. My family needs me too much. But, then again, so does Julie. What am I going to do?*

Julie used the free time she now enjoyed to visit her two teachers and friends, Esther and Claudia. She had been writing them faithfully from the road and sending them all the newspaper clippings and reviews. At first, Esther Lieber had been a little disturbed when Julie accepted the job as a vocalist with Paco Castell. Before Julie left town to join Paco in Hartford, Esther had asked her pupil to come to her studio for a long talk.

Patting the blue velvet sofa that faced out on her beautiful garden, Esther motioned for Julie to join her there. "Julie, my dear. Please, be honest with me. Are you quite certain you want to give up your career on the Broadway stage? I'm not sure you'll get the opportunity to do full justice to your voice, singing with a band. That's not what I trained you for."

"Oh, Esther, I understand how you feel about my future on the stage, and up until now I agreed with you. But an opportunity like this might never come along again. You know how I've always admired the big Hollywood musicals, especially the ones with Paco Castell.

Well, what he's offering me now is a chance to get out of the chorus and bit parts and become a featured vocalist with his orchestra."

Taking her teacher's hand, Julie squeezed it fervently, her eyes dancing with excitement as she visualized her future. "Can you imagine how glamorous it will be to be playing in famous nightclubs and hotels all over the country and maybe all over the world? Just think, I'll be out there singing in front of a big band all alone, instead of being just another chorus girl. Paco Castell has made so many pictures and discovered so many stars. I'm bound to get noticed much quicker this way than waiting and hoping for another Broadway show to turn up."

Esther understood Julie's youthful enthusiasm and ambition. It was one of the things she admired about her young student. But having heard of Paco Castell's reputation, she was skeptical about his integrity and his real motivation in signing her. But when Julie begged her to understand that she would be fulfilling a dream by singing with Paco Castell's orchestra, Esther reluctantly gave Julie her blessing but cautioned her to practice so as not to forget what she had learned.

Claudia had also voiced certain reservations when Julie paid a visit to her studio. "Julie, what will happen now with your acting career? You've shown such promise as an actress. How can you interrupt your studies?"

Julie tried to explain her situation. "Claudia, I love to act and I intend to continue my studies, but I can't let this opportunity slip by. It might never happen again."

Realizing that Julie was determined, Claudia had embraced her warmly and wished her well.

Now that the tour had come to an end, Julie's days were filled with activity as she waited for Paco to return from California. One afternoon, as she entered the apartment, Julie heard the telephone ringing off the hook when she opened the door. Quickly, she ran to answer it.

"Julie, for God's sake, where were you? I've been calling all day."

Irritated that she was constantly being asked to account for her whereabouts, Julie answered testily, "I was visiting my singing teacher, Paco, and running some errands. I can't sit around all day waiting for your calls."

Catching the annoyance in her voice, Paco was instantly contrite. "Forgive me, my precious one. I was anxious to reach you because I have good news. I'll be arriving in New York on Sunday night. My divorce is finally proceeding smoothly and my mind is clear, so I can now concentrate on the future."

Julie's blood ran cold when she heard this. She knew only too well what Paco had in mind. Soon he would be free, and that meant he could pursue her openly. How was she going to handle him?

"Another important thing that I wanted to discuss with you," Paco continued, "is the South American tour. Have you spoken to your parents?"

"No, Paco, I haven't. My mother and father have been so happy being back together again and living a normal life, I just don't have the heart to press them for an answer right now."

"Julie," Paco said, with mounting irritation, "you must give me an answer. Rogers and Cowan, my press agents, are calling me every day about the trip. We must send off the publicity no later than next week."

"Oh, Paco, it's so difficult. You know I want to go. I'm just not sure if I can convince my mother and father."

"Well, why can't you go alone? My brother and Marion will be along. You like her don't you? The two of you could room together."

"Oh no, Paco. My parents would never agree to that."

"Well, my dear," Paco answered cunningly, "you know how much I want you for the tour, but, if your parents refuse, as much as I would hate to do it, I would have to find someone else to replace you."

Paco knew exactly what effect his threat would have on Julie, and he was right because when she hung up the phone she was practically in tears. Kicking off her shoes, she curled up on the sofa and tried to think straight.

Replace me. Oh, no. Just when my career is starting to take off. I can't let that happen. I want to make this trip too much. Paco had described over and over again how exciting it would be traveling to Rio and Buenos Aires and what an impact he felt she would make. How could she possibly let a chance like this slip through her fingers?

Leaning her head back on the couch Julie heaved a sigh of utter despair. The turmoil brewing inside of her could never be resolved without her parents being hurt. Julie sat there for a long while and watched the afternoon sun disappear as dusk settled over the city. Her parents would be arriving home at any moment and she knew that she could no longer delay the inevitable confrontation.

A short while later, when her father heard Julie's request, his nor-mally gentle face tightened into a steely mask of anger. "Leave home again and go to South America?" he thundered. "No, it's out of the question. You just got home."

Rose glanced around and put her fingers to her lips.

"Sam, don't shout. The neighbors will hear, and besides, you're frightening Julie."

Julie sat huddled in a living room chair, her face ashen. Although she had geared herself for their resistance, this was worse than she had anticipated. Her father was adamant about keeping his family together.

"Sam," Rose said, as she watched her husband pace the room. "For God's sake, sit down so we can discuss this quietly. Let Julie explain everything. You never gave her a chance to finish."

Julie, grateful for her mother's intervention, summoned up all her courage as she continued to try and convince her father.

"Dad, Paco wants to play a few dates in the East to break in the material for South America. He mentioned Boston and Washington, D.C., as two of the cities, so maybe you could even join us on the weekends. He has also promised to raise my salary to one hundred and fifty dollars a week."

Julie watched her father's stern expression, hopeful for some positive reaction, but his face looked grim and unrelenting.

"So what?" Sam asked sarcastically. "Will that compensate me for another three months of loneliness?"

"No, Dad, of course not but it'll only be for eight weeks, and then we'd be home."

"Julie, you're such a gullible child. After South America there will be someplace else that seems exciting to you and then on and on. This is no life for us. I'm not the kind of man who can leave his business and go traipsing around the country following his wife and daughter. I want a home. You could work right here in New York and everyone would be happy."

Julie listened to her father's reasoning and knew that what he said was probably true. But she couldn't quit now. It would mean living cooped up in this same apartment with her father's impossible restrictions. She couldn't go back to that same life. Not after having tasted freedom.

"Dad, I beg you. Please, let us go. If things go well we can all go to California permanently once Paco starts making pictures. You've always said how much you'd like to leave New York."

Rose, sensing an opportunity to voice an opinion, joined in. "Sam, darling, be reasonable. Before we leave the country we could see you on weekends like Julie suggested, and before you know it, we'd be home."

"Rose, what has happened to all your promises, not only to me, but to Esther? Just the other night you cried like a baby about your mother's poor health. You said you were afraid something might happen to her, and you wouldn't be there."

"I know, Sam, and you're right. I'd probably never forgive myself. But Julie has worked so hard to come this far. I want to give her this opportunity. It means so much to her."

With that, Sam knew that he was beaten. Shaking his head wearily, he threw up his hands in despair.

"All right, all right, you win. I can't fight the two of you. But, I want to clarify one more thing before I agree. I read in the papers that Paco's wife is in Reno getting a divorce. I want you to promise me that you'll make sure he behaves like a gentleman at all times, and if he doesn't, you'll come home immediately."

Addressing his next remark to Rose, he cautioned her. "Rose, I'm relying on you to take care of Julie. Don't get carried away by all the glamour and excitement. If something happens to her, I'll hold you responsible."

Turning rapidly on his heels, he left the room.

Julie, who had been practically holding her breath during the entire episode, heaved a sigh of relief. She had gotten a reprieve. For how long didn't matter. She would be going to South America. The next obstacle confronting her would be Paco, and she was certain that he would prove to be much more difficult than her father.

CHAPTER
16

They had now been back on the road for three weeks and already it was apparent that conditions had greatly improved since their last trip. For one thing, they were traveling by plane instead of bus, and instead of the one-nighters, which Julie hated, they were playing two-week engagements.

The Show Room at the elegant Shoreham Hotel in Washington, D.C., where they were now appearing, was jam-packed every night with an impressive array of top government officials. There were also dignitaries from various foreign embassies, especially those from Latin America and Spain who had been long-standing Paco Castell fans. They were extremely impressed with Paco's new discovery and showered her with compliments when Paco introduced her to them after the show. When they found out that she was not of Latin origin, they were amazed. Her near perfect pronunciation of Spanish and her newly acquired Latin style in dancing could have fooled anyone.

During the day, when not rehearsing, Julie and Rose would go on long tours through the beautiful city. It was September, the perfect month for sightseeing. Congress was back in session and the city was teaming with excitement. Julie wanted to see everything—the Lincoln Memorial, the Jefferson Memorial, the Washington Monument, and of course, the White House. Julie and Rose stood outside the long fence that surrounded the grounds and gazed at the beauty and splendor of the stately mansion. That evening, just before the show, Julie enthusiastically described everything she had seen to Paco, especially the White House.

She was awed when he told her that only last year he had performed for Harry Truman at the White House at a state dinner, and she wondered if she would ever have the opportunity to sing in front of a president.

As Sam had promised, he joined his family in Washington their first weekend there. At first, he had been reluctant to go, claiming he couldn't leave the business and that it was foolish to incur added expense. But Rose would have none of it.

"Sam, you're just being stubborn. The fare isn't expensive, and it'll give us some time together, almost a little vacation."

Once he arrived, Sam was glad that he had come. Not only did he get to see Rose, but this also would be his first opportunity to see Julie performing with the band.

Even though Rose had tried to prepare him for what to expect, when he finally saw his daughter onstage, he was totally dazzled by her beauty, poise, and talent. She exuded a sensuality that had an even stronger impact because of her total unawareness of it. The audience response to her performance was very enthusiastic, and Sam felt a surge of pride in watching her. But he also had a chance to study Paco carefully during the performance, and Sam instantly recognized the proprietary look of a man who is smitten by a woman and anxious to have her as his own. This disturbed and angered him. Without him there to protect Julie he wondered if Rose would be strong enough to stand up to a man like Paco Castell. Rose was as ambitious for Julie as Julie was for herself, and he feared that this ambition might easily get in the way of her judgment.

On the night preceding their closing at the Shoreham, Julie was just about to change into street clothes, when there was a knock on her dressing room door. As usual, Rose was backstage, helping Julie with her clothes and keeping an eye out for Paco. Julie opened the door and found the maître d' standing there with a short man who had thinning blond hair and appeared to be in his late forties.

"Miss Lauren, I'm sorry to disturb you, but this gentleman is a friend of Mr. Castell's and we can't seem to find him. We thought he might be in your dressing room."

"No, Maurice, I'm sorry he's not here. Have you tried his suite upstairs?"

"Yes, Miss." But before he could continue, the man who stood beside him spoke up. "Miss Lauren, my name is Johnny Meyer. I'm an old friend of Paco's, but actually it's you that I've come to see."

Julie invited him in and introduced him to her mother.

"If I may call you Julie," he said, "let me come directly to the point. I just saw the show and I think you're terrific. Have you ever thought about a career in motion pictures?"

Thought about it, Julie wanted to shout, *I've thought about nothing else since I was five years old.*

"Well," Julie answered, "I've always dreamed of going to Hollywood and making pictures. As a matter of fact, Paco has promised to feature me in his next RKO film."

"Forget about Paco for the moment. I'm talking about you—alone. I happen to represent someone, whose name I cannot divulge at this time, who is very interested in having you come to California for a screen test."

Julie had to lean against the dressing table to support herself because suddenly she felt weak in the knees. She had no idea who this man was, or who he was representing, but he seemed dead serious.

"Mr. Meyer, please sit down. I don't know what to say. I never expected anything like this, and to tell you the truth I'm speechless."

"Well, Julie," he said, studying her face. Up close she was even more beautiful than she appeared onstage. "I've been in to see you perform three nights in a row now, and my boss in California knows all about you. If you say the word, I will make arrangements for you to go to the Coast to make a screen test."

Julie was getting more excited by the minute. *Screen test, Coast,*— magical words to her ears. "Mr. Meyer, it sounds wonderful. But," she said, glancing over at Rose, "I'm sure I couldn't go to California without my mother."

"That's no problem, Julie. We're aware that you're quite young, and therefore, we would expect your mother to accompany you. What else is bothering you?"

Julie looked around nervously, her mind racing. "I don't know how Paco would feel about this," she explained. "He's planning a tour to South America at the end of November and expects me to come with him. I don't think he'd agree to my leaving, and I certainly wouldn't do anything without his approval."

Rose, who had remained silent, felt that it was time for her to find out more about this man and who he was representing. Gently easing Julie out of the way, Rose confronted him.

"Mr. Meyer, before we discuss a trip to California or anything else, I would have to know who you work for and what studio he is connected with."

Fixing his gaze on the mother, he astutely realized that she would be a tough cookie to deal with. *But, he thought, I've dealt with difficult situations before, and for someone who looks like Julie, it would be well worth the effort.*

"Of course, Mrs. Lehman. I understand perfectly. The studio is RKO, and the man I work for and who owns the studio is Howard Hughes."

It was now Rose's turn to be speechless. Grasping Julie's hand, she stared at him. Howard Hughes, a man so famous that even the most unsophisticated knew who he was—aviator, billionaire, and the discoverer of Jean Harlow and Jane Russell. Her mind began to race wildly. This could not only be Julie's big chance for motion pictures, but also a means of getting her away from Paco Castell.

A moment later there was a knock on the door, and without waiting for an invitation, Paco walked in. Quickly surveying the scene before him, his face darkened with dislike and anger as he lashed out. "What the hell are you doing here, Johnny? Are you still pimping for Howard Hughes?"

Julie and Rose gasped when they heard this, but Johnny Meyer's mouth just curved into a sardonic grin. Pulling a gold cigarette case out of his pocket, he opened it slowly and removed a thin brown cigarette.

"Still the same old Paco. Mr. Charm until he gets angry. Then he becomes a crude bum."

Paco's face reddened, and for a minute he looked as if he would strike Meyer, but somehow he managed to control himself. "Why don't you get the hell out of here," he warned, "before I really lose my temper. I don't know what crap you've been telling them, but remember, I know you from the old days."

Ignoring Paco, Johnny Meyer flicked open his gold lighter and casually lit his cigarette.

"Julie, I have to go now, but one of my associates, Walter Kane, will be calling you tomorrow. Think my offer over. Walter will accompany you to California. He is prepared to make all the necessary arrangements and can also answer any questions you might have. It's been a great pleasure meeting you both. Good night."

Brushing by Paco, who looked ready to explode, he left the room.

As soon as the door closed Paco released his pent-up fury on Julie.

"What did he mean about a trip to California?" he yelled. "What has he been telling you?"

Julie had never seen Paco so angry and his rage frightened her.

"Please, Paco, calm down and give me a chance to explain."

Rose had to bite her lips to keep from screaming back at him. *How dare he treat my Julie like this?* Rose fumed silently to herself. *If he doesn't simmer down I'll really give him something to yell about.*

Paco reluctantly sat down on the chair that Meyer had just vacated, and with his eyes never leaving her face, he waited for Julie's explanation.

Julie nervously began to repeat the conversation that had taken place. When she finished there was silence as she waited for Paco's response. When he spoke Paco took pains to soften his tone, remembering that he had to convince not only Julie, but also her mother that they would be making a mistake.

Rising, he took Julie's hand in his and looked up pleadingly at Rose.

"Julie dear and Rose, you're both intelligent women. You must be sensible. I know this guy Johnny Meyer. Everyone knows him. He has a bad reputation. He scouts all over the country for beautiful young girls for Howard Hughes. He arranges a phony screen test for them and sets them up for Hughes."

Looking at their incredulous faces, he continued. "If you don't believe me ask my agents, Freddie or Larry. They can confirm that what I'm telling you is the truth."

"But, Paco," Julie asked. "If that's true why would they agree that my mother could accompany me? They must be serious about a screen test. And maybe, if it's successful, they will offer me a contract."

Rushing on, before Paco got the wrong idea, she added, "That doesn't mean that I couldn't do the South America tour. You know I don't want to leave the band. If I make the test during the weeks we have off before South America, I wouldn't even miss a day."

Paco was growing steadily more irritated, even though he was trying hard to conceal it.

"You're not listening to me, Julie. Don't you understand that Hughes is not interested in your talent. He has beautiful girls stashed away in apartments and hotels all over Los Angeles. He pays them salaries and most of them have never even see the inside of a studio. I now have a contract with RKO. Why can't you be patient and wait until I make my picture? I promised you that I would feature you in my musical numbers." Reaching for her hands, he said, "Julie, I care about you and I'm trying to protect you."

"I know, Paco, and please believe me, I'm grateful. But this would mean more than just my future as a singer. If the test is good, it would give me a chance to show I'm an actress."

Paco abruptly pulled away and glared at her.

"Actress," he sneered sarcastically. "Hollywood is full of actresses. Haven't you heard of casting couches?"

By then Rose decided that it was time for her to intervene. Julie was no match for him.

Looking him straight in the eye, and hoping that he would get her full meaning, Rose spoke her mind. "Paco, I think I can tell if someone is a phony and has ulterior motives toward my daughter. Remember, I'm her mother and I'm fully capable of protecting her. You've been very nice to us and obviously Julie is grateful and wouldn't want to disrupt your plans. But if this Walter Kane does call and offers Julie a concrete screen test, and if you give her your consent, and hopefully your blessing, then I think she should take it. I'm sure you wouldn't want to stand in the way of what might be a great opportunity."

Paco's patience began to erode when he saw that his words had obviously made no impact. With disgust plainly evident on his face, Paco rose and faced Julie. "I've had enough of this stupidity. I've told you my feelings about Howard Hughes based upon my experience. If you and your mother choose to ignore my warnings then go ahead. But be sure you're back in time to start the tour. I've spent a lot of time and a great deal of money in publicizing your appearances and building you up, and I don't want to be left out in the cold. The impresario in South America expects Paco Castell and his entire show and that includes you."

Julie couldn't understand Paco's anger. She had every intention of fulfilling her commitment to him. Furthermore, even with a screen test, there was no guarantee that she would be put under contract. It was just a chance, but one she had to take.

Paco turned and left the room without saying another word. As he walked down the hall to take the elevator back to his suite, he was seething with jealousy. He didn't know who to blame more—his agents, who he suspected might be involved in some way, or that bastard Meyer. Entering his living room, he decided to call his agent in California. When he reached him at his office, Paco exploded.

"Lew, for Christ's sake, what's going on? First you put me with a studio that makes lousy musicals instead of with MGM where I belong. And now those pricks are trying to steal my vocalist."

Lew Wallace, the head of MCA, patiently tried to convince Paco that they had nothing to do with Johnny Meyer's visit.

"If that's true, then call Hughes and tell him to back off."

"Paco," Lew tried to explain. "We can't do that. No one tells Howard Hughes what to do. Do you want us to jeopardize your three-picture deal just because of a girl singer? Be sensible. Chances are she'll never get the test, and even if she does, nothing will come of it."

"Then call her and her damn mother and tell them that. She won't believe me. Maybe she'll believe you."

Paco slammed the receiver down, angry and frustrated at this sudden turn of events. Just when everything seemed to be going well in his patient pursuit of Julie, this cropped up. *I wish my lawyer hadn't told me to stay clear of California until my divorce is final.* Ripping off his tie and jacket, Paco walked into the bedroom and dropped down on the bed as he reviewed his options.

First, I'll have to call her father in New York and try and convince him what his daughter is letting herself in for. If that doesn't work, and her father can't persuade her to change her mind, then I'll call my lawyer, Harold, in California and tell him to take charge of matters out there. It wasn't the best solution, but he didn't know what else he could do. Feeling somewhat relieved that he now had a game plan and possibly an unwitting ally in Sam Lehman, Paco stretched out on his bed and tried to relax. But he was unable to get Julie out of his mind. *Why am I going through all of this,* he thought. *There are plenty of beautiful girls who would be more than happy to be with me. She's beautiful, yes, but so are many others who are far less complicated and would certainly give me less problems.* Suddenly another thought crossed his mind. *Could it be that this child who doesn't even realize she is a woman has stirred something in me that I didn't realize existed until now?* The thought disturbed him. The closest Paco had ever come to real love had been Lola Caldero, his first wife, but that relationship had been very differ-ent. They had both been very young and still struggling when they met. She had worshipped Paco and tried to ignore his many indiscre-tions. After they were married, he quickly grew tired of her and her incessant jealousy and openly began to seek other companions. Even after their divorce Lola still hoped that when Paco grew tired of his other women, he would one day come back to her. Paco never deceived himself into thinking that his next two marriages had been anything more than relationships based entirely on passion, and they, too, had ended badly. Now he found himself confronted with this young and ambitious girl whose strict upbringing and difficult parents were making his life miserable. Paco felt tormented because he desired her, and he was frustrated by her seemingly constant rebuffs. As he stared vacantly at the ceiling, he tried to tell himself to be patient a little longer. *Probably nothing will come of it and she'll come right back. But I swear on my mother's grave that if anyone touches her I will kill them. When she finally comes to me, and she will, I want her to be pure and untouched.*

With this resolved in his mind, Paco realized suddenly that he was hungry, and leaning over, he picked up the phone and ordered his dinner.

CHAPTER 17

"Julie, are you ready?" Rose called out from the kitchen. "Dad is waiting downstairs in the car."

Hearing no response, Rose tried again. "Julie, hurry. We'll be late."

Adjusting her hair under the white felt hat her mother had purchased for the trip, Julie studied herself for the last time in the mirror. Her face was glowing with the natural flush of youth and excitement that no rouge could ever duplicate.

"I'm coming, Mom. Just give me a minute."

Well, Julie, she thought, *this is it. You're on your way. This is what you've dreamed about all your life—what you fantasized about those long months that you lay here in this very room, too ill even to walk to the bathroom. Now, in less than an hour, you'll be on a plane that will fly you to the place that dreams are made of—Hollywood.*

"Julie," Rose yelled impatiently as she entered the bedroom. "I'm not going to call you again."

When Julie still hadn't moved, Rose shouted in exasperation, "Julie, for God's sake, what are you daydreaming about? We've got to go."

"Okay, okay, Mom. I'm ready." Picking up her purse and gloves, she put her arm around her mother and flashed her a dazzling smile. "Let's go, Mom. California here we come."

On their way to the airport, Julie and Rose were so excited about what lay ahead of them that they were scarcely aware that Sam had said hardly a word. While his wife and daughter kept babbling about all the movie stars they hoped to see, Sam was engrossed in his own thoughts, especially his telephone conversation with Paco a few days earlier. At first Sam had been confused when Paco called him urgently from Washington, D.C. But Paco came quickly to the point.

Reaching him at the office, Paco had pleaded, "Sam, your wife and daughter won't listen to me, so it's up to you to make them see the light."

"Paco, I don't know what else I can do. They're so thrilled about the screen test and this opportunity. What more could I say? I don't want to break Julie's heart."

"Is it better if those bastards break her heart?" Paco asked. "Listen, Sam, we're grown men and we know what other men are like. Hughes just wants to get her out there for one reason—he wants her for himself. She isn't the first girl they've done this to and she won't be the last. As far as a screen test is concerned, I doubt if she'll even get that far. Walter Kane is nothing more than a glorified pimp for Howard Hughes, and this is the man you're turning your daughter over to."

Sam was so confused he couldn't think straight. Everything that Paco was saying sounded logical. But was it the truth?

"Paco, look. Let me think about this a few days. Right now I don't know what's right or wrong and I have to sort it out in my mind. I'll make my decision when Julie and Rose return to New York."

After hanging up the phone, Sam sat there desperately trying to evaluate everything that Paco had said. He would not do anything now, he decided, but once they were home he would discuss the matter carefully with Rose.

But when the engagement was over and they returned to New York from Washington, Julie was so enthusiastic about the screen test and the possibility of a future contract, that Sam didn't have the heart to deny her the chance. Still harboring reservations, Sam agreed that they could go. Whatever concerns he felt about Howard Hughes were overshadowed by the fact that they were going to California and far away from Paco Castell, for whom he still had a lingering mistrust. He reasoned that if Julie *did* get signed to a contract, he could then move to California with them, where he would be in a better position to guide Julie's career and, at the same time, put an end to their painful separations. As Sam pulled the car up to the curb at the TWA terminal, he prayed that he had made the right decision.

After adjusting their seat belts, Julie and Rose carefully removed their jackets to make sure their flower corsages would not be crushed. Looking around the plane they were amazed that outside of Walter Kane they were the only passengers aboard the huge TWA plane. Unbuckling her seat belt, Julie turned around and tapped him gently on the arm.

"Excuse me, Mr. Kane. Do you know if we'll be taking off soon or are we waiting for other passengers to arrive?"

Glancing at his gold watch, Kane said, "No one else is expected, Julie. We're only awaiting clearance to take off."

Confused, Julie persisted. "But there are so many empty seats."

Smiling, he astonished her by saying, "Julie dear, Mr. Hughes doesn't care about empty seats. He owns TWA. In fact, he sent this plane expressly to take you and your mother to California. Now just relax and enjoy the trip."

Julie whispered her amazement to her mother. Rose too was astounded. "Imagine, Julie, a whole plane for us. Wait 'til the family hears about this. They'll never believe it."

During their flight, they were treated like royalty and it seemed in no time they had arrived in Los Angeles. The limousine that awaited them was the largest car that Julie had ever seen. When they were seated inside Julie touched the seats. The upholstery was like velvet. There were bottles of liquor stacked behind a little cabinet and glisten-ing crystal glasses in every size.

Other than inquiring whether there was anything they needed, Walter Kane hadn't spoken much during the plane trip. His telephone conversation with them before they left New York had clarified to some degree some of the reservations Sam Lehman had felt regarding the trip. He explained what would happen once they arrived. Julie would test for a musical called *Two Tickets to Broadway*. Beforehand, she would be coached in preparation for the test, and if the outcome was successful, she would then be signed by the studio to a seven-year contract starting at seven hundred and fifty dollars a week. Even Paco's agents at MCA were satisfied that these were standard terms and conditions for a studio contract. If, for whatever the reason, the test was not made, or was not successful, Julie was resigned to returning home, being no worse off for the experience. In any case, everyone reassured her that she would be back in New York in ample time to make the South American tour with Paco.

As the limousine made its way from the airport to their hotel, Julie and Rose stared out the windows, hoping to glimpse some famous Los Angeles landmarks. Like any tourist, the sites they most associated with Hollywood were Grauman's Chinese Theater, with its famous footprints and, of course, the famous "Hollywood" sign perched high up in the Hollywood Hills.

But their drive from the airport took a different, but even more impressive route. The car drove past huge gates that led to the incredible mansions of Bel Air. Julie recognized the name instantly because Paco had told her of his beautiful house there; the one that he had fought over so desperately with Laura, and had finally succeeded in winning back. Julie had to pinch herself to make sure she wasn't dreaming when Walter Kane pointed out the famous Beverly Hills Hotel. She was an avid reader of movie magazines and had seen dozens of pictures of movie stars dining in the Polo Lounge and hanging out at the pool. Even the tall palm trees lining the streets looked more majestic than in films, and as the sun filtered through their leaves it cast a golden glow over the city. Everything seemed golden to Julie— from the bronzed faces of people they passed in the streets of Beverly Hills to the shiny dome of the famous restaurant the Brown Derby. It was thrilling to finally be there, and it was an experience that she would never forget.

When the car pulled up in front of their hotel, the Town House, Julie had no idea what part of town they were in except they had left Beverly Hills and were somewhere on Wilshire Boulevard. She was anxious to get oriented because she and Rose hoped to do some sightseeing in their free time. As they approached the desk to register, Walter Kane suddenly appeared with keys in his hand.

"Julie, there's no need to sign in. You're already registered. Here are your keys." Taking her arm, he guided her toward the elevator. "I'll come upstairs with you to make sure you're both comfortable. The bellman will bring your bags."

When Julie opened the door of their suite she couldn't believe her eyes. Turning to Kane she was about to thank him, but he was already at the telephone calling the manager.

"This is Walter Kane in suite 406 and 408. There are not enough flowers here. I specifically told you from New York that I wanted yellow roses—lots of yellow roses—in every room." Turning to them he asked, "How do you like the accommodations, Julie? Will you and your mother be comfortable here?"

"Oh, Mr. Kane. It's just breathtaking. I had no idea that Mom and I would stay in such a beautiful place. Thank you so much."

Julie peeked into the huge bedroom, and even a hasty glance assured her it was the most elegant place she had ever seen. It was larger than their apartment in New York, and it even had two bathrooms, a luxury Julie had never had!

Patting her cheek, Kane told her, "Nothing is too good for our future star. Now, you and Rose get settled and order some dinner. Mr. Hughes would prefer that you eat in your rooms. We don't want the press to get wind of your whereabouts. The studio wants to keep you under wraps until after the test is made. Then the publicity department will see to it that you are launched properly."

He started to leave, but suddenly he stopped at the door. "Be sure and order whatever you want and don't worry about the expense. Just sign your name. Everything will be taken care of. And by the way, Julie, you needn't bother to call Paco or your father in New York. I will inform them personally that you and Rose have arrived safely."

"Thank you, Mr. Kane," Julie answered. "Also, could you please tell them what hotel we're in? We didn't give them any information before we left, and they'll probably want to call us. I know that Paco wants me to see his house while we're out here."

"Sure, Julie, no problem. Now relax. Have a good evening. I'll call you first thing in the morning."

With nothing to do but unpack and order dinner, Julie could now leisurely inspect their new surroundings. The living room was furnished simply, but elegantly. The walls were covered in a creamy brocade, and there was a marble fireplace in the center wall flanked by french doors on either side. Opening the door, Julie stepped out on a small terrace that overlooked the pool. There were lush bougainvillea vines trailing down the sides of the wall that surrounded the adjacent gardens. Julie stood there a moment and closed her eyes. The pungent smell of jasmine was in the air, and Julie took a deep breath, filling her lungs with its sweetness. So far California was even more beautiful than she had expected, and they had only been there a few hours.

Closing the door behind her, Julie walked back into the living room and joined her mother in the bedroom. Rose was busy unpacking and humming "A Pretty Girl Is Like a Melody." She had already slipped out of her traveling clothes and put on a robe. For the first time in months, her face was relaxed and she seemed happy.

"Mom, here let me help you. You should have called me."

"It's okay, *mamale*. It's such a pleasure to have all this space to ourselves. Did you know there are two bathrooms?"

"Yes, I saw them when we came in."

Opening the door, Julie looked around. "I guess this is the master bath," she said, running her hand over the cool marble counter.

"Yes, and look at the size of the tub. It's as big as a swimming pool. Just feel the towels, Julie. They're so big and soft."

Julie helped her mother place their clothes in the drawers, and by the time they had finished, Julie and Rose were famished. Flopping down on the beige satin-covered sofa near the fireplace, Julie reached for the menu. With Paco, they were always very careful to order things that weren't too expensive. They never wanted him to think they were taking advantage of him. But tonight, Julie felt daring. It was their first night in Los Angeles and they would splurge.

Much later, after a sumptuous dinner of shrimp cocktail, sirloin steak and french fires, peach melba for Julie and cheesecake for Rose, Julie leaned back and sighed happily, "Hasn't this been an incredible day, Mom?"

"Yes, Julie, it certainly has been, and I bet I've gained five pounds."

Julie laughed. "No, you haven't, Mom. You just picked at your food. I ate like a pig."

"You—can afford it. I can't."

Suddenly, a pensive look came over Rose's face. "I wonder how Dad is? I'm surprised he hasn't called."

"I'm sure he's fine, Mom. Mr. Kane told you he was going to call him to tell him where we are and that we're okay."

"I know, but it's not like Dad not to call me after such a long trip. I hope he's all right and that nothing is wrong with Grandma Esther."

"Mom, please don't worry. If something was wrong he would have called you."

Rose sighed. "I guess you're right, Julie. Well," she said, reluctantly getting up from her comfortable chair, "I think we should get ready for bed. Mr. Kane will be calling you early and you should look rested."

As Rose started for the bedroom, she asked, "Are you coming, Julie?"

"In a minute, Mom. I just want to go out on the terrace for a few minutes. It looks so beautiful out there."

"All right, but don't be long, and come inside if it's chilly."

Julie stepped out into the cool night air and gazed into the darkness. In the distance, she could see the twinkling lights of homes, and she wondered if that was Beverly Hills. As she leaned against the railing, she could hear music drifting up from the piano bar below in the courtyard. *A rhumba,* Julie thought pensively. *One of Paco's compositions.* Humming softly to herself, she began to think. *It's strange Paco hasn't called. I know how jealous he is and how much he hated my coming here. I would have thought he'd be on the phone the minute he knew where we were. But it's late in New York and he's probably still angry. He's sure to call tomorrow.* Closing the door behind her, she turned off the light and returned to the bedroom. Julie removed her clothes quietly, so as not to disturb her mother. *Better get some beauty sleep myself. Tomorrow will be a big day.*

Back in New York, even though it was one o'clock in the morning, a frantic Paco was dialing Sam Lehman's telephone number. He heard it ringing, once, twice . . .

"Answer, goddammit, answer."

Three times . . . Suddenly, a tired voice answered, "Hello."

"Sam, it's Paco."

"Paco," Sam answered, a note of fear creeping into his voice. "What's wrong? Has anything happened to Rose and Julie?"

"That's what I was hoping you'd tell *me.* Have you heard from them?"

"No, I haven't. But I assumed they called while I was out. I came home late from work and went straight to bed. I would have called them but I don't know where they're staying. Do you?"

"No, and that's what's bothering me. I've called the Beverly Hills Hotel, the Beverly Wilshire, the Hotel Bel-Air—everywhere. They're not registered."

Sam couldn't tell from Paco's voice whether it was genuine concern for his wife and daughter's well-being that he felt, or just anger that he wasn't in control. But whatever it was, Sam now joined him in expressing his fears.

"Paco, I'm worried. What do you think we should do?"

"We'll have to wait 'til morning when I can contact my lawyer. In the meantime, I have MCA on the Coast looking for them. Dammit, Sam. I *told* you what they were letting themselves in for. Why didn't you stop them?"

"Paco, be reasonable. How could I stop them? Until now everything has been aboveboard."

"All right, Sam, go back to sleep. They're probably fine. I'll have some answers in the morning. In the meantime, call me if you hear from them."

"I will Paco, and you do the same. Good night."

Both men hung up the phone thinking their own thoughts. Sam was concerned about his wife and daughter's health and welfare. Where were they? Why hadn't they called? Paco, on the other hand, was passionately jealous and fearful that somehow he might be in danger of losing Julie.

The next morning, promptly at nine o'clock, the phone rang in Julie's suite. It was Walter Kane.

"Good morning, Julie. Did you have a good sleep?"

"Oh yes, but we've been up for hours. Change of time I guess."

"Yes, of course," Walter answered. "Can you meet me down in the lobby, say, in about forty-five minutes?"

"Of course, Mr. Kane. We'll be there."

Exactly at nine forty-five Julie and Rose stood near the front desk, waiting for Walter Kane to arrive. Minutes later in he strode, wearing a dark gray pinstripe suit with a white carnation in his lapel. "Good morning, ladies. You both look very beautiful. Shall we go? The car is outside." Piling into the car, Julie was excited, anticipating her visit to the studio.

They had been driving for almost half an hour and Julie was beginning to get fidgety. So far, Walter Kane had been engaging her mother in idle chatter and had made no mention of where they were going or her upcoming screen test. She still had no idea when it was to take place and what would be expected of her. The only thing he kept emphasizing was the need for them to avoid the press. Julie was confused. *I'm not famous,* she thought. *No one knows who I am, so why all the secrecy?* Another thing kept bothering her. He hadn't mentioned whether he had spoken to her father and Paco. She was hesitant about asking him but decided that as soon as they got back to the hotel, she would call home.

Minutes later, the car pulled up in front of a small building that looked like a private home, and they all got out. Julie looked around, and it seemed to her that they were in a residential area, but where, she didn't know. Walter Kane took her arm and guided her up the steps. There was a sign near the doorbell—Dr. Marvin Sheldon, D.D.S. Julie and Rose looked at each other in amazement. What were they doing here? Julie was about to ask, but Walter Kane, anticipating their question, answered it for them.

"Julie, I guess you're wondering why you're here?"

"Why, yes, I was. I thought we were going to the studio."

Pressing the buzzer he began to explain. "Before we proceed with your screen test, Mr. Hughes would like to check out a few things."

By now they were inside the waiting room, which was empty except for the receptionist. Motioning for them to be seated, Kane continued.

"Julie, the camera can be very cruel. It picks up little things and magnifies them greatly. Your teeth, which may appear all right onstage, could flaw your appearance if they're not perfect. That's why we want Dr. Sheldon to check them out before you go before the camera."

"But, Mr. Kane," Rose said almost indignantly. "Julie's teeth *are* perfect. Just look at her smile. She never even had to wear braces."

"I know, Rose, they do look good, but I have to follow Mr. Hughes's orders. Don't worry. It won't take long, and then I'll take you both to lunch."

Just then a tall man wearing a white jacket appeared in the doorway, and, after introducing himself, asked Julie to come into the office. Julie did as she was asked and spent the next hour having her teeth poked at and X-rayed. All the time she was sitting there she kept thinking, *This is ridiculous. There's nothing wrong with my teeth. What am I doing here?*"

When the examination was completed, Walter Kane accompanied them back into the car, and a short while later they arrived at a small restaurant where a table was awaiting them. The lunch was delicious, and though they saw no celebrities dining there, Walter Kane told amusing celebrity stories to make up for it.

After lunch Julie finally summoned up the courage to ask when she was going to start preparing for her test. "Mr. Kane, I would love to get the script as soon as possible so that I can study it."

"Julie, there's plenty of time for that. We don't want to rush you before you're ready."

Noticing the look of disappointment that crossed her face, he said, "Now, dear, I don't want you getting anxious or upset. Remember what I said about the camera. It catches everything."

Julie nodded and looked at her mother. Rose hadn't said much during lunch, but Julie knew her mind was working. *Is she thinking what I am? This is not exactly what we expected?*

Julie was silent during the drive back to the hotel. When they parted Walter Kane patted her hand and told her, "I won't tire you out anymore today. Get some rest tonight and have dinner sent up. Tomorrow we want to take some photographs of you, and then I'll take you to RKO."

Finally, Julie thought with great relief. *I was beginning to think there was no RKO.* Thanking him, Julie and Rose entered the hotel. When they arrived at the front desk, Rose asked for the keys and messages.

"I'm sorry, ma'am. There's nothing in your box."

"But that's impossible. I was expecting a call from my husband in New York."

The young girl behind the desk turned around and looked again. "No messages."

Rose looked confused and upset. She glanced at her watch. It was four o'clock—seven P.M. in New York. Surely Sam would have called by now. As they rode up in the elevator, Julie, too, was perplexed. Paco called her every day and sometimes twice a day. Now, nothing. Was he still too angry to speak to her, or was it that he just didn't care? She began to get concerned about her job. *Has he found someone to replace me with the band?* she thought. *No, that's ridiculous. He couldn't have done that so quickly. He'll call later. I'm sure..*

Rose took off her shoes the minute she entered the suite and went into the bedroom to call Sam. He might still be in the office, but if not, she'd try the apartment.

Placing her call with the hotel operator, Rose waited for a response. A few minutes later the operator came back on the line and informed her that the circuits were busy and they would have to try later. Frustrated, Rose joined Julie in the living room.

"Mom, did you reach Dad?"

"No, I tried but I couldn't get through."

"Well, it's still early. How about going for a walk? Or maybe we could take a taxi to Grauman's Chinese Theater."

Rose hesitated. "Well, I did want to speak to your father, but I can try again later. Wait until I put on more comfortable shoes and we'll go."

Julie freshened her face and brushed her hair, excited that finally she had someplace to go. When her mother was ready and they were about to leave the suite, a man suddenly appeared seemingly out of thin air and approached them. Startled, they stepped back and were about to slam the door in his face, when he stopped them.

"Mrs. Lehman, don't be frightened. My name is Jack Carlisle. I work for Howard Hughes."

"You almost scared us to death. What do you want?"

"I'm sorry. Didn't Mr. Kane tell you about me?"

"No, he didn't."

"Well, I'm sorry ma'am. I'm here to guard you. Mr. Hughes would prefer that you and your daughter not leave the hotel unless you're with Mr. Kane. If you need anything, I can get it for you."

"We don't need anything," Rose answered angrily. "We just want to get out and do some sightseeing."

"Well," he paused. "I'll have to call Mr. Kane about that. Could I use the phone?"

"No, you can't. Just please get out. But when you *do* call Mr. Kane, please tell him I'm very disturbed. We don't like being held prisoner."

When he left, Rose slammed the door and stared at Julie. "Well, how do you like that? We're not supposed to leave the hotel unless we get their permission. Julie, I never thought I'd say this, but maybe Paco was right. Something about this whole deal is very fishy." Crossing the room, she picked up the telephone, more determined than ever to reach Sam. Sam Lehman picked up the telephone after the first ring. "Sam, thank God you're in. I was afraid I'd miss you."

"Rose, I've been sitting here frantically waiting for your call. Where are you?"

"I'm in Los Angeles at the Town House. Didn't Walter Kane tell you?"

"Nobody has told me anything. Paco and I have been going crazy worrying about you and Julie. He's had everyone in Los Angeles looking for you. What hotel did you say you're in?"

"The Town House. I don't know what part of town this is, but it looks like it's off the beaten track."

"Well, that's not important," Sam answered. "How are you and Julie and how is everything going?"

"We're fine. But this whole business is very strange."

Rose filled Sam in about what was happening as best she could without worrying him further. When Sam heard about their restrictions as far as leaving the hotel, he became furious.

"But, Rose, why would you accept that? You're a grown woman. You should know better. Why would you let that guy stop you from leaving?"

"Sam, it's not that easy. I don't want to spoil anything for Julie. Tomorrow she's supposed to go to RKO and take pictures. I don't want to make waves. Not yet."

"Well, I'm damned angry that Walter Kane never bothered to call me and that he lied to you."

"Listen, Sam. Don't worry. I'm on my guard. Let's see what happens tomorrow. If I don't call you by six o'clock my time—then you call me."

"All right, Rose. Please give my love to Julie. I miss you very much."

"Me, too. I guess you'd better call Paco and let him know where we are. Julie was a little concerned about the tour."

"I will, Rose, as soon as I hang up. Good night, dear."

Rose returned the receiver and sat down on the sofa. She needed time to think. Julie was in the bedroom watching the "Show of Shows" on TV and seemed content for the moment. No need to upset her needlessly. *Tomorrow when Walter Kane picks us up, he'd better be prepared to clarify what's going on. Is Julie going to make a screen test? And if so, when? Furthermore*, she thought determinedly, *no more guards outside the door. We expect to be permitted to come and go as we please.* Satisfied with her decision Rose joined Julie in the bedroom.

"Baby, I just spoke to Dad and he sends his love."

"Thanks, Mom. Has he spoken to Paco?"

"He's going to call him now. It seems that Kane forgot to call them and they didn't know where we were."

"Oh, so that's why Paco hasn't contacted me."

"Believe me, Julie, once he knows you're here he'll be calling every hour. You know how he is."

Julie laughed.

"Yes, Mom, I do. Well, as long as everything is all right I feel better. Are you hungry? I hope so, because I am. Let's order dinner."

But later, as Julie prepared for bed, she began to worry why she still hadn't heard from Paco. He now knew of her whereabouts so why the silence? Was it possible that Paco had grown weary of dealing with her problems and had decided to find a replacement for her? Julie prayed that wasn't the case and that he would forget his anger and call her.

The next morning, on their way to the photographer's studio, Rose waited for an opportune moment to confront Walter Kane and get some answers.

The limo finally pulled up to a store on Melrose Avenue and everyone got out. Julie and Rose followed Walter Kane into the store, but they were bewildered. Now where were they? A man came out and greeted them and asked them to come to the back. Once inside, they saw a large room with a white backdrop and lights and a camera already in place.

Walter Kane came up to Julie and introduced the photographer. "Julie, this is Paul. He will be taking your pictures. If you'd like to touch up your makeup, there's a dressing room on your right."

Julie took her makeup case and obediently went into the room. *This is weird,* she thought as she reapplied her makeup. *Why am I taking pictures here instead of at the studio? This place looks like a dump. Even the camera looks old-fashioned.*

Outside Rose was engaged in a serious conversation with Walter Kane. He was trying to reassure her that they were free to move about as they liked and that "of course you're not prisoners."

"Well, I don't know what you'd call it. A guy pops out of nowhere and tells us he has to call you to get your permission to let us out."

Walter brushed an imaginary spot off his immaculate suit and smiled at her.

"Rose, we were just trying to take care of you and Julie. You're unfamiliar with Los Angeles and we feel responsible for your well-being."

Rose was dissatisfied with his explanation, but decided to accept it and move on to her next question. "What about the screen test? Julie has to be back in New York by next Monday. Today is Tuesday and we don't seem any closer to a test than we were two days ago."

"Rose, please don't be so impatient. Later today I'll take you both out to RKO and show you around the lot. In time we'll start Julie with a drama coach." His response was so calm and reassuring that Rose had to content herself with that answer for the moment.

Two hours later a tired but happy Julie was back in the car and on her way to RKO. She was thrilled that she finally would get to see a real movie studio. The car passed through the main gate and stopped in front of Sound Stage 9. Walter Kane got out and opened the door for them.

"Here you are, ladies. Just like I promised you. Now if you follow me I'll show you around the set. We have to be quiet. Janet Leigh is filming."

Julie and Rose followed him to a door, and once the red light went out, they accompanied him inside. There were people everywhere—each one performing a different task. A few men were working at a long makeup table touching up actors' faces, while the cameraman checked lights. Several hairdressers were busy combing the hair of five or six beautiful young women. Over in the corner Julie recognized Robert Taylor sitting by himself, studying a script. Walter Kane asked them to wait there, and minutes later he beckoned for them to join him. Next to him, dressed in a long white chiffon gown and looking positively radiant was Janet Leigh. Walter introduced them.

"Miss Leigh," Julie said admiringly, "I can't tell you what a big fan I am of yours. I've seen all your pictures, and you look even more beautiful in person." Thanking her graciously, and complimenting Julie on her own beauty, she excused herself and went into her trailer. Julie was impressed with her charm and natural manner, and hoped that one day soon she too would be part of this special world.

The rest of the day was spent touring other departments—publicity, music, wardrobe. Julie didn't get to meet any other stars, but she wasn't disappointed. She was certain that in the following days, while preparing for her test, she would see many others.

Returning to the hotel that afternoon, Julie felt a little more optimistic. At least today she had moved one step closer to her goals. Walter Kane did not accompany them back to the hotel, explaining that he was needed at the studio. Julie and Rose found themselves alone in the car for the first time since they had arrived. Julie took advantage of this and asked the driver if he could stop at Grauman's Chinese Theater on the way back to the hotel. She was determined to see the footprints of famous stars before she left California, and this might be her only chance.

When they arrived at the famous theater on Hollywood Boulevard, Julie and Rose rushed around excitedly, looking for their favorite stars. Almost immediately, Julie found what she was searching for.

"Mom, look over here. I've found Betty Grable's footprints." Rose joined her and watched as Julie placed her own foot in the famous star's footprint. "Gosh," Julie said. "Her feet are so small or else mine are too big."

They spent nearly an hour there, going from star to star, and all the while Julie kept wishing that someday she would be famous enough to have a place of honor there.

Later that day when Rose checked the front desk, there were still no messages, but now she wasn't concerned. Sam would be calling anytime now, for it was almost six o'clock, but Julie's face fell when she realized that Paco still hadn't contacted her. As they started to walk to the elevator, Rose felt someone tap her arm. She looked up and saw an attractive white-haired man standing next to her.

"Mrs. Lehman?"

"Yes, I'm Mrs. Lehman."

"My name is Harold Ross. I'm Paco Castell's attorney. May I have a few words with you and Julie?"

Recognizing his name as someone Paco had mentioned before. Rose smiled warmly at him. "Mr. Ross, we were just on our way upstairs. Would you care to join us?"

"Yes, I would. I'd like to speak to you both in private."

Suddenly, out of the shadows the bodyguard that Walter Kane had assigned to them stepped in front of Harold Ross.

"Excuse me, sir. May I ask where you are going?"

Harold Ross was speechless for a moment, but quickly regained his composure. "Mrs. Lehman, do you know this man?"

"Yes, I do. He's the guy who watches our door to see that we don't leave."

"Excuse me a minute, Mrs. Lehman."

With fury in his eyes, the lawyer motioned the bodyguard aside, and in a voice that left no doubts as to who was in charge, said, "Listen, mister. I don't know who the hell you are, or who hired you, but I am Miss Lauren's lawyer, and I would advise you to get out of here right now."

The younger man studied the situation and decided the best course of action would be to leave. He quickly backed off, but instead of leaving the hotel, he went directly to the telephone.

Harold Ross joined Julie and Rose, who had been observing the scene curiously, and they went upstairs. Once they were in the suite, Harold Ross came directly to the point. "Mrs. Lehman, are you aware that you and your daughter are not registered here? And when anyone calls asking for you they are told you're not staying at this hotel?"

"What," Rose shouted increduously. "You must be mistaken."

"No, Mrs. Lehman, I'm not. Paco has been trying to reach you ever since you spoke to your husband last night, but no one will admit you are here. I've called myself and was told the same thing. In desperation

Paco finally called me and asked me to seek you out in person and find out what's happening."

Although she was shocked at his disclosure, Julie was relieved that Paco had indeed been trying to reach her. Rose started to pace the floor. "I can't understand it. Why would they do such a thing?" Turning to the lawyer, she asked, "Mr. Ross, what should we do?"

"Mrs. Lehman, please let me handle this."

Picking up the phone he asked for the manager. "Mr. Lewis, this is Harold Ross. I am Paco Castell's attorney and a close personal friend of Mrs. Lehman and her daughter. Yes, they're in 406. People have been calling the hotel asking for Julie Lauren or Rose Lehman and have been advised by the switchboard that there are no guests with that name registered. I don't know what the problem is, but I would strongly urge you to rectify it . . . *immediately.*"

Satisfied that he had succeeded in convincing the manager that he meant business. Harold Ross turned his attention back to Julie and Rose. "Mrs. Lehman, I'm sure that you'll be getting your calls now. But that's not my only concern."

Still shaken by this unpleasantness, Rose asked him what he meant.

"I just learned this morning that Howard Hughes owns this hotel, and that a very beautiful Italian actress has been holed up here for several months. I've also been told that she hasn't worked in any films or even been seen much around the hotel. It would appear that she's here for only one reason—to be available to Hughes. Under these circumstances, I would urge you to be extra careful where Julie goes, who she sees, and, under no circumstances, let her out of your sight."

"But what about the screen test? Do you think that it's for real, or was Paco right? Did they just want to get Julie here for Howard Hughes?"

"Mrs. Lehman, truthfully, I don't know. The man does own RKO and it's possible they could be serious about a test. But from what you've told me about your last two days here, and what I already know about Hughes's reputation, I would suspect that their reasons for bringing her here are, at best, questionable. Look, why don't you wait and see what happens tomorrow." Reaching into his pocket he produced a piece of paper. "Here's my card and home telephone number. Call me anytime, night or day. I can be here in twenty minutes."

Rose and Julie thanked him profusely for his kindness and concern and assured him that they would keep in close touch.

Too disheartened by the day's outcome, Julie barely touched her food that night. She had no idea what tomorrow would bring, but one thing was certain. Unless there were some positive steps taken, and soon, she probably would be returning to New York without having made a screen test. Shortly after dinner, Julie received the long awaited telephone call from Paco. He tried to hide his delight in telling her "I told you so," but he was obviously pleased that his predictions seemed to be coming true. He urged her to come home immediately, but Julie wouldn't give in.

"Paco, I have to wait at least another day before I make up my mind. Walter Kane promised me that tomorrow I would start coaching in preparation for my test. I can't quit now. If I did, I'd always wonder if I had made a mistake."

Unhappy with her decision, Paco made her promise she would keep in touch with his lawyer. He had been advised by his agents to keep out of the situation personally, because his own contract with RKO could be in jeopardy if he interfered.

After Julie's conversation with Paco, Rose settled down on the couch with her sewing kit in hand. There was a dress of Julie's that needed hemming and she hoped it would help her to relax. Julie decided to take a hot bath, which was her favorite way of unwinding. As she poured the bath salts the hotel provided into the rapidly filling tub, she glanced at her partially naked body in the mirrors that covered almost the entire bathroom. God, I look as pale as a ghost! *Maybe I can catch some sun before leaving California*, she thought. As she soaked in the soothing water, Julie could feel the tension slowly leave her body. Resting her head back, she tried not to think of anything—the test, Paco, South America, her future. *I wonder what other girls my age are doing tonight*, she thought wistfully. *They're probably out on a date or going to a prom or a movie—things that I've never experienced.* Julie sighed, but she wasn't unhappy. She had made her choice and she had no regrets.

Her thoughts were abruptly interrupted by the ringing of the telephone in the next room. *Who can that be?* she wondered. *I've already spoken to Paco and Dad wouldn't be calling so late. It must be at least ten-thirty.* Grabbing a robe, she dried herself quickly and went to answer it. But her mother was already speaking to someone in an agitated voice.

"Listen, Dr. Siegalman. I don't care what Walter Kane told you.

My daughter is not nervous, and she definitely does *not* need any medication. Thank you and good night."

Rose turned around and faced Julie, who was now sitting on the edge of the bed.

"Can you believe that?" Rose asked. "This doctor was told by Kane that you're anxious about the screen test and feels that maybe he should see you and give you something. I should have told him you're anxious about *not* getting the screen test."

The more Rose thought about it, the more agitated she became. "What kind of doctor calls at this hour? It's almost eleven o'clock. Ever since we've arrived it's been one surprise after another."

Julie couldn't answer because she, too, was confused. "Well, let's not worry about it, Mom. You handled it perfectly." Suddenly very tired, Julie climbed into bed and got under the covers. "The bath made me sleepy, Mom. I'm going to bed."

"I am, too, Julie. I'm just going to wash my face and slip into a nightgown."

An hour later, both Julie and Rose were roused from a sound sleep by a loud knocking on their door. Julie, being a very light sleeper, was the first to hear it. Thinking at first that the noise must be somewhere else, she turned over. But the knocking became more persistent. Now even Rose heard it, and sitting up straight in bed she turned on the light and glanced at the clock.

"Who the hell could that be at this hour of the night?"

Putting on her robe and slippers, Rose walked into the next room, with Julie right behind her.

"Who is it?" Rose called from behind the door.

"Mrs. Lehman, it's Dr. Siegalman. Could I see you for a few minutes?"

A look of exasperation crossed her face. "Do you know what time it is?"

"Yes, Mrs. Lehman, and I'm sorry. But Mr. Kane insists I talk to you and Julie tonight."

The urgency in his voice prompted Rose to do something that ordinarily she would have never done. Motioning for Julie to get her robe on, she let him in.

Once inside he again apologized for the late hour, as he took the chair offered to him. "Mrs. Lehman, as I told you before, Mr. Kane, acting on Mr. Hughes's behalf, wants to make sure that Julie is in good health."

"And I told *you* over the phone, doctor, my daughter is in perfect health."

"I'm sure she is, but we would feel much better if you would allow me to examine her."

"Examine her?" Rose yelled at him. "Examine her, for what?"

"Well," he stammered, uncomfortable by her reaction. "I just want to make sure that what you say is true. Mr. Hughes likes everything to be perfect."

Furiously, Rose crossed to where he was sitting and pointed her finger in the direction of the door.

"Doctor, I would like you to leave here immediately or I will call the manager. I don't know what kind of game you people are playing, but I don't want any part of it. First, they send my daughter to a dentist she doesn't need, and now in the middle of the night *you* come here to give her God only knows what kind of examination. I'm fed up with all of this and you can tell that to Walter Kane *and* Howard Hughes. Now, get out of here before I really lose my temper."

Hoping to regain some dignity, Dr. Siegalman stood up and started to leave but not before saying, "Mrs. Lehman, I resent what you are implying. I happen to be a highly respected physician in this town and I only came here to help."

"Well, go help someone else. We don't need you."

As soon as he was gone Rose kicked the door shut with her foot and locked it. "That's it," she said furiously. "We're leaving."

Julie had not uttered a word during all of this, but when she heard her mother say that they were leaving she tried to calm her. "Mom, take it easy. Why are you so angry? He left when you asked him to. Maybe they really were concerned about my health."

"Oh, Julie, you're still a child. Sometimes I forget that because you look so grown up." Pulling her down on the sofa beside her, she took her daughter's delicate hands in hers. "Sweetheart, you'll have to trust me. That doctor was here for no good. No respectable physician would come to a hotel in the middle of the night, when he was already told by me hours ago that we didn't need him. They know there is nothing wrong with you. You're not nervous, you're not ill. Then why was he here?"

Julie's big eyes stared up at her mother's face. "Why, Mom?"

"Because my intuition and experience tells me he wants to make sure," and now Rose hesitated for a moment searching for a delicate way to put it, "that you're a virgin."

Julie gasped when she heard this. "What? Oh no, Mom, you must be mistaken. That can't be why he was sent. You're wrong." Julie was so distraught that Rose thought she might begin to cry at any moment.

"Julie, baby, listen to me. I can't be sure. But for the life of me, I can't think of anything else. They must check out the poor girls who come here alone like a racehorse they're going to buy—their teeth, their bodies, and I guess in some cases, if they're very young, like you, their virginity. Thank God I was here, those bastards."

"But, Mom," Julie asked plaintively, "I'm not even sixteen. Why would anyone doubt my . . . virginity?"

"Because, sweetheart, not every girl your age is still a good girl. They know you've been traveling with a band. They know Paco Castell and his reputation. They put two and two together and got bimbo."

"Oh, Mom," Julie cried. "I'm so miserable. I wish we had never come here. It's worse to have seen a little bit of heaven and now to have to leave it all."

Turning away, Julie ran into the bedroom and flung herself on the bed. The tears she had been holding back now came streaming down her face. "It's not fair," she cried bitterly. "I was sure this was going to be my big chance."

Rose came to sit by her daughter's side and tried to comfort her. "Julie, it's not the end of the world. You'll have plenty of other chances. Okay, so this didn't work out. You're young, you're beautiful, you've got talent. Everyone tells you that. Your life is just beginning."

"Beautiful," Julie spit out disgustedly. "My looks only seem to get me into trouble. People, especially the men, don't give a damn about talent. All they care about is looks."

"Julie," Rose commanded. "Turn around and look at me."

Reluctantly, Julie rolled over and looked at her mother's face.

"Now, listen to me, Julie. It's better to be beautiful than just average. Believe me, it opens a lot of doors. Once those doors are open, people—decent people—will recognize that besides having beauty you have talent. You also have sweetness and brains and integrity. You can't let this incident discourage you. There will be plenty of other opportunities."

Julie stopped crying and was trying hard to believe that what her mother was saying was true.

"Now," Rose said, brushing Julie's hair away from her damp fore-head, "dry your eyes and let's try and get some sleep. Tomorrow we'll make our plans."

Weary and discouraged, Julie pulled the blanket over her and dropped off into a fitful sleep. They were awakened early the next morning by the sound of the phone ringing. Julie stretched her arm out and reached it first. It was Walter Kane.

"Good morning, Julie. Are you awake?"

Julie put her hand over the receiver and whispered to her mother, "It's Walter Kane."

Rose reached over and quickly took the phone from Julie's hand. "Mr. Kane, this is Rose Lehman. I have to talk to you. Could you meet us up here in about an hour? Fine, we'll expect you."

Rose put down the receiver and got out of bed. On her way to the bathroom she called out to Julie, "Baby, order some breakfast and then start packing. Walter Kane will be here in an hour."

Julie glanced around the room that she would soon be leaving. Sadly she ordered room service and started to pull her clothes from the closet. She wondered what Walter Kane would say when her mother confronted him. *Would he deny everything? Tell them they were being foolish? That there was a screen test awaiting her?* Julie didn't have long to wait for an answer. They had just finished their breakfast, when there was a knock on the door. Rose went to answer it and ushered Walter Kane into the room.

As he approached Julie, he looked at her appraisingly. "My dear, how lovely you look. Are you ready for today? I thought we'd have lunch at the Brown Derby and then I would take you both sightseeing."

Not a word, Julie thought, *about last night's mysterious visit or about the drama coach he promised for today.*

Rose quickly intervened. "Mr. Kane, we've now been here for four days and I don't think you have any intention of making a screen test with my daughter."

Kane started to protest, but Rose stopped him. "Furthermore, I don't like what's been happening since we arrived. Late last night your so-called doctor paid us a visit, and as far as I'm concerned, that was the last straw. Julie's not sick and you know it. First, the secrecy about our whereabouts and a guard outside the door. Then, telephone calls telling people we're not registered. This whole thing stinks. My husband and I have discussed this situation and we would like to have two tickets back to New York immediately."

Walter Kane stood there, an incredulous look on his face. "Mrs. Lehman, I don't know what to say except I think you're being very hasty. These things never happen quickly. It takes a while to get a young inexperienced girl like Julie in shape for an important screen test. Weeks, maybe, sometimes months."

"That's not what was told to us in New York."

"Well, once you got here we decided Julie needed to be groomed before she could make a test. Look," he said, smiling up at her, "if being away from your husband presents a problem to you, we could arrange for a chaperone for Julie while she's out here."

"I'll bet you could," Rose answered sarcastically. "But that's not the problem and I think you know it. Besides being disturbed by the strange way you handle things, Julie has a commitment to begin a tour with Paco Castell shortly and she can't wait any longer."

"Well, Mrs. Lehman, Mr. Hughes is going to be very disappointed when he hears this."

"Maybe he will, but I can't help that. Now, if you could just give us our tickets we would like to leave today."

Walter Kane began to pace up and down nervously. "Today may be impossible. It's already past ten. I'm not sure we can make arrangements that quickly. Aren't you being a little unreasonable?"

"If you think I'm unreasonable now, then wait until I tell Paco's attorney, Harold Ross, what happened last night. Would you prefer that?"

Now, visibly angry at Rose's veiled threat, Walter Kane answered her brusquely. "Mrs. Lehman, I have nothing further to say. I will have two airline tickets delivered to you within the hour. You had better be prepared to leave by this afternoon."

With that, he walked rapidly to the door to let himself out, but not before hearing Rose announce, "Don't worry, we're ready now."

CHAPTER 18

Julie and Rose's departure from Los Angeles was far less different from their departure from New York five days earlier. This time there were no corsages, no hugs and kisses. Just a dismal feeling of failure. As Walter Kane had promised, their plane tickets had arrived less than an hour after he had left their suite. There was no limo waiting for them, so Rose and Julie took a taxi to the airport, where they boarded a crowded TWA plane. During their long journey home both mother and daughter tried valiantly to engage in conversation, but their attempts proved futile. Neither one felt much like talking. They were too engrossed in their own thoughts. Rose was trying to put the entire episode out of her mind and plan ahead for their future trip to South America. She was terribly concerned about leaving Sam once again, but she was committed to accompanying Julie, who needed her now more than ever. Julie, on the other hand, was still too bitterly disappointed by what had happened to even think of the future. In the back of her mind she couldn't help but wonder if, perhaps, her mother had acted too rashly. *Maybe,* she thought, *the doctor incident, the security guard, and all the other strange occurrences were not unusual at all?* But the question that kept gnawing away at her was whether she had messed up not only this opportunity but also any future she might possibly have in motion pictures. Gazing at the cloudless horizon, she wondered if her mother's actions would also make it impossible for Paco to use her in any of his future pictures at RKO. She feared that they would, but there was nothing she could do about it now. She knew that Paco was pleased that his predictions had come true and that she was coming back to him. After her mother had called home to advise her father what time they would be arriving, Julie called Harold Ross and told him what had happened and that they would be leaving California immediately. A short time later, Paco called her from New York, exhilarated by the news that they were coming home.

Without bothering to inquire if she was upset or disappointed by the turn of events, Paco burst out jubilantly, "Julie, I'm so excited I'll be seeing you soon. Once you see what a sensation you're going to be in South America, you'll forget all this stupidity."

Now, as Julie sat waiting for the hours to pass, she prayed that what Paco said was true. She needed something wonderful to happen to her now to ease the pain of her Hollywood fiasco.

The drive home from the airport was solemn. Although she was happy to see her father, Julie couldn't shake off her depression. She was relieved not to have to answer any questions. She didn't want to have to rehash the whole thing over again. All she wanted now was to find a place in their small apartment where she could be by herself.

They had been home for a little over a week, and slowly the painful memory of Hollywood had begun to fade. As Julie had anticipated, her first encounter with Paco after her arrival in New York had been difficult. When she entered the rehearsal studio Paco was waiting for her. As soon as he spotted her he came over at once and embraced her.

"*Querida*, it is so good to see you again. You don't know how much I've missed you. Here, take your coat off and come sit next to me. Would you like some coffee?"

Julie removed her coat and gave it to Luis, who had just entered the room.

"No, Paco. Thanks, I'm fine. I've just finished breakfast."

"So," Paco said, taking her hand. "Now that you've been home awhile and have had a chance to think this Hughes thing over, do you realize what a foolish girl you've been?"

Oh God, Julie thought, *here it comes. I knew he wouldn't wait too long before reminding me.* His remark brought back all the pain she had been trying to forget and, looking at Paco beseechingly, she tried once again to explain. "Paco, I know you think I was foolish, and maybe I was. But, if I hadn't gone I would have always wondered whether I had passed up a great opportunity."

Paco looked at her in amazement. "But I told you that those bums were up to no good. Starting with that worm Meyer all the way up to Hughes. Why don't you give me credit for knowing this business and what Hollywood is really like?"

Paco stood up, suddenly angry at himself again for not having stopped her and even angrier at Julie for not listening.

"Julie, I've been a star for many years, and I know better than you or your parents, for that matter, what's best for you."

Julie sat there and tried to avoid his eyes, too shattered and intimidated by Paco's wrath to say anything in her defense.

Seeing how devastated Julie was sitting there, her large eyes ready to burst into tears at any moment, Paco suddenly stopped his tirade.

"Julie, I can see how upset you are, so we won't discuss this any longer. But, you have to promise me one thing."

Julie looked at him and nodded her consent. At that moment she would have promised him almost anything if only he would stop castigating her.

"In the future I want you to listen to my advice, and don't ever fight me when I tell you not to do something."

Julie said nothing. Just as it was with her father, she found it easier to agree with him than to argue.

"Now," Paco said, satisfied that he had made his point, "let's talk about South America."

A week later, as Julie reached into the closet to pull out her green wool dress, she wondered about the meeting scheduled that morning at MCA. At Paco's request, she was on her way to see Freddie Barnett, who was handling their South American tour. Freddie wanted her to meet Lew Wallace, who was head of the agency and normally headquartered on the West Coast.

Julie dressed slowly, taking more time than usual with her makeup and hair. She hoped to impress Lew Wallace because he could be instrumental in helping her with a motion picture career, if she hadn't already ruined her chances. Slowly turning around in front of the full-length mirror that hung on back of the closet door, Julie inspected herself. Making sure that her stocking seams were straight, and satisfied that she looked her best, Julie picked up her wool coat and slipped it on. Even though the past few days had been mild, November could be a tricky month and she couldn't afford to catch cold—not with the tour looming at the end of the month. Before leaving the apartment, Julie checked her purse to make sure that she had enough money. Even though she had been earning a pretty large salary for a girl her age, her mother was still reluctant to part with any more money than was absolutely necessary. There were many times when Julie found herself downtown with not enough money to buy lunch. There had been one humiliating experience after rehearsal when she had miscalculated and found herself fifty cents short when it came time to pay her check at Childs Restaurant. Fortunately, the young waitress, sensing her embarrassment, spoke to the manager on her behalf. He accepted her assurance that she would be back the next day with the balance. Julie had felt shamed by the whole incident, but when she tried to explain this to her mother, it fell on deaf ears. Rose doled out only what she felt was reasonable, and that was that.

As Julie was about to enter the impressive MCA offices on Madison Avenue and Fifty-seventh Street, Lana Turner, one of Julie's idols, was just leaving. Julie had never seen anyone quite as beautiful or glamorous. The movie star was dressed all in white, her turban only partially concealing her famous platinum hair. And though the weather was still mild, a white mink coat was casually draped over her shoulders. Her pale, but luminous skin glowed in the sunshine, and as she passed Julie, she smiled, demonstrating her famous dimple. Julie stared at her admiringly and was tempted to follow her back out the door and into the street. But she knew that if she did, she would be late for her appointment. Reluctantly she turned and found her way to Freddie Barnett's office.

"Mr. Barnett is on the phone, but he'll be with you shortly," his secretary said.

Julie sat down on the sofa opposite the desk and looked around. The office was furnished like a private home with exquisite antiques and paintings everywhere. The walls were painted a dark green and the rug looked like velvet—it was so soft. Julie removed her coat and folded it neatly across her lap. A few minutes passed, and just as the secretary was about to usher her into the office, Paco arrived. He looked very dapper, dressed in a navy blue pinstripe suit with a red carnation tucked in his lapel. He was not wearing a coat and his face was flushed from the wind.

"Ay, querida," he beamed, embracing her. "I'm glad you are here. Let's go in."

Freddie was seated at his desk when they entered. Quickly he rose and came around the desk to shake hands with Paco, and to give Julie a quick kiss on the cheek. Julie glanced around the splendid office and immediately saw a very tall man standing by the window. Turning, he smiled and came over and extended his hand to Paco.

"Paco, it's good to see you. It's been a long time. When are you coming back to the Coast?"

"As soon as you guys get me some work. Speaking of that, what's happening with my RKO deal? Do they have a picture for me yet?"

"We'll get to that in a minute, Paco. But first I'd like you to intro-duce me to this lovely young lady."

Paco, who had almost forgotten Julie was there, turned and took her arm. "Julie, I would like you to meet Lew Wallace." Julie smiled up at him and shook his hand.

"Would you believe that when I became a client this guy was working in the mail room?" Paco continued, with a laugh. "Now look at him. He's a big shot out in California, and who do you think helped make him a success? . . . Paco Castell."

Lew Wallace wasn't a particularly handsome man, but there was something ruggedly appealing about him. He had a quiet dignity and elegance—qualities that Julie admired very much. In a way, he re-minded her of a much younger George Abbott.

Once they were all seated, Paco again brought up the subject of RKO. Freddie would have preferred to discuss the many details con-cerning the upcoming tour, but Paco intended to take full advantage of Lew's presence.

"Lew, now that the contract is finally signed, what do you think RKO has in mind for me? I was hoping they would have a project for me right after South America. It's been too long since my last picture."

Aware that Julie was listening attentively, Paco then asked, "Did the office tell you what happened to Julie a couple of weeks ago out on the Coast? The Hughes thing?"

Lew studied them both for a minute. Paco sat there with a smug expression, while Julie stared at him, her eyes intently searching his face. *Poor child,* he thought. *She's obviously scared to death that she may have done something to jeopardize Paco's relationship with RKO.*

"Lew," Paco persisted impatiently. "Did you hear me?"

"Yes, Paco, I'm fully aware of what happened to Julie in California, and I'm sorry that she was exposed to that kind of nonsense."

"It wasn't my fault," Paco answered sarcastically. "I warned her not to go, but she wouldn't listen to me."

Julie fidgeted nervously in her chair, feeling both embarrassment and anger. *They're talking about me as if I wasn't in the room*, she thought, *as if I were invisible.*

"Mr. Wallace," Julie said hesitatingly. "I'd like to ask you a question. Do you think my mother acted too hastily by insisting we go home? I'm so confused I don't know what to think."

Lew got up and walked over to Julie and resting his lean frame against the desk, he looked down at the distraught girl. "Julie, I don't think your mother acted rashly at all. In fact, she exercised good common sense. Since you left California we've done some investigating on our own, and my sources, whom I consider very reliable, have come up with some interesting information."

Pulling up a chair next to her, he continued. "We found out that several of the suites in the hotel where you were staying have two-way mirrors."

Julie looked at him bewildered, not quite sure what he meant. "Two-way mirrors?" she asked. "What does that mean?"

Before Lew could answer, Paco jumped up and shouted furiously, "It means those bastards were watching you constantly and probably saw you naked."

Julie looked at the three men, still not fully comprehending what she had just heard.

Lew Wallace gently took Julie's hand, a scowl crossing his face. He was irritated by Paco's unnecessary bluntness, but because he was an important client, he controlled himself.

"Julie, what I'm trying to explain to you is that most probably your activity in the apartment was being monitored some of the time. If what I was told is true, then it's more than likely that there were mirrors in the bathrooms and perhaps somewhere else where you could be observed without your knowledge."

The full impact of what he said suddenly dawned on Julie, and a wave of shame swept over her. Her thoughts flashed back to the beautiful bathroom, and she remembered how she had luxuriated in the bathtub each night and then dried her naked body in front of the mirror. Like any young girl, she had posed and studied herself in what she thought was total privacy. But now she realized that all the while she was being spied on by strangers. It was ugly and degrading and the thought of it made her sick. Julie dropped her head into her hands and closed her eyes, desperately trying to block out the memory of that humiliating experience.

"Oh, God," she mumbled huskily, trying not to cry. "How could they have done that to me?"

"Julie dear," Lew urged her, "please try not to let this upset you so. It was indeed an unpleasant situation, and I can imagine how you must feel. But you can't let this incident destroy you. Thanks to your mother's good instincts you left before anything else happened—perhaps something that you might not have been able to handle."

Paco, who had been watching Julie and listening to his agent's explanation, suddenly stood up. "Lew," he shouted, unable to contain his anger any longer. "All you talk about is *her* bad experience. What I want to know is how does all of this affect *my* deal with RKO? Did this mess with Julie screw it up?"

Lew Wallace stood up as well, enraged by Paco's outburst. "No, I don't think it will affect anything. But, Paco, where the hell is your sensitivity? Can't you see how upset this girl is? Why don't we talk about this later?"

"Later. When later?" Paco asked testily. "You'll be on a plane back to the Coast tonight and I want to know something now."

Julie wasn't listening. She was in a daze. All she wanted to do was run somewhere and be by herself—anywhere but sit in that office facing those men.

"Paco," she said, rising and pulling on her coat, "I'm not feeling too well. I think I'd like to go home now."

"Julie, where are you going? You can't leave now. We have to talk about South America."

"Oh, Paco, you don't need me. Just call me later and let me know when we start rehearsals."

Julie turned around and, smiling apologetically at Lew Wallace and Freddie, who were both watching her, said, "Please forgive me for leaving, but I really have to go. Mr. Wallace, thank you for all your kindness and honesty. I really appreciate it. Good-bye Freddie, I guess I'll be seeing you very soon. Thanks again."

As she started to leave, Paco got up and put his arm around her protectively. "*Querida*, you're right. You do look a little pale. Go home now. I'll call you later."

Julie nodded, but as she closed the door behind her she could hear

Paco's voice. "Okay, Lew, now that she's gone, tell me the truth. Did Julie and her mother fuck up my deal?"

Julie left the office, dazed by what she had heard. No one had prepared her for the kind of world she had entered. *No*, Julie thought, *that's not true. They did try to warn me. Esther, Claudia, even Paco, and I wouldn't listen. But how could I believe Paco about Howard Hughes when all along he's hardly concealed his own passion?* She remembered the stolen kisses, the endless endearments, the lustful glances. Julie had assumed that Paco's reasons for trying to prevent her from going to California were based on his possessiveness and jealousy. As Julie wandered aimlessly up Fifth Avenue, she wished that she had someplace to go to other than home, and someone she could talk with, other than her parents. She didn't want to burden her teachers with any more of her problems. They had already given her so much of their time. Then who? Marshall—no, he had his own troubles. Ever since he returned home from the war he had gone from job to job, searching for something that might secure his future. But he couldn't seem to make up his mind what he wanted to do with his life. Even though she knew he loved her dearly, he just wasn't the kind of person she could turn to for help. Her aunts, her grandmother— out of the question. Grandma Esther was in and out of the hospital constantly now. Julie certainly wouldn't want to bring her any more *tsouris*. She already had enough trouble.

Oh well, Julie thought as she glanced up at the street sign and saw that she was already at Seventy-ninth Street, *I might as well go home.*

Fortunately, the apartment was empty. After putting her coat away, Julie pulled out some music Paco had given her to study. But she was still too distracted to concentrate. During her long walk home, she still hadn't decided whether to tell her parents about what she had learned that morning from Lew Wallace. But now, as she sat staring into space, she suddenly knew she would have to tell her parents the truth and not leave out anything, because Paco would be certain to do so the first opportunity he got.

Julie worked hard all afternoon going over new lyrics in Spanish, repeating them until they were perfect. Gradually, she began to feel better about everything. She consoled herself with the fact that in a few weeks she would be going to a foreign country for the first time, and if Paco was right, she might achieve a big success. As far as RKO and movies were concerned, she would have to wait for Paco to tell her what had happened at MCA after she left. She was certain he would not be concerned about sparing her feelings and therefore would tell her the truth.

It was early evening when Julie heard the door slam. "Hi, Mom," she called out. "I'm here in your bedroom, working."

Instead of her mother her father's tall image appeared in the door-way. He looked tired as he began removing his coat. "It's me, baby. I'm home early. Where's Mom?"

"I don't know, Dad. The apartment was empty when I came home. I guess Mom's out shopping."

"Where else?" Sam said chuckling. Stretching out his arms, as he had done ever since she was a little girl, he said, "Well, how about a kiss from my beautiful daughter?"

"Of course, Dad, I'm sorry," Julie said running over and giving him a hug and kiss on his cheek. "Dad, your face is cold. Would you like me to make some coffee while we wait for Mom?"

"Yes, sweetheart. I'm just going to wash up first."

Just as they were about to sit down, Julie heard the key turn in the front door. "Mom," Julie called out. "We're here in the kitchen. Dad's home."

Rose walked in, her arms loaded with bundles that she quickly set down on the counter. "Sam, are you all right? How come you're home so early?"

"The place was quiet today. They're getting ready to set up the showroom for buyers, so I thought I'd come home and surprise you."

"Good," Rose said as she pulled off her coat, her face flushed from the cold air. "I went to Macy's this afternoon; they were having a sale. As soon as I put these things away I'll make dinner."

As Sam went to his usual spot in the living room with the evening paper, Julie helped her mother in the kitchen. After they had finished dinner, Julie decided it was time to bring her parents up-to-date on what was happening.

As Julie retold the story to her parents about the mirror and the spying, the same feeling of shame she had experienced that morning washed over her again, and she felt herself on the verge of tears. Her father sat there in stunned silence while her mother paced up and down the small kitchen, trying to figure out what to say. She was angry and shocked. But she was also a fighter. She was determined not to let this defeat her daughter any more than it already had.

Suddenly, she stopped pacing and announced defiantly, "You know what I say, Julie? I say to hell with those sick perverts out there. Whatever they saw, they saw, and we can't change that. Just put it out of your mind and be grateful to God that they never got a chance to harm you."

Sam, on the other hand, now that the initial shock had passed, was furious. *Those bastards,* he thought. *They are no better than the sleazy guys who constantly hang around the garment district trying to take advantage of the models.* Sam felt guilty that he had permitted Julie to go to California, especially in light of Paco's telephone calls and repeated warnings. This now made him feel he had acted irresponsibly. But there was nothing he could do except to try and comfort his daughter. Unfortunately, he had already agreed to the South American tour, and it was too late to back out now. But he was determined that when they returned, it would be a different story. Career or no career, Julie would have to abide by his decisions. Their lives could not continue on like this. He was sick of all the disruption their traveling had caused. But most of all, he was sick of being alone. He needed his wife, physically and emotionally, and he needed his daughter. If somehow he couldn't make Rose and Julie understand this, then he knew a showdown was inevitable.

CHAPTER 19

Please fasten your seat belts and observe the No Smoking sign until we are in the air and the captain has turned the sign off."

The pretty Pan American stewardess who made the announcement searched the aisle, trying to get a better look at Paco Castell. She had been in the galley in the back of the airplane when the group had arrived, but she heard all the whispering among the other passengers.

"Isn't that Paco Castell?" a lady asked, tugging at her sleeve.

"I believe it is, ma'am. He and his entire orchestra are on our flight to Cuba."

It took quite a while to get all the musicians and performers settled down in their seats. Everyone was excited about the trip and anxious to get started. Only Paco, Julie, Rose, Marion, and Luis were seated in first class. The rest of the orchestra and entertainers were in the coach section and occupied practically the entire plane.

Before leaving, Paco had taken great care in preparing his show. He had once again chosen José and Estella, his favorite dance team; his male singer, Miguel, who had made such a hit on the last tour; and a new group of incredible tap dancers he had seen in a nightclub in Chicago. He knew they would be a sensation in South America, where they just adored Negro entertainers. Joining them on each lap of the tour would be a local comedian to round out the bill.

Settling into their seats, Julie took out a book and some magazines while Rose reached into her carry-on bag for her knitting. Julie began to rub her left arm, for it still ached a little from her smallpox vaccination. She was surprised because it had been more than a week since she had received the injection and no one else seemed to complain of any pain.

Paco and Luis were seated directly across the aisle from Julie and were already engrossed in working on the travel schedule. Marion sat directly behind Julie and appeared to be loaded down with papers regarding hotel reservations and press appointments.

As the plane lifted off and slowly started its ascent, Julie remembered her father's parting words to her: "I hope this trip turns out to be everything you've dreamed about and more. I'm going to miss you and Mom terribly, especially since I won't be there to celebrate your sixteenth birthday with you. I pray to God that you will both be safe and that no harm comes to you."

At the sight of her parents' sad faces, Julie was stricken with remorse. As much as she had looked forward to this trip, she now prayed the time would pass quickly so that her parents could be reunited. When the time came for them to board the plane, Julie felt a sense of relief that her mother and Paco would be there to protect her. Since her trip to California, she had felt very vulnerable and was frightened of being alone. Paco had been very helpful to her in the hectic weeks that preceded their departure. He instructed Marion to find a dressmaker, who eventually made Julie two beautiful sequined gowns that were very striking and sexier than anything she had previously worn. Since they would be appearing mainly in theaters and nightclubs, Paco also helped Julie prepare a suitable repertoire. Their appearance in Rio would coincide with Carnival, and Julie was thrilled that they would be part of the celebration.

As Julie and Rose settled down in their seats, Paco glanced over at Julie, now engrossed in a magazine, and thought, *Dios mio. She's getting more beautiful every day. How I'd love to be sitting next to her so I could hold her hands in mine. I would have given anything to have had her all to myself on this trip. If I could have her alone with me in the tropics, without her mother constantly around spying on us, I'm sure that she would have eventually come around. Mierda,* he almost shouted out loud. *How much longer can I take this? I want her so badly I can't think of anything else.* He needed to put his obsession with Julie out of his mind. Paco thought back to his last conversation with Sam before leaving New York. Sam had insisted on having a private talk with him before giving his final permission for Julie to make the trip. Reaching Paco by phone late one night at his apartment, Sam had come directly to the point.

"Paco, I don't think the money that you're paying Julie is enough. The expenses on the road practically eat up her entire salary. I'm sure that things in South America are probably even more expensive. I must ask you to give her a raise or else, I'm sorry, but I can't let her go."

Paco listened quietly until Sam had finished and then his temper exploded. "What do you mean she can't go? I've spent a fortune on publicity for her, besides new arrangements and gowns. Now, at the last moment, you decide to hold me up?"

"Paco, I'm not trying to hold you up. I just want what's fair."

"I pay their hotel bills. Isn't that enough?" Paco growled into the receiver.

"No, Paco, it's not. Listen. My whole life has been disrupted because of you. Either give her a raise or agree to pick up all their other expenses. We won't be able to save any money if she continues on like this."

Paco realized that Sam had him over a barrel and there was nothing he could do at this late date. Besides, she was more than just a singer to him, even though her father had no way of knowing that. In a steely voice Paco agreed to pay for all their expenses within reason.

"Are there any other last-minute requests?" Paco asked sarcastically.

"Yes, Paco, there is one more thing," Sam answered. "You're in business to make money and I'd like to be in business, too. I have decided to become Julie's manager, and I would like your office to send Julie's checks directly to me. I will provide my wife and daughter with whatever they need."

Manager, Paco thought. *That's a laugh. What makes him think he's qualified to be a manager? He's just a greedy man trying to get all he can.* Paco had been tempted to reveal his conversation with Sam to Julie but decided against it. There would be time enough for that later.

Paco's earlier good humor as they embarked on the trip had now vanished, and turning to Luis he instructed him to go see how the rest of the group was doing. "Tell them to stay all together when we land. We're having a press conference at the airport and they'll want plenty of pictures of everyone."

Luis quickly did as he was told. He could tell that Paco was in one of his moods and he didn't want to become the butt of his anger. He also knew what was bothering his brother. It was Julie. *Dammit,* he thought as he made his way down the aisle. *Why is he so obsessed with this girl? Now, Laura, she is a woman, not a child like this one. But on the other hand, what a bitch. Well, I just hope he leaves me out of it. I don't want to get involved in another one of Paco's romantic affairs.*

The four hours it took to reach Havana seemed like four days to Julie. Bored with her magazines and impatient to see land, she constantly leaned over to ask Paco how much longer it would take. She was looking forward so much to her first visit to a foreign country. The way Paco described Cuba, it sounded like paradise, and Julie could hardly wait to begin this glorious adventure.

The Havana newspapers would later report that the arrival of Paco Castell in Cuba was probably the biggest event since General Fulgencio Batista became president. Because of Paco's enormous popularity and his reputation as the greatest exponent of Cuban music in the United States, his appearance there had been eagerly anticipated.

There were hundreds of people waiting at the airport in Havana when they arrived. When Julie stepped to the open door of the plane she was immediately enveloped by the warm tropical air, a sharp contrast to the winter weather they had left behind in New York. As they made their way down the steps and into the crowd, a band began playing Paco's theme song and enthusiastic admirers thrust bunches of flowers into Julie's arms. Julie's throat tightened with emotion at the incredible display of warmth and admiration from the fans who had gathered there to greet them. When they reached the terminal, the press began to encircle Julie and bombard her with questions. It was difficult for her to understand much of what they said because they spoke so quickly and with an accent she was unfamiliar with. Surrounded by several dignitaries and the local impresario, Paco stood there with a broad smile on his face. He was enormously pleased with the reception he was receiving, and encircling Julie's waist with his arm, he proudly introduced his new "discovery."

"*Señores,* when you see my little 'New Yorkina' on the stage, you will fall in love with her."

Julie was overwhelmed by all the attention being accorded her, and the first chance she got she whispered to her mother, "Isn't this incredible, Mom? Aren't you glad we came?"

Rose nodded, though her thoughts were still with Sam back in New York.

After forty-five minutes and hundreds of photographs, Paco indicated it was time to go, and the whole group was led outside to a waiting bus. They piled in enthusiastically, obviously excited about the warm welcome that they, too, had received. Paco, Julie, and Rose were ushered into a white limousine that had a VIP card on the windshield. The drive from the airport to the Hotel Nacional, where they would be staying, took only half an hour, but Julie wouldn't have minded if it had taken all day. She was fascinated by the beauty of the city. Everything looked so clean, so white, similar to Los Angeles in a way, but much more lush and tropical.

When they pulled up under the portico in front of the Hotel Nacional, there was a huge banner that said *Bienvenidos Paco Castell y su gran orquestra*. *Well*, Julie thought, *this really is a welcome*. It was unlike anything she had seen since she had started traveling with Paco. As they entered the enormous lobby, music greeted Paco's arrival and a waiter immediately came up to them and offered them frozen daiquiris served on a silver tray. Julie and Rose refused them, though Julie had to admit they did look appetizing. The presidential suite had been reserved for Paco, and after promising Julie he would call her later, he went upstairs with a few members of the press who were anxious to interview him. The rest of the company was staying nearby at the Hotel Florida. Julie had passed it on the way, and although it looked very nice, it was hardly the impressive and elegant Hotel Nacional. Julie knew that if it weren't for the fact that Paco took a personal interest in her, she would undoubtedly be in the other hotel with the rest of the group. She hoped that they wouldn't resent her because of this display of favoritism. But most of all she prayed that they wouldn't read something else into the situation. Even with her mother along as chaperone, Julie could sense an undercurrent of gossip among the musicians. She couldn't blame them. Most of them had been with Paco a long time and knew his reputation, especially with his vocalists. *Well*, Julie thought, *I can't help that. They'll eventually realize that I'm different.*

When the bellman opened up the terrace door in their room to show them the view and Julie looked out at the incredible panorama of sand and sea, she could understand why Havana was such a magnet for countless tourists each year. The water was not just blue but a bright aquamarine, and as she looked down at the white beach below the hotel, she could see that it was filled with bronzed bodies, most of them tourists she guessed, because as Paco had pointed out on the plane, "High-class Cubans, especially the ladies, never sit in the sun. They value their porcelain skin too much."

Julie was overwhelmed by the view and called to her mother, "Mom, come over here and look outside. It's just beautiful."

Rose joined her daughter on the terrace and put her arm around Julie's waist. "You're right, Julie, it's like paradise. I just wish your father were here to enjoy it with us."

If Julie was enchanted by Havana, she was totally overwhelmed by the place where they would be appearing. The Club Tropicana was famous all over the world, and years later Julie would look back and still remember it as the most beautiful nightclub she had ever seen. The entire stage and seating area were outdoors with a sliding roof to provide shelter if it rained. The bandstand was flanked on each side by huge white staircases that led up to a platform on top and then back down to the stage itself. The whole area was filled with palm trees and flowers, and off to the side of the stage, there was a waterfall that cascaded down into a lagoon. The bandstand was on a revolving stage, and Paco told her during rehearsal that for the show she would make her entrance on the bandstand as it moved slowly into the spotlight. Julie was excited, but also terribly nervous. This would be her first performance in a foreign country, and with all the glowing advance publicity she had received, she hoped that she wouldn't disappoint them.

As lovely as the Tropicana seemed during rehearsal, when they arrived before the show the next night, it was even more dazzling. The club presented their own review nightly and it featured gorgeous show girls, dancers, singers, and a local comedian. That same show would precede the appearance of Paco Castell, who was the star attraction. As Julie anxiously waited to go on, she and Rose watched the other entertainers from the side of the room. Julie had never seen such scantily clad dancers and show girls—not even on the Broadway stage. They had beautiful bodies, though a lot more *zoftig*, as Rose described them, than American girls, and they certainly didn't mind showing off their physical attributes. Julie looked down apprehensively at the gown she was wearing. In New York it had seemed very sexy, but here, in comparison to what the Cuban girls wore, it looked very tame. Of course it was as daring as Rose would permit.

Paco was right when he had predicted that the Cubans would love

Julie. The audience that night, and on each succeeding night, was very generous with their applause. They whistled and carried on with great fervor the minute she walked out onstage. Julie wasn't sure whether it was her talent or her looks that they admired more. But, whatever it was, they enthusiastically demonstrated their approval. Even though they had heard the same songs hundreds of times before interpreted by other entertainers, they seemed quite taken with Julie's renditions. Paco explained their reaction after the show.

"*Querida*, the Cubans find your slight American accent when you sing in Spanish quite charming. But what amazes them most is the way you move. They can't believe you don't have Latin blood in you." Julie accepted Paco's explanation, and each night she did her utmost to give the audience her very best.

Because Latins began their evenings much later here than in the States, there was only one performance a night. This gave Julie lots of free time to explore Havana during the day. She and Rose visited all the historical places the hotel concierge suggested, including the famous Moro Castle and the glorious beach at Vadadero. But the biggest thrill of all was the luncheon in Paco's honor that she and Rose attended. The owners of Bacardi rum, who were close friends of Paco's, hosted an elegant gathering of some of Havana's most prominent aristocracy. The luncheon took place at the Havana Beach and Yacht Club and the setting was breathtaking. The room overlooked the sea and the tables were decorated with exotic flowers that filled the room with heady fragrance. The men and women arrived dressed elegantly, and everyone, much to Rose's delight, spoke English. After being intro' duced to Julie, many of them who had already seen the show compli' mented her, not only on her beauty and talent, but also on her ability to converse in Spanish, which they found unusual for an American. Julie liked being included in this very sophisticated, international soci' ety, and though she was still very shy and clung closely to Rose and Paco, she hoped that one day she would really "belong."

After a few more days of sightseeing with Paco and Rose, Julie decided to relax and spend some time at the hotel swimming pool. It was difficult for her to read or sun herself for any length of time because guests who recognized her kept coming over and asking for her autograph. Not that Julie minded it. She was thrilled by all the atten' tion she was receiving. *A far cry*, she thought, *from that horrible summer in the Catskills*. As Julie reflected on her good fortune she looked over at Paco, who was stretched out on a chaise lounge basking in the sun.

Thank you Paco, she thought, *for making all of this possible.* Feeling her eyes on him, Paco suddenly stood up and came over to her.

"You must not take too much sun, my beauty. You have to be careful of the tropics. The rays are much stronger than you think."

Julie looked up at him. He had lost a few pounds, and with his deeply tanned skin and blue eyes, he looked much more fit than when they first met.

"You're right, Paco. I'll be careful. My skin does burn easily, and I certainly wouldn't want to arrive in Rio de Janeiro with my skin peeling."

Noticing that Rose was happily nowhere in sight, Paco sat down on the chaise next to her. Leaning over her body, as if he were about to brush an insect off her face, he whispered tenderly, "Do you have any idea how beautiful your body looks glistening in the sun, and how slowly but surely you are driving me mad?"

Julie looked at Paco and read the desire in his eyes. He was doing everything in his power to seduce her, and although he was not the kind of man she had always pictured in her dreams, his worldliness and magnetism were undeniable. She was beginning to understand why so many beautiful women had succumbed to his charm. Julie could feel the heat of his body next to her skin and with it came the first stirrings of an emerging sensuality. Confused by these feelings, she lay there motionless, afraid to be touched, yet unable to move. Amazed that Julie hadn't bolted out of his arms, as she usually did when he pursued her, Paco moved closer, suddenly encouraged.

"*Querida,* would it be possible for you and I to have a late dinner alone tonight after the show? There are so many fabulous places in Havana that I would like to show you."

Before Julie could answer, she could hear her mother calling her. "Julie, I think you've had enough sun for today. Let's go in."

Paco immediately sprang to his feet, cursing under his breath. *Hijo de puta madre. Son of a bitch. What timing that woman has.*

Excusing himself, he went back to his chair and picked up the magazine he had dropped.

Rose, meanwhile, glared at her embarrassed daughter. "What the hell was he doing lying next to you like that? What was he saying?"

Julie looked around anxiously to see who was sitting nearby. When her mother's temper flared up, so did her voice. "Mom, please don't shout. He was only here a minute. He wanted to know if we wanted to join him for dinner."

"We," Rose scoffed. "I'll bet it wasn't *we*. It was *you*. Listen to me, young lady. I don't want to see that man that close to you again. Do you understand me? Now pick up your stuff and let's go in."

Julie did as she was told. She always did what she was told, but, more and more, she was beginning to resent it.

Her mother had been very edgy the past few days, complaining about the heat and the food. But Julie knew that wasn't the real reason. They hadn't heard from her father except for a brief phone call the day they arrived and that was ten days ago. Rose wrote home every day, and although she had been warned that the mail was slow, she had expected at least one letter by now.

The days seemed to fly by, and suddenly, before they knew it, the time had arrived for their last performance at the Tropicana. And what a memorable evening it was! The club was jammed. People had been lined up in the streets for hours waiting to come in, even though they were aware that there was no place to sit. They were so anxious to catch Paco Castell's last appearance in Havana, they didn't mind crowding around the huge bar just so they could see the show. Julie put everything she had into her performance and when she finished her last number the crowd began to scream *otra, otra*. Julie didn't have another song prepared, but at Paco's suggestion, she repeated another chorus of "El Cumbanchero," which brought a roar of approval from the audience. After they had quieted down, Julie gave a short farewell speech to the audience in Spanish, thanking them and all the Cuban entertainers in the show for their kindness and hospitality. Her eyes still glowing from all the applause she had received, Julie said, "*Muchisimas gracias, señoras y señores. Estoy un poco triste que terminamos esta noche pero espero de regresar muy pronto.*" Her few mistakes in Spanish were so endearing to the rather jaded audience that they all gave her a standing ovation. It couldn't have been a more rewarding experience and it left Julie with beautiful memories of Cuba that she would never forget.

When they departed the next day, it was with a touch of sadness, at least as far as Julie was concerned. She had sampled her first taste of what a foreign country was like, and she loved it. Because of Paco, she had been introduced not only to society people, but artists, writers, and famous composers. Julie had entered a world that not only fascinated her but also one in which she was beginning to feel more and more comfortable and accepted. This, Paco assured her, was only the beginning. The best was yet to come.

* * *

The Copacabana Beach in Rio was everything Julie had expected and much more. As the plane circled the coastline, she was able to catch a close look at the fabled white beach that stretched along the entire city. In the distance was the awesome Sugar Loaf Mountain with its statue of Christ standing majestically atop the mountain—his arms outstretched, as if embracing the city. When the plane landed, the crowds that greeted their arrival were as large as in Havana, and even more enthusiastic. The city was in the process of preparing for Carnival, and although it was still weeks away, you could feel the electricity in the air. *What a place to celebrate my birthday and the New Year,* Julie thought as she entered the Copacabana Palace Hotel, which was where they would be staying. Wearing a cream-colored dress that accentuated her golden tan perfectly, Julie received many admiring glances as she and Rose waited to check in. Paco had told her that the women in Brazil were the most beautiful in the world. *Well,* she thought as she looked around her, *from what I've seen so far, the men aren't too bad either.*

The first thing Rose did when she reached the front desk was to inquire if there was any mail waiting for them. Since leaving Cuba they had made one brief stop for three days in Caracas, Venezuela, and in all that time since she had left New York, Rose had only received two letters from Sam. That wasn't like him, and she hoped that nothing was wrong at home.

After they were shown to their room, instead of rushing out to see the city, as was her custom, Julie decided to lie down and rest for a while. For the past few days she had been feeling very tired, which wasn't at all like her. But she attributed her weariness to all the traveling. Removing her clothes, Julie slipped into a robe and stretched out on the bed. The weather was very hot and the humidity almost unbearable. *Maybe a nap will pick me up,* she thought as she closed her eyes.

Rose also decided to lie down, but not because she was tired. She was depressed and missed Sam terribly. Even the thrill of being on the trip and the pride in seeing her daughter so successful could not elevate her spirits. *Well,* she thought as she kicked off her shoes, *we're almost halfway through this tour. Rio, then Uruguay, Buenos Aires, and then, God willing, home.* Rose was surprised at how much she was looking forward to going home. As much as she had wanted to make this trip, she realized that her place was back home with her husband.

As Julie's birthday approached, and preparations for Carnival began, excitement began to mount. To Julie's amazement and delight, she had been chosen to reign over the Carnival as queen. She had received an enormous amount of Press since her arrival, and her beauty and charm had captured the hearts of the Brazilians. According to their impresario, it was the first time in the history of Carnival that an American girl had been chosen as queen. She would be expected to ride on a special float depicting the friendship between the United States and Brazil. Of course, she would continue to perform nightly with Paco and the band at the famous nightclub Night and Day.

The Brazilian audiences were very demonstrative in their apprecia- tion of Julie's talent and, being hot-blooded Latins, also her beauty and youthful sensuality. The entire show proved to be a huge success and Paco was already discussing a return engagement for next year.

Still feeling slightly under the weather, Julie hoped that when the time came for Carnival she would have the stamina to participate in the parade. Carnival lasted eight days and the school of samba bands and floats played continuously twenty-four hours a day for two days. Besides that, there were at least two costume balls where they would be expected to perform. Rose had reservations about all this work and she had no hesitation about voicing them to Julie.

"Julie, you can't be expected to sing and dance at the club at night and ride all day and part of the night on the float. You're exhausted already. You'll get sick if you don't get some rest."

"It's okay, Mom," Julie reassured her. "I can handle it. This is too great an honor to pass up."

The morning of her sixteenth birthday Julie jumped out of bed early. Even though it had been close to four A.M. when Rose had finally turned out the lights, Julie had been too excited to sleep. Not wanting to disturb her mother, she had tiptoed quietly to the terrace and looked out over the city. There was hardly anyone walking on the Copacabana Beach—only some trash collectors picking up the debris from the day before. Julie began to think, *In a few days it will be 1952.* Everything was happening so fast she couldn't believe it. *I'm finally sixteen and so much has happened to me this past year. I wonder where I'll be next year at this time, and with whom.*

Rose stirred and opened her eyes. Glancing over at Julie's bed she saw that it was empty. Then she saw her daughter's slim silhouette standing on the terrace. *My little girl,* she thought as she looked at the lovely young woman who stood gazing at the sea. *Wasn't it only yesterday when the nurses brought in my little "miracle baby" and placed her in my arms? Even then she was so beautiful and so good. She hardly ever cried, not as a baby and not when she was ill those long, terrible months. Oh, Julie, she prayed. I want you to have a good life. Everything your heart desires. I wish to God Sam were here to celebrate with us,* she thought sadly, as doubts and fears were still flooding her mind. His last letter to her had been warm and loving, but something seemed not to be right. It wasn't anything he said that worried her. It was what he didn't say. *To hell with the money,* she thought suddenly. *Today's our daughter's birthday and I'm going to call him.*

Although it was still early, Julie could feel the intense heat of the sun beating down on the terrace. Turning, she quietly made her way to the bathroom, but the sound of her mother's voice stopped her.

"It's okay, sweetheart. You don't have to tiptoe around. I'm up. Come over here and let me give you a big hug and kiss, my sweet sixteen-year-old girl."

Julie ran over to her mother's bed and they cuddled for a few minutes, just like they had when she was a little girl.

"So, how does it feel to be sixteen?" Rose asked. "Have you noticed any wrinkles yet?"

"Oh, Mom," Julie laughed. "You love to tease me. I know that according to you and Dad I'm still a baby, but remember, you got married when you were my age."

A sharp fear stabbed at Rose's heart. "Julie, don't compare my life to yours. I was out working at fourteen, supporting my mother and sisters. Besides, things were different when I was a girl."

"But, Mom, I've been working since I was thirteen and I'll bet I'm as mature as you were at my age."

Rose sat up suddenly, flustered and upset at the direction the conversation was taking. "Julie, it's different. You didn't have to work. You wanted a career. You have a mother and father, thank God, who would have taken care of you if you had preferred to go to college. But you wanted show business. I married your father because I had no real talent and no hopes for a career. Besides that, I fell madly in love with him, and even though I was pretty, what future was there for a girl like me, other than a husband, a home, and children? You're different. Why are we even discussing this now? Let's just agree that we both grew up fast and that you are mature for your age. Now, sweetheart, let's talk about what we're going to do today to celebrate your birthday."

Julie embraced her mother again and said, "Mom, I hope that one day I'll have a daughter who is as close to me and loves me as much as I love you. Now, if you would order breakfast for the both of us, I'll grab a quick shower. I don't want to waste even one minute of today."

When Julie arrived at the club that evening to start preparing for the show, José and Estella greeted her backstage with a big hug and kiss.

"*Felice cumpleaños,* Julie. You finally made it. We have this little gift for you. It's not much, but we hope you like it."

Julie kissed them and unwrapped the tiny package. Inside was a small gold medal with Saint Christopher on one side and a Star of David on the other.

"Oh gosh, it's beautiful. But you shouldn't have spent so much money."

"It wasn't that much, Julie," Estella said, fastening the thin delicate chain around Julie's neck. "You know that Saint Christopher is the patron saint of travelers. We hope your mother won't object to your wearing it. You can wear the Jewish star on the outside."

"Oh, she won't object," Julie said, as she admired the lovely medal in the mirror. "Thank you so much for thinking of me."

As soon as they left, Julie changed into her robe and sat down to begin the nightly ritual of putting on her stage makeup. Her mother had urged her to go on ahead of her. She was still trying to get a call through to Sam in New York, but she promised to meet Julie later at the club. Fortunately, the impresario had provided transportation for their nightly trips back and forth, so Rose wouldn't have to deal with the local taxis. Julie had learned to adapt quickly to foreign cities, but Rose was still terrified by unfamiliar places and different languages.

It's been a wonderful day so far, Julie thought as she brushed face powder over her flawless complexion. After breakfast a huge bouquet of yellow roses had arrived from Paco with a tender note. "Happy Birthday to the loveliest girl in the world. *Tu eres la mujer más linda de todo el mundo, y te quiero mucho.*" When Rose asked her to translate the Spanish, Julie told her that he had called her the most beautiful girl in the world, but she was careful to leave out the "I love you very much" part.

When she called Paco's suite to thank him, he didn't inquire what her plans were that day, but that didn't surprise her. Julie knew he was planning some kind of celebration for her after the show that evening. He had tried to keep it a secret but Marion had let it slip inadvertently. Julie was happy to have the day alone to spend with her mother. She knew that her mother was feeling down about leaving Sam at home and Julie felt that shopping might take her mind off her troubles. In spite of their limited funds, Rose insisted on buying Julie a present. "After all," she explained. "You're only sixteen once. You should have something to remember this day."

The hours they had spent happily together flew by, and now, back at the club, Julie studied herself in the dressing room mirror. Just a few more strokes of the brush to her long hair and she would be ready. *If only my stomach didn't feel so queasy,* she thought uneasily. *I don't know what's wrong with me. Maybe it's nerves.* There was a gentle rapping on the door, and when Julie opened it, Paco came into the room—a huge smile illuminating his face. His eyes darted around, searching for Rose, and when he realized that she was not there, he swiftly came over and embraced Julie.

"Did you really like my flowers, *querida?*"

"Oh yes, Paco. They are so lovely. My room smells like a garden. I tried to call you when we returned, but you were out."

"Yes, I was busy doing some interviews at the radio station. Did you have a good day?"

"Oh, yes. We went shopping and Mom bought me a lovely aquamarine heart. She found a jeweler who gave us a great deal. He didn't speak English and, of course, we don't speak Portuguese. But, leave it to my mother. Somehow she found out that he was Jewish, so she was able to negotiate with him in Yiddish."

Paco smiled as he listened to Julie describe her day, but his mind was elsewhere. He was intensely aware of the silky robe that clung to her body like a second skin. Suddenly, he could feel his own body responding to her sensuality. Moving closer to her, he put his arm around her back arching her up to him. Julie, uneasy by his closeness, pushed firmly against his chest as she tried to free herself.

"Paco, please. I have to finish dressing. It's almost time for us to go on."

"You're right, Julie. I'll go. But after the show do not make any plans. I have a surprise for you." Suddenly, without warning, he took her in his arms and kissed her passionately. "Julie," he murmured into her hair. "I've waited for this day a long time. Tonight, we will celebrate my beautiful one."

After he had gone, Julie hastily repaired her smeared lipstick and tried to steady her trembling hands. She lived in constant fear that one day her mother would surprise them when Paco was being amorous, and Julie was terrified of the scene that would ensue.

The show that night was exhilarating, and Julie felt the audience was especially responsive to her. She was still euphoric when, later that evening, Julie entered the restaurant flanked by Paco and her mother. As she approached the tables to greet her friends, a group of samba musicians started playing "Brazil." For this special occasion, Julie had chosen to wear a turquoise silk dress that not only comple-mented her skin and red hair but also showed to perfection her new aquamarine heart, which lay nestled in the hollow of her throat. Paco had purposely delayed their departure for the restaurant so that the rest of the group could get there ahead of them. There were flowers and candles on the tables, and bottles of wine were already open and in the process of being sampled by the thirsty assemblage. Julie took a seat at the head of the table, which had been reserved in her honor, and as soon as they were settled, the waiters began to serve. When Julie reached for her napkin, she noticed a small, beautifully wrapped box resting on her plate. She instantly knew that this must be a gift from Paco, and glancing over to him, she smiled.

"Is this for me?"

"Of course it is. Would you like to open it now?"

"Oh yes," Julie answered enthusiastically. "I love presents and I hate to wait."

Julie hastily unwrapped the box, and when she saw what lay inside, resting in a black velvet case, she gasped. "Oh, Paco, it's so beautiful. I've never owned a ring before and this is the most beautiful one I've ever seen."

Everyone seated at the table stopped talking as they watched Julie happily admiring her gift.

Paco sat there pleased with himself. His instincts had told him that she would be impressed with the aquamarine stone he had picked out for her. It was set in a simple, but elegant, gold setting, and as Julie turned to show it to her mother, he began to plan how he could get her alone later that night. Rose wasn't at all happy that Paco had chosen a ring as a gift for her daughter and she hoped that he and the others would not read any special significance into it.

Rose looked quite lovely that evening and, in the soft lighting, could have passed as Julie's older sister rather than her mother. But hard as she tried to participate in the gaiety, she still couldn't forget about Sam. Frustrated because she had been unable to reach him, either at the office or at home, she had finally given up in despair and joined Julie at the club. *Where in the hell is he?* Rose asked herself as she listened to the gaiety surrounding her. *Doesn't he realize it's Julie's birthday?* Anger began to replace the worry she had felt earlier, and she resolved that she would write him a long and nasty letter when they returned to the hotel.

After they had finished eating, and all the toasts to Julie had been made, the Brazilian musicians resumed playing and most of the group got up to dance. Paco reached for Julie and when they began to samba everyone stopped dancing and began to applaud. Paco was an expert dancer, and once Julie was in his arms, the fatigue she had been experiencing these past weeks seemed to disappear as she whirled to the sensuous music. Paco was not too happy about having to relinquish her to other partners, especially Miguel, who he suspected of having a secret crush on Julie. Occasionally, on the bandstand, Paco would catch him gazing at Julie with a look that could only be interpreted as desire, and Paco didn't like that one bit. He was sure that Julie was unaware of this, but he decided that as much as he liked his singing, Miguel would be dismissed as soon as the tour was over. When Paco finally reclaimed her, he steered Julie away from the tables and whispered in her ear.

"Can you meet me on the beach later tonight after we return to the hotel? I must spend a little time alone with you."

Julie's body instantly stiffened when she heard his request. "Paco, I just can't. My mother would never approve. You know that." Julie watched Paco's smile fade and she pleaded with him. "Please don't be angry and try to understand."

Paco remained silent for a moment as he sought to control his impatience and displeasure. "Julie, I'm not angry, but please don't ask me to understand. You're not a baby anymore. I don't know what's wrong in your seeing a man alone for a few minutes. For God's sake, I'm not going to rape you."

"Paco, please," Julie begged. "This has been such a wonderful evening. Please, don't spoil it for me."

Julie turned and returned to her table, where Rose was waiting for her. It was late and Julie could see that her mother was very tired.

"Mom, would you like to leave now? It's been a long day."

Rose smiled at her daughter gratefully. "I've been ready for the last hour."

Paco, who had followed Julie back to the table, heard Rose's remark and offered to escort them back to the hotel. After bidding the others good-bye, they left the restaurant just as the sun was beginning to rise over Sugar Loaf Mountain.

When the concierge gave Rose the key to their room, he also handed them an envelope. "Mrs. Lehman, a telegram arrived for your daughter while you were out."

Rose hastily grabbed the yellow envelope and went to join Julie, who was waiting at the elevator.

"Julie, there's a telegram for you," she said, ripping open the paper before Julie could take it. "It's from Dad," she said, smiling broadly. "I knew he wouldn't forget."

Rose turned it over to Julie, greatly relieved to have finally heard from Sam. The message read:

> *Happy Birthday to the most wonderful daughter in the world.*
> *My heart is with you and Mom tonight and every night. All*
> *my love, Dad.*

Julie was thrilled to have heard from her father, not only for herself, but for her mother, who she knew was suffering. Arm in arm they made their way back to their room, exhausted but happy to have ended the day on such a positive note.

New Year's Eve in Rio had been so exciting that Julie was doubtful anything could top it. But several weeks later she would agree with all the others that *nothing* could compare with Carnival in Rio. Even the famous Mardi Gras in New Orleans paled in comparison. The night the festivities began, thousands of Brazilians lined the streets, having flocked to Rio from other cities for this spectacular event. The floats, which had taken many months to construct, were lavish. After viewing them, Julie was certain that there couldn't be one flower left in Rio because all of them had to have been used to decorate the already extravagant floats. Everyone, from every walk of life, was dressed in costume, and they were determined to outdo one another in ingenuity and brevity. Prizes were to be given the last day of Carnival for the most original costume, and Julie was relieved that she wouldn't have to be the one to judge which was the best. They were all so outstanding. There were also prizes to be awarded to the different school of samba bands for best original song, and even though he wasn't Brazilian, Paco was accorded the honor of being chosen as one of the judges. The stores and most of the restaurants had closed early the first day of Carnival and the Hotel Copacabana was jammed with people lining the balconies in order to get a better view of the parade. The floats would pass directly in front of the hotel, down the famous Copacabana Beach, and on to different locations throughout the city. Paco had insisted that Rose remain in the hotel with Marion and Luis to watch the parade from his suite.

"Rose, be reasonable. It's no use going with Julie in the car to the starting location. Obviously, you can't sit with her on the float and it will be impossible for you to get back to the hotel for hours because of the traffic."

Rose had reluctantly agreed, only because Paco would be accompanying Julie. He and the orchestra would be riding on a separate float behind her, but Paco promised to watch out for her in case the crowd became unruly. As Julie prepared to leave the hotel, Rose couldn't believe her eyes. She had never seen her daughter look so beautiful. The Carnival Committee had commissioned a gown to be designed for her together with a gold and silver crown befitting her role as queen of the Carnival. The gown was made of white tulle with hundreds of tiny silver sequins, which shimmered like stars in the sky, scattered over the dress. The bodice was low cut and strapless, embroidered with tiny seed pearls and rhinestones, and across her shoulder, Julie was to wear a banner that read "Rainha do Carnival."

The weather was oppressively hot and even the onset of evening had not cooled off the city. Julie's face was very flushed as she put the finishing touches to her makeup. The hotel hairdresser had been summoned to help her arrange her hair for the parade, and he employed all of his artistry to create an elaborate hairdo that enhanced Julie's beauty. As Julie rode down the elevator with Paco and her mother, she couldn't help but notice the anxious expression on her mother's face.

"Mom, please don't worry. I'll be fine. Paco and the band will be right behind me, and I'll be joining you and the others later on at the club. Don't forget to watch for me. I'll wave to you as we go by."

Rose squeezed Julie's hand for good luck, trying gamely not to show her anxiety. "I'm not worried, dear. I'm just a little concerned about your health. You've been so tired the last few days, and you haven't been eating much either. Now you've got hours ahead of you of smiling and waving during the parade. On top of that, you've got the show to do later on at the nightclub."

Paco took Julie's arm as they emerged from the elevator and into the throngs of people crowding the hotel lobby. "Rose, she'll be fine," he assured her while guiding Julie toward the entrance and into the waiting car. "Why don't you go back upstairs to my suite? Marion is there and Luis will be joining you as soon as he gets the band on the bus." Rose kissed Julie good-bye and went back into the hotel, escaping the noise that was growing louder every minute.

It took more than an hour for them to reach their destination, which under ordinary circumstances would have been a fifteen-minute drive. Their driver kept turning around and muttering excitedly in Portu-guese, and Paco explained that he was cursing the traffic, the Carnival, and life in general. When they finally arrived, Julie was hoisted up on the float that would carry her through the streets. At the far end there was a miniature replica of Sugar Loaf Mountain and the Copacabana Beach and in the front was a scaled-down copy of the Statue of Liberty. The flowers that covered the sides and top were red, white, and blue with the flags of Brazil and the United States standing side by side, also made completely of flowers. Julie took her place on a chair made to resemble a throne. *This is not too bad,* she thought as she looked out at the crowds. *At least I get to sit.*

Unfortunately, that was not to be the case because as they started to move slowly along their designated route the people in the streets screamed for Julie to stand. They wanted to see all of her, and even though she couldn't understand what they were saying, their gestures clearly indicated what they wanted. The music and wildly sensual dancing had incited the crowd to a frenzied pitch. By the time Julie's float approached the front of the Copacabana Hotel, her face ached so from smiling and throwing kisses, she didn't think she could possibly go on much longer. But she knew she must. The crowd expected it.

As Julie passed beneath the terrace where she knew her mother would be standing, she looked up and waved frantically. The people who were running alongside were making so much noise Julie couldn't hear anything but her name being shouted over and over again. "Julie, Julie." It was like a dream—a fantasy that was being played out in one of the most beautiful cities in the world. Tonight was special, magi-cal—something she would never forget.

Later, when Julie returned to the club, she found her mother waiting for her. As Julie hastily stepped out of her Carnival costume and donned her regular evening gown, Rose wiped her moist and tired face.

"Julie, you look exhausted. How are you going to do a show now?"

"I'll be fine. I just have to catch my breath for a minute and have something cold to drink."

Rose fussed over her daughter and tried to cool her down. She was helpless to do more because Julie would never consent to missing a show. From that night on, until the day they left Rio, Julie's life became a whirlwind of activity. Night turned into day with brief pauses only to shower, change clothes, grab a quick bite to eat, and then begin the cycle all over again. Paco's stamina never seemed to waiver, and Julie marveled at his ability to function with so little sleep. At Rose's insistence, Julie went to bed right after the show and remained there until she had to reappear at the next function. Not only had the crowds in the streets *not* diminished, but they seemed to be steadily increasing in preparation for the last night. The last performance, which took place in the stadium, drew thousands of people, who danced and sang throughout the evening with wild abandonment. It was a fitting climax to what had been a triumphant engagement. Julie and the other performers summoned every bit of strength to give their all, and the crowd went wild. Julie looked out at the adoring faces in the audience and mentally snapped a picture that would remain with her for the rest of her life. She would never forget Brazil, and the Brazilians would never forget Julie Lauren.

CHAPTER
20

Julie, would you check and see if the bellman brought up all the bags?" Rose asked as she eagerly ripped open Sam's long-awaited letter. The mail from home had been waiting for her upon their arrival in Montevideo, Uruguay. As Rose scanned the pages, devouring every word, Julie picked up her makeup case and brought it over to the dressing table. *I'd better freshen up before going to the theater,* Julie thought. *Paco said we might be there late rehearsing for tomorrow's opening.* After their huge triumph in Rio, Julie wasn't sure if anything could equal it. But if the huge crowd waiting to greet them at the airport was any indication of the enthusiasm awaiting their appearance, then they were sure to be a success. As Julie began removing her makeup from the case, the phone rang.

"Julie, how soon can you be ready? We want to leave for the theater." Paco's voice sounded very impatient, and Julie knew why. On their closing night in Rio, he had once again invited her to dine alone with him to celebrate their success, and as usual, Julie had refused. This time Paco's patience had run out and he had been sulking ever since.

"Paco, I was just about to unpack, but I can do that later. When do you want to leave?"

"I'll meet you down in the lobby in half an hour."

Julie was about to tell her mother that she was leaving, when suddenly a wave of nausea swept over her. Dropping into a chair, she bent her head over between her knees. She could feel beads of perspiration trickling down her neck as she tried to control the terrible feeling that engulfed her. Rose, who had just folded her letter and placed it in her purse, glanced up and saw Julie huddled in the chair. Alarmed, she ran over and put her arm around her daughter's shoulder.

"Julie, what's wrong?" she cried. "Are you sick?"

Julie nodded, still too dizzy to look up.

Rose leaned down and grabbed her daughter's hands. They were as cold as ice. "Sweetheart, tell me what's wrong. We'll call the doctor."

Suddenly Julie looked up and shook her head violently. "No, Mom, please. I just felt sick to my stomach for a minute. I'll be all right."

"Stay right where you are," Rose said as she headed for the phone. "I'll get you some ginger ale."

"Wait, Mom," Julie called out weakly. "Paco's downstairs waiting for me. We have to get to the theater right away. I can get some ginger ale downstairs at the bar on the way out."

Rose ran back and pleaded with her. "Julie, you can't go out now. You're sick. You must be coming down with something. Let me call Paco and tell him you're going to miss rehearsal."

"Please, Mom. I'll be fine once I get some air. I've got to go. They're expecting me." Julie got up slowly. She was still shaky, but at least she was able to stand. Remembering her father's letter, she asked, "What did Dad have to say? Is everything all right at home?"

"Yes, dear," Rose answered. "Don't worry about anything. Wait here. I'll get my purse and go with you."

"No, Mom, it's really not necessary for you to go to the theater. You know how bored you are at rehearsals. Why don't you unpack while I'm gone? My gowns must be a mess. When I get back we can have a light dinner and get to bed early." Julie suddenly regretted having mentioned food, because just the thought of eating made her feel queasy. *Maybe by the time I get back, I'll be myself.*

Reluctantly, Rose let her go but cautioned her to take it easy and to come back immediately if she felt sick again. When Julie left, Rose took out her letter from Sam and read it again. "Rose," he had written, "the weather in New York is cold and miserable. We haven't had a ray of sunshine in days. I was thinking of going to Miami for a few days. One of the men in the office has reservations and has asked me if I'd like to join him. You and Julie won't be back until the middle of February and right now business is slow, so maybe I should take him up on his offer." As Rose read these lines, an uneasy feeling came over her—part apprehension and part resentment. *Isn't that just like him,* she thought. *For years I've been begging him to take us to Florida in the winter and he's always refused. Now all of a sudden he decides to go.* Rose suddenly put down the letter, angry at herself. *Stop it, Rose. You're just being selfish. He's home alone and miserable while you're off traveling to exotic places. Why shouldn't he get away if he has the opportunity?* Rose finished the rest of the letter and put it away. *I'll write him after I finish unpacking and urge him to go. He deserves a rest.* That resolved, Rose once again began to think of Julie. *What in God's name could be wrong with her? She looked absolutely green before she left. I should never have let her go, but she's so stubborn sometimes. She hates to miss even a rehearsal, much less a show. When she was on the Broadway stage she worked when she was sick even though we begged her to stay home. Well, I can't sit here worrying. If she's no better when she gets back, I'll have Paco call a doctor.*

Paco hardly spoke a word to Julie during their drive to the theater. She couldn't help but notice his grim expression when she got in the car, and after traveling with him these past months, she was certain his mood was not likely to improve quickly. As she gazed out the window admiring the pretty city of Montevideo with its wide tree-lined boulevards, she tried not to think of how nauseous she was still feeling. The ginger ale had helped some, but she still felt far from perfect.

Hordes of photographers were awaiting their arrival at the beautiful Teatro Reina in the center of Montevideo's theater and nightclub district. Paco helped Julie out of the car, and as they made their way into the theater, one of the reporters stepped in front of Julie's path and asked her, "Señorita, are you and the maestro romantically involved? Is it true you are going to be his next wife?"

Julie was dumbfounded by the question and wondered where in the world he could have gotten that kind of information. She had no time to speculate further because Luis pushed them aside and closed the doors behind them. Julie was grateful not to have to answer any questions. Her discomfort was intensifying, and now her only desire was to get through rehearsal as quickly as possible and return to the hotel.

Sitting in the darkened theater watching Paco rehearse the other acts, she suddenly felt Marion slip into the seat next to her. Noticing her unnatural pallor, Marion expressed her concern.

"Julie, you don't look well. Is something wrong?"

Julie smiled wearily. "I don't know, Marion. I think I may be coming down with the flu or something."

"Why don't you tell Paco. You really don't need to rehearse, you know. I could take you back to the hotel."

"Thank you, but I'd better try out the microphone. You know how Paco is about sound."

"Well okay, honey. But just let me know if you change your mind." She started to leave, and Julie stopped her.

"Marion, Paco hasn't told me anything about our itinerary and how long we'll be playing here."

Marion opened her notebook and checked her calendar. "Let's see. We'll be in this theater for a week; then we'll play Punta del Este, the beach resort outside of town for three days; then we return here for the remainder of the week."

Julie sighed, praying that whatever was bothering her would not interfere with her work.

As they drove back to the hotel later that evening, Paco appeared to be in a better frame of mind. He was exhilarated by the advance sale of tickets and the amount of money he would be making on the tour. As they entered the Hotel Princesa, Paco put his arm around Julie.

"Julie," he said, cupping her chin with his hand. "It's late. I think you should go right up to your room, order room service, and get some sleep. Tomorrow will be a very full day. We have a press conference at one and the first show is at seven P.M."

As Julie turned to leave, Paco had an afterthought. "This morning I received an invitation from an old friend of mine from Argentina, Alberto Dodero. He has an incredible house in Punta del Este. He's asked me to have lunch with him and some other people when we get there next week. When I told him about you, he suggested that I bring you along."

Before Julie could answer, Paco read the question he saw in her eyes. "Yes, Julie, it's okay to bring your mother along."

Julie managed to get through the opening and the next few days without anyone suspecting that she was ill. But it wasn't easy. Her appetite had decreased sharply, but in order not to scare her mother, she forced herself to eat and pretend she was well. The Uruguayan audiences were unrestrained in their approval of the show, and the critics wrote glowing reviews of Paco's showmanship and of his ability to find such talented performers. As was their pattern, Julie and Rose dined with Paco after the show, but now Luis and Marion joined them. Paco was cordial to Rose and affectionate with Julie, but he had not made any romantic overtures since Rio. Julie was relieved. Feeling the way she did physically, she was grateful not to have the additional strain of having to deal with Paco's advances and her mother's antagonism. Julie had refused to see a doctor, hoping that whatever was bothering her would go away by itself. After her childhood illnesses, she had an almost irrational fear of all doctors. As they prepared to leave the Hotel Princesa for their trip to Punta del Este, Julie slipped two aspirins into her purse just in case she needed them. *If I don't feel better by the time we return to Montevideo, I'll have to give in and see a doctor. We still have the trip to Buenos Aires ahead of us and I certainly don't want to miss that.*

The hotel in Punta del Este was similar in style to the Hotel Nacional in Cuba, but even more elaborate. As Señor Ramos, the general manager of the hotel, showed them around, he pointed out the different amenities. After they toured the magnificent gardens, the manager escorted them to their room, which overlooked the sea. Paco had opted in favor of going directly to his suite, having no need to tour the hotel, since he had been there before with Laura. Once they were alone, Rose looked around the splendid accommodations and had to admit that the trip so far had offered them the chance to experience things that otherwise they might never have seen.

"If only you felt better," Rose said, touching Julie's forehead to see if she had any fever.

"Mom, please don't nag. I told you I feel fine. I'm going to unpack and take a bath. I should have plenty of time to take a nap before the show."

The audience that filled the hotel ballroom to capacity that evening was unaware that Julie had any health problems. From the moment she set foot on the stage, Julie felt completely in control. Her earlier successes in Rio and Cuba, plus the instant rapport she had begun to experience with the audiences in Montevideo gave her the confidence she needed to relax and enjoy herself. Even though Spanish was not her native language, she was still able to chat comfortably with the people seated ringside. When she sensed an opportune moment during her performance, she allowed her natural sense of humor to come through, and this further endeared her to the Latins. When she took her bows at the end of her last song, she was glowing from the enthusiastic reception she had received. Paco watched the expression on the people's faces over his shoulder as he conducted the orchestra and was pleased that his earlier instincts had been confirmed. The young girl he had found and groomed was fast developing into a marvelous performer and was turning out to be an unexpected success. And of course, this made Julie even more desirable to him.

Qué suerte. I'm lucky, he thought as he watched her leave the stage. *I have not only found myself a magnificent young creature, but also a great attraction for my orchestra.*

Later that evening, Paco showed her around the casino.

"Julie," he said, taking her arm proudly. "Come with me. I want the Uruguayans to see my American beauty up close."

Julie had changed into a white chiffon cocktail dress with a billowy skirt that showed off her tiny waist. Rose had helped to pin up her hair and fasten a gardenia just above her ear. Julie had added an extra dab of rouge to her cheeks to offset her pallor. The energy she had expended during the show had not yet returned, and though she wouldn't admit it, she did not feel well.

As they entered the beautiful casino, with its red velvet walls and crystal chandeliers, Julie couldn't help but stare at the beautiful women and elegant men who were intently gambling. Paco pointed out the different games going on at the tables—roulette, twenty-one, and the "best game of all" according to Paco, chemin de fer. They looked terribly complicated to Julie, but even if she could have understood them, she still wouldn't have played. Julie could never understand how people could risk losing hard-earned money. Even the prospect of winning didn't tempt her, and when Paco placed some money in her hand and told her to put it on a number, she refused.

"I don't like to lose, so I had better not play."

Paco laughed as he sat down at the roulette table. Patting the empty seat next to him he said to her, "Well, if you don't want to play, then at least sit next to me for good luck. I won't stay long. Then we can join the others for supper."

Paco won a considerable amount of money in a short time, and after cashing in his chips, he escorted Julie to the dining room where Rose and the group were waiting. He was in an excellent mood and entertained everyone with stories about his early childhood. No one got to bed until very late and Julie fell asleep instantly, exhausted by the day's events.

Julie and Rose slept late the next morning. There was no need to rush, as the car taking them to the home of Paco's friend, Alberto Dodero, would not be picking them up until noon. When Julie and Rose joined Paco in the lobby the car had not yet arrived, and while they waited, Paco told Julie and Rose a little about the man they were about to meet. Dodero was Argentinian and one of the richest and most powerful men in South America. He was currently using his home in Punta del Este as his main base of operations, having become persona non grata during the current Peron regime. Like many others, he had incurred Eva Peron's displeasure, and even though she was rumored to be seriously ill with cancer, her dominance and power were still felt throughout the country, where she was both loved and feared. Alberto was currently happily married to a former American show girl named Betty, who was, according to Paco, "a great broad."

Suddenly a bellman approached them. "Señor Castell, the car has arrived."

Julie looked down at her dress, hoping it would be appropriate. She had chosen to wear a sleeveless pale lavender silk dress with a matching jacket. Her mother had picked it out with her at Macy's in New York just before they left. It had been left over from the previous summer, and on sale, therefore making it more affordable. Paco was dressed all in white, except for his tie, which was a startling blue. With his tanned skin and blue eyes he looked very attractive.

When they reached the front entrance of the hotel, the most beautiful car Julie had ever seen was waiting for them. When they climbed in, Julie looked at the exquisite interior of the car. The upholstery was a rich golden tan, the color of expensive luggage and the wood paneling had a deep rich patina. There was a small mirror on her left side near the window and, beside it, a crystal bud vase containing a yellow rose. There were no markings inside to indicate what make of car it was, so Julie asked Paco softly so the chauffeur wouldn't hear.

"Paco, this car is incredible. What kind is it?"

"My dear, this is a Rolls-Royce and just one of the many cars that Alberto owns."

A Rolls-Royce, Julie thought. My God, if Dad and Marshall could see us now. Julie felt like a queen as they proceeded along the country road to their destination. Even the pains in her stomach had subsided, and she hoped that it was a sign she was getting better. A short time later, the Rolls-Royce passed through black wrought iron gates and continued along a winding driveway that led to the house. Surrounded by huge trees was a sprawling Mediterranean-style villa painted the softest coral with balconies at almost every window. As the chauffeur helped Julie and Rose out of the car, a man came running down the steps to greet Paco. Throwing his arms around him, he gave Paco a big hug, his eyes beaming with delight at the sight of his old friend.

"*Paquito, mi hermano*, it's been a long time. Let me see what the years have done to you."

Standing back he looked at Paco, shaking his head approvingly. "You dog. You haven't changed at all. How do you do it?"

Paco grinned knowingly and extended his arm to introduce Julie and Rose, who were standing there in the sunlight, admiring the magnificent house.

"Alberto, I would like you to meet my new singer, Julie Lauren, and her mother, Rose."

Alberto bowed his head and kissed both ladies' hands. Glancing up at Julie, he gazed at her with the kind of look that only a man who has known many beautiful women would have. Turning to Paco he gallantly said, "Paco, you lucky devil. I don't know who is more beautiful, the mother or the daughter."

Julie blushed and thanked him for the compliment, but Rose fidgeted around nervously. As much as she enjoyed being surrounded by such beauty and elegance, Rose still felt uncomfortable with strangers, especially foreigners.

Alberto led them through the marvelous tiled entry and into the gardens where the other guests were gathering. Julie immediately recognized a tall lanky man dressed in tennis clothes who was leaning up against a tree. Julie pulled her mother to one side.

"Mom, don't look now but you won't believe who's here. Gary Cooper." Rose started to turn, but Julie held on to her arm. "Not now. It's too obvious. Wait until he's not looking."

Julie turned her attention back to Paco, who was still involved in an animated conversation with Alberto. When he saw Julie, he placed his arm around her possessively.

"Well, Alberto, what do you think of my little Julie?"

"I think she not only lives up to your description of her, but, my friend, I think you did not do her justice. She is exquisite."

Julie smiled shyly at his kind words and thanked him for inviting them to his home. Moments later a beautiful blond woman, who Julie judged to be somewhere in her thirties, joined them. There was a casual elegance about her that Julie admired instantly. She was dressed in a white silk blouse that was tailored to perfection and her matching silk pants flared out gently, almost like an evening skirt. Her complexion was flawless and so was her jewelry. Around her neck were several strands of lustrous pearls, and as she extended her hand in greeting, Julie couldn't help but notice a huge sparkling square cut diamond on her finger.

"Betty, darling. Look who's here. Paco. Give him a big kiss."

His wife happily obliged, giving him several hugs and kisses, laughing and talking at the same time. "Paco, where have you been? Why haven't you been back to see us before now? The last time we saw you was during your trip here with that bitch wife of yours. Are you divorced yet?"

Paco and Alberto started to laugh. "*Cuidado, mujer*, you talk too much," Alberto cautioned her good-naturedly.

"That's okay, Alberto," Paco said. "Betty can say anything she wants. Besides, she's right. Laura is a bitch. In answer to your question, beautiful one, I expect my divorce to be final any day. Now, I would like you to meet a countryman of yours. My new vocalist, Julie Lauren."

Betty sized up the young girl standing in front of her and decided that she liked her. There was a sweetness and vulnerability about her that was very appealing. She leaned over and kissed Julie on both cheeks.

"It's a pleasure to meet you. Welcome to Casa Dodero. Has anyone offered you anything to eat or drink?"

Without waiting for a reply, she took Julie by the arm and summoned a butler. "Jorge, bring some hors d'oeurves and wine for my guests. Do you like wine, Julie?"

"No thank you, Mrs. Dodero, but a Coke would be fine if you have one."

"Mrs. Dodero? Shit, baby, just call me Betty. I don't go for that formal crap. I'm just a down-home girl at heart."

Suddenly, Julie remembered that she had left her mother standing alone. "Betty, I would like you to meet my mother. She's right over there."

"Your mother?" Betty said laughingly. "I don't believe it. You brought along a chaperone? I'll bet Paco just loves that."

"My mother had to make the trip. I'm only sixteen and this is my first time out of the country."

"Sixteen," she gasped. "This time Paco has really outdone himself."

Noticing Julie's pained expression, Betty hastened to apologize. "Don't mind me, Julie. I'm very outspoken, but that's what makes me different from all of Alberto's other broads. I don't take any crap from him and he loves it. Now come on, baby, and introduce me to Mom."

As the afternoon progressed, Julie was introduced to the other guests. Most of the people there already knew Paco, and judging by their appearance and the jewels that the women wore, Julie had to assume that they were very wealthy. She also got to meet the American Consul General to Uruguay and his wife, who were very cordial. But the moment Julie had been waiting for came when Paco introduced her to Gary Cooper. Up close, he was even more handsome than on the screen, and very gracious. Even though she had just met him, he seemed genuinely interested in hearing about her background and plans for her career. He told her he was taking a much needed rest, having just completed his latest movie, *High Noon*, with a young and beautiful new actress, Grace Kelly.

When the butler announced that lunch was being served on the patio, Paco escorted Julie and Rose to their seats. Rose found herself seated next to a businessman from New York, which pleased her, for it would at least give her someone to talk to in English. Gary Cooper was seated directly across the table from Julie, and next to him, a good friend of his from the States, Countess Dorothy Di Frasso. Although she was neither beautiful nor young, the countess possessed great vitality, and men found her very attractive. The jewelry she was wearing was dazzling, and though it was somewhat excessive for a casual lunch, she managed to carry it off. Her colorful vocabulary and great sense of humor easily dominated the conversation at the table.

As Julie watched her admiringly, Paco leaned over and whispered, "There used to be a rumor circulating in Hollywood that before Cooper married Rocky, he and Di Frasso were lovers. But that was long ago and now they're just good friends. She was extremely helpful to Gary when he was starting out in pictures. She inherited a fortune from her father and I've heard that one of her lovers was the gangster Bugsy Siegel. One thing is certain, Julie she's a woman with powerful connections."

When Julie looked down at her place setting she couldn't believe the amount of flatware. There were several forks, knives, and spoons in all sizes. Everything was in gold, including the enormous centerpiece, which was brimming with flowers.

As the impeccably dressed butlers in their white jackets and white gloves began to serve lunch, Julie glanced around nervously at the others to see what utensils they were using. There were too many to choose from and Julie didn't want to make a mistake and embarrass Paco. As the laughter and wine began to flow, the conversation at the table became a mélange of different languages. Seated on Julie's left was an extremely handsome and dashing young man who everyone addressed as "Rubi." She later learned that his full name was Porfirio Rubirosa and that his first wife had been Flor Trujillo, the daughter of the president of the Dominican Republic. They had been divorced after a brief marriage, and he was currently wooing the American heiress Barbara Hutton, who was also there and seated next to Alberto Dodero. Julie watched and listened carefully, trying to absorb as much as she could from this sophisticated crowd.

Julie stole a quick glance at her mother to see how she was faring, but Rose hadn't touched anything as yet. She could guess what her mother was probably thinking. *If only they'd serve some mushroom and barley soup and some pot roast instead of this* chozerai. Rose always classified anything that wasn't good Jewish cooking as *chozerai*—garbage. Rubirosa was very attentive to Julie during lunch, but being a Latin he was fully aware that Paco Castell was a jealous man and he was therefore careful not to do anything to inflame him. As dessert was being served, he leaned over and asked Julie something that had been puzzling him all afternoon.

"My dear, I know you have been singing with Paco for only a short while and that you are quite young. Tell me, where do you come from and how did you learn to speak such good Spanish?"

Julie smiled at him and answered with the first thought that came into her head. "Well, in answer to your question, I was born in Brooklyn, raised in Manhattan, and I learned Spanish in self-defense."

The handsome Latin laughed at her response, delighted and somewhat envious of Paco that one so young could possess such poise and humor.

When lunch was finally over, Alberto rose from his chair to make a toast to his guests. Raising his glass, he singled them out individually and thanked them for joining him and his wife for lunch. When it was Julie's turn he became especially effusive.

"Julie, my dear, you are undoubtedly the youngest among us today and certainly one of the loveliest new visitors ever to grace our home. Now, ladies," he said, laughing, "don't be angry with me. You are all very beautiful and you know it. But Julie is a newcomer to this country and, therefore, we must make her feel very welcome."

The others at the table applauded their approval, including Paco, who looked like the cat who had swallowed the canary. Alberto asked Julie if she would like to say something before they left the table to go into the library for coffee and brandy. Julie looked at Paco apprehensively, hoping he would help her, but he just smiled and waited for her to speak.

Shyly Julie rose from her chair and addressing her hosts she thanked them in Spanish for their hospitality and kindness and for making her and her mother feel so welcome. Then, as if it were an afterthought, she added, "Espero que ustedes vendran al hotel a ver nuestro espectáculo, antes que terminamos."

Amid much applause and congratulations on her Spanish, a very embarrassed Julie sat down. *What was I thinking of, asking these people to come and see the show?* As the guests started to disperse, Julie moved her chair back and was about to get up when Paco leaned over and gave her a kiss on the cheek.

"That was a very sweet little speech, *mi preciosa*. Everyone here is very taken with you. Now, I think we'd better start back. We have a show to do tonight, and business has been so great, we'll probably have to do two shows for our closing tomorrow night."

Julie gathered up her jacket and purse and with Paco and her mother went in search of their hosts to thank them and bid them good-bye.

"Alberto," Paco said, as he shook his friend's hand at the doorway. *"Muchisimas gracias* for everything. Where is Betty?"

"Here I am, you horny son of a bitch. I was just finding a bed for Barbara Hutton to lie down on. She's had a bit too much vino as usual."

Paco kissed Betty and said, "Julie and I want to thank you for a wonderful day."

"It was nothing. It was our pleasure having you here. I'm sorry you have to leave so soon. Most of our guests will be staying on for dinner."

Suddenly, without warning, Betty reached for Julie's arm and pulled her to one side while calling over her shoulder, "Alberto, keep Paco busy for a minute. I want to talk to Julie."

Steering her toward the car that was waiting in the driveway, she said, "Julie, you seem like a really sweet young kid, and because I like you, I want to give you some advice."

Julie looked at her questioningly.

"I've known Paco a long time. In fact, even before he married Laura. Taking into consideration what I know about him, I think I should warn you to be careful."

"Careful of what?" Julie asked.

Betty Dodero leaned against the shiny fender of her car and lit a cigarette while she considered what she was going to say. "Look, Julie, it's obvious that Paco has the hots for you, and what Paco wants, he usually gets."

Julie blushed, embarrassed that a perfect stranger would not only speak so bluntly to her but would have guessed in just a few short hours the kind of predicament she was in.

"Julie, you must be aware that your mother watches him like a hawk, and don't think for a moment that she doesn't know what he's up to."

Before Julie could protest, Betty stopped her. "Honey, what I said before about Laura was the truth. She *is* a selfish and greedy bitch, but life with Paco was not a bed of roses. He gave her a hard time when it came to other men, even before she started fooling around. Everyone knows he's insanely jealous and has a fierce temper. You may not be interested in him, but if he's determined to have you *nothing* will stand in his way. Don't say anything now. Just think about what I've said and be on your guard. I'd hate to see you hurt. We *gringas* have to stick together, especially when we're up against those Latin bastards. Now, let's go back before they think we're plotting a murder."

Arm in arm they joined the men and Rose, who was standing there waiting impatiently. "What have you two been up to?" Alberto asked. "Paco is anxious to get back to town."

"Just girl talk, *mi amor*. I told Julie that I was putting together a group to come see their closing show tomorrow night. We want to give Paco a grand send-off before he returns to Montevideo."

Kissing them good-bye, she started to return to the house and her guests, but as the car pulled away, she yelled to Julie. "Take care, Julie. We'll see you tomorrow night."

Paco could barely wait for the car door to close before asking Julie, "What was all the whispering about? What was Betty saying to you?"

"Nothing important, Paco. She just wanted to tell me which shops at the hotel are the best. She also insisted that if I want to buy something, I should mention her name and tell them that she's a friend of mine."

Julie dared not look at Paco's face because she feared he would know that she hadn't spoken the truth. If he suspected Betty's true feelings about him and knew of her warning, he would have been furious.

Rose concentrated her gaze on the landscape. She knew for certain that Julie was lying and she could guess the reason why. She had sized up Betty Dodero instantly upon meeting her and had decided that she was one smart lady. There was no doubt in her mind that she had been giving Julie some sound advice concerning Paco. She only hoped that her daughter would listen.

Paco also was aware that Julie had not told him the truth, but he decided not to press her. He knew how dazzled she had been by this afternoon. More and more, with each day that passed, she was being swept away by fascinating people who not only possessed great wealth and enormous power but, in many instances, great fame as well. He was now firmly convinced that nothing that either her mother or anyone else could say would persuade her to give up a life-style that he knew she found challenging and exciting. *She may not realize it yet,* Paco thought, *but the die has been cast. She could never be happy going back to her former life.*

CHAPTER
21

·

Paco carefully studied the itinerary that Luis had handed him as they left Punta del Este on their way back to Montevideo. Everything seemed in order. They would finish their remaining days in the Teatro Reina and then head for Buenos Aires. Paco turned around in the car and glanced at Julie, who was sitting in the back with her mother. She didn't look well. Suddenly it dawned on him that she had lost some weight and her color was not good.

"Julie, is your stomach still bothering you? You haven't said a word since we left."

Julie hesitated before answering him. She was feeling much worse, and now, beside her terrible nausea, she had developed a sharp pain on her right side. She didn't want to worry her mother, but she wasn't sure if she could continue on much longer without some kind of medication to ease the pain.

"I'm not feeling great, Paco," she answered feebly. "Perhaps I *should* see a doctor when we reach Montevideo."

Suddenly, Rose was very frightened. This was the first time Julie had admitted that she was sick, and it scared her. Here they were, in a foreign country, and far away from home and Sam. Julie had been such a sickly child that even the thought of another illness could send Rose into a state of panic.

"Julie," Rose pleaded. "I begged you to see a doctor a week ago but you refused. Now, you may be really sick."

"Please, Mom," Julie begged. "Don't frighten me. I thought I was getting better but I guess I was wrong. I'm sure it's just a bug."

"Of course, Julie," Paco agreed. "That's all it is. As soon as we get to the hotel we'll find a doctor. I'll call Alberto Dodero and get a recommendation from him."

By the time the physician reached the hotel, Julie was in excruciating pain. She was feeling so wretched she couldn't even tolerate the ginger ale Rose had sent for and had thrown up so many times in the last hour that her throat and stomach were sore. When the doctor walked in their room, Julie was lying on the bed too weak to even lift her head. After introducing herself, Rose led him to where Julie was lying.

"Señorita Lauren, I am Dr. Diaz. I received an urgent phone call from Señor Dodero. What seems to be the matter?"

As the doctor spoke he swiftly reached for her wrist and felt her pulse. Julie explained the symptoms that she had been experiencing the past weeks—her lack of energy and nausea and now the sharp pain in her right side. The doctor listened carefully while studying her face. Her color was sallow, and because of her constant vomiting, she appeared to be terribly dehydrated. He then requested that she open her robe so that he could examine her. Rose stood by silently, grateful that at least the doctor could speak English.

The moment his fingers touched the spot Julie had pointed out, she let out an involuntary scream. Rose rushed to her side, her face stricken. "Doctor, what is it? What's wrong with my daughter?"

Julie was trying hard not to cry, but she couldn't hold back the tears that were now streaming down her face. She was not only in pain, but was now frightened.

"Doctor, that really hurt. Is it my appendix?"

"No, Julie, it's not your appendix." Covering her gently with the blanket, he patted her head. "Please, try to rest. I'd like to speak to your mother."

Dr. Diaz signaled to Rose that he would like to speak to her privately, and they went into the hall. "Mrs. Lauren, I don't want to alarm you, and naturally I can't be certain until we take some tests, but I think your daughter may have hepatitis. Her liver appears to be enlarged and her eyes are slightly jaundiced. Has she had a virus lately or shots of any kind?"

Rose stood there, stunned. She didn't even know what hepatitis was, but she did know that an enlarged liver was serious. Dazed and frightened, she tried to think back.

"No, Doctor. Before this trip she was perfectly fine." Suddenly, it dawned on her. "My God, she did have a smallpox vaccination before we came to South America. We all did. Julie started to complain about not feeling well about a week after we left the States."

"Well," the doctor responded, pulling out a pad and pencil from his jacket, "as I said before, I can't be sure, but it's possible she may have contracted hepatitis from a contaminated needle. I'm going to write a prescription for something to relieve the nausea and vomiting and I would suggest you bring her to my office tomorrow morning so I can run some tests."

Rose thanked him and they both went back into the room where Julie was waiting for them, fright written all over her face. "Mom, what is it? Is there something seriously wrong with me?"

Before Rose could reply, Dr. Diaz reached down and took her delicate hand in his. "*Señorita*, please don't worry. You're going to be fine. I've given your mother a prescription for some medicine that should help you. Tomorrow we'll try to get to the bottom of this."

Taking his case from the table, he bid them good-bye and left the room, promising to see them at his office the next morning. As soon as he was gone, Rose sat down next to Julie and stroked her forehead, hoping to calm her fears.

"Julie, darling. Please try to relax and don't be frightened. I'm going to Paco's room to give him this prescription and then I'll be right back."

Julie nodded her head weakly, trying not to think of her condition and what might be wrong with her. When Rose returned to their room after delivering the prescription to Paco, Julie was dozing fitfully. Quietly, so as not to disturb her, Rose sat down in the easy chair near the window and tried not to let her own fear run away with her. *Please God*, she prayed silently, *don't let her be sick. She's had more than her share for someone so young. Oh, Sam*, she thought, *we need you so. What am I going to do?*

Upstairs, in his luxurious suite, Paco was pacing the floor nervously. He had sent Luis downstairs to try to find a *farmacia* that would be open, but that wasn't his only concern. From what Rose had said,

Julie's condition could be serious. *Mierda*, he thought. *What am I going to do if Julie can't perform? We still have four days to go and the place is sold out. And what about Buenos Aires? All the advance publicity has already gone out announcing her appearance. The press and the public are expecting my new discovery—the redheaded American girl who was queen of the Carnival in Rio and who has taken the Latins by storm.* Angrily he picked up the phone and called his impresario, Pablo Montoya.

"Pablo," he bellowed into the receiver. "We may have a problem. Julie is sick and we won't know just how bad it is until tomorrow. You'd better make yourself available to me at a minute's notice."

"But, Paco," Pablo answered, sweat breaking out on his face. "The place is all sold out. We have two shows booked every night and could even do a third if you wanted. Paquito, I don't have to tell you how important she is to us. The entire show is great, but you know what an impact Julie has made. It's not only her talent. The audiences are wild about her beauty and charm. You just can't let her miss the shows. We need her."

Infuriated by Pablo's whining about Julie's importance to the show, and frustrated that she might be letting him down, Paco angrily replied, "Pablo, remember who you're talking to. That audience is there to see me. *I'm* the one they've admired in motion pictures and on records all these years. Vocalists come and go, but there's only *one* Paco Castell."

Pablo knew better than to disagree with Paco. "*Sí, maestro*, I know. Of course, you are the star. But you know the Latins. They love beautiful women."

"Well, find me a replacement. I don't care how good she sings. Just make sure she's beautiful and sexy." Paco slammed down the receiver just as Luis came back into the room. "Well," Paco asked, "did you find a *farmacia?*"

"*Sí, mi hermano.* There was one that's open all night just down the street. I just delivered the medicine to Rose."

The next morning Paco accompanied them to the clinic where Dr. Diaz had his offices. After drawing some blood and examining Julie more carefully, the doctor asked them to wait in the outer room for the tests to be completed. Shortly, he called them back into his office. They feared the worst when they saw the grim expression on the doctor's face.

"I'm sorry," he told them, "but I can now confirm what I suspected all along. The *señorita* does indeed have hepatitis and yellow jaundice.

I would suggest that she either enter a hospital here or return to the United States as soon as possible."

Paco jumped up, anger written all over his face.

"What do you mean, return to the States? We're right in the middle of a tour and Julie is my featured vocalist. I've spent a fortune on publicity. She *has* to perform."

The doctor sat back in his chair and folded his arms across his chest. "Señor Castell, I am only giving you my recommendation. Of course you are free to do as you wish. If the *señorita* feels she can perform, then that is up to her. My professional opinion is that she should go home immediately and see her own doctor for treatment. This is not an illness that should be treated lightly."

Julie sat next to her mother too stunned by the news to say anything. It was like a nightmare. All the terrible memories of being sick and bedridden came rushing back to her.

Rose leaned over his desk, her body trembling with fear and apprehension, as she asked him, "Isn't there anything you can give my daughter now? It might take a few days before we can get back to New York."

"Mrs. Lauren, your daughter needs to be treated in a hospital. With her type of hepatitis, the jaundice will become quite intense and she would be more comfortable under complete medical supervision. The medication I've given her can probably tide her over until you can get her home."

Thanking him, they left his office and headed back to the hotel. Rose refrained from making any comment about Paco's outburst in the doctor's office because she knew it would upset Julie. But she planned on speaking to him privately once Julie was safely back in bed.

Paco kept on looking at his watch, concerned about the show that was only hours away. *Goddamn doctors,* he thought. *What do they know? She doesn't look as sick as he said she was. She just needs a little rest and some medicine.*

When Julie and Rose returned to their room, Julie undressed quickly, got into bed, and turned her face to the wall. The pills the doctor had given her had helped to calm the sick feeling in her stomach, but nothing could ease the pain in her heart—the terrible guilt of having let Paco down when he had been so good to her. If only she could finish out the tour. She wouldn't mind anything after that—hospitals, doctors, she would endure it all. If only she didn't have to quit.

While Julie rested, Rose put a call in to Sam in New York. As usual, the operator said there would be a delay, so Rose kicked off her shoes and sat down on the chair near Julie's bed, trying to collect her thoughts. As soon as she reached Sam she would speak to Paco about arranging their trip back home. Rose must have dozed off because when she awoke, the room was dark and she could hear someone knocking at the door. Searching for the light switch, she called out, "Just a minute. I'm coming. Who is it?"

"It's Paco, Rose. Please let me in."

Rose opened the door and motioned for him to be quiet. Julie's eyes were closed, and she didn't want him to wake her.

"I was waiting for my phone call to Sam to come through," she whispered. "And then I was coming to see you."

"Rose," Paco said urgently. "You've got to help me."

"Help you?" she asked suspiciously. "What do you want?"

"Rose, we're in a terrible predicament. Pablo called. The theater is packed and he thinks there could be serious trouble if Julie doesn't appear."

"Appear?" Rose asked through clenched teeth. "She can barely stand up. She hasn't eaten for two days and she's as weak as a kitten. She's sick, Paco. I'm just waiting to speak to my husband, and then I want to take her home."

"Rose," Paco pleaded, steering her over to the window as far away from Julie as they could get. "All I'm asking is that she make an appearance at the theater. Just one song so the public can see her. You don't know Latins the way I do. They can get very nasty if they don't get to see what was advertised."

"Then let them get nasty. That's not my concern. I'm not going to wake a sick child just so that you and your impresario can get rich."

Rose didn't realize it but her voice had been steadily rising, and Julie, hearing her mother's voice, sat up in bed.

"Mom, Paco, what's going on?" Suddenly, Julie remembered—the show. "Paco, what time is it? I have to get dressed."

They both rushed over to the bed as Julie attempted to stand up. Rose reached her daughter first.

"Julie, get back into bed. You're sick and you are not going to do the show tonight."

Paco leaned over her, a smile on his face as he grasped her hand. "Julie dear, I've been trying to convince your mother that you *must* appear this evening. Everyone is expecting you, and you wouldn't want to let them down, would you?"

Julie was too groggy from the pills to realize what was happening. But, she knew she had to do the show. Paco expected it.

Sensing her vulnerability, Paco continued. "If you could just come to the theater and make a quick appearance. That is all I ask of you. I promise that I will have Luis put you in a car immediately after the show and take you back to the hotel. By tomorrow we hope to have found a replacement for you until you are well."

Rose started to protest, but Julie threw aside the covers. Paco had said the magic word—*replacement*. No one was going to replace her. This job meant too much to her. She was going to the theater no matter what.

"Paco, I'm going to get dressed. I'll meet you downstairs in half an hour."

"Are you crazy!" Rose screamed. "You're sick."

"I'll be okay, Mom. Please, help me get ready."

Rose stared helplessly at Julie and then shot a look of pure hatred at Paco. *You won this time, you bastard,* she thought. *But this will be the last time.*

"All right, Julie. I'll let you make an appearance, but remember. No singing or dancing." Turning to Paco, Rose said, "I want you to make arrangements for us to leave as soon as possible. Do you understand?"

Paco nodded his head in agreement. He would placate the bitch for the moment. Anything to get Julie to the theater.

Julie managed to get her makeup and hair fixed so that she looked presentable, but nothing could conceal her eyes. The pupils were still amber, but the white had disappeared and had been replaced by a sickly yellow—the first sign of jaundice.

No one spoke in the car, and when they arrived at the theater Luis and Marion were there to meet them. Marion was shocked when she saw Julie's condition, and she helped Rose take her to the dressing room. Paco went directly to the stage, as he was already dressed, and moments later the opening number began. Julie had to summon up all her strength just to put on her evening gown and finish her makeup. She didn't dare think of her pain or nausea. If she did, she would never get through the show. She sat there quietly waiting for them to call her. Minutes passed and suddenly there was an urgent knocking on the dressing room door. Marion opened it and the short and perpetually perspiring Pablo stormed in.

"Julie, Paco sent me to get you. The public is clamoring to see you. Come quickly."

Julie heaved a big sigh and started to follow him, but Rose grabbed her daughter's hand and reminded her sternly, "Julie, remember what I said. Just smile and say that you're not feeling too well and come right off."

Julie walked out into the wings, and when Paco saw her standing there he gave her his usual big introduction and started her music. Julie hesitated. She felt very weak and she wasn't quite sure if she could make it. Paco kept looking over to her, waiting for her entrance, but Julie held on to the curtain for dear life. Paco suddenly left the stage and went to see what the delay was.

"Julie, you missed your cue. Come on."

Julie stood rooted to the spot, afraid to move while she felt so faint. "Paco, I don't know if I can handle it. I feel dizzy."

"Julie, I've had enough of this nonsense. You're just giving in to yourself. Come on."

Pulling her arm, Paco practically dragged her out on to the stage, and when the spotlight hit her, the audience went wild. The guys in the balcony whistled and screamed her name, and somehow Julie got through the song. When she finished she received thunderous applause. Julie turned to Paco. She was feeling very weak and just wanted to say a few words and bow out gracefully. But Paco immediately went into her next number. This song called for her not only to sing but also to dance a fast rhumba. Julie didn't know what to do. There was no time to make a decision. Her professionalism told her she must try to perform. As the beat accelerated, Julie's feet and body moved faster and faster to the music. She completely lost track of where she was and what she was doing. She only knew that she had to keep up with the music. The rhythm section began to beat wildly as Julio, the conga player, started dancing in a circle around her. The crowd reached a frenzied pitch. They kept chanting "canta, baila, peliroja"—"dance, sing, redhead."

Then suddenly it was over. Julie tried to take a bow, but the room began to spin around her. Desperately she headed for the safety of the wings, and when she reached the black velvet curtain her legs gave way and she fainted.

Julie didn't realize until much later, when she was back in the safety of her bed, that it was Miguel's strong arms that had prevented her from falling. He carried her back to her dressing room and placed her gently on the couch. He had been standing in the wings waiting to go on when he saw Julie struggling to continue, and he knew by the pained expression on her face that she was in trouble. Miguel had been afraid to speak to Julie during the trip because of Paco's unwarranted jealousy. But when he saw her frantic attempt to reach the side of the stage, he was glad he was there to help her.

Rose was hysterical when she saw Julie's condition and begged Marion to get help. When Julie opened her eyes and saw her mother's concerned face, she bravely tried to smile.

"Hi, Mom. I guess I'm a tough act to follow. Who can top fainting?"

"How can you make jokes when you've just nearly given us all a heart attack?" Rose asked, angry at her daughter's foolishness, yet relieved that she was awake.

Luis, who had been trying to reach Dr. Diaz, came forward. "Julie, I have not been able to contact the doctor, but I left a message at his home."

"Thanks, Luis. I don't know what happened to me. One minute I was singing and dancing and then all of a sudden I lost control."

"I think the best thing we can do is to get Julie back to the hotel," Marion suggested. "By that time we can hope Dr. Diaz will have contacted us."

Paco was still onstage performing. He had seen Julie teetering on the verge of collapse, but when he saw Miguel reach for her he decided to continue. His credo was "the show must go on."

When Rose and Julie, accompanied by Luis and Marion, reached their room, the telephone was ringing. Leaving Marion with Julie, Rose ran to grab it, thinking it must be the doctor.

"Hello, Rose, it's Sam. How are you and Julie?"

Just hearing his voice triggered all the emotion she had been trying to conceal and Rose started to sob into the telephone. "Oh, Sam," she cried. "I'm okay, but Julie is very sick."

"Sick. Oh, my God. What's wrong with her?"

"She has hepatitis and yellow jaundice. We just came from the theater."

Sam gasped, unable to comprehend how all of this could have happened so quickly. "Why didn't you call me before and let me know?"

"I tried calling you, Sam, but we couldn't get through. I wrote you in my last two letters that Julie had been feeling under the weather, but you never answered. I guess you were away."

A deep feeling of guilt came over Sam, and not knowing how to handle it, he lashed back at Rose. "I got your letters, Rose, but you never said that it was anything serious. Why didn't you come home immediately when she first started feeling sick?"

"Oh, Sam," Rose cried. "I never dreamed it was so serious. She took a turn for the worse in the last twenty-four hours."

"Rose, try and stay calm. What are you going to do?"

"We're waiting for the doctor now. It's late here and I hope we can reach him tonight."

"Rose, dear," Sam said tenderly. "I'm sorry that you and our baby are going through all of this alone. I wish I could help. After you see the doctor, call me and let me know what arrangements you've made to come home."

"I will Sam, I've got to go now. The doctor may be trying to get through. I'll call you tomorrow. If you don't hear from me, then call us here at the hotel. I love you."

Luis had been standing in the hall, waiting for Rose to get off the phone. "Rose," Luis said, glancing at his watch. "I have to get back to the theater. The show will be over soon and Paco will need me. Marion will stay with you if you wish."

"Go ahead, Luis, and please tell your brother to come here right after the show. I must speak to him."

On their way back to the hotel, Luis filled Paco in on all that had happened since Julie had precipitously left the stage. Paco was angry, and the urgent "command" that he see Rose immediately only made it worse. The audience had turned unruly when they discovered that Julie was not returning with more songs. Most of the people out front were unaware that Julie had fainted because Miguel had caught her so quickly. When intermission was over, they fully expected Julie to come back, and when she failed to appear, they made their displeasure clear. It was in this frame of mind that Paco knocked on Julie's door after dismissing Luis with instructions to call a nearby restaurant and order his dinner.

Julie was in her bed when her mother opened the door to let Paco in. She felt too weak to do anything but smile wanly from her pillow. Marion had gone downstairs to the hotel kitchen to see if there was some clear soup available. Julie had not eaten anything for almost twenty-four hours, and the lack of nourishment, coupled with her constant nausea, was taking its toll.

Paco, who was still dressed in his tuxedo, came into the room and went directly to Julie's side. "Julie, my dear. I'm so sorry you are ill. I would have come offstage immediately, but I saw that Miguel was standing nearby and I knew he would help you."

Sitting down on her bed, he took her hand in his. "The audience was very upset when you didn't return. I had to explain that you weren't feeling too well." Smiling, he patted her cheek. "You see what a success you have made because of Paco? They were all clamoring for Julie. Now you must rest and get well."

Unable to restrain herself any longer, Rose, who had been standing by silently listening to Paco, suddenly flew into a rage. Running over to the bed, the petite but sturdy woman grabbed Paco's jacket and with one swift motion pulled him to his feet.

"You son of a bitch," she screamed. "How could you do this to my daughter? First you taunt her about replacing her, knowing full well what effect that would have. Then you deceitfully promise that all she has to do is make a quick appearance. She was in excruciating pain, but you forced her to go to the theater. If you really cared about her you would never have let her go."

Hysterically, Rose began to beat her fists against his chest. "You miserable lowlife. What did you do when she got there? You dragged her out on stage and then played music that would have exhausted her even if she was well. Then when she fainted, instead of rushing off immediately to see if she was alive or dead, you continued on like nothing had happened. You don't give a damn about anyone but yourself."

Totally out of control now, she continued to scream. "If I were a man, I'd give you a beating you'd never forget."

Paco pulled her hands away from him and backed up to the door. His face was contorted with rage and his fists were clenched at his sides. But it was his eyes, seething with hatred, that scared Julie and caused her to jump out of bed.

Running over to them, she pleaded. "Mother, Paco. Please, stop it."

Enraged, Paco screamed. "Tell your mother not to touch me again or I'll forget I'm a gentleman."

"A gentleman," Rose screamed, lunging for him again. "You don't know the meaning of the word. You're just an arrogant, selfish son of a bitch."

"Mom," Julie begged, clutching her side. "Please don't say anything else. I can't stand this fighting."

"If you can't stand the fighting," Rose said, "then tell this animal to give us our tickets so we can go back home where we belong."

"Who the hell wanted *you* here in the first place?" Paco yelled. "You can leave whenever you want."

Rose sprang up again like a cornered animal and would have attacked him if not for Julie, who stood in the way.

"Stop it, stop it both of you," she screamed. "I can't take any more of this." Sobbing, Julie tried to steer her mother to the opposite side of the room and away from Paco.

Suddenly the door opened and Marion came back into the room. She didn't have to be told what was happening. She had heard the screaming and crying as soon as she emerged from the elevator. When Julie saw her enter the room, she broke away from her mother and ran to her.

"Marion, thank God you're here. Please help me."

Marion put her arm around the frightened girl and tried to calm her. "Julie dear, you're sick. You must get back into bed."

"Of course she's sick," Paco said furiously. "And it's all because of that crazy mother of hers. She just tried to attack me. What the hell have I got to do with Julie being sick? I just want to finish this goddamn tour in peace."

"The tour," Rose said bitterly. "That's all he thinks about—that and money. What about my daughter's health?"

"Marion," Paco shouted, "give her the damn tickets and arrange for the hotel bill to be paid immediately."

Straightening his tie and smoothing back his hair, he said. "That's the appreciation I get for taking a nobody and trying to make her a star. Without even consulting me, her mother decides to leave, taking with her the girl I've spent a fortune on, publicizing and promoting. Does she give a shit about my feelings and the show? No. Does she care that she's leaving me without a girl singer? No. Well, no matter what happens, Julie or no Julie, I plan to finish this tour." With a grandiose wave of his hand to Julie, who was lying in her bed, quivering with pain and fright, he left the room.

After reassuring Rose that she would return shortly with their air-line tickets, Marion too departed.

"Julie," Rose pleaded. "Please don't look at me like that. I had to tell him what I thought of him. It's been boiling up inside of me for months. The man is no good. Can't you see that?"

"Oh, Mom, all I can see is that I'm not only sick but I've also lost my job and probably my greatest chance for the future."

"Your future doesn't depend on him, Julie. Why are you so blind?"

Julie couldn't answer because, suddenly, her body was racked by a sharp pain that caused her to cry out in anguish. "Oh, my God, Mom. It hurts. What's keeping the doctor?"

"I don't know, baby. He still hasn't called. Here," she said, taking a pill from the bottle of medicine near the bed. "Take this. Maybe, it will help you."

The rest of the night Rose never left her daughter's side. As Julie tried desperately to find a comfortable position so she could doze, Rose made her plans. She would try to get a plane to New York right after Julie saw the doctor. As soon as they made their final arrangements, she would wire Sam. As the morning light began to filter through the sheer curtains, Julie stirred. Rose looked at her daughter and was shocked by her appearance. She hadn't noticed last night, but in the harsh glare of daylight, she could see that not only Julie's eyes were yellow but also her entire face and body.

Julie groaned with pain and began to scratch her arms and legs. At first it was gradual, as if she were trying to get at a mosquito bite, but it grew more intense. Suddenly, Julie was desperate, frantically trying to scratch her body.

"Mom," she screamed. "Help me. I'm itching all over."

Rose was helpless. She didn't know what to do. Why was Julie itching so much? "Where, baby? Show me where it's bothering you."

"All over," Julie cried. "It's driving me crazy."

Leaping out of bed, Julie ran into the bathroom. Turning on the taps in the bath tub, Julie started to rip off her nightgown. Rose ran after her.

"Julie, what are you doing? I don't think you should be taking a bath."

"I have to, Mom. I can't stand the itching."

By the time Dr. Diaz reached their room, both Rose and Julie were frantic. The itching had gotten so bad that Julie beseeched her mother to help her scratch, and when their fingernails proved ineffective, Julie grabbed her hairbrush and began scraping her body like a person possessed. Rose tried to stop her, but Julie, driven by the unrelenting agony, was hysterical.

The doctor had only to glance at the pitiful young girl and he knew instantly that she had taken a turn for the worse. The jaundice was causing the unbearable itching and regrettably there was little he could do to help her. Sedatives were out of the question because they might further damage her already enlarged liver, and there was nothing topical he could give her for relief. She either had to go home or to a hospital immediately. Reaching for the phone, he quickly asked the operator for Paco's room. The operator informed him there was a "Do Not Disturb," but the doctor persisted.

"You must wake him. It's an emergency."

When Paco finally answered, his voice reflected his irritation over being awakened. But the doctor was brutally frank and came right to the point.

"Señor Castell, Julie is very sick. We must get her to the States immediately or hospitalize her here."

"She can't go to a hospital here," Paco answered brusquely. "I'm leaving for Buenos Aires tomorrow. She'll be all alone in a foreign city. I cannot be responsible for her once we leave, and we won't be coming back."

"Then you must arrange for transportation today," Dr. Diaz answered, amazed at the man's lack of feeling. "In her condition I doubt if a regular airline will take her, even though she is probably not contagious anymore. We will have to see if there is an ambulance plane available. The Red Cross does have that kind of service in cases of emergency."

Paco told him that he would get his brother to work on that possibility immediately and promised to stay in touch with the doctor.

The hours that followed were worse than any illness Julie had ever endured. When a normal hairbrush ceased to give her any relief, she begged her mother to use the wire brush that Rose used to clean their suede shoes. Julie ran it across her body so fiercely, the bristles left tiny tracks of blood in their path. She didn't care. Crying, she prayed to God for relief, but it didn't come. Her only moments of respite were when she was soaking in the soothing bath water. Julie lay there, immobilized, too weary to even cry anymore.

Somehow the hours slipped by and soon it was time to get ready to leave. Rose was packed and dressed long before Julie awoke from a fitful sleep. Slowly she helped her fragile daughter dress for the long journey home. The doctor had arranged for an ambulance to take them to the airport, and all that remained was for Rose to gather up their last-minute belongings. Julie was barely aware of what was going on. She was in a stupor, her energy drained because of the pain and itching.

Luis and Marion paid them a visit just before the ambulance arrived. It took every ounce of willpower for Marion not to cry in front of Julie, as she bid her good-bye. She was extremely fond of this young girl, who had entered their lives less than a year ago, and who had captivated everyone with her sweetness. Luis handed Julie a letter from Paco explaining that his brother did not want to risk another confrontation with her mother and therefore could not say good-bye to her in person. It was with a heavy heart that Julie looked around the room for the last time before leaving for the airport. She had started this trip with such high hopes. And with each new success in the different countries they had performed in, the memory of her Hollywood experience had grown dimmer. The honor bestowed on her in Rio had been the crowning glory, and Julie had been eagerly looking forward to Buenos Aires, the "Paris" of South America. But now she knew it was not meant to be. She was leaving with not only her health in jeopardy, but her relationship with Paco irreparably damaged. Julie had no idea of what lay ahead of her, but as the ambulance door closed behind her, she was afraid that it was also closing on her career.

CHAPTER 22

Julie stared at the white walls in her hospital room. They were bare, except for a large painting of a bowl of fruit that looked as if it had been painted by a second grader. She had been in Doctors' Hospital for two weeks, ever since being brought there by ambulance upon her arrival in New York. Though still very weak, she was beginning to regain some of her strength, and the jaundice that had tormented her so was finally starting to fade. Julie was still being fed intravenously, and that, coupled with the endless blood tests, had caused havoc with the veins in her arms and legs. She was still too exhausted to read, so Rose had brought her radio from home, and that helped to ease her feeling of desolation.

Sam had been anxiously waiting for them at the airport terminal when they arrived. The painfully thin and haggard young girl who was carried from the plane did not look at all like the smiling and robust girl he had said good-bye to several weeks ago. In the first critical days of her confinement, Sam barely left Julie's side. It was only when he was thoroughly assured by the doctors that she was out of danger that he finally returned to work. As sick as she was, Julie hated being in the hospital, and the doctors were very evasive when she asked them how much longer she would have to be confined. The leading specialist in liver-related disorders, Dr. John Somach, who had been brought in for consultation by their family doctor, was very gentle, but frank.

"Julie, you've been a very sick girl. You developed serum hepatitis weeks ago, and by the time you came to us, your liver was dangerously enlarged. I don't want to scare you, but if it weren't for the fact that you are so young and healthy, you might have died."

Not scare me, Julie thought. *What could be worse than dying?*

Julie could see how relieved her mother was to be back home, but as cheerful as she pretended to be every time she visited the hospital, Julie could sense that something was wrong.

There was an obvious strain between her father and mother, and Julie couldn't understand why. They both spent hours at her bedside, but they spoke mostly to Julie and barely to each other. *Perhaps I'm imagining it,* Julie thought. But the feeling persisted. Her brother and his wife came by often, as did her aunts, who showed up with all kinds of food, none of which she could eat. Julie hadn't heard from Paco since she left and it pained her that during all this time he hadn't made any effort to contact her. His parting letter to her had been very brief.

"Julie, *mi preciosa,*" he wrote. "I'm sorry things turned out so badly. Your mother's vicious attack on me was totally unwarranted. I did nothing to hurt you. I only had your best interests at heart. You know how important you are to me, but I cannot continue working with you under these conditions. Think carefully about your future with me. I will see you when I return. *Con todo mi amor,* Paco."

His return, Julie thought as she reread his letter. *He should be coming home any day now. Will he call? I wonder.*

A week later Julie was well enough to sit up in bed and had started to eat small portions of food. One afternoon, as she was finishing lunch, her mother walked in. Julie knew instantly that something was wrong. It was obvious that her mother had been crying. As Rose neared the bed, trying bravely to smile, Julie asked her what was wrong.

"Nothing, baby," she said, kissing Julie's forehead. "I'm just having a bad day. I guess it's because I miss you so much. The apartment seems so empty without you."

"Mom, I'm lonesome too. I wish I could get out of here. But, that's not what's bothering you. Please, tell me the truth."

Rose turned her head away so that Julie wouldn't see her tears, but Julie knew her mother too well and was suddenly alarmed by her behavior.

"Please don't turn away. You've *got* to tell me what's upsetting you."

Suddenly, it was as if a dam had burst as Rose started to unleash all her pent-up emotions. With tears streaming down her cheeks, Rose poured her heart out to her daughter.

"Julie, I wanted to spare you this, but I can't keep it to myself any longer. Your father has been having an affair with another woman." Rose sank down on the bed and began to sob.

Julie was too stunned to move. *No,* she thought. *It's not possible; not my father. She must be mistaken. My father loves my mother. He wouldn't do a thing like that.*

"Mom, I don't believe it. Who told you this? They're lying—whoever they are."

Rose raised her head and looked at her daughter. "I wish it was a lie, but it was your father who told me."

Julie was too shocked to say anything. She just stared at her mother in disbelief as Rose continued. "Remember when your father took the trip to Florida? Well, he wasn't with one of the men from the office. He was with a woman."

Julie started to speak, but Rose stopped her. "Oh, Julie, it's all my fault. I should never have left him alone for so long. A man needs his wife near him, not shlepping all over the world. Oh, don't think I'm condoning his actions. When I first found out I wanted to kill him. But, then, I thought about it and I realized how much I still love him and need him. Oh Julie," she cried, pulling her daughter close to her, "he said it happened because he was lonely. He swears it's over now, and that he'll never see her again. Your father says he loves me and is begging me to forgive him. I don't know what to do."

How strange, Julie thought. *All of a sudden I feel like I'm the mother and she's the daughter.*

As Rose continued to cry softly, Julie tried to comfort her. "Mom, please try to compose yourself. You're going to make yourself sick carrying on like this."

Rose sat up and took a handkerchief out of her purse. Slowly, she began to wipe her eyes. "I'm sorry to burden you like this, *mamale,* especially when you're not well yet. But I'm too ashamed to tell anyone—even my sisters, and I guess I needed someone to talk to."

Julie stroked her mother's hair. "It's all right, Mom, I understand

and I'm glad you confided in me. I've suspected for weeks that some-thing was wrong."

Suddenly, Rose sat up and looked at her daughter. "Julie," Rose said nervously. "You must promise me you won't say anything about this to your father. It would kill him if he thought you knew. I don't know what he would do."

Julie had to think carefully before answering. Now that she knew the truth, how could she ever face her father again and not feel differ-ently about him? But she would have to try. She couldn't hurt her mother any more than she had already been hurt, even if it meant pretending that nothing had happened.

Embracing her mother tightly, she promised. "Don't worry, Mom. I will never say a word or do anything that would make Dad suspect I know. I swear it."

And Julie kept her word. Not once during her father's daily visits did she demonstrate all the pain and resentment that was churning inside of her. She reasoned to herself that if her mother could put the whole horrible episode behind her and forgive him, then Julie would try and do the same.

As Sam walked along the long hospital corridor on his way to Julie's room, his thoughts were not only on his daughter's illness but back in the apartment, with Rose. Shortly after their return from South America, when Sam could no longer bear the burden of his deception, he had confessed everything to Rose and had begged for her under-standing and forgiveness. At first, she had been too wounded to accept his explanation that his indiscretion with another woman had come to pass only because of his great loneliness. And rightly so. His behavior had been inexcusable. Rose was still a beautiful woman and Sam was certain other men found her attractive. But he never once doubted her complete fidelity. He knew that her devotion to him would be unwavering no matter how long they were separated. Sam had begged Rose to shield Julie from the truth. He couldn't bear to see the love and admiration that had always shone in his daughter's eyes turn to disappointment and, possibly, hate.

Quietly, Sam opened the door to Julie's room, fearful of waking her if she was asleep. As he tiptoed into the room, he saw that Julie was awake but lying very still with a faraway look on her face.

Tenderly, he leaned over and kissed her cheek. "Hi, sweetheart. How are you feeling today?"

Julie looked at her father with such sad eyes that Sam thought his heart would break.

"Better, Dad. I was just waiting for the nurse to come in with my dinner. Not that I feel much like eating. I'm so sick of this place."

Sam pulled up a chair close to the side of her bed and sat down. "Julie, dear, you have to eat so you can get your strength back. You've been a very sick girl. But the food can't be the only thing that's bothering you. You looked so unhappy just now when I walked in."

"You're right, Dad. It's not just the food. I'm tired of being sick. It's not fair that this had to happen just when I was doing so well in South America."

"Everything happens for the best, Julie. I'm sorry you got sick, sweetheart, but if it had to happen at least you got a chance to see what kind of man Paco Castell really is and I hope it opened your eyes. Baby, please be patient a little longer. Once Mom and I get you home, you'll forget all about hospitals and sickness and everything bad that's happened to you. In fact, when you're feeling up to it, we could all go on a little vacation."

Julie sighed and turned her head away. In the distance she could see the lights of the city's skyscrapers illuminating the horizon. How she longed to be out there, performing in some glamorous spot, instead of having to lie here in bed. Her father refused to understand that going home to the life she had led before meeting Paco seemed unbearable to her now. Too much had happened. It wasn't only her disillusionment with her father. It was much more. *Even if Paco never comes back into my life,* Julie thought, *how can I go back and live the way I did before I met him? I've come too far. And, what if Paco does come back and wants me to continue, I can't ask my mother to jeopardize her marriage again for my career. Even if she agreed, Paco would never accept it. He told me so in his letter.*

"Well, Julie," Sam asked, "you haven't answered me. How does a vacation in some warm climate sound to you?"

How about Florida? Julie was tempted to suggest. *You never took me and Mom before. Maybe now that you know the best spots you would show them to us?* But Julie said nothing. She had made a promise to her mother, and no matter how difficult it was going to be, she would keep it.

"Dad, why don't we wait until Dr. Somach discharges me before we make any plans. Right now all I want to do is get out of here."

Sam patted her hand and got up from his chair. "You're right, sweetheart. Plenty of time later to discuss this. I think I'd better go now. Mom has dinner waiting, and you know how she hates it when I'm late."

Sam leaned over to kiss her, but something in his daughter's expression, and the coolness he felt in her response, made him stop. Suddenly, he bent down and embraced her frail body and held her tightly. There were so many things he would have liked to have explained to his child, but he lacked the courage. Releasing her, he gently smoothed her hair back from her face and tried to console her.

"Julie, baby. Don't let all of this get you down. I know how you hate being sick, but you're a fighter, and you'll overcome this just as you did before when you were a little girl. Try and be brave. Mom and I will be back tomorrow."

Sam kissed Julie and left the room, anxious to get home and see Rose. *Oh, what a fool I've been*, he thought as he strode briskly toward the elevator. *I should have stood my ground and never have let them go out on the road with that bastard. He's to blame for all our troubles. None of this would have happened if only Rose and Julie had stayed home.* As Sam walked out of the hospital into the cool evening air, his hate for Paco was so overwhelming that had he come face-to-face with him at that moment, he felt he might have done something violent.

A few days later, just when Julie began to despair of ever hearing from Paco again, the door flew open and in he walked, smiling at her as if nothing had ever happened. With long quick strides, he approached the bed and reached down to embrace her.

"*Querida*," he said, studying her face for signs of her illness. "You are looking so much better than the last time I saw you. I've just returned home and rushed right over to see you. These past weeks I have been so worried about my little Julie. Are you feeling any better?"

Julie was so startled by his sudden appearance, she barely knew what to say. "Yes, Paco. I'm much better now. In fact the doctors think there's a possibility I may be discharged by the end of the week."

"Leave here at the end of the week? That's great news," Paco beamed. "Now, I have some good news to report. My divorce from Laura has just become final. At last I am a free man."

Julie looked at him in amazement. *If I live to be a hundred, I will never understand this man*, she thought. *I didn't hear from him for almost a month and the last time I saw him he and my mother were cursing each other. Now he waltzes in here and tells me that he's a free man, like nothing ever happened.*

"Well, Julie," Paco asked, tracing his finger along the curve of her soft cheek. "Don't you have anything to say?"

"Paco, I don't know what to say. You never even called me once during these past weeks and I've been so terribly sick."

Paco's expression turned contrite. "Julie, my beautiful one. How could I call you? Do you remember the circumstances under which you left? Your mother wounded me very deeply. I didn't want to call the hospital and have her throw that kind of abuse at me again."

Suddenly, he smiled benevolently at Julie. "But, I am a very forgiving person and I am prepared for your sake to make peace with her. After all, she may be my mother-in-law."

Julie gripped the sides of her bed in panic. "Paco, wait a minute. You're going too fast and not giving me a chance to think."

"What is there to think about? I'm crazy about you. You've known that all along. If you were a different kind of girl we could travel together and let our relationship develop slowly. But you won't even let me touch you. You refuse to permit yourself to experience the sexual fulfillment that every woman desires and needs. So, if I cannot have you any other way, I'm prepared to marry you."

Pausing, he leaned down over her and nestled his face in her hair. "If you become my wife," he murmured huskily, "I will show you what ecstasy really is. You will blossom into the woman you were meant to be. Oh, Julie, I've waited so long and I want you so much."

Julie tried to sort out in her mind what he was saying. His offer of marriage was hardly the kind of romantic proposal she had always dreamed about. *He wants me, he desires me, but does he love me? He's never once used that word. And, how do I feel about him? My father has never even let me date. What do I know about men, much less marriage? Do I care for him enough to estrange myself from my parents, because I'm certain that's what it would mean. And, am I ready for marriage?*

"Julie," Paco said, sitting up suddenly. "You haven't answered me."

"Oh, Paco, please don't rush me. I need more time."

"Well, there isn't too much time, Julie. I'm not only speaking about us personally, but also our future together professionally. I'm sure you understand that we cannot go back to where we were before. I will not travel with you and your mother. I want you, not only on the stage but in my bed. There is no other way, and you must decide."

Bending down again, he reached for her mouth, feeling her soft moist lips trembling under his pressure. Slowly, his tongue began to explore the inside of her mouth, at first gently, but as his passion heightened, then with more urgency. His breath began to come in short gasps as his mouth attempted to devour her lips. Julie, suddenly frightened by his passion, tried to pull away.

"Please, Paco," she murmured breathlessly. "Someone might come in."

"To hell with them," he said urgently, pulling her back into his embrace.

With all the strength she could muster, Julie pulled herself free. "No, Paco, please. You must go."

Paco got up and tried to regain his composure. He couldn't understand why, but she had the power to arouse him sexually more than any woman he had ever known. "Julie, I can't go on like this. You must speak to your parents and make a decision. My patience is at an end."

Turning to leave, he gave her his ultimatum. "I will call you tomorrow. I must have your answer by then."

"No, Paco," Julie said. "I can't discuss this with them while I'm still in the hospital. Wait until I get home and I have a chance to think about what you've told me. I promise to give you an answer soon."

Reluctantly, Paco agreed and left the room. As he walked down the hospital corridor on his way to the elevator, he barely missed bumping into Rose, who was standing near the nurses' station. Paco was deep in thought and would not have relished coming face-to-face with his "adversary." A year ago when his battles with Laura had reached a climax and he finally realized that divorce was inevitable, the idea of ever remarrying again would have been unthinkable. But when Julie came along everything changed. At first he had hoped that his infatuation with her would have resulted in just another affair, with no commitment on either side. But that notion had soon proved to be futile due to her parents' constant vigil and Julie's own restraint. As Paco pressed the elevator button, he heaved a great sigh. *Yes, my Julie,* he thought as he entered the crowded elevator. *You will surely say yes and somehow convince your parents. Now that you have experienced my world, it would be impossible for you to return to your former life. We both know that.*

Julie dropped her head back on the pillow, exhausted by her confrontation with Paco. So much had taken place since she had returned home. First, the news of her father's infidelity and now the sudden reappearance of Paco and his unexpected proposal. Her disillusionment with her beloved father weighed heavily on her, as did her frustration because she had vowed to keep it forever a secret. Now Paco had issued her an ultimatum, which would force her to choose between her career and marriage with Paco, or returning home to her parents and the restricted life she had lived before. She had reached a critical crossroads in her life. Her decision might affect her whole future.

CHAPTER 23

Rose stood in the middle of the living room, nervously wringing her hands, her face flushed with anger as she faced a frightened Julie. In contrast, Sam sat practically motionless in his favorite chair near the window. His expression was grim as he tried to digest the news he had just heard from his daughter.

"How dare you even mention that man's name to us," Rose screamed, "after what he's done to you? I can't believe you could stand there and tell us he wants to *marry you*. Well, young lady, let me tell you something. It'll be over my dead body."

Julie looked helplessly at her father, hoping he might be more reasonable, but that was not to be the case.

Solemnly, Sam said, "Julie, you know that I don't get hysterical like your mother, but I do agree with her completely. What you have asked us to consent to is out of the question. You are only a child, and even if you were older, I would never let you marry someone who has no morals and no conscience. Frankly, I'm surprised that you would ask, knowing what kind of man he is."

"Dad, he already explained why he couldn't interrupt the tour when I got hepatitis. The theaters were sold out for months. It would have been impossible for him to quit."

"I suppose forcing you to perform when you were jaundiced and in pain was not his fault either," Rose shouted at her. "And not going to the airport to make sure you were taken care of, or calling the hospital and offering to pay any of the bills were just further indications of what a devoted and caring man he is," Rose added sarcastically.

Julie sat there, powerless to stop the bitterness and anger that her announcement had triggered. She had been home from the hospital for three days, and although she looked fit enough, her weight was still below normal and she tired easily. Her doctors had told her that it would take a year of carefully watching her diet and being sure she got enough rest to achieve a complete recovery.

Attempting once more to plead her case, she turned to her mother. "Mom, you were with me on the tour. You saw my success. How can you ask me to give it all up? I'd have to go back to where I was before I met Paco. That would mean making the rounds again. Auditions and more auditions. With Paco I was already on my way to becoming a star."

"You can be a star without him," Rose answered bitterly.

"But how long would it take me and how could I be sure? You know how difficult it is to get a Broadway show. At each audition there are dozens of girls up for the same part."

Sam stood up suddenly and sat down beside his daughter. "Julie, forget about your career for a minute. We're talking about your life— your future. Do you understand what being a wife means? I seriously doubt it."

"Dad, all I know is that I want to be a part of Paco's world—the people I met and the acceptance I received were incredible. You weren't there, so you can't understand it. But I just *can't* give that up."

"Julie," her father asked her pensively. "Do you love this man?"

"Love," Rose said scornfully. "What does a sixteen-year-old know about love? How could she love a man like him? He's had two wives and God knows how many other women. Oh, God, how I hate him. He's ruined our lives."

Julie put her hands over her ears and implored her mother. "Mom, please don't scream. It doesn't help matters."

Sam looked at Julie and repeated his question. "Julie, do you love him?"

Julie searched her mind for an answer to her father's question. Since her mother's shocking disclosure of her father's indiscretion, her faith in him had been so shattered that she found it difficult to believe that true love really existed.

Realizing that her father expected a reply, Julie said, "Dad, I don't know what you mean by love. You've never permitted me to date, and though I've had a few innocent 'crushes' on different boys, you know better than anyone that there has never been anything serious. I feel that deep down inside of me Paco cares for me and would protect me."

"But what about you?" her father asked. "Do you care for him?"

Julie looked into her father's eyes and tried to answer his question honestly. "Dad, he's an exciting man. I feel 'alive' when I'm with him."

"But that's not a good enough reason for a woman to marry a man," Rose interrupted. "What about love and children? God forbid," she added, murmuring under her breath.

Julie blushed at her mother's question and turned away. She hadn't given any real thought to what marriage might entail. She preferred to think of Paco as someone with whom she shared many common inter-ests. He liked to travel. He was sophisticated and knowledgeable, not only about music, but about art as well. He spoke many languages and was known the world over. She respected and admired his achieve-ments. *Weren't those good enough reasons to marry?* she asked herself. There were even times, when he wasn't being too aggressive, that she felt herself responding to his embraces. Having no knowledge of what sex was really like, except for fragmentary conversations with the girls in her shows, she hoped that when the time was right she would be ready to assume the responsibilities of marriage. She really had no choice. If she had any doubts before, the last few days at home since leaving the hospital had thoroughly convinced her that living at home would be impossible.

"Julie," her mother said impatiently. "Did you hear what I said?"

"Yes, Mom, I did and I'd like to answer you. But I can't predict what will happen later. I just know that this is what I want to do."

Furiously, Rose turned on her heels and stormed out of the room. Sam paused a moment, shook his head sadly, and followed his wife into the bedroom.

Well, Julie thought with a sigh of relief. *At least they listened to what I had to say.* But she knew the battle was far from won. Her parents wouldn't capitulate that easily. This was the first time in her life that Julie had ever defied her parents and taken a stand, and it was a role she didn't take to easily. She hated to cause them unhappiness, and she still ached with compassion for her mother's predicament. But she desperately wanted to return to the band and begin making up for lost time.

The weeks that followed were filled with anguish for both Julie and her parents. After each unpleasant scene there were tears, recrimina' tions, and threats. Her parents warned her that if she didn't abandon the idea of marriage, they would personally confront Paco and warn him that she was still a minor to make sure he stayed away. Torn between Paco's ever-increasing pressure to give him an answer and her parents' unyielding position, Julie grew desperate. She knew Paco's patience was coming to an end. He was considering many different offers of engagements and there was the RKO movie that was still in the offing. It was now mid-April and he told her he planned to return to California by June. The tension at home became unbearable with her mother's constant screaming and her father's refusal to even discuss the situation. Julie longed to escape her parents' unending tirade against Paco, and her chance came one evening when her parents were out. Julie met Paco for an early dinner at the Stork Club, and as soon as they were seated, he told her of his plans.

"Julie, I have been giving our future considerable thought and have come up with a plan. We could be married here in New York sometime in May and then fill in a few engagements on our way back to the Coast. *Querida*, I know that doesn't sound too romantic, but we could take a honeymoon later—perhaps even go abroad. Would you like that, my darling?"

Julie was startled. *That's so soon,* she thought. *How can I possibly carry this off? He still refuses to accept the fact that my parents are bitterly opposed to a marriage.*

Paco moved closer to her and whispered tenderly into her ear."If what I said doesn't convince you how much I want you, then, maybe this will." Reaching into his pocket, Paco pulled out a black velvet box and placed it on the table in front of her. Julie stared at it, her heart beating wildly. Paco leaned back on the plush settee and smiled confidently as he waited to see her reaction. "Go ahead, my beautiful one. Open it."

Julie picked up the box and opened it slowly, savoring the moment. When she saw the contents, she couldn't conceal her delight. "Oh my God, Paco. It's so beautiful. I've never seen anything like it."

Julie was so overcome with excitement that she was totally unaware of the interested glances from the other patrons seated in the restaurant. Most of the people there had recognized Paco Castell instantly when

he walked in and were curious about the beautiful girl who accompanied him.

Her hands trembling, Julie removed the diamond ring that lay nestled
in the satin lining and looked at Paco in wonderment. "I can't believe
this is for me," she said, turning it around admiringly in the candlelight.
"I never expected anything like this."

"Try it on, Julie, and see if it fits," Paco said, fully aware of the
impact his gift had made.

Julie's slipped it on her finger and her eyes filled with tears of joy.
To her it seemed like the largest diamond in the world, although, in
fact, it was barely three carats and imperfect both in color and clarity.
But to this sixteen-year-old, it was as beautiful as any of the diamonds
that she and her mother had gazed at longingly in the windows of
Cartier or Van Cleef & Arpels. With grateful and adoring eyes, Julie
reached for Paco's hand and leaned over to kiss him gently on his
cheek.

"Oh, Paco, if only I could wear it. It's so beautiful I hate to take it
off."

"Why should you take it off? It's your engagement ring."

Julie swallowed hard, desperately seeking a way to tell him that the
problem with her parents had not yet been resolved. "Paco," Julie
said tentatively. "My parents still haven't given me their permission."
Hurriedly, she added, "You know I've been pleading with them for
weeks, but they think I'm too young to get married." She had purposely
ignored the rest of their objections, knowing how much that would
infuriate him.

"Why don't you let *me* talk to them? If they sincerely want your
happiness, they should welcome the chance for their daughter to marry
a man who would not only take care of her but also be in a position
to advance her career."

"No, Paco," Julie said quickly, fearing that any intervention by Paco
would only make matters worse. "Let me try again."

Looking down at the ring sparkling on her finger, she assured him
of something she still wasn't convinced she could accomplish. "I'm
sure that my parents want my happiness, and if you'll just be patient
a little longer, I think they will eventually consent."

The final confrontation between Julie and her parents took place a
week later. While placing some underwear in Julie's drawer, Rose
found the ring. Her volatile nature made her want to lash out immediately at Julie, but she decided to wait until Sam came home that

evening. After hurriedly filling Sam in with her discovery, Rose summoned Julie to their room.

"What does this ring mean, Julie? And don't give me any of your
stories."

Offended by her mother's accusation, Julie said, "Mom, you know
that I don't lie."

"Then why didn't you tell us about this ring, which, by the way, is
a piece of crap."

"I was afraid of what you and Dad would say."

"Julie," Rose yelled furiously, clutching her heart. "You are going
to put me in my grave. I can't take this anymore."

The tension and pressure that had been building for weeks had
finally taken their toll, and Julie started to cry uncontrollably. "I can't
take it anymore either. Please, please, I beg you. Let me go."

With both his wife and his daughter in a virtual state of collapse,
Sam decided to act.

"I'm sick and tired of all the misery your association with Paco has
caused us. You want to be happy. Well, your mother and I are entitled
to some happiness too. After all these weeks I can see that there's no
reasoning with you. You're still under age and legally I could stop you.
But I've decided against that. Therefore, after giving this considerable
thought, I have reached a decision. We will give you our consent to
marry on one condition."

Julie looked at her father with tear-streaked eyes. "What condition,
Dad?" she barely whispered.

Sam paused before answering. He was remembering his conversation
with Rose weeks ago when Julie had first mentioned marriage to Paco
and they had discussed their options. He had told her, "Rose, you
knew from the very beginning how opposed I've been to Julie's association with Paco Castell. Because you badgered me and, against my
better judgment, I allowed you both to go out on the road with a man
whom we have both come to know is no good. Because of that mistake,
we're now facing an even bigger problem. Despite everything we've
said, Julie thinks her life will be over if we don't give her our permission."

Rose had listened to Sam while feeling great remorse. "Sam, you're
absolutely right. A lot of what we're going through *is* my fault. I
encouraged her because I thought Paco could be a shortcut to success.
But I realize now that there will be a big price to pay."

"Rose, if we can't convince her to change her mind, then we must at least protect her interests and perhaps our own. Julie is too young and inexperienced to handle money, and that bastard not only knows that but will take advantage of that fact. We may eventually have to give our consent because we can't go on living this way. But if we do, then I want to make damn sure that no one gets ahold of her money. Right now she's not making that much. But if she becomes famous, who knows, there could be a great deal of money involved. We know Julie's too trusting to be allowed to handle her own finances. Therefore, I will have to do that for her."

Privately, Sam had reasoned to himself, *I've never been able to give Rose all the luxuries in life she's always dreamed of. Working for other people will never make me a rich man. But if Julie does succeed in a big way, maybe it will help to make our own lives a little easier.*

Now turning back to Julie, who was anxiously waiting for his answer, he said, "Julie, these are my conditions. If Paco is going to have the pleasure of having my beautiful daughter as his wife, then I insist that he sit down with me and discuss an appropriate financial arrangement."

His eyes as cold as steel, Sam began to outline his demands. "To begin with, you will not continue to work for him at the same salary that you have been receiving. That's out of the question. Furthermore, I expect to become your business manager and receive a commission. That man is robbing us of our daughter, and therefore I feel that we are at least entitled to be taken care of financially. This arrangement will also benefit you, as I will be protecting your money."

Julie stared at her father in amazement. She couldn't believe her ears. Though grateful that her ordeal was finally coming to an end, she was shocked that her future was being discussed as if her father were selling the car or some other material possession. She couldn't care less about money. She would be happy to give her parents anything they wanted. She would have done it anyway, even if her father hadn't demanded it. Julie loved her parents and wanted them to have all the luxuries that money could buy. She had always prayed that her career would enable her to provide them with the comforts she felt they deserved. Perhaps as Paco's wife, she would realize that dream.

CHAPTER
24

Julie, for God's sake, put a smile on your face. You look like you're going to a funeral instead of to your wedding."

Julie's sister-in-law, Marsha, had been trying in vain for the past hour to brighten Julie's mood and help her prepare for the wedding that was now only moments away. The fact that Rose had not participated in any of the arrangements, not even in the selection of the short white dress that Julie had chosen to wear, had put the burden of helping Julie totally on Marsha's shoulders. She didn't mind, but her advanced pregnancy prevented her from doing too much. The sight of Julie's large, sad eyes riveted on the door, waiting and hoping for her mother to come in, tore at Marsha's heart. Rose and Sam had reluctantly agreed to attend, but Rose had absolutely refused to help in any of the preparations. When her son and daughter-in-law urged her participation, her refusal was adamant.

"She's made her bed. Now, let her lie in it. Paco Castell calls all the shots, so he can take care of the wedding too. Dad and I promised her we would attend, but that's *all* we are going to do." And then Rose burst into tears.

"All those years," Rose wailed on, "watching my baby suffer during her illnesses—praying for her, nursing her, making sure that nobody harmed a hair on her head. And how does she thank me? By marrying a man old enough to be her father."

Marshall tried to calm his mother as best he could. Although it had been years since he had personally been subjected to one of Rose's outbursts, he could still remember how unintentionally cruel his mother could be when she was in pain. And he knew that his mother was feeling more pain now than at any other time in her life. He felt great compassion for her. His father, on the other hand, was handling the situation quite differently. Sam had barely spoken to Julie since his discussion with Paco. Paco had readily agreed to all of Sam's ultimatums, only too happy to now have a weapon to use against Julie's parents at the appropriate time.

Paco's suite at the Waldorf-Astoria, where the ceremony was to take place, was decorated with dozens of pale pink roses. Marion had taken care of the details at Julie's request when it appeared certain that Rose would not get involved. Only the immediate family would be present. That meant Rose and Sam, Marshall and his wife, and Paco's brother. The only outsider would be Marion, who had worked for Paco for twenty years and therefore qualified as family. Paco, with Marion's help, had arranged for a small reception to be held in the Empire Room right after the ceremony. The Empire Room was not being used just then as a dining and dancing facility because the Starlight Roof had just reopened for the season. In addition to a few old friends, Paco had invited his agents, lawyer, and business manager to the reception. Julie had hoped, in the absence of any of her friends, to have some band members present. But Paco refused, replying brusquely that they didn't belong there.

As Julie stared at herself in the mirror, she couldn't stop thinking about how differently she had fantasized her wedding. In her childhood dreams, she was wearing a long white gown with an enormous train and a beautiful veil with yards and yards of tulle. She had bridesmaids and a flower girl and everything was perfect. Her parents' pride was reflected in their faces as her father gave the bride away. The reality brought tears spilling down her creamy skin. Other than her parents and Marshall and his wife, none of the other family would be attending. Not her aunts and uncles and not even her grandparents. They had all spoken to her and sent their love, but none would agree to come because of her parents' opposition to the marriage. Julie could easily understand the absence of her Grandma Esther. Her health had been in a steady decline and she was now bedridden most of the time. But she had not deserted Julie. During Julie's last visit to her grandmother's apartment a week before the wedding, instead of an expected tongue lashing, her beloved grandmother took her in her arms and comforted her when Julie broke down and cried.

"*Sha, mama sheyner,* don't cry. Your mama and papa will forgive you. They love you and only want what's best for you."

"Oh, Grandma," Julie cried. "I don't want to hurt them. I don't know what to do. I just feel grown up and Daddy won't accept that. I want to make something of myself—be someone. Paco loves me and will take care of me. I know he's much older but I'm more grown up than people think."

As Julie poured her heart out to her sympathetic grandmother, expressing her hopes and frustrations, suddenly it seemed to Esther that it was not Julie speaking but her daughter Rose. Her mind flashed back to this same room so many years ago when a young and vibrant Rose, sitting in the very same chair, had voiced the same desires and ambition to "be somebody." *They are so alike,* Esther thought as she stroked her granddaughter's hair. *Fire and burning ambition.* But because she had been unable to achieve success in a career, Rose had settled for marriage and a home and children. *Julie wants more,* Esther thought sadly, *and she thinks this man can give it to her. I hope to God she's right.*

"*Veint nischt,* my child. Don't cry. You are a good child and you will always have my blessing. I will pray to God to look after you and guide you. There is only one thing I ask."

"What is that, Grandma?"

"Don't ever forget your religion and your commitment to God. Wherever you go through life and whatever you do, remember your heritage and be proud of it."

Resting her head on her grandmother's soft breast, Julie promised her, "I will never forget, Grandma. And, I swear I will make you proud of me."

All eyes were on the pale and delicate young girl who walked into the living room accompanied by her unsmiling father. If one didn't know better, they might have thought she was on her way to a high school dance, instead of her wedding. As she approached her beaming and excited groom, her hands, clutching a tiny bouquet of tea roses mixed with baby's breath, trembled. The judge who was to perform the brief ceremony stood in front of the marble fireplace that was draped in flowers. The late afternoon sun was filtered by the sheer curtains that framed the windows but still cast a golden glow on the bride as she repeated her vows. Later, Julie would have little recollec-tion of the ceremony. The tension that filled the room was felt by everyone, except perhaps Paco, who was overjoyed to have finally won his prize. Once the judge had pronounced them man and wife, Paco took his fragile and beautiful bride in his arms for a long and passionate kiss. Rose and Sam looked away, unable to witness Paco embracing their daughter. Luis immediately popped open the champagne that had been cooling in the ice bucket and raised his glass to propose a toast.

"To the bride and groom. A long and happy life together."

Everyone lifted their glasses except Rose and Sam, who stood there unsmiling. Marshall, aware of his parents' discomfort and his sister's strain, put his arms around Julie. "Well, old girl, welcome to the club. Marsha and I hope you will be happy."

"Thank you, Marshall," she whispered to her brother.

When the tiny wedding party entered the Empire Room, they were greeted by violins playing Paco's theme song. Julie smiled at Paco, sud-denly encouraged that her wedding might be festive after all. Still clutch-ing her bouquet, she accompanied Paco as he started to greet the assorted guests. Before coming downstairs, Marsha had helped her remove the delicate lace mantilla and beautiful Spanish comb that Julie wore during the ceremony. Her long red hair now flowed gracefully on her shoulders and framed her youthful face. The lace bodice of her ballerina-length dress showed off her tiny waist and accentuated her rounded and firm breasts. Her only jewelry, besides her gold wedding band, were pearl earrings that Marion had lent her and her diamond engagement ring. Several tables had been set up around the dance floor, and after being congratulated by Paco's business associates and their wives, Julie took her place next to Paco at the bridal table. Her father and mother were already seated, and as Julie sat down she could sense their desire to leave as quickly as possible. Julie looked at her mother hoping for a word or a gesture that would make Julie feel less guilty. But it was not to be.

"Mom," Julie said as Paco turned to his brother and began talking. "You look absolutely beautiful. I've never seen that dress before. Is it new?"

"No, Julie. I wore it to your opening in Chicago. Don't you remem-ber?"

"Oh, yes, I forgot. But you look even better in it now."

"Well, it's because I'm so happy," Rose answered sarcastically. "It's exactly the kind of wedding day I've always dreamed about for my only daughter."

Julie looked away, fighting back the tears that seemed ready to fill her eyes at any moment. *It's no use,* she thought. *I've made them miserable and they'll never forgive me.*

While dinner was being served, Julie turned her attention back to Paco, who had been discussing their travel plans with Luis. She caught the tail end of their conversation.

"Make sure our bags are picked up no later than six P.M. tomorrow. I want to have a run-through with the orchestra when we arrive in New Orleans tomorrow night."

Julie tugged at Paco's arm. "Paco," she asked. "I thought we weren't leaving until Monday?"

Putting his arm around her shoulders, he whispered into her ear, "We must leave tomorrow evening, *mi querida.* Not too much time for a honeymoon, but we will make up for it." Breathing heavily against her skin, he added, "We have tonight and part of tomorrow. The suite is ready, your clothes are already there, and I have champagne waiting for us."

After dinner a large wedding cake was rolled out, and Julie and Paco rose to cut the first slice. Raising his glass, Paco made a toast to his bride and guests.

"First, I want to toast my beautiful wife. *La mujer más guapa del mundo.* Then, we would like to thank all our friends and family for being here."

Paco took another sip of wine and looked at his guests. "Now, I know you will understand if we leave early. My beautiful bride is tired and we must travel tomorrow."

Reaching down, Paco took Julie's arm and lifted her to her feet. Julie walked around the table and, one by one, kissed everyone good-bye. When she reached her parents she thought her knees would give way. As much as she had wanted her freedom to pursue her own destiny, now that she had it, she was frightened. She wanted to feel her parents' arms around her and to know that she had their love and approval. Suddenly she wanted to go home and be their little girl again. But because of her own doing, that chapter of her life was over. She would always be their daughter, but she would never again be their little girl. Despite their cool response, she kissed them on the cheek, and hugged them one final time, and with a pain that reached down to the very core of her soul, she left the room to begin her new life.

CHAPTER
25

Julie lingered as long as she could in the bathroom of the luxurious apartment that was now her home. She could hear Paco moving around in the bedroom and the unmistakable sound of champagne being turned and chilled in the ice bucket. Julie gazed thoughtfully at her reflection in the mirror. She had washed her face clean of the minimal makeup she had worn to her wedding, and her long hair gleamed from the vigorous brushing it had just received. Julie had donned a long ivory silk nightgown, a gift from Paco, that was by far the most expensive and sexiest nightgown she had ever worn. It clung to her sensuously, accentuating every curve of her rounded body. On a hook behind the door hung the flimsy lace peignoir that accompanied the gown.

"Julie, *mi amor*. Are you coming out?" Paco called. "The champagne is ready and I have some caviar."

Julie's hands were clammy as she carefully removed the negligee and slipped it over her gown. *Oh God*, she thought. *I can't delay this any longer. I have to go out no matter how nervous and scared I feel.*

Opening the door, Julie walked hesitatingly into the room. Paco, who was bending over, pouring some champagne into a glass, sensed her presence and stood up. When he saw Julie standing there, bathed in the soft glow of lamplight that made her negligee even more transparent, he gasped at her beauty.

"*Dios mio*," he murmured huskily, his eyes devouring her body. "You are too beautiful to be real."

It took only a moment for him to reach her and pull her forcefully into his arms. When he felt the warmth of her body, which trembled under his touch, his passion rose, inflamed by his desire to possess her. Quickly his mouth found hers while his hands frantically sought to remove her clothes. The urgency of his kisses and the hardness she felt as he pressed his body against her frightened Julie. She tried to push him away gently so that she could catch her breath, but Paco was too strong and unyielding. Frantic now to have her, he practically dragged her to the bed, and in the struggle, her negligee dropped to the floor. Pressing her down on the smooth softness of the comforter, Paco paused only long enough to throw off his silk robe and hurriedly tear off his pajamas. Embarrassed by his nakedness, Julie averted her eyes as he lowered his powerful body over her and began to lunge at her with tremendous force.

"*Ay, mi amor*," he gasped. "You have made me a wild man. I have never seen anything as beautiful as your body."

Rubbing her supple breasts with his hands he groaned, "Take that damn nightgown off. I want to touch your skin."

Julie looked at him with startled eyes. She hadn't expected him to be so violent. Paco knew she was a virgin, and she had hoped that he would be gentle and understanding. Aroused by his raging desire, Paco suddenly decided he could no longer wait. With one powerful hand he ripped at the silk that separated his body from hers, and as the material gave way, Paco lunged for her once again. Julie felt nothing but panic as this wild stranger rubbed his body up and down over the entire length of her body. His passion had reached a frenzy, and as he moaned he called her name over and over again. Suddenly, with one final spasm and a cry of relief, it was all over, and Paco dropped down beside her on the bed, totally spent. Julie could feel something wet and sticky on her stomach but she was afraid to move. With one hand she reached for the remnants of her nightgown and tried to cover herself. Paco lay there, his face flushed, with beads of perspiration dropping from his now satiated body. Reaching for her hand that lay limply on the coverlet, Paco apologized.

"*Perdoname, querida*, I couldn't wait. You excited me so, I had to come. Do you forgive me?"

Julie didn't answer. What could she say? *Is that what making love is all about? Do all men act like that? What am I supposed to feel?* she wondered silently. As innocent as she was, she still knew enough about sex from speaking to other girls to realize that Paco had never penetrated her and yet he had reached his own sexual climax. Julie closed her eyes, hoping to block out what had just happened. She had never envisioned her wedding night like this—so totally devoid of tenderness and loving endearments.

Paco stood up and went into the bathroom. Julie could hear the water running. Minutes later he came back into the room, and suddenly she could feel her body being gently rubbed with a washcloth.

"Oh, my beautiful little Julie. What a mess I have made. Let Paco clean you up."

Julie kept her eyes tightly closed and let Paco wash her. After he had dried her body, he slipped on his robe and went over to the bucket where the champagne sat, ready to be poured. While his back was turned, Julie seized the opportunity to grab her negligee, which lay on the floor, and covering herself as best she could, she quickly ran into the bathroom. Gazing at herself in the mirror, her reflection revealed someone who seemed like a stranger. Julie stared at her disheveled hair and flushed face and she could already see red marks on her body— evidence of where Paco's strong hands had touched her. Draping herself in a large bath towel, she opened the door and walked hesitatingly back into the bedroom.

Paco was sitting on the bed, propped up against the pillows and sipping champagne. Smiling at her, he patted the bed and called to her.

"*Querida*, come and have some champagne and caviar."

Instead, Julie opened the closet and began to rummage around, searching for a nightgown and a heavy robe. Once she found them she went into the bathroom to change, and when she emerged, she went over to the opposite side of the bed from where Paco was sitting.

"Julie," Paco said, placing a plate near her. "Here is some caviar. It is delicious. I will pour you some champagne."

"No thanks, Paco. I'm not hungry. In fact, I'm rather tired. It's been a long day."

Taking off her robe, she slipped into bed. Paco continued to sip his champagne slowly, and when he finished, he removed the plate and turned out the light. As he got into bed beside her, he reached out to touch her, and finding her body covered, he said impatiently, "Julie, for God's sake, take off that ugly nightgown. You are not a schoolgirl anymore. You're my wife. I don't want you to wear anything to bed."

Nervously, Julie removed her nightgown and pulled the sheets up tightly under her chin. She lay there without moving, but her heart was beating wildly. *Please God,* she prayed silently. *Let Paco fall asleep. I don't want him to touch me again tonight.* As if in answer to her prayers, Paco leaned over and kissed her cheek as he tried to stifle a yawn.

"*Querida,* I want to make love to you again, but the champagne has suddenly made me very sleepy. You go to sleep now and tomorrow morning your Paco will awaken you with his kisses."

Gratefully, Julie returned his light kiss, turned onto her side, and curled her body into a tight ball. The large tears that had been hovering in her eyes dropped down on her outstretched arm. *Is this what the girls in school giggled about and couldn't wait to experience?* Julie thought. *It can't be. There's got to be something more.* Instead of the gentleness and love she had been expecting, and what she had been promised, she had experienced nothing more than a few minutes of lust by a man who could obviously satisfy himself by just touching her. *Oh God,* she thought, biting her lips to keep from crying out. *What have I done?*

PART
II

CHAPTER 26

Steve Burton glanced at his watch impatiently and frowned when he saw the time. *Dammit,* he thought. *They should have been here by now.* Steve knew the reason his parents were late—his mother. Sylvia Burton had been fighting his marriage ever since Steve had announced his intention of marrying Sharon Davis immediately after his graduation from law school. That news had dealt his mother a blow that she had not expected. At least not so soon. She and her husband, Louis, had scrimped and saved so that their only child could have a decent education, and now, when his future looked so promising, he was taking on the burden of a wife.

To make matters worse, he had chosen a girl they felt was totally unsuitable for their son. There was nothing about Sharon that Sylvia liked. In the few times that they had been in her company, they found her to be cold and very manipulative. Not that Steve couldn't take care of himself. He was not only intelligent but also totally in charge of his life and had been since a very early age. He knew what he wanted ever since he was a boy, and once he charted his course, he always accomplished everything he set out to do. But Steve had changed ever since he started seeing Sharon on a regular basis. She was very strong willed, and his parents feared that his marriage to her would create a breach in their relationship with their son.

Steve decided he would wait another fifteen minutes, and if his parents didn't show, he would proceed without them. Although he knew of his mother's antagonism for Sharon, he was determined not to let her dominate his life. He had to admit, though, that there were times when Sharon would say and do things that made him wonder if they were really suitable for each other. But he had committed himself, and he was not going to back out now.

Sharon was a pretty girl and extremely bright. She came from a good family who dearly loved their daughter but didn't completely understand her. Steve enjoyed a better relationship with her parents than Sharon, who, at times, was barely civil to them. He first became attracted to Sharon after meeting her at a party on a weekend visit home from Cambridge. Unlike most of the young girls he had dated, Sharon seemed more mature and settled, and they soon found that they shared many of the same interests.

Steve had always enjoyed great success with women and, although not conceited, was well aware of his attractiveness to the opposite sex. His handsome, rugged face atop a lean six-foot frame was well developed from years of intense physical activity. He had always enjoyed boxing and baseball and, before entering law school, had even toyed briefly with the idea of pursuing a career in professional baseball. But his ambition for a political career convinced him to abandon those thoughts and to continue on with his education. In Steve's final year at Harvard Law School, besides maintaining his position in the top ten percent of his class, he also served as editor of the *Harvard Law School Record* and had so greatly impressed his highly esteemed professor of criminal law, Sheldon Gluck, that the professor wrote a letter to the prominent New York jurist Samuel Lebowitz, urging him to help Steve launch his career after he graduated. Sharon and Steve soon began to see each other on a steady basis, and gradually Sharon replaced all the other girls in his life. She had a good position as a secretary at a New York advertising agency, but early in their relationship had made it very clear that she had no ambitions for a career. All she wanted was to marry and have a family, and this appealed to Steve. Their steady dating soon turned into a serious commitment, which did not please his parents, especially his mother. Sylvia Burton sensed in Sharon a steely determination to marry Steve, and she wasn't at all convinced that it was purely for love. In fact, knowing of Sharon's strained relationship with her parents, she seriously doubted whether Sharon was even capable of any strong emotion. Although Sharon tried her best to convey the feeling that she was deeply in love with Steve, Sylvia Burton feared that something was missing and that her son might eventually be hurt. The more his mother fought the impending marriage, the more determined Steve became that his will, and not his mother's, would prevail. So, his decision firmly set, Steve pursued his plans to marry Sharon with or without his parents' blessing.

Leaving the door to his room at the Waldorf-Astoria slightly ajar, Steve walked down the hall to see how Sharon was progressing in her preparations for the ceremony. Just then, a beautiful, young, redheaded girl walked toward him followed by a porter laden with baggage. She smiled. As he caught her eye, Steve smiled back and, his green eyes twinkling, said, "Looks like you're going on a long trip."

The girl blushed and answered, "As a matter of fact, I am. I'm going on my honeymoon."

Honeymoon, Steve thought in amazement. *She looks like she's barely out of grade school!* "Well, good luck," he said as he continued down the hall. When he reached Sharon's room he knocked gently on the door.

"Honey, how are you doing?"

"Steve, I'm almost ready but don't come in. It's bad luck."

"All right, darling, but try to hurry. I'll be waiting for you downstairs in the Empire Room. The rabbi is already there."

"Please, give me another ten minutes, Steve," Sharon answered. "You know I hate to be rushed."

Steve turned and walked back to his own room to see if he had forgotten anything. As he approached, he could hear his mother's voice coming from inside.

"Louis, I wish you hadn't forced me to come. I have nothing to say to that girl, and Steve knows it. She's never made any attempt to become my friend. She got what she wanted—my son. Why should I pretend something I don't feel?"

"You have to, Sylvia, if you want to make your son happy. He loves her. That should be enough for you."

Pretending he hadn't overheard this exchange, Steve entered the room and greeted his parents. "Mom, Dad, I'm glad you're here. It was getting late and I was worried."

Sylvia walked over to her son and embraced him, love shining in her eyes. "Of course we're here. Where else would I be when my only child is getting married?"

Relieved, Steve kissed his petite, prematurely gray mother and gave her a hug. Then, glancing at his watch, he said, "We'd better go. The guests have been there for quite a while. Sharon will be down shortly."

Steve and his parents made their way to the Empire Room, where the ceremony and reception were to take place. When they reached the entrance Steve excused himself and asked his parents to go on in and take their places.

"I'll join you in a minute. I want to see a friend of mine first."

Freddie Barnett was standing by the huge bronze doors leading to the entrance of the Empire Room, smoking a cigarette. Steve had met him through one of his classmates, and they had quickly become friends. Steve was delighted that Freddie, who traveled a great deal, had been free to accept the invitation to the wedding.

Joining his friend at the door, they shook hands and Steve asked him, "Freddie, how come you're not seated? We're just about to start."

"I was just about to go in. I've been here for quite a while. As a matter of fact, I should have stayed at the hotel overnight. I attended another wedding here last night. A client of mine got married—again."

"Oh, really," Steve asked curiously. "Who?"

"Paco Castell."

"The bandleader? Jesus, how many times has that guy been married?"

Freddie smiled. "Oh, three or four. Who knows? But this one is the youngest and certainly the most beautiful."

"How young?" Steve asked.

"Sixteen."

"Sixteen? She's just a kid. Why would a girl that young marry a man so much older? She must be either a nut or a bimbo."

"She's hardly a bimbo, Steve. Actually she's a very sweet and innocent kid. But then I'm not sure why anyone gets married."

Patting Steve's shoulder, Freddie smiled broadly and walked into the Empire Room to take his place among the guests.

Steve looked around nervously, and realizing that the time had come, he took a deep breath and followed his friend into the room to take his place under the *chuppa* to await the arrival of his future bride.

CHAPTER
27

Julie, wake up. The seat belt sign has just been turned on. We will be landing in Los Angeles very shortly."

Julie opened her eyes and saw Paco gathering up his papers. Straightening the skirt of her beige wool suit, she fastened her seat belt and gazed out the window. Paco assumed she had been sleeping, but Julie had been thinking back to her last trip to California and how different everything had been then. She kept remembering how excited she and her mother had been, wearing their beautiful corsages, and how filled with hope for her future in movies. *Little did we dream that in less than a year I would be returning here as a married woman. Married woman* . . . Julie looked at the wedding band on her finger and slowly turned it around, as if to confirm the fact that she was truly married. She still couldn't get used to the idea. They had been so busy and had traveled so much since leaving New York two months before that Julie had never gotten the chance to feel like a bride. Their daily routine was practically the same as it had been when she was accompanied by her mother. Except that strangers now addressed her as Mrs. Castell and she was accorded a new respect as the wife of a famous bandleader. And she now shared a bed with Paco. Each night after the show was over and they had returned to their suite, Paco's need to make love to her was so great he barely gave her a chance to undress. *If only he would caress me gently and try to arouse me so that I too could feel something,* she thought. But that was not the case. All night long on the bandstand, he would whisper promises of bliss. But the moment the door closed behind them he would undress quickly, and before she could remove her clothing and put on her robe, he would stop her. He told her he preferred to undress her slowly so he could savor the beauty of her body. Bit by bit he would remove her gown, her stockings, all her undergarments, until finally, when he could not bear it any longer, he would fall on top of her in an orgasmic frenzy that always left her unaroused and unfulfilled. This scene would repeat itself night after night, and each time Paco would assure her that the next time their lovemaking would be different. But it never was. Occasionally, Paco would try to explain.

"Julie, my love. I don't know what's wrong with me. It has never been like this with any other woman, and I have had many," he boasted. "Maybe it's because I waited so long for you, and now that you are mine, you excite me too much. You see my darling," he laughed, "you are too beautiful for your own good. But I promise you that once we reach Los Angeles our real honeymoon will begin and I will teach you what lovemaking is all about."

Julie wondered if what Paco promised her would ever come to pass. It bothered her that he was only interested in his own gratification, and she instinctually knew that it wasn't normal. Not having anyone to discuss this with, neither her mother nor a close girlfriend, Julie had no choice but to sadly accept the life she had chosen for herself.

Suddenly, her thoughts were interrupted as she felt the wheels of the plane touch the ground and eventually roll to a stop. When the stewardess announced that it was time to deplane, Julie gathered up her things as Paco closed his briefcase. As he took her arm and led her down the aisle toward the exit, Julie could see that he was very excited.

Squeezing her arm with pleasure, he told her, "Julie, I promised you we would be coming home to California, and here we are. Wait until you see my beautiful home. That bitch Laura thought that she'd wind up with it in the divorce settlement, but she was mistaken. Now it will be the home of my beautiful bride."

Paco had not exaggerated in his description of the beautiful house that was surrounded by magnificent trees in the best part of Bel Air.

It was much more than Julie had expected. There was the obligatory swimming pool and a championship-size tennis court with a viewing pavilion almost as large as her former apartment. The master bedroom was decorated in soft shades of peach with delicate accents of the palest green. The French doors that filled one entire wall overlooked private gardens bordered in roses of every color. Adjacent to the bedroom were two large dressing rooms and baths, each decorated in a different color. When Julie opened the mirrored doors to her suite, she couldn't believe what was behind them. There were shelves of every size lined in fabric the same shade of peach as the bedroom, and racks that nearly reached the ceiling that could hold at least a hundred pairs of shoes. There was space especially constructed for evening gowns, dresses, suits, and trousers. *In fact,* Julie thought as she inspected everything, *I barely have enough clothes to fill even one side of this closet.*

The marble bathroom with its enormous tub and separate shower was magnificent. The dressing table with its deep drawers was just perfect to accommodate creams and lotions. *What exquisite taste Laura had,* Julie thought as she looked at all the detail and care that had gone into making this a woman's dream. *No wonder she didn't want to give it up.* The rest of the house was equally impressive. Paco took her from room to room, describing each piece of antique furniture and painting with the pride usually exhibited by a parent showing off his children. Inga and Peter, a Swedish couple, ran the house to perfection. Besides cooking and cleaning, their duties included caring for Paco's and Julie's clothes. Julie had never had servants before, and she was too shy and inexperienced to know how to direct them. But they were so well trained that they were able to anticipate their employer's every need, and Julie liked them immediately. Julie longed to call her parents in New York so that she could describe the splendor she was living in, but, because of the bitter feelings she knew they still harbored, she decided to wait awhile. Instead, she would write and send them pictures of the house and grounds, hoping to impress them.

As the weeks passed, Julie slowly started to adjust to her new life and new home. Almost a month had gone by since their arrival in California, and Julie grew more surprised each day that Paco hadn't mentioned future bookings, since he hated to remain idle for long. He had given the band a short vacation so that they could spend time with their families. His own energies were now totally focused on getting a commitment from RKO. Almost every day Julie would hear him berating his agents for not coming up with a film. According to them, the problem rested with the studio heads, who were cutting back on the production of musicals because they were too costly to make. Julie still harbored her own fears that she would be excluded from any motion pictures that Paco would make because of the Hughes fiasco.

After six weeks, Paco decided to take matters into his own hands and throw the "party of all parties" to make Hollywood aware that Paco Castell was back in town. Before speaking to his press agent, Warren Cowan, who would handle the star-studded guest list, Paco compiled his own list of every studio head and executive who could be important in reestablishing him in the movie industry. Excited by his plans for this gala party, Paco took Julie aside when she asked him if she could help.

"*Querida,* you do not have to do anything. Warren will prepare a guest list of all my friends at MGM and the other studios. Romanoff's, one of the best restaurants in Beverly Hills, is going to cater the affair, and I personally will arrange the decorations." Julie listened attentively to Paco's plans, thrilled at the prospect of meeting so many famous people. But she was slightly disappointed that no one asked her opinion about anything. She knew that she lacked experience as a hostess, but she felt she had creative ideas about decorating and would have loved to have been given an opportunity to express them. Julie wondered if she would ever be permitted to assume her role as mistress of the house. Paco insisted on treating her like a child telling her that all she was required to do was look gorgeous.

Paco even urged her to go out and buy the sexiest dress she could find. "But not too expensive," he warned. "I hate extravagance. Besides, with your figure you could wear anything and it would look like a million dollars. I want to knock them on their asses when they see what Paco has married, and I guarantee you that when word gets around about this party, people will be fighting to be invited. With all that publicity, the studio will be eating out of my hand."

After weeks of preparation, the night of the party finally arrived. Julie was very nervous and kept fussing with her hair, frustrated that tonight of all nights it refused to behave. Downstairs, the caterers were putting the finishing touches to the tables in preparation for the famous guests who would be arriving shortly. *We're lucky the weather is great,* Julie thought as a warm breeze drifted through the open window in her dressing room. Paco had been concerned that the evening might be cool, even though it was July. "California is unpredictable," he cautioned her when she consulted him about what she should wear over her new gown. But they were experiencing what the native Californians called a Santa Ana, and their guests would be comfortable on the huge terrace in back of the house, where dinner was to be served.

Picking up her comb once again, Julie decided to sweep most of her luxurious hair over to one side and secure it with a large white flower covered in tiny white sequins. It would match her new gown, which was still hanging in her closet. She had found it on sale at I. Magnin, one of the best stores in Beverly Hills, and had fallen in love with it the minute she tried it on. The white silk jersey gown complemented her golden skin and caressed her figure in just the right places without being vulgar. The grecian design left one shoulder bare and the soft folds of fabric, held together by a tiny rhinestone clasp, draped beauti-fully down over her bodice and fell gracefully to the floor. Just as Julie was satisfied that she had secured the flower firmly in her hair, she heard Paco's voice.

"Mi preciosa, are you almost ready?"

Paco entered her dressing room, and when he saw Julie wearing only her panties, he stopped.

Julie instantly recognized the look in his eyes and hastened to cover herself, but it was too late. Paco, who was all dressed except for his trousers, pulled at the belt of his silk robe as he reached for Julie.

"Dios mio," he muttered to himself, as he stood there pressing his body tightly against her, breathing in her fragrance. "You look and smell like a rare and exquisite flower."

Gently, at first, he kissed her sensuous lips, and then, feeling the softness of her mouth, his kisses became more demanding.

"Please, Paco," Julie pleaded, while trying to extricate herself from his embrace. "You're ruining my makeup and it's taken me an hour to fix my hair. Our guests will be here soon."

"To hell with them," Paco said, pulling her down on the carpeted floor. "They'll wait. This won't."

When Paco finally went back into his own dressing room, Julie sat down at her makeup table and tried to repair the damage. As she once again pinned the flower into her hair, Julie was troubled. So far, the sexual part of her marriage had not been what she had anticipated, and her frustration was growing. She had expected that a man of Paco's great experience would have been a patient and tender lover. Instead, his lust made her feel she was only an object for his own gratification. *Maybe it's my fault,* she thought. *If only there was someone I could confide in.*

As the rooms started to fill with famous people, Julie clung tightly to Paco's arm for security. After introducing her proudly to Robert Taylor and Esther Williams, who were there with their respective spouses, Paco turned to greet other friends, patting a short gray-haired man on the shoulder and calling him L.B. Julie found herself being introduced to the famous head of Metro-Goldwyn-Mayer, Louis B. Mayer. One by one they all came—Errol Flynn, Tyrone Power, Bogart and Bacall—all glamorously attired. Julie didn't know who to look at first. Lana Turner, wearing a silver evening dress, arrived with her date, a handsome dark-haired actor, and Clark Gable, one of Julie's idols, had a beautiful blond in tow. It was like a dream, and Julie just hoped she wouldn't wake up and find herself back in the chorus, thumbing through a movie magazine. Paco looked very dashing in his tuxedo as he drifted through the throngs of assembled friends and associates. He was in a very good mood, obviously happy to be back again in his beautiful home with a young and gorgeous new wife who was attracting admiring glances from both men and women alike. A group of mariachis were playing familiar Mexican songs outside on the terrace, where Rita Hayworth, resplendent in a pale green gown, was dancing with a handsome man who seemed very taken with her.

Julie couldn't take her eyes off her. Rita Hayworth was the embodiment of everything that Julie admired and hoped to achieve. As the evening wore on and dinner was finally served, Julie was thrilled that she was to be seated next to Cary Grant. Not only was he one of the best-looking men she had ever seen, but, as she was soon to discover, one of the kindest. Sensing her nervousness, he immediately put her at ease.

"My dear," he said in his famous British accent, "I've been very eager to meet you. All the men this evening have been ogling you, and the ladies are quite frantic to find out your age."

Smiling his boyish smile, that Julie had seen so many times on the screen, he leaned back in his chair and studied her. "I would guess that you can't be more than eighteen. Am I right?"

Julie smiled back at him, her shyness momentarily gone because of his friendly manner. "I'm trying to look older so that I can get a job in films but, actually, I'm only sixteen."

Grant let out a whoop of delight that caused the other people at the table to look in his direction.

"Sixteen," he said, lowering his voice so as not to violate her confidence. "That Spaniard you married keeps finding girls younger and younger, and in your case, more beautiful."

Julie blushed, thrilled that he found her so attractive. Smiling impishly at him, she said, "Oh, Mr. Grant, Paco didn't marry me for my looks. He admired my mind."

This time Cary Grant really started to laugh and, squeezing her hand, told her, "You're not only beautiful, but funny and smart—all the ingredients needed to take you to the top in this town. And that's where you're headed, my girl."

After dinner, instead of leaving early, as Paco's press agent told her people in the industry usually do, most of the couples got up to dance to a Latin band that Paco had put together for the party. Julie left her table to join Paco, who was seated at another table engaged in a deep conversation with his agent and another man. She had gone only a few steps when she was stopped by a very tall, gray-haired young man, who she recognized instantly.

"Excuse me, Mrs. Castell. My name is Jeff Chandler and I was wondering if you would care to dance with me? I was watching you and Paco on the dance floor before dinner and I think that you could make even a clumsy guy like me look good."

Julie smiled up at him. He wasn't good looking in the conventional sense, but up close his virility was overwhelming. But the most compelling thing about him was his voice. It was not only deep and resonant, but terribly sensual. Realizing she was staring, Julie hastened to say, "I'd love to dance with you, Mr. Chandler, but please call me Julie."

The actor politely took Julie's arm, and together they made their way to the crowded dance floor. After a few tentative steps, Jeff relaxed and smoothly glided Julie around the floor in a slow rhumba. She was enjoying herself enormously. Her charming partner confided that he loved to dance but that his wife preferred watching from the sidelines. When the number was over he led her off the floor and told her how much he enjoyed dancing with her. "If I don't get a chance to see Paco, please thank him for lending me his beautiful wife, and thank you, Julie, for a wonderful evening."

As soon as he left, Julie went back to Paco's table, but he was gone. Before she could seek him out, a familiar face appeared at her side sporting the famous grin that had made so many female hearts flutter.

"Julie, my dear," he said, giving her a kiss on the cheek. "It's so good to see you again. I heard that you took ill after we saw you at the Doderos in Montevideo."

Julie smiled at him, happy that he remembered her. "Oh, Mr. Cooper."

"Gary," he corrected.

"Gary," she said, smiling at him. "It's true, I was very sick for a while, but I'm much better now. I'm so happy to see you again."

"I'm delighted, too. Oh, by the way, I hear congratulations are in order. Paco is a very lucky man. Where is he, by the way? I'd like to thank him for a great party."

"I was just about to look for him myself. The last time I saw him he was talking to some men."

"Oh, yes. I saw them out on the terrace. He was talking to Charlie Feldman, honey, a very important agent in this town. Well, if I don't catch up with him, please thank him for me."

Giving her a warm hug, the lanky actor took off in the direction of the bar, and Julie turned her attention once again to finding Paco. He had insisted they sit at separate tables during dinner, and though Julie had no idea of the time, she guessed it was getting pretty late. Finally as the crowd started to thin out, except for a few stragglers still lingering at the bar, Julie caught a glimpse of Paco standing at the other end of the living room. She quickly made her way to his side, intending to thank him for making her so happy with this wonderful party. Everyone she had met had been so kind that they had helped to ease some of the anxiety she had experienced earlier. As she approached Paco she could see that something was wrong. Gone was his earlier look of happiness and excitement. His blue eyes had narrowed into angry slits and his face was flushed. When she reached him she gently put her hand on his arm and asked him, "Paco, where have you been? I've been looking for you. Most of the guests have gone."

Throwing off her hand roughly, he turned on her with a fury that made Julie's heart race. "You couldn't have been looking very hard, my dear. But, maybe that's because you were too busy dancing cheek to cheek with that two-bit actor. Don't you think I saw the two of you?"

"Paco," Julie gasped, shocked at his tone. "We weren't dancing cheek to cheek. He told me he knows you and he was very polite. In fact, you must know that his wife was at the party. He wanted to thank you for letting me dance with him."

Paco grabbed Julie's wrist so hard she almost cried out in pain.

"Listen to me, Julie, and don't ever forget what I'm going to tell you. I am a Latin and I do not like my wife dancing with other men unless they have my permission."

Gripping her to him even harder, his menacing eyes never leaving her face, he warned, "Do you understand me? I have just been through one episode with a wife who flirted with every man around. I will not accept another. Goddammit, you will not embarrass me in front of my friends. Do you hear me?"

Humiliated and hurt by his unfair accusation, Julie began to cry. She hadn't done anything wrong, and Jeff Chandler had acted like a perfect gentleman. Paco often asked her to dance with friends of his. Why was he carrying on so about something so innocent? Julie tried to stifle her tears, but she couldn't. There was too much pent-up emotion.

Abruptly, Paco released his grip and told her to stop sniveling and acting like a child. "I haven't done anything so terrible to you. I'm sorry you're upset, but you brought it on yourself. I don't like other men touching my wife."

Julie sank down on the sofa and tried to compose herself. She sat there motionless for what seemed like a long time, staring at the red marks Paco's fingers had left on her wrist. She heard the front door close, and except for the butler's footsteps, the house was now silent. All the guests had obviously left and Paco started to pace the room, picking up the empty wineglasses, which had left circles on the furniture.

"Careless, no-good bastards. They come here to eat my food and drink my booze and I don't even have anything to show for it." Suddenly, he stopped pacing and angrily shouted, "Do you know what my sons of bitches agents said tonight when I cornered them about my RKO deal? They said the studio would not be making any musicals in the near future and that they would pay off my entire contract. Do you believe those *hijos de putas*? After all the money I've made for those bastards in this town, they're treating me like dirt."

Julie said nothing. She was still too upset about Paco's unfair treatment of her. *Besides,* she thought, with a sinking feeling, *what can I say? I'm more disappointed than he is that he won't be making any pictures. I'd hoped that when Paco did make films there would be a spot for me. But now I guess that's not going to happen. Thank God I'm not the reason they're paying him off. He would have never forgiven me.*

Julie stood up and in a weary voice said, "Paco, I'm very tired. If you don't mind I'd like to go to bed."

Paco seemed hardly aware of her now. He started to pace again, his mind already racing ahead with new plans to bolster his career.

Julie stood there waiting for a reply, and when Paco didn't answer, she said softly, "I'm going upstairs."

When Paco looked up at her there was a new expression in his eyes. One of great expectation and excitement. "Julie, I've just decided what we're going to do. I'm going to accept that fabulous offer I received a month ago to tour the Far East. The money they're offering is incredible and the publicity will give my career the shot in the arm it needs."

Julie stared at him in disbelief. Gone was the half-crazed man who had confronted her only minutes ago. She was now looking at a different person. Someone with a new purpose and goal. The transformation was incredible. She now understood that part of the fury he had unleashed against her was not because of anything she had done, but because of the intolerable frustration he felt over his career. He had been a star for a long time and was not prepared to accept anything less.

Suddenly, it dawned on Paco that Julie had been telling him something a few minutes ago, but he didn't remember what. In a voice that belied his earlier anger, he said sweetly, "You must be tired, sweetheart. Go upstairs to bed. I want to make a list of the things I need to tell Luis to do in the morning. We will call the orchestra back to California and begin rehearsals immediately."

Taking her hand, which minutes before he had bruised in his jealous frenzy, he kissed her palm. "Oh, Julie, this trip will be sensational. You know, I'm a big record star over there. They love my music. There will be standing room only. You will love it."

Paco didn't even notice when Julie quietly left the room. He had removed his jacket and was seated on the couch, busy making notes in the reminder pad he kept with him at all times.

Julie took off her high heels and walked slowly up the stairs. All the energy and enthusiasm she had felt earlier in the evening was gone. Paco's unwarranted jealousy had not only frightened her, but also demonstrated how quickly his mood could change without provocation. As she wearily opened the bedroom door she wondered whether she could learn to cope with this complicated and difficult man.

CHAPTER 28

Julie stretched her long slender body on the enormous king-size bed that she shared with Paco. She loved the feel of the silk sheets that Inga meticulously changed every day. It was a luxury that she was unaccustomed to and she wondered if Laura had picked them out. Even though Paco's former wife had removed all of her personal belongings at the time of the divorce, there were still traces of her everywhere—the sheets, the towels—little details that only another woman would notice. Even her heady fragrance still lingered in the closets, and sometimes it almost made Julie feel like an intruder.

Julie glanced at the crystal clock at the side of the bed. It was ten o'clock—she had slept much later than usual. But the party and its aftermath had drained her, and she had no desire to get out of bed. She hadn't heard Paco come to bed last night and now that she was awake she saw he was already gone. *Probably working on the tour,* Julie thought. It still amazed Julie that Paco could function with so little sleep. He seemed to thrive on hard work, and new deals in the making always supplied him with fresh energy. Reluctantly, Julie relinquished the luxury of her bed. When she opened the silk drapes that covered the French doors, bright California sunshine filled her eyes. The gardens were ablaze with color, and in the distance, she could hear the gardeners mowing the enormous lawn in front of the house. Julie grabbed her robe from the chaise lounge and went into her dressing room. *If only Mom could see this,* Julie thought sadly as she ran her hand along the marble counter. *Imagine, this room is all mine and at home we all shared a bathroom less than half this size.* Julie should have felt elated, but she didn't. *I guess I just need someone to share this excitement with,* she thought as she slowly brushed her hair. Feeling the pangs of homesickness, she decided to call home later in the day. In a way she dreaded it, because ever since her marriage, the few conversations with her parents had left her feeling depressed. But she still felt it was her duty to call home no matter how cold her parents acted. As Julie slipped into white shorts and a cotton blouse, she looked at her wrist and suddenly she remembered the ugly scene that had taken place the night before. She was beginning to realize that Paco's temper was like a bomb just waiting to explode and that she would have to be careful not to ignite the fuse.

As she approached the beautiful breakfast room that overlooked the pool, Julie could hear Paco's voice. He was speaking on the telephone. He nodded to her as she sat down and Julie saw that he was in a good mood. He finished his conversation with a hearty chuckle and turned his attention to her.

"*Buenos días, mi amor.* Did you sleep well? I tried not to disturb you this morning. Your beautiful face looked so peaceful. By the way, that was Ty Power on the phone. He was telling me what a great time he had last night. I've had a dozen calls so far this morning and flowers just arrived from L.B. Didn't I tell you that this party would be one of the best this town has seen in a long time? I'm sure that it will pay off. The hell with RKO. It's not the only studio in town. After our tour of the Orient, and all the publicity it will generate, I'll be back in demand, bigger than ever."

Noticing Julie's attire, he asked, "What do you plan to do today, *querida?* Would you like Peter to drive you into Beverly Hills?"

"No. I think I'll just spend the day at home and relax. It's so beautiful outside."

"You're right, darling. Stay at home with Paco. I get lonely when you're gone." He took a last sip of his coffee and came around the table to kiss her.

"I have to make some calls," he said as he reached down with one hand and felt the softness of her breast, which was slightly visible in

her low-cut blouse. "But I'll see you at lunch *mi amor* and maybe later
. . ." He left the rest unsaid, but Julie knew all too well what he meant.

After finishing her light breakfast, she took a book from the library
and found a comfortable chair on the terrace near the swimming pool.
She spent what was left of the morning enjoying the peaceful surroundings, and when the sun became too intense, she toured the lush gardens
and waterfalls in front of the house. *No wonder Laura fought so hard
to keep this.* Julie sighed. *Even though this place is like paradise to me,
I could never imagine myself fighting over material things.* As she was
about to go inside to change, a car drove up the long circular driveway
and stopped in front of the house. A tall attractive man got out of the
car and came toward her. She recognized him as one of the men Paco
had been speaking to on the terrace last night. Julie ran down the broad
terrace steps to greet him.

"Hello, Julie. I'd like to introduce myself. I'm Ray Burns, one of
Paco's agents. We didn't get a chance to meet last evening."

"Another agent," Julie blurted out before thinking. "I thought I had
met all of them. Your office must have more agents than clients."

He laughed as Julie blushed, embarrassed that she had spoken that
way. "Please forgive me, Mr. Burns. I didn't mean that the way it
sounded. It's just that I've met so many of Paco's agents here and in
New York that sometimes I get confused."

"That's perfectly normal, Julie. We do have a large office and staff.
But I assure you we have an even larger list of clients."

"Oh, I know you do," Julie answered. "And I'm proud to say that
I'm one of them."

"We're very pleased about that, Julie, and my associates think you
have a big future."

Julie smiled happily at him, and as they both approached the entrance
to the house, Peter, anticipating their arrival, opened the front door
just as Paco came rushing out of the library to greet his guest.

Placing his arm around his shoulder, he said, "Ray, come on in and
have a drink. I see you've already met Julie."

"Yes, Paco, I have. She was on the terrace as I drove up."

"Good, let's go into the library. You mentioned on the phone that
you had something you wanted to discuss with me."

As they walked into the elegantly paneled library, filled with Paco's
awards and memorabilia, Julie took this as a signal to leave. Whatever
business they were about to engage in, she doubted if she would be
needed.

"Mr. Burns, if you'll excuse me. I think I'll run upstairs and change. It was nice meeting you."

Ray Burns put his hand out, as if to stop her. "Julie, please don't leave just yet. What I have to say will interest you too."

Julie looked at Paco to see if this suggestion met with his approval. His silence indicated that she was welcome to stay, so she sat down on the leather sofa and tucked her legs under her. Paco sat down behind his huge desk, waiting to hear what news his agent was bringing.

"Paco, Julie, the office received a call this morning from Herman Hover, the owner of Ciro's. He'd like you to appear there."

Julie's ears perked up instantly. Paco had taken her dancing there last month, and she had been enormously impressed. It was famous not only as a nightclub but also as a meeting place for the Hollywood elite.

"What date does he have in mind?" Paco asked, his mind calculating quickly how he could fit this engagement in before the Orient.

"As soon as you're ready. If the band arrives in time, you could open next week—play a two-week engagement and still leave on time for the tour."

Paco's eyes glistened with excitement as the agent laid out the plans. He hadn't played Ciro's for a few years, and if this engagement turned out to be anything like the last, it would cause a sensation. His fans in Hollywood would jam pack the place every night. What a triumph it would be.

"All right, Ray. If he meets my price then tell him we have a deal. But be sure you get him to commit to go all out in promoting this engagement."

"Don't worry about that, Paco," Ray said as he rose from his chair. "I'll get on it right away. I better get going. Hover is anxious for an answer."

He started to leave, but stopped for a moment. "I hope you're excited, Julie! This engagement could help your career a great deal."

Paco quickly came over to her side and put his arm around her possessively. "Of course she's excited. She's going to be the sexiest woman that ever walked on that stage. The whole town will be talking about her by the time we get through."

Julie wondered about Paco's remark as she entered her bedroom and began changing her clothes. Only last night he had carried on like a madman just because she had innocently danced with Jeff Chandler. Today he was talking about grooming her to be the sexiest woman to ever walk on a stage, without the slightest twinge of jealousy. She was confused. Didn't he realize the more provocative she appeared, the more attention she would attract from the opposite sex? As far as she was concerned, she wanted to be regarded as a performer and not just a sex symbol.

Things progressed very quickly from the moment Paco accepted the engagement. The band, which had been hastily reassembled by Luis in New York, arrived and immediately began rehearsing for the opening. Paco made arrangements with an MGM dressmaker to sew some new gowns for Julie. He wanted her to project an even sexier image for her Hollywood debut, and the gowns he selected left little to the imagination. Julie welcomed the activity. Having no friends in California, it felt good to be back rehearsing every day and spending time with José and Estella, who would also be appearing in the show. As the opening drew nearer Julie's excitement intensified. Paco made sure that every single member of the press would be present, and he personally called them ahead of time to plug his upcoming tour.

When the big night finally arrived, Julie suddenly experienced an unexpected attack of nerves. She had been nervous all day as the stage crew fussed with the spotlights and sound. When she returned home late that afternoon she had barely eaten a bite of the light supper Inga had prepared for her on a tray. There was too much at stake for her that night to think of anything but what she had to do. Now, only forty-five minutes away from show time, Julie fidgeted in her dressing room, as she redid her hair and makeup until she was satisfied that she looked presentable. Paco, on the other hand, was so relaxed he was able to mingle casually before the show with friends in the crowded room, which was filled to capacity. Almost everyone who counted was there—actors, producers, directors, studio heads, and the two most powerful women in town—Louella Parsons and Hedda Hopper. They were eager not only to witness Paco Castell's return to the Hollywood scene but also curious to get a glimpse of his new wife and vocalist.

As the musicians ascended the bandstand in their colorful ruffled blouses and took their places, Paco looked in to see how Julie was doing.

"*Querida*, you can't believe what's going on out there. It's like a madhouse. Gable is down front and so is Lana. Cary Grant, Betty Grable—you name it, they're all there." Paco's face was glowing. Julie hadn't seen him this happy since South America.

Her hand began to shake as she put down her powder puff. "Paco, please don't tell me more. I'm already so nervous I can hardly remember my name. What if they don't like me or if my voice cracks? What if I forget the lyrics?"

Paco turned her around and lifted her face up to his. His eyes were deadly serious as he faced her. "Listen to me, Julie. Forget about your voice and lyrics and all that crap." Grasping her chin, he swung her around to face the mirror. "Look, Julie, and what do you see?"

Julie looked at her reflection, but all she could see was a nervous and frightened girl who was about to face an incredibly sophisticated audience.

"Julie, get that scared look off your face. Don't you realize how beautiful you are and what an impact you're going to make?"

"But, Paco, there are plenty of pretty girls out there—much prettier than me. I want to impress them with my talent as well as my looks."

"You will, my darling, you will. But right now that's not what they're expecting. Julie, you have the most famous Latin band in the world behind you, and what they're going to witness is a gorgeous sexy woman who can move and dance like no one else can. Your singing voice is just fine and I'm sure that they will appreciate that. But your interpretation of my music and how you sell it as a performer is what counts. Now, go out there, my beautiful one, and knock them dead."

Julie smiled gamely as she watched Paco leave to join the musicians onstage. *He couldn't care less about what kind of singer I am or how important it is for me to be considered more than just a pretty face,* she thought. *I'll just have to go out there and do the best I can.*

"Ladies and gentlemen," a voice called out from the back of the room. "Herman Hover takes great pride in presenting the one and only Paco Castell and his orchestra."

A roar of applause and whistles greeted Paco as he walked out for his first number. The band started playing one of his greatest hits, and when the number was finished and the applause had died down, Paco thanked everyone for their warm welcome. After a few minutes of amusing banter, he gave the signal for the band to go into another song, which he had recorded years before with Bing Crosby. Julie watched Paco from a tiny opening in the curtain behind the bandstand. His face was all smiles, and the audience was responding enthusiastically to his music. Suddenly, she realized her cue was coming up and her body froze with fear. *Please God,* she prayed silently. *Don't let me be a flop tonight.*

Moments later, she heard her introduction. "*Señoras y Señores,* it is my great pleasure to present to you my new discovery and beautiful wife—Miss Julie Lauren."

Julie took a deep breath, and with all the strength she could muster to keep her knees from knocking, she walked out into the spotlight.

The audience gasped when they saw her. The gold lamé gown that was fairly simple in design clung to her rounded curves as if it had been painted on. There was a slit in the skirt that revealed her long slim legs as she walked to the microphone. The only ornamentation were strings of emerald green bugle beads that hung down like fringe on her shoulder straps. The combination of the burnished red gold of her hair falling loosely down her back and her tawny skin was startling. She could sense the audience's approval immediately and her instincts told her that unless she really messed up her songs, she was home free.

As she started her first song, the audience was so busy discussing her looks, they didn't seem to pay much attention to her singing. But when she launched into a slow ballad in Spanish they quickly quieted down, and the response when she finished was more than she could have wished for. As much as the audience appreciated her singing, when she started to undulate to the Latin music and danced a fast rhumba accompanied by the two male percussionists, they really went wild. Even this sophisticated crowd got caught up in the exciting rhythms. Julie gave the best performance of her young life, and with her hair whirling around her face, reminded them of Rita Hayworth in *Gilda*. Pausing between songs to catch her breath, she greeted the audience.

"Hello everyone, and thank you," she said.

Someone in the back yelled out to her half-jokingly, "Hey beautiful, you sure have a great voice."

Julie's sense of humor took over. Not missing a beat she answered, "Yes, I noticed you've been watching my voice all evening."

The audience screamed with laughter at her remark and Julie laughed too. She had never been so happy. Her earlier nervousness was gone, and she felt entirely at ease basking in the acceptance she felt from the audience. When her performance was finally over, Julie went backstage to wait for Paco. She was too excited to change and she wanted to get Paco's reaction. Holding on tightly to Estella's hand, Julie waited anxiously. She knew that she had done well, but she still needed Paco's confirmation. When the applause finally died down, he left the stage and joined her.

Quickly, he removed his jacket, soaked through as it was because of the hot lights, and embraced her. "Didn't I tell you that you would be a sensation? Paco knows his public."

"Oh, Paco, it was more than I ever dreamed it could be. Are you really pleased?"

"Of course I'm pleased, and you'll get even better. We will tour all over the world and we will be quite a team. As long as you follow my direction you'll continue to be a success. I've created other stars and I will do the same for you. Now go and change, *preciosa*. We should go out and mingle with the public. They're all anxious to meet you."

CHAPTER 29

Paco's predictions about the impact their appearance would make at Ciro's all came true. The day after their opening, there were glowing reviews, not only in the newspapers, but also in the bibles of the entertainment industry, *Daily Variety* and the *Hollywood Reporter*. They were effusive in their praise of Paco's music and showmanship, and all of the critics agreed that he had been away from the Hollywood scene far too long. But the plaudits heaped on Julie far overshadowed even Paco's triumph.

"Julie Lauren is Paco Castell's latest discovery," the *Herald-Examiner* exclaimed, "and boy is she a winner! Her singing and dancing wowed the star-studded audience that jammed Ciro's last night. Studio execs would be smart to grab her for films. She's a natural."

The press compared her with everyone from Rita Hayworth to Lana Turner, and they almost unanimously proclaimed Julie Lauren a girl fast on her way to becoming a star.

Naturally, Paco was pleased by Julie's success. After all, hadn't he discovered her and taught her everything she knew? But already certain reservations about her success started to set in. Especially when his press agent called him a few days later about Julie.

"Paco, Louella and Hedda each want to interview Julie for their column, and Harrison Carroll of the *Examiner* is running a cute story today. By the way, Herman Hover wants more pictures of Julie for the front of Ciro's."

"I will think about this and call you back, Warren," Paco said as he hung up, disturbed by the attention being focused on Julie. He was concerned that things were moving too quickly. Underlying that concern was a fear that if the studios got ahold of her he might lose control. The Howard Hughes episode was still too fresh in his mind.

As the days progressed, it seemed that Julie's every waking moment was so charged with activity that she barely had time to come home, change, and get to the nightclub. Paco accompanied her everywhere, and even though the interviews were scheduled for her alone, Paco's presence could hardly be ignored. All the columnists ended up interviewing both of them, except Louella, who told Paco in no uncertain terms, "Paco, stay the hell out of the room for Christ's sake. I already know everything about you. I want to speak to this child alone."

At first, Julie was intimidated by the formidable and powerful columnist. She had been told by everyone that if Louella didn't like you, look out. But Louella treated her kindly, which totally disarmed Julie and prompted her to answer Louella's rather probing questions openly and honestly.

Inviting her to sit beside her on the couch in her sun-filled living room in Beverly Hills, Louella began the interview by asking Julie, "How did your parents react when you told them you were going to marry a man old enough to be your father?"

For a second Julie was startled by the bluntness of her question and hesitated before answering. Deciding that she had nothing to hide, Julie answered the columnist with the humor and candor that were part of her nature. "Miss Parsons, they accepted it quite calmly. My father hit the ceiling and my mother simply said she was going to put her head in the oven."

Louella Parsons threw her head back and laughed until tears ran down her cheeks. She had interviewed them all, from Carole Lombard to Liz Taylor, but she had never come across a young girl who had impressed her more.

"My dear," she said kindly. "You are a delight. Don't ever lose that spark and your sense of humor. They will serve you in good stead throughout your life."

As a result of that favorable interview there was an even greater curiosity by the Hollywood crowd to see "Paco Castell's sexy and talented child-bride," as Louella had labeled her.

The preparations for the Far East tour were on schedule, and Julie was sad that she would be leaving California just when things were going so well. Paco, however, was anxious to go. His agents had been unable to get another picture deal for him, even though the Ciro's engagement had generated enormous publicity. Their answer, when badgered by Paco, remained the same: "Paco, the studios are just not making those big-budget musicals right now."

In light of this, Paco was astounded by the telephone call he received from Lew Wallace early Monday morning, the beginning of their last week at Ciro's.

"Paco, this morning I received a call from Bill Goetz over at Universal. He and Edie were at Ciro's on Saturday night and they were very impressed with Julie. Bill thinks she has a great quality and they would like to test her for a contract with the studio."

For the first time in his life Paco was at a loss for words. He couldn't believe his ears. This was not a Howard Hughes ploy just to entice a beautiful girl. William Goetz was not only the head of a studio, but a serious man, highly respected in the industry and married to Louis B. Mayer's daughter. This man meant business, and he wanted to test Julie. *Goddammit,* he thought. *What the fuck have I created? Instead of me they want her. What am I going to do?*

"Paco, are you there?" Lew asked. "Did you hear what I said?"

"Yes, I heard you, Lew. And are you aware that in less than two weeks we leave on an extended tour of the Orient that *your* agency arranged? Do you expect me to change my plans now at this late date? Or maybe you think I should leave my wife here alone in Hollywood with all these vultures?"

"Paco, take it easy. They want to test her this week. If they like her then we'll negotiate the deal and you can leave for your trip just as planned. If the test is no good, then there's no harm done. Either way, you leave on time."

Paco slammed the receiver down on the hook without answering, knocking a beautiful and costly piece of porcelain to the floor.

"Hijos de putas," he murmured under his breath. *Just when every-*

thing is going the way I want it, those sons of bitches screw it up. Well, he thought as he went in search of Julie, I'd better tell her the news myself before they get to her. I've got to make her understand that I won't put up with any nonsense. She's my wife now and screen test or no screen test, she'll be on that plane with me when we leave for Japan.

CHAPTER 30

S teve Burton opened the door to
the apartment he and Sharon were renting on West Eighty-seventh
Street and immediately removed his jacket and tie. The oppressively
hot and humid July weather was making New York intolerable, and
without air conditioning, their tiny apartment felt like an oven.

"Sharon," he called. "I'm home." But no one answered.

She must be out shopping, Steve thought as he poured himself a tall
glass of ice water and sat down on the couch. *Just as well. I need time
to think.* His interview that morning had gone exceedingly well, but
before giving an answer, he had to examine all the pros and cons of
the offer very carefully. He felt that his decision could very well affect
his entire future. Leaning back on the couch, he began to reflect on
the events that had taken place since his marriage to Sharon in May.
After passing the bar, instead of accepting a job with a Wall Street
law firm, Steve had signed on as campaign manager for the former fire
commissioner of New York, the celebrated Jacob Grumet. Judge Grumet had been Thomas E. Dewey's chief assistant during Dewey's racket-
busting days as U.S. attorney for the southern district of New York.
Grumet, who was running for re-election to the court of general sessions, had selected Steve at the recommendation of Leonard Probst,

probation commissioner for the State of New York. Steve was understandably thrilled to have been chosen at such a young age and with
no prior political experience. A political career had been his dream
ever since he was a boy and he and his mother had imagined what it
would be like if one day he became a judge and maybe, even, governor
of the State of New York.

During the course of the campaign Steve was introduced to Frank
Hogan, district attorney for New York county and undeniably one of
the most effective and respected district attorneys in New York City's
long history. As the campaign progressed and Steve's encounters with
Hogan became more frequent, Hogan became increasingly impressed
with Steve's abilities and very quickly endorsed Grumet's assessment
of Steve's potential in the political arena. Then just today, with the
campaign finally over, Hogan had invited Steve down to his office
to determine his interest in an appointment as an assistant district
attorney—surely the dream of any young lawyer aspiring to a political
career in New York because it provided the best possible stepping-stone
for advancement. And yet Steve had certain gnawing reservations.
Throughout the campaign he had come in contact with many political
leaders, including the notorious Carmine De Sapio, the long-reigning
head of Tammany Hall. Steve became increasingly aware that many
of the more successful politicians employed tactics that were abhorrent
to him. From the "inside" Steve had discovered a seamy side of politics
that he was never aware of before, and disillusion soon set in. Just the
thought of having to cultivate these types in order to further his career
became increasingly repugnant to him. As Steve contemplated Hogan's
offer over and over again in his mind, he was very much undecided.

Steve was jolted out of his thoughts by the telephone ringing.

"Mr. Burton, please. Howard Reinheimer calling."

Steve sat up, instantly alert. "This is Mr. Burton."

Seconds later Howard Reinheimer's cultured voice greeted him.
"Hello, Steve. How are you doing?"

"Just fine, Mr. Reinheimer. I've been very busy working for Judge
Grumet."

"I know, Steve. I've been keeping track of you since our last meeting."

Steve remembered that meeting very well. It had taken place right
after he graduated from Harvard Law School. Steve had been interviewed for a possible position with Reinheimer and Cohen—perhaps
the most prestigious theatrical law firm in the country. Even though

Steve felt he had acquitted himself very well, there just was no opening at the time.

"Steve," he continued, "I've been hearing some very fine things about you, and if you're still interested in joining our firm, I would like to have a chat with you. Are you free for lunch tomorrow?"

Having almost given up any hope of ever again hearing from this highly respected law firm, whose dazzling client list included such entertainment industry giants as Rogers and Hammerstein, Lerner and Loewe, and Kaufman and Hart, Steve could barely restrain his exuberance.

"Mr. Reinheimer, I'm delighted that you called and I would very much like to have lunch with you."

"Good. Then why don't you meet me at the Schubert Theater around noon tomorrow. Oscar and Dick are auditioning some actors for replacements in *The King and I*. Pick me up there and we can run over to '21' for lunch."

Steve was euphoric when he hung up the phone. He could hardly believe what was happening. Just this morning he had been offered an appointment to Frank Hogan's office, and now, out of the blue, this telephone call from Howard Reinheimer. This could make the decision he had been wrestling with even more difficult. Steve suddenly looked around. The apartment had started to grow dark with the onset of evening, and as he began to turn on the lights, Steve looked at his watch. It was getting late, and he was impatient for Sharon to return home so he could tell her the good news. *Maybe,* he thought, *after discussing it with Sharon, I'll have a fresh perspective.*

Steve didn't have long to wait, for moments later he heard her key turn the lock and Sharon walked in. Her normally pretty face was grim and unsmiling as Steve greeted her at the door.

After embracing her, Steve took the packages she was carrying and said, "Honey, I've been so anxious for you to get home. I've had quite a day and I'm dying to tell you about it."

Sharon gave Steve a half-smile and headed straight for the bedroom. As Steve followed her, she said, "Steve, can we talk about whatever is so important after I take a shower? I've been out all day, and I feel so hot and sticky. I just can't stand staying in these clothes another minute."

Steve looked at his wife of eight weeks in bewilderment. She had been aware that he had an important meeting scheduled that morning. He would have thought that she would be terribly anxious to hear

about something that could affect her future as well as his. Steve's
earlier enthusiasm was suddenly extinguished, and at that moment, he
no longer felt like discussing the district attorney job or even mentioning the telephone call from Howard Reinheimer.

"Sure, Sharon," he said, trying to hide the hurt from his voice. "Go
ahead and take your shower. My news can wait."

Steve went back into the living room and sat down. He didn't like
what he was thinking. *Sure,* he reasoned to himself, *she wants me to
be a success. But the sad fact is that she lacks any exuberance and
passion. Ever since our marriage she seems more and more incapable of
demonstrating any deep emotion. She says and does all the dutiful things
expected of a wife, but I want more. I not only need a wife, but a
companion—a friend—someone to joke with and have fun with—someone who won't think I'm a fool if I act silly sometimes. Where is that
girl?* Steve wondered to himself. *Did she ever really exist, or did I create
her in my own mind?*

Sharon emerged from the shower, and after drying her hair, she
slipped on a thin bathrobe and went directly into the kitchen to prepare
Steve's dinner. She herself had no appetite, having had a late lunch.
Besides, she thought as she set the table, *it's just too damn hot to eat.*
Glancing into the living room she saw Steve sitting there, staring
vacantly into space.

"Steve," she called. "Dinner will be ready in a few minutes. I've
fixed salmon croquettes and a salad. Is that okay with you?"

Steve looked up, but there was a distracted look on his face. He had
been totally immersed in his thoughts. "What did you say, Sharon?"

"Croquettes, Steve. They'll be ready soon."

"Sure. Whatever you have is fine."

A few minutes later he joined her in the tiny kitchen and sat down.
"Now, Steve," she said as she placed the food on the table and sat
down opposite him, "what was it that you wanted to tell me before?"

Steve looked up at his wife's face, hoping to see a sign of genuine
interest, but it just wasn't there. Gone was the elation that he had felt
earlier in the evening, and now he was the one who didn't feel like
talking.

"Steve, you're daydreaming again. What was it you were so excited
about telling me?"

Steve picked at his food, avoiding her eyes. "Sharon, why don't we
let it wait until tomorrow? You seem to be tired and frankly, so am I."

Sharon seemed relieved as she rose from the table.

"As you wish, Steve. Actually, I'm not hungry right now so maybe I'll go lie down for a while. I bought a fan for the bedroom."

Steve was glad that he had managed to avoid discussing his plans while he was in this frame of mind. There would be plenty of time after his meeting with Reinheimer to review all of his options with Sharon. Steve was anxious to involve Sharon in all his career decisions in order to insure that his marriage would work. He hoped that she would at least meet him halfway.

After dinner, Steve turned off the lights and gathered up his papers from the living room table. With the windows opened wide, there was now a cool breeze drifting through the apartment. When he opened the bedroom door, he saw that Sharon was already fast asleep, her dark hair spread out on the pillow. Slipping quietly out of his clothes, he lay down beside her and closed his eyes. As he slowly drifted off to sleep, his thoughts were on his meeting the next day and what the outcome would mean for his future.

The next morning Steve dressed carefully for his luncheon date with Howard Reinheimer. Sharon had left earlier to keep a dental appointment and have lunch with some friends. At breakfast she hadn't pressed him for any information and Steve decided to wait until after his meeting before discussing his options with her. Steve chose his favorite gray suit and a conservative tie that he hoped would lend him a distinguished air. He was still a month away from his twenty-fifth birthday and did not want his youth to stand in the way of a possible offer from the firm, if that indeed was what they had in mind.

Steve left the apartment and hailed a taxi to take him to the Schubert Theater. When he arrived there, it was so dark inside that Steve had to blink several times in order to adjust his eyes to the darkness. Slowly he found his way down the aisle. Up on the stage, a beautiful dark-haired girl had just started to sing in front of the black velvet curtain. As Steve approached Howard Reinheimer, he felt a tinge of excitement. The lawyer was sitting next to Richard Rogers and Oscar Hammerstein, two of America's most celebrated and successful composers and producers in the theater. Steve had come into contact with many important people, but none in the entertainment industry, and like many others, he was in awe of creative talent. Steve had often tried to imagine what it might be like to represent such renowned figures.

Extending his hand he greeted Howard Reinheimer. "I hope I haven't kept you waiting?"

"Not at all," Reinheimer responded. "Let me introduce you to Dick and Oscar. Gentlemen, I would like you to meet Steve Burton, who I hope may soon be joining our firm."

"Howard was just telling us about you and the fine work you did on Judge Grumet's campaign," Hammerstein said, shaking Steve's hand.

"Thank you for the kind words," Steve said, taking a seat.

He soon found himself totally absorbed by the auditions. After some time, he felt a hand on his shoulder indicating that it was time to go.

"Steve, Dick Rogers has kindly offered to drop us off at '21'. I asked him to join us, but he's meeting Dorothy at Le Pavillon."

Steve followed the others out to the car, which was parked in front of the theater. As he got in the silver Rolls-Royce, he made a mental note to mention it to his mother. He knew that she would be impressed by things like that. She had high hopes for her only child, hopes that included recognition of her son's talent and all the trappings that went along with success.

When they reached the restaurant and, after they were seated, Howard came directly to the point. "Steve, I know that you've been politically active in the past few months. Have you decided to pursue that as a career or would you be interested in going into private practice?"

"As a matter of fact," Steve answered proudly, "Frank Hogan has just offered me a position as assistant district attorney but, for a number of reasons, I must confess to having certain misgivings. Frankly, I had almost ruled out the prospect of joining a law firm at this time. But your firm does offer many unique opportunities, and if asked, I would seriously have to consider it."

"Well, Steve, I have already discussed the possibility of your joining the firm with my partner and associates and they enthusiastically endorsed the idea. Why don't you think about it and get back to me as soon as you have sorted this out in your mind." With that agreed to, both men settled down to enjoy their lunch.

When Steve reached home late that afternoon, Sharon was already there. Hearing him enter the apartment Sharon called out from the bedroom, "Steve, I'm in here. You'd better hurry and change. We're meeting the Berensons for drinks and an early dinner. By the way, call your mother. She's phoned several times."

When Steve entered the small but attractively furnished bedroom, Sharon was seated at her dressing table rubbing some cream on her hands. He could see that her makeup was freshly applied and she had pinned her dark hair up into an attractive French twist. Steve sat down at the edge of the bed and loosened his tie.

"Sharon, could you come over here? I have something I would like to discuss with you."

Sensing the urgency in his voice, Sharon turned around and came over to the side of the bed. "What is it, Steve? You look so serious. Is something wrong?"

"Nothing's wrong, Sharon. In fact, things couldn't be better." Taking her hand he gently pulled her down to sit beside him. Slowly he began to reconstruct the events of the past two days—the meeting with Hogan and the offer from Reinheimer. As Steve described his conversation with both men, he began to feel an even stronger conviction that fate was pushing him in the direction of the law firm. But before telling her that, he waited to hear her reaction.

Sharon stood up and walked over to the window. After thinking for a moment, she turned back to him. "Steve, I don't know what to say. They both sound like exceptional opportunities. But haven't you always had your heart set on a career in politics?"

"That's true, Sharon, but you must be aware of how disillusioned I've become in the past months."

Walking back to the bed, Sharon faced her husband. "Just because you saw one side of politics and came across some people who didn't meet your standards doesn't mean that all politicans are bad," she stated firmly.

Sharon was somewhat thrown by this unexpected news and she wasn't quite sure if she approved. She hadn't anticipated this turn of events, and somehow, the thought of Steve giving up a promising political career, where he could possibly reach great heights, to enter a theatrical law firm unsettled her. The prospect of being the wife of a famous judge, senator, or who knows, even governor—as her mother-in-law often said—obviously appealed to Sharon much more.

Sensing Sharon's ambivalence, Steve tried to present the entire picture to her. "Sharon, what you say is true, but you have to understand that this firm's practice may be unlike that of any other in this city or even the country. They not only represent many of the most famous entertainment figures in the world, but a number of the most dynamic and important executives in the industry. I can see boundless opportunities opening up for me."

As he spoke, Steve's belief in what he was saying lifted him to his feet. His eyes sparkling with enthusiasm, he pulled Sharon up to him and stated with resolve, "Honey, I hope you can understand my feelings and approve because I've reached my decision. I have a great feeling about this position." Taking her hands in his, he said, "Trust me, sweetheart, I know I'm doing the right thing."

Sharon managed to muster a weak smile even though she wasn't convinced that he was right. "All right, Steve. If that's what you want then it's fine with me. Now, you must hurry or we really will be late."

Turning, Sharon picked up the dress that lay across the bed and resumed dressing.

Well, Steve thought as he started to change his own clothes, *not exactly the exuberant response I was hoping for, but maybe that will come in time.* As he turned the shower on he knew that he had two important telephone calls to make the next day—Frank Hogan and Howard Reinheimer. He had made his decision, and with it came a flood of relief. Happily he stepped into the shower and started to sing.

CHAPTER
31

As the studio makeup man put the finishing touches to Julie's makeup, he could feel her body trembling beneath his fingers. "Calm down, honey. You're going to be a nervous wreck by the time you reach the set. Look, I've seen a lot of girls come in before a screen test. Some of them are beautiful and others are just attractive, but they have a certain spark. You seem to have it all. I watched your makeup and wardrobe tests yesterday and you looked like a million bucks. Even though you didn't speak, your vitality came through. Now relax and just remember that the camera can be your friend if you let it."

Julie tried to follow his advice, but it wasn't easy. So much was riding on the outcome of this test—a seven-year contract and possibly her future in pictures. Paco had been no help the past few days as she prepared for the test. In fact, his attitude was so negative and he seemed so ambivalent about wanting her to have a film career that she wondered why he had gone to the trouble of presenting her so prominently at Ciro's. Just last night, after the show, he had gone on endlessly about how foolish she was to want to tie herself down with a studio as a contract player when she could be a star with his band. She could remember his very words. "At Universal you'll be just one of many starlets who are given small roles and eventually fade away. With me, you can perform in the best places all over the world— something those other girls can't do. Then, later, after you're firmly established as a star, you will be able to name your own price at any studio in town."

Julie chose not to remind him that many of Universal's big stars had indeed started out as contract players. Only yesterday she had been introduced to Rock Hudson and Piper Laurie, who were both rapidly becoming extremely popular. She also knew that Tony Curtis and many others had started their careers there as contract players. Why couldn't she have that same success? Julie's thoughts were suddenly interrupted by the makeup man tapping her shoulder.

"Honey, they're ready for you. You go on ahead and I'll meet you on Stage Fourteen."

Julie followed the assistant director, who had been sent to summon her, and they walked through the early morning sunlight to the sound stage. Julie braced herself, for not only was the crew awaiting her arrival, but Paco as well. He had accompanied her to the studio early that morning and had insisted on being present during the test. She wished he hadn't. She was already nervous enough, and his presence certainly wouldn't help. If only she could feel that he was in her corner. But in her heart she knew he wasn't. An inner voice told her he wanted her to fail. The next few hours went by very quickly. Julie knew her lines, and her leading man, one of the young actors under contract to the studio, was very supportive. She was doing a scene from a new film scheduled for production sometime in the very near future. Her role was that of a young Mexican girl in love with a soldier during the era of Pancho Villa. At first, the director was concerned about her red hair not being right to portray a Latin girl, but after consulting with the studio hairdresser, they decided to have her wear a black wig.

"Look, Julie," the director told her during the makeup test, "I know that you're leaving shortly for a tour with Paco so I don't want you to go to the trouble of dyeing your hair. But if the test is good and you get the part, I'm afraid you'll have to sacrifice your red hair. I don't like the way wigs photograph on the screen. They look phony."

Julie would have dyed her hair green to get a part like this in a movie, but she was grateful that he was considerate enough not to insist that she do it now just for a screen test.

When the director finally said "cut and print that," Julie heaved a huge sigh of relief. They had gotten what they wanted after only three takes. The director and cameraman came over to congratulate her, and the makeup man, who had been watching her closely from behind the camera, gave her a wink of approval. Julie gathered up her heavy peasant skirt and walked over to Paco. She couldn't tell what he was feeling because he had a stoic expression on his face.

"Paco, how was I? Did you like the test?"

"Who the hell was that jerk they got to play with you? I could barely understand him."

"He was playing the part with an accent," Julie explained. "I thought he was good."

"Well, I thought he was *mierda*," Paco answered testily.

"Paco, they weren't testing *him* for the picture, they were testing *me*. How did I do?"

"You were good, but I hate you in black hair."

That's a hot one, Julie thought. *Isn't he the one who wanted me to dye my hair black when I joined the band, just like his former vocalist, Ruby Gonzalez?*

"Well," Julie said, trying to hide her disappointment at Paco's lack of enthusiasm. "It's only a wig. In a few minutes I'll be a redhead again. I had better change now so we can go. I have a lot to do before the show tonight."

Paco got up and walked with her to the trailer where the wardrobe lady was waiting to help her undress. *Dammit*, he thought. *She's good—a natural-born actress. And she looked so young and gorgeous. I hated it when that actor put his arm around her. If she photographs half as good as she looked in person, they're going to sign her. What will I do then? I've got to convince her that she'll be making a big mistake burying herself under contract to a big studio. It's my only chance. If I can't convince her*, he plotted as he waited for her to change, *then maybe I can persuade Lew to make such outrageous demands that it will scare them off.*

For two days Julie anxiously awaited word on the outcome of her test. Finally, the day before their departure for Tokyo, the call came.

Julie was at home when the phone rang. Something made her grab the receiver on the first ring. She had been practically glued to the telephone since the test, and she desperately wanted to hear the news—good or bad—before Paco.

Lew Wallace's secretary put him through immediately. "Julie, congratulations. They loved the test and they want to make a deal."

Julie hugged the receiver tightly to her chest, trying not to cry. She had almost given up hope of hearing anything before they left and this news was like a dream come true. "Oh, Mr. Wallace, I can't believe it. Thank you, thank you so much."

"You're welcome, Julie, but you're the one who convinced them, not me. Now you go ahead with your plans and make the tour. We'll handle the details concerning your contract, and as soon as the papers are in order, we'll send them to you for your signature. You can be sure that my associates will make the best possible deal for you. Please tell Paco the good news and tell him I'll call him later."

Julie hung up and danced around the room. Her first instincts were to call her parents in New York. She knew her mother would be ecstatic and maybe, just maybe, this would help mend the gap in their relationship. Just as she was about to reach for the phone, Paco walked in. He was dressed in his silk robe and was carrying some publicity pictures that were being sent ahead. He leaned down and kissed Julie's forehead as he placed the photos on the table.

"*Qué pasa?* I heard the phone ring. Who was it?"

Julie enthusiastically repeated the conversation, all the while watching Paco's reaction. Instead of the expected outbreak against the wisdom of accepting a seven-year contract, Paco listened quietly until she had finished.

"Congratulations, Julie. I know this is something you've always wanted. I just hope you're not making a mistake."

Julie looked at him, suddenly confused. *Why isn't he reacting the way I thought he would,* she wondered. *Is he really sincere and happy for me or is this just the calm before the storm?*

"Thank you, Paco," Julie said gratefully. "I promise that I'll try not to let this interfere with our work together. I can still sing with the band and tour with you. If they want me to be in a film, maybe you could play in Los Angeles at the same time. Herman Hover has told you a hundred times that you can name your own dates at Ciro's."

Paco studied his bride carefully. She was obviously trying to placate him so that she could get her own way. But that wouldn't work. She would soon find out that Paco Castell would call the shots—not Julie Lauren. As he adjusted his silk ascot in his dressing gown, he studied himself in her full-length mirror.

"I needn't remind you," he told her, "that I expect you to be available whenever and wherever I need you. You have a responsibility to me, not only as my wife, but as an important member of my show." Turning around to face her, he added, "If it hadn't been for me you wouldn't have had this opportunity, and I hope you appreciate that and respect my wishes. I must come first in your life."

Julie readily agreed. More than anything in the world she wanted harmony in her life, and if this meant working twice as hard, then she was prepared to do it.

Paco kissed her cheek and went back into the bedroom to finish his packing, but as he laid his clothes on the bed for Peter to pack, he began to plan how he could still remain in control. *I'll just make sure that whenever they need her she'll be away on tour with me. Sooner or later they're bound to get disgusted with her and place her on suspension. I know the way the studios work. If she's not available, and I'll make sure she won't be, they'll eventually drop her.*

CHAPTER 32

The unprecedented success of Paco Castell and his show in Japan encouraged his representative there to extend the tour beyond Hong Kong to include Manila. Paco was delighted. It would mean not only a lot more money and a new market for a return engagement, but also accomplish something even more important. It would keep Julie away from the studio. As Paco sat in the living room of their luxurious suite in the Peninsula Hotel in Kowloon across the bay from Hong Kong, he planned their itinerary.

"Let's see," he said to Luis, who was handling the plane reservations, "we have another week here and then we fly out immediately to Manila. You'd better go on ahead, Luis, and help arrange the publicity. Be sure the record company has plenty of albums available at the theater. We ran out in Tokyo."

Luis listened attentively and made notes. Paco expected his instructions to be followed to the letter. Julie walked in from the bedroom, where she had been resting, stretched her arms, and flopped down on the sofa. She had intended to do some shopping for presents for the family, but she had fallen asleep. Even though the terrace doors were open and there was a huge ceiling fan whirling noisily overhead, the heat was still oppressive. Julie found herself tiring easily—the doctors had warned her to expect it as the aftermath of her bout with hepatitis. Right now she had to conserve her energy for tonight's performance. They had been working practically night and day in intense heat and humidity since arriving in the Orient five weeks ago. Two shows a night in the theater, one late show at a nightclub, and during the day, appearances at army bases and press interviews. It was an impossible schedule that had left the entire company exhausted. Everyone was looking forward to a much-needed rest. Everyone, that is, except Paco, who was charged with energy and already thinking ahead to future engagements.

Since their arrival in Hong Kong, Julie hadn't heard any news from her agents regarding a future film, but she wasn't terribly concerned. She knew that she was in good hands. The contract that Lew Wallace had sent them in Tokyo was essentially the standard seven-year deal, with two exceptions. The starting money was far more than Paco had told her to expect, and for that, she was delighted. She knew that her father would be too. Another unexpected bonus, and one that only a powerful agent like Lew Wallace could have accomplished, was permission for Julie to travel with Paco and not have to attend the acting classes that were required of all contract players. This was a big concession on the part of the studio because they always insisted on having their starlets on the lot, not only to train them, but to use them for publicity. It not only benefited the studio, but also helped launch the new actors. Julie was certain that without that concession Paco would never have allowed her to sign the contract. He still felt that she was making a mistake and didn't mind reminding her of that whenever he could. But despite his objections, Julie had signed the contract and mailed it back to Los Angeles. Now, as she sat on the sofa, gazing pensively out the window at the small boats in Hong Kong harbor, she wondered how long it would be before the studio summoned her back.

"Julie," Paco called. "You're so quiet. Come and sit over here, *querida*. I've been so busy arranging our schedule I'm afraid I've been neglecting you."

Pulling her bathrobe belt even more tightly against her body, Julie went over to join Paco. Luis would be leaving at any moment and she certainly didn't want to arouse Paco's desire. As she rested her head back on the soft cushion, she reflected on her marriage. *After six months our sex life is no more satisfying to me now than it was when we got married*, she thought. Paco, on the other hand, seemed deliriously happy and desired her constantly. Julie's frustration had grown to the point that she felt she had to discuss it with someone or burst. One night before the show, she started to say something to Estella, but embarrassed by the questions she knew her friend would ask, she stopped herself at the last minute. But Estella, sensing Julie's despera-tion, began talking to her, and in doing so, she inadvertently divulged something she had been keeping secret for a long time. Estella revealed that when Julie became ill in South America, Paco had quickly replaced her with another girl he found in Argentina. This girl, "a cheap-looking bimbo," according to Estella, moved into Paco's suite as soon as Julie left and had remained there for the rest of the tour. At first, Paco had attempted to use her as vocalist with the band, but after the first couple of nights it was evident to everyone that the girl's talents must lie in another direction, because she certainly wasn't a singer.

Julie's first reaction upon hearing this was anger and humiliation. Paco had professed great love and caring for her when he returned from South America, when all the time that she lay sick in a hospital he had been amusing himself with another woman. For a while Julie wrestled with the idea of confronting him and demanding an explana-tion, but then she decided that it would serve no purpose. They had not been married then. But this hurt her deeply. The two men closest to her—her father and her husband—had both betrayed her. Would there ever be any man she would be able to trust?

Julie was abruptly reminded of Paco's presence when he took her hand.

"I've been talking to you, Julie. Would you like to go to Macau when we finish here?"

She looked at Paco and tried to focus on what he was saying. She hadn't realized that she had been so deeply lost in her own thoughts. "I'm sorry. I was daydreaming. What did you say?"

"I said, my dear, would you like to take the boat to Macau for two days at the end of the week? We have some time off before we go to Manila."

"Oh, yes, Paco. I've heard that it's a beautiful place. It might be fun."

"Very well, *querida*. I'll arrange it."

Paco suddenly became aware of the thin bathrobe that Julie was wearing and the thought of her inflamed him. "Why don't you go and relax in the bedroom. It's much cooler in there with the shades down. I'll join you in a minute. I could use a nap too."

A nap, my Aunt Sophie, Julie thought. *That's the furthermost thing from his mind.* She was about to enter the bedroom when she heard the doorbell ring. Peeking out, she saw Paco answer it, and a moment later the bellhop handed him a telegram. Frightened that there might be something wrong at home—Grandma Esther maybe—Julie ran back into the room.

"Paco, what is it?" Julie asked as Paco started to open the envelope.

"I don't know, *querida.* Just be patient a minute and I'll read it."

Julie watched Paco's expression anxiously to see what the telegram contained. As he read the message, his eyebrows turned up at the outer corners and his eyes narrowed as they usually did when he was angry. When he finished he looked up at her furiously and thrust the telegram in her hand.

The message read:

> *Julie, imperative that you return to California no later than September 1st. Universal wants you for the role of Manuela in* The Story of Pancho Villa. *They need you for two weeks of rehearsal prior to eight weeks of shooting. Excellent opportunity for screen debut. Same director who shot your test. Please wire confirmation immediately. Regards to you and Paco. Lew Wallace.*

Paco had started pacing the floor and muttering furiously to himself in Spanish. When she finished she turned to him, concern in her eyes, and asked him what was wrong.

"What's wrong?" he yelled. "Didn't you promise me that nothing would interfere with our work together?" Mimicking her voice, he said, " 'Paco, don't worry. I'll only accept a role when it's convenient for you.' Well Goddammit, it's not convenient for me. We've still got a job here in case you're interested and a week in Manila."

"But, Paco," Julie answered timidly, nervous at his displeasure. "The telegram said September first. That means I would be returning home only three days earlier than you. Couldn't you just fill in for me for three days?"

"Who the hell is going to fill in for you after all the publicity I've sent out? I warned Lew not to pull that crap on me. He knows how important you've become to the show."

"Please be reasonable," Julie pleaded. "Mr. Wallace didn't know you were extending the tour. He thought that we would be heading home by then."

"Well, we're not. And I'm going to wire him that you're not avail-able on that date."

Paco started for the phone, but Julie forestalled him.

"Paco, please don't be rash. This is my first movie and it's a great part. I had a chance to read the whole script when I was preparing for my test. If I don't come home they might choose someone else."

Paco shook himself free and reached for the phone. "I know the studios better than you. They never start when they say they will. No, it's out of the question. You'll have to finish the tour."

Julie knew that it would be useless to argue with him when his mind was made up. Turning, she went back into the bedroom and closed the door. Pulling up the blinds, she opened the windows and looked out at the boats in the harbor. *Oh God,* she prayed. *Please don't let me lose this opportunity. I want it so much.*

As soon as she left, Paco immediately called the front desk and sent his agent a negative reply. When he finished he sat down and contemplated what his actions would be if the studio insisted. *The hell with them. I'll just demand that she finish out the tour. She's my wife now. She wouldn't dare refuse me.*

Two nerve-wracking days went by of urgent messages between Paco and Lew Wallace, and the matter was still not resolved. The strain was beginning to take its toll on Julie, who looked pale and wan, but just when she was about to give up hope, she received a telephone call from California.

Lew Wallace was seated at his magnificent antique English desk in Beverly Hills when his secretary informed him that his call to Hong Kong was ready. "Julie, I can't stall the studio any longer. They will replace you if you're not back on the first. Actually, they wanted you here a week earlier, but I convinced them that because you were on tour and had a commitment they would have to wait. But the first is their cutoff date. You've got to come home."

"Oh, Mr. Wallace, I want to, but Paco is furious. He says I can't go."

Lew Wallace paused, his own anger beginning to rise. "Julie, is he there? Please, let me talk to him."

Julie left the room and called Paco to the phone. Her only chance was for Lew Wallace to convince him. She watched as Paco took the receiver wordlessly and listened to Lew Wallace for a few minutes. Then, his face distorted with rage as he slammed the phone down, Paco turned and faced a frightened and anxious Julie.

"All right, you can go. But, I warn you. This is the last time you're going to leave me holding the bag. First, South America and now this. I'm not going to play second fiddle to your career."

Storming out of the room, he went into the bedroom and slammed the door. Julie didn't follow. She knew it would be better to stay away from Paco when he was in this frame of mind. He had been hostile to everyone since receiving the telegram two days ago. Now, he would unleash his fury on anyone who crossed his path.

Instead of feeling elated that she would soon be returning home to make her first movie, Julie felt dejected. Why couldn't Paco realize that she had no intention of shirking her responsibility? She loved singing with the band and was grateful to him for everything. And what did he mean "the last time he'd be left holding the bag"? Didn't he realize that the only reason she had to leave him in South America was because she was desperately ill? She sighed. *I'd better give him a chance to cool down before going inside*, she thought. *Thank God we'll only be separated for a few days. I don't think Paco's temperament and his insane jealousy could tolerate any more than that.*

Anxious to share her good news with someone, Julie got up and walked over to the desk, took out some writing paper, and began to write. "Dearest Mom and Dad. Guess what's happened? I'm going to Hollywood to make my first movie."

CHAPTER
33

Julie carefully removed all the last vestiges of her heavy makeup and studied herself in the mirror. Her recently dyed black hair contrasted starkly with her pale skin and amber eyes, and the effect was startling. Even though most people found it attractive, it had taken Julie quite a while to get used to her dark tresses, and now that the picture was finally completed, she looked forward to returning to her natural hair color. Suddenly she realized that she would have to rush if she were to get back to the set in time for the cast party. Paco was already there, as were the other members of the cast, who during the last eight weeks had become almost like a family.

Everyone from the producer on down had done their best to make her feel comfortable during the long hours that she had spent on the set, and Julie was very grateful for their kindness. Even though her role was not as important as that of the popular Mexican actress Sarita Montez, it still gave her a chance to prove that she could act. Those who'd seen the rushes had been very pleased with the performance she had turned in and predicted a bright future for her in films. As Julie applied a light dusting of powder to her clean face, the door to her trailer opened and her dresser, Marjorie, peeked in.

"Julie, can I help you with anything? I would have been here sooner, but I had to bring some of your costumes back to wardrobe."

"Hi, Marjorie. You're just in time. Could you zip me up?"

"Sure, honey. Here, let me get that for you."

Her dresser helped Julie on with the green dress that she had chosen to wear that evening and smoothed the silken folds over her slim body. Julie dabbed her lips lightly with some lipstick and surveyed the results. It felt good to be back in her own clothes after wearing the cumbersome costumes required for the role of Manuela. Only her dark hair seemed out of place, but by tomorrow that would be gone and she would feel more like herself.

With a final glance at the mirror, Julie gathered up her purse and wrap and hastened to join the others. She only hoped that Paco would be in a good mood and not spoil her evening.

After greeting the head of the studio, Bill Goetz, who always made it a point to come down and congratulate the cast and crew, Julie joined the other cast members. Even though Paco held her around the waist possessively most of the time, Julie still tried to relax and enjoy the compliments and attention she was receiving. A short while later, Paco glanced at his watch and gave Julie a sign that he wished to leave, so she made her good-byes and accompanied him outside. The weather was still balmy, even though it was November, and the studio was deserted except for a few extras who were lined up at the casting board, looking at the call sheet for the next day.

The Cadillac convertible that Paco had purchased upon his return from the Orient was waiting where he had left it earlier in the day, and as he helped Julie into the car, Paco breathed a sigh of relief. The picture was finally over and he would once again have Julie all to himself. He had rushed through the last three days in Manila like a man possessed. Julie's departure for Los Angeles had left him in a state of despair, and not even his daily telephone conversations with her could lighten his mood. His throat would tighten and he would feel his blood pressure rise when he thought of his precious flower alone in Hollywood surrounded by handsome actors and conniving directors. He knew that they would make passes at Julie, and although he also knew that she was not a bitch like Laura, who adored the chase, nevertheless he couldn't help speculating—*she's young, ambitious, and very vulnerable. I should not have let her go.*

As they left the studio and made their way across the San Fernando

Valley and back to Beverly Hills, Paco asked, "Would you like to stop at Romanoff's or Chasen's for a bite to eat?"

"Not really, unless you're hungry. They had so much food at the party I couldn't eat another bite. Besides, I'm a little tired."

"Well, I'm not surprised," Paco answered. "You've been getting up at five o'clock in the morning for two months and working pretty late some nights. I'm glad I've been free to pick you up at the studio every day."

"I know, Paco, and I'm grateful that you've been so understanding and patient." But when Julie turned her head away, she couldn't help but wonder about his real motives. He allowed their houseman, Peter, to drive her there in the morning, but he inevitably showed up on the set just before lunch and stayed there for the entire day, watching her every move.

With one hand on the wheel, Paco put his other arm around Julie and pulled her closer. "*Querida*, now that the picture is over and you're free to travel, I have made some plans for our future. While you were busy I arranged bookings for Chicago, St. Louis, Boston, and New York. But, the most exciting news of all is a European tour that I have been thinking about. It would begin next spring and take us through the entire summer. Would you like that, my beauty?"

Julie was surprised at the news. This was the first she had heard of any future tour, and the very thought of traveling immediately, without even a short vacation, unnerved her. She was tired and had hoped to rest, at least for a little while. *Stop it*, she quickly reminded herself. *Paco's been idle, waiting for you to finish this film and you know how he hates that. Don't be selfish. If that's what he wants to do, then do it willingly and don't complain.*

Smiling warmly at him, Julie said, "Paco, that sounds exciting. And I'm thrilled we'll be going to New York. I'm terribly anxious to see my parents. It's been such a long time."

"Good," he said as he lifted her hand to kiss it. "Then we should be ready to meet the band in Chicago on Monday."

Monday, Julie thought. *That gives me only three days—to change my hair, prepare my gowns, and pack.* Suddenly Julie felt very, very tired. Then another terrifying thought occurred to her. *What will happen when the studio needs me for publicity before the movie opens? They have already indicated that I should make myself available to help promote the film. Oh God, why didn't I think of that before? But I can't worry about that now. I'll have to face that problem when I get to it. Right now I must make Paco's needs my first priority.*

Julie and Paco left the following week right on schedule, and as the tour progressed the days quickly turned into weeks and the weeks into months. They had played so many different nightclubs and hotels that sometimes during the night, if Julie awoke suddenly, she would have difficulty remembering what city she was in. She thought often and longingly of California—their beautiful home and the happy time she had spent there making the film.

As their return to New York drew closer, Julie became increasingly apprehensive about seeing her parents and wondered how they would act once they were reunited. During telephone calls home they had become increasingly affectionate and obviously delighted with the fact that she was finally making a movie. But not once did they ask about Paco. She hoped that during her brief stay in New York harmony would prevail between her parents and husband and that the animosity they felt would not cause another battle. In her last conversation with them they told her they were planning a trip to Florida right after her birthday and the Christmas holidays. Julie was thrilled and greatly relieved that the money she was sending them was making their life a little easier. Now, if only she could win their approval. Sighing softly, Julie finished her makeup and was about to put on her evening gown, when Paco walked in.

"*Querida,* you'd better hurry. There are a lot of drunks out there and I want to start the show early."

"I was just getting into my gown, Paco."

"Here, let me help you."

As he helped slip the flimsy fabric over her body, he nuzzled his face into her hair. "*Dios mio,* you smell good," he said huskily as his hands lingered over her rounded breasts. "Oh, Julie. I wish we had more time. I would take you here and now."

"No, Paco, please," Julie said slipping away from his grasp. "We have a show to do. You said you wanted to start early."

Smiling ruefully at Julie, he said, "You are right. I must go now, but do a good show and remember what I told you to do in 'Chiu Chiu.' Throw your hair back from your face like Rita Hayworth. It will drive the men crazy."

As the door closed behind Paco, Julie heaved a deep sigh of relief.

These were the moments she dreaded the most—when Paco's lust made him forget everything else. If she hadn't resisted, he would have taken her right here in the filthy dressing room with only moments to spare before the show.

Straightening her gown, Julie put on what she hoped was her Rita Hayworth face and went out to face the noisy crowd.

CHAPTER 34

Steve Burton couldn't sleep. His argument earlier in the evening with Sharon still preyed on his mind. *Dammit*, he thought as he tossed in bed, trying to find a comfortable position. *I tell myself don't fight. If she's hostile or uptight about some-thing try to ignore it.* But that logic didn't always work, and when his inner resolve gave way, he blew. *God knows*, he thought as he watched the flickering shadows from the open window in their bedroom create strange images on the ceiling, *I'm not always the easiest person to live with. My hours with the law firm have been long, and I realize I'm away from home a couple of nights a week because of business dinners. But, nevertheless, I've tried to make Sharon happy. I've explained to her over and over again that it won't always be this way. But when my associates in the firm are busy with other clients, they rightfully expect me to handle my share of the load.*

Steve was not even sure that his work was the real culprit. Sharon seemed so restless and bored. *Maybe she should have continued to work until we had a baby. A baby.* Steve's face softened as he contemplated that prospect. *That would be wonderful and maybe the answer to all our problems.* He knew that Sharon desperately wanted to conceive, and when each passing month told her that she was not yet destined to be a mother, her disappointment and frustration grew. *But*, Steve thought, *I'll keep trying to reassure her that we're both still very young and have lots of time ahead of us. With Christmas almost here, maybe I can cheer her up so that we both can enjoy the holidays.* Resigned to the fact that sleep was eluding him, Steve slipped quietly out of bed and tiptoed into the living room. Not even bothering to switch on a light, he stretched out on the couch and began to reflect back to earlier in the evening when he had arrived home. He still wasn't sure how their argument had begun but he remembered walking through the door, brushing the snow off his coat, and calling out to her.

Not hearing an answer he removed his damp coat and went into the bedroom. Sharon was busy at her desk writing. She looked up at him as he approached her and instantly he was aware that she was not in a particularly good frame of mind. Deciding to ignore the tiny scowl that creased her otherwise unlined face, he put his arms around her and kissed the top of her head.

"Hi, honey. Sorry I'm late, but I had to finish up some papers before I left. Did you have a good day?"

"Same as usual," she answered, turning back to the list she had been working on before he came in.

Hoping to shake her out of her mood, he asked, "Well, in that case, why don't I take my bride out for dinner? You look like you could use a night out."

"Oh, Steve," she answered almost impatiently. "I've already eaten. I didn't bother to wait for you because lately I never know what time you're going to show up."

"Sharon," Steve said, trying to keep the irritation out of his voice, "you know if I'm going to be very late I always call you ahead of time." Glancing at his watch, he added, "Sweetheart, it's only seven-thirty. Why don't I grab a bite to eat here and we can still catch a movie. I'm really anxious to see *From Here to Eternity*."

Sharon looked up at her husband's handsome face and was about to consent but suddenly changed her mind. "Steve, thanks, but I'd rather not if you don't mind. I'd like to finish my list and the invitations for our New Year's Eve party."

Realizing that Sharon had no intention of going out, Steve reluctantly sat down on the bed and began to loosen his tie.

"Oh, is that what you were doing when I came in?"

"Yes, and I'd like to get them in the mail by tomorrow. It's already a little late."

Sharon pulled a loose strand of hair off her face and picked up a barrette that was on the desk and fastened it into her long brown hair. Steve watched her and wished that she would let her hair hang softly instead of pulling it back. Her shiny thick hair was one of her best features, and Steve loved to run his hands through its silky texture. Looking at his young wife busy at her desk, Steve felt a sudden surge of tenderness. Jumping up, he went over to her, and unfastening her barrette, he let her hair fall loose as he took her into his arms.

"Sharon, to hell with the invitations. I want to make love to you."

Sharon seemed uncomfortable in his arms.

"Steve, please. I must finish."

"You'll finish later. I'll help you. Come, darling," he said as he gently steered her toward the bed.

Sharon didn't resist him, even though she was not feeling particularly romantic. It wasn't just that he had been a little late that evening—that she could have accepted. Lately, for some strange reason, she had begun to resent him. If she could have delved honestly into her own feelings, she would have found that her unhappiness stemmed from the fact that Steve seemed so happy and content with his career, while she had nothing really to occupy her time. Her days were empty. She had never enjoyed a good relationship with her parents, and now even the few girlfriends she knew were already pregnant and happily involved awaiting their babies. Even though Steve was understanding of her feelings and compassionate, she still felt so alone.

"Sharon, darling," Steve said as he embraced her slender body. "What's wrong? Don't you want me to make love to you?"

Sharon looked into her husband's face, which was flushed with desire. "Oh, Steve, you know I do. I just don't know why I'm so unhappy."

"Maybe I can make you feel better, darling. Let me try."

Steve kissed her lips and throat and tenderly began to make love to her. He could feel her respond, but the fire that he had always hoped to ignite still eluded him. He wasn't sure if Sharon was deliberately holding back a vital part of herself in fear of exposing her vulnerability, or if she was just incapable of feeling great passion—in or out of bed. Whatever the reason, it continued to frustrate him. Before his marriage to Sharon his brief interludes with other women had always terminated because he felt no emotional commitment. But while the affairs had lasted, both parties had enjoyed highly satisfying sex. And yet with Sharon, the woman he was in love with, it wasn't like that. Sharon performed her wifely duties, but at times it seemed as if she was only going through the motions halfheartedly.

Steve continued making love to her, but the passion he had felt earlier had ebbed. Rolling away from her, he lay there quietly, without moving.

Sharon looked at his face and realized that she had disappointed him. "Steve, I'm sorry. Really I am. I just wasn't in the mood tonight."

"No problem, Sharon," he said as he avoided her eyes.

He grabbed his robe form the back of the door, put it on, and gathered his clothes from the floor, where he had shed them earlier. "I'm going to get something to eat. Do you want anything?"

"No, Steve, thanks. There's some chicken still warm in the oven. Do you need any help?"

"No, I can manage."

Steve ate his dinner slowly, and in the silence of the kitchen tried to recapture his earlier mood. When he returned a little while later, Sharon was back at her desk, busily piling the finished envelopes into a box for mailing.

"There," she said, heaving a sigh of relief. "They're all done. I invited about twenty-five couples—most of our friends, plus Mr. Reinheimer and Mr. Cohen and their wives. I thought this would be a good opportunity to meet your bosses."

Steve sat down on the bed and picked up his briefcase. He began pulling out some papers he intended to review. "That's fine, Sharon. They may have other plans, but I'm sure they'll stop by for a drink. By the way, you don't have to mail my parents' invitation. My dad is stopping by the office tomorrow, so I'll just give it to him."

Sharon looked up at Steve, bewildered. "Steve, I didn't invite your parents, or mine for that matter. It's not that kind of evening."

He looked up from his papers, disbelief in his eyes. "What kind of evening is it, Sharon? It's New Year's Eve for God's sake and the first real party we've ever given in our home. Most likely my parents won't even come. But that doesn't mean we shouldn't give them the courtesy of inviting them—and your parents, too."

Sharon's face tightened into an angry mask as she faced him. "Well, I'm sure as hell not going to invite my parents. You can bet on that. But since you're carrying on so, I'll send your parents an invitation, though I think they'll feel out of place among all our friends."

Steve stood up and came over to her, his temper flaring. "Dammit,

Sharon. Can't you even pretend that you like my folks? They've never done anything to you."

"Oh, Steve," Sharon answered testily. "Why don't you cut out all this bullshit. You know damn well that your mother hates my guts."

"That's not true," Steve said. "She's made many attempts to get close to you, but you continue to shut her out. It's not a one-way street, you know."

Sharon reached for the box of invitations that were on the desk and angrily dumped them on the floor. "Here, you take charge of these. I don't give a damn *who* you invite or whether we even *have* a New Year's party."

Stepping over the envelopes that were scattered over the floor, Sharon stormed into the bathroom and slammed the door.

Steve just stood there, fury in his heart. *Control yourself*, he told himself. *She's acting irrationally. Don't get trapped into saying something you'll regret.*

Steve angrily pulled the bedspread off the bed and lay down. He had originally intended to review the work he had brought home from the office, but now he couldn't concentrate on anything but his problems with Sharon and what he could do to solve them. Cupping his hands behind his neck, he tried to sort out his life and where he was heading. *I'm making great strides in my career*, he thought, *and meeting a lot of important people. My salary is pretty good, considering the fact I've only been with the firm less than a year. Then what in the hell is wrong? Why am I so unhappy?* The answer that kept coming back to haunt him was always the same. Sharon. He hated to admit that, since it was exactly what his mother had predicted even before he married her. What he had said earlier was true. His mother *had* tried to break through Sharon's reserve and treat her warmly as a daughter, but Sharon rebuffed all her attempts. *Then what is the answer?* Steve wondered. *Should I own up to the fact that I might have made a mistake and get out, or should I be patient and give my marriage more time?* There could only be one answer. Try and see it through. Divorce was not something he believed in. He would have to hang in there and pray that they had a baby soon. Maybe then, Sharon would feel fulfilled and open her heart and become the wife he needed. He desperately hoped that his wish would be granted.

CHAPTER 35

"S am, come quickly. Julie's on the phone." Sam Lehman put aside his newspaper and went into the bedroom, where Rose was engaged in an animated conversation with his beloved daughter.

"Yes, Julie, Dad's here. He'll get on the phone in a minute. Where are you?"

"I'm in New York," Julie said happily.

"New York?" Rose gasped. "Why didn't you tell us last week that you were arriving so soon? We thought you'd be here next week."

"I thought so, too, Mom, but Paco has decided to play the Copacabana over the holidays so we came back to rehearse some new material."

"Oh, baby, I'm so anxious to see you and so is Dad. We've missed you so much. Where are you staying?"

"At the Waldorf Towers, Mom. Paco still has his apartment there."

"Yes, I forgot," Rose said bitterly, remembering instantly that the last time she had seen her daughter had been at that farce of a wedding. "Well, at least you'll be home for your birthday, sweetheart." Rose tried hard to keep the hate she felt for the man who had taken her daughter away out of her voice. "We should do something to celebrate. I'll call Marshall and Marsha."

Glancing over at Sam she could see that he was grimacing impatiently for her to relinquish the phone so that he could speak to Julie.

"Wait, *mamela*. Dad is practically pulling the phone out of my hand. I'll call you later. I have so many things I want to ask you."

She reluctantly handed Sam the receiver. "Julie, baby, I've missed you so much. How do you feel? Have you gained any weight back? Have you heard from the studio since we last talked to you?"

"Wait, Dad," Julie laughed happily. "One question at a time. I feel fine, and yes, I've put on a couple of pounds. No, I haven't heard from Universal about the release date yet, but I'm sure they'll contact my agents soon."

"When do we get to see you, Julie? Can you come by the apartment tomorrow evening after I get home from the office?"

Julie paused for a moment, thinking. "Gosh, Dad, I don't know. I'll have to ask Paco what his plans are. But if not tomorrow, then definitely the next day. We have a lot of unpacking to do, but I'm certain we can come by."

Bristling at the sound of Paco's name, Sam said, "I'm not interested in seeing *him*. Mom and I just want to spend some time alone with *you*."

Julie's throat tightened with anxiety. Here it was—just what she had been dreading. The unending conflict between her parents and her husband. *What am I going to do?* she thought. *They refuse to budge, and if Paco finds out that they still harbor such bad feelings about him he'll be furious.*

"Look, Dad. I have a better idea. Why don't you and Mom come here tomorrow night and have dinner with us at the hotel? That way, Mom won't have to cook and I can show you all the newspaper clippings and photographs of the movie."

Now it was Sam's turn to be stuck for an answer. There was such a plaintive sound in Julie's voice. He knew that she was being torn between her devotion to them and her loyalty to Paco. But God, how he detested that man and how he hated to be in his company. "Julie, darling, let me discuss it with Mom and we'll call you later. We're thrilled that you're home and don't worry—we'll get to see each other soon."

Sam put down the receiver and looked into his wife's questioning eyes. "Rose, it's no use. We're going to have to be in that bastard's company sooner or later. So let's get it over with. Just forget about him and let's see our daughter as often as possible while she's in New York. God knows how long it will be before we see her again."

In her beautiful apartment overlooking Park Avenue, Julie carefully replaced the receiver on the telephone. She was deeply troubled. *No matter how hard I try, I'll never be able to have any real peace. My parents hate Paco and he hates them and it will always be that way. Now where does that leave me?* she wondered sadly. *Right smack in the middle—just where I've always been—trying to make everyone happy.*

In future years, Julie would always think back with great sadness to that cold December day when she turned seventeen. She knew it was a bad omen when the telephone awakened her at the Waldorf Towers at eight A.M. and she heard her brother's voice.

"Sis, I'm sorry to call you this early. I know that you don't get to bed until very late, but this is kind of important."

"It's okay, Marshall," Julie answered sleepily. Cupping her hand over the telephone, she quickly glanced over to Paco, who had not stirred. *He could sleep through World War III,* Julie thought, *but I'd better not take a chance.* "Wait a second, Marshall. I'll take this call in the living room."

Grabbing her robe, she hurried into the other room and closed the door. Picking up the extension, she said, "Okay, what's up?"

"Honey, I thought I'd better warn you in advance. Mom and Dad are not planning on coming to the Copa tonight to celebrate your birthday."

"What?" Julie asked, fear gripping her heart. "Is something wrong? Is anyone sick?"

"No, it's nothing like that, Sis. Look, did something happen between Paco and them since you've been back? Did they have a fight or something?"

"Nothing in particular," Julie answered, trying to think back. "Just the same old story. *They* think that he's trying to manipulate me and *he* thinks they're selfish and demanding. What did they say to you?"

"Well," her brother answered, as tenderly as he could, "they called my house late last night and said that they've had enough. They refuse to 'spend another night in that man's company.' When I asked them what was wrong, all Dad would say is, 'that monster is ruining my daughter's life and I'm not going to sit around and watch it.' "

"Oh, Marshall," Julie cried. "I don't know what to do. I guess they're angry because at dinner the other night Paco was discussing a European tour, and they think that he's taking me out of the country just to ruin my chance in pictures. They're convinced that Paco is too dominating and is trying to intimidate me. But I never dreamed that they would react this way and refuse to celebrate my birthday with me."

"Look, honey, I don't want to get into your private life. I have my own troubles as far as Mom and Dad are concerned. But are you sure that what they're saying isn't a little bit true? After all you *are* very young and inexperienced and Paco does tell you what to do every minute of the day."

"But, Marshall, for years and years, so did Mom and Dad. No one has ever given me the chance to think for myself. Oh, Marshall, I don't know what to do. When they tell me something it sounds right. But when Paco tells me his side, he sounds right too. I just wish they'd all leave me alone."

"So what else is new?" Marshall chuckled ironically.

"For God's sake, don't laugh," Julie pleaded. "I'm miserable enough already and today is my birthday."

"Honey, I'm not laughing, believe me. I feel for you and I'm sorry that you're going through this. Listen, you go back to bed and try not to worry. I'll go over to the apartment and try to convince them to show up at the club tonight. Maybe they'll listen."

"Tell them that we'll be leaving town again next week and I don't know how long I'll be gone. Oh, Marshall," Julie pleaded, "please make them come."

"Don't worry, sweetheart. I'll do my best. In any case, Marsha and I will be there. I love you, Sis, and don't you ever forget that."

"I love you too, Marshall, and thank you."

Julie hung up the phone and stared aimlessly into space. Sleep was out of the question now, for she had to think. *Should I call them or not?* she wondered. *No, I'd better not. I might say the wrong thing. Better let Marshall try and reason with them. I won't say anything about this to Paco. It'll just set him off and give him an opportunity to say something nasty.*

Hours later Julie peeked out at the jam-packed room in the Copacabana and tried to find the table she had reserved for her family. There were so many people already seated and the dance floor was so crowded she could barely see the tables at ringside. Marshall hadn't called back since their early morning conversation, and she hoped that it was a good sign that he had accomplished his task. Unable to venture out any farther than where she was standing for fear of being seen in her evening gown, Julie went back into the dressing room. She was alone with only the loudspeaker blasting out the music the band was playing for company. Paco was up on the bandstand, playing the last set before the show. Next door, through the thin wall that separated their dressing rooms, Julie could hear the chatter of the beautiful Copa girls, most of whom were barely older than she. *They're so happy and carefree,* Julie thought. *All they talk about is their boyfriends and the places they're going after the show.* None of them appeared to be seriously motivated to pursue a career. They only seemed intent on cashing in on their good looks by marrying a rich man and getting out of the business as soon as possible. In a way, Julie envied them. No worries, no responsibilities. Just two shows a night of prancing around in skimpy costumes then being carted off to a late dinner. All at once, Julie felt older than those girls. She was not only married, but committed to a career. Suddenly she felt robbed of her youth. Could it be that her parents had been right?

Moments later, Julie became aware that the music had stopped and the audience had quieted down. She could imagine the scene outside. The waiters would be placing the last drinks on the tables before the show began. Julie Podel, one of the Copa's bosses, might be standing near the entry growling at the captain to "get that goddamn drunk out of here before I punch his face." And Jack Entratter, the other chief honcho, would be checking to see if Frank Sinatra, a Copa regular, and his party had arrived.

The sound of the drumroll startled Julie, even though she had heard it hundreds of times before. Taking a deep breath she turned out the light in the dressing room and opened the door. The club was dark except for the palm trees that lined the back of the bandstand and the candles that flickered on each table. Inching forward in the dark, Julie reached the steps that led down to the stage. She paused and waited there.

The resonant voice of the master of ceremonies suddenly filled the room. "Ladies and gentlemen, the Copacabana is proud to present the exciting music of Paco Castell and his orchestra, featuring the beautiful Miss Julie Lauren."

The spotlight hit Julie exactly as they had rehearsed, and when the audience saw her standing there in her flame-colored gown that gave her red hair an even greater intensity, they screamed and applauded their approval. Slowly, to the beat of the sensual music, Julie descended the stairs, moving her hips slightly to the music. Her smile showed off her dazzling white teeth, and her amber eyes glowed with excitement. As she made her way to the microphone, she could hear the murmuring going on in the audience.

"God, she's gorgeous, but she's only a baby."

"Paco sure knows how to pick them."

"Do you think she's a natural redhead?"

Julie just smiled and floated to the center of the stage. She felt good. This was where she belonged. These people loved her. And if she was good they would love her even more at the end of the evening. This was what she had been training and struggling for all her life. The response of the crowd was like a warm embrace, and she never wanted it to end. Her eyes began to focus on the crowd. It seemed that everybody who was anybody was out there tonight. Then, suddenly, she saw her table. Marshall and Marsha were smiling at her, pride mirrored in their faces. Next to them two empty seats stared at her defiantly. The chairs said "we told you they wouldn't come. We know it's your birthday and you're playing to an enthusiastic crowd in one of the greatest nightclubs in the world. It's just too bad. You disobeyed them and married that terrible man, so you must be punished." Julie opened her trembling mouth and with her heart bursting with pain sang the first line of her song. "You are deep in my heart and will be forever."

CHAPTER
36

Julie stood on deck and watched the Statue of Liberty slowly fade from sight as the *Queen Mary* moved out of New York harbor and into the open sea. Paco stood at her side, signing autographs for some fellow passengers, who were thrilled that a famous celebrity was sailing on the same ship.

"Oh, Mr. Castell," a lady with an outrageous red hat and a huge corsage pinned on her shoulder said, "you're the third celebrity we've seen so far since we came on board. Of course the other two went directly to their cabins, but we did get a glimpse of them coming up the gangplank."

The portly man who stood beside her was obviously her husband. "Yeah, Paco, no mistaking the Duke and Duchess of Windsor all right. God, is that broad skinny."

Julie couldn't help but smile at that comment. People said the strangest things about celebrities, and she often wondered what they said about her behind her back.

Suddenly, the foghorn belched out a loud noise that startled Julie. "What was that, Paco?" Julie asked nervously.

"Nothing, *querida*. You'll get used to it. Come, it's getting chilly. Let's go downstairs."

He started to leave, but the woman standing next to him pulled at his sleeve. "Oh, Mr. Castell," the red hat gushed. "Won't you introduce me to your daughter? She's so lovely."

"She's *not* my daughter," Paco said through clenched teeth. Under his breath, Julie could hear him mumble *stupid bitch*. "She's my wife!"

Embarrassed, the woman suddenly backed off, but her husband came to her rescue. "Well, you sure know how to pick them, Paco old boy."

Paco grabbed Julie's arm and pulled her toward the door. "If that's the kind of idiots we're going to come in contact with this voyage, then we'd be better off having our meals in our stateroom."

"Oh, Paco," Julie said as they hurried through the corridors still filled with people holding their champagne glasses. "The man you called the steward said we're eating in the VIP dining room. He called it the Verandah Grill, and it only seats one hundred people. Most of the people dining there are either celebrities, socialites, or regulars who have crossed many times." Julie chattered away, hoping to break his mood. "I'm sure you won't be bothered by lots of people."

"I hope you're right. Five days is a long time to be cooped up."

As they entered their stateroom they had to pick their way carefully through the huge baskets of flowers that had been sent by business acquaintances of Paco. There were boxes of candy and fruit sitting on the table, and over in the corner, champagne was being chilled in a bucket of ice. Julie was so thrilled to be sailing to Europe on this luxurious ship that she didn't have time to dwell on the disappointment she felt because her parents hadn't been there to see her off. She had spoken to them from the road frequently since the horrible night of her birthday and had seen them briefly in New York a week before her departure for Europe. But they had never discussed the incident and Julie never mentioned the Copacabana or the pain they had caused her by their absence. Julie had begun to come to grips with the realization that she was powerless to change things, and therefore, she attempted to put it out of her mind. She desperately wanted to be happy. After all, she was young, it was spring, and she was on her way to Europe and a new adventure.

The *Queen Mary* offered all the amenities of any large luxury hotel, and Julie knew there would be more than enough activities to keep her busy during the voyage. Paco, on the other hand, started to grow restless during their second day at sea. After being served a sumptuous breakfast in their stateroom, he and Julie toured the promenade deck and visited the shops that lined the arcade. The passengers were all elegantly attired in sport clothes, and Julie spotted many faces she had seen in the society pages. After lunch, she told Paco that she would like to take a swim in the indoor pool. Paco told her to go alone, preferring to relax in a chair on the upper deck. With nothing to occupy his time and no one he really cared to converse with, he soon grew bored with his book and began to look at his watch, impatient for Julie to return. When she finally appeared, her cheeks glowing from the vigorous exercise and her body beautifully encased in white shorts and matching halter top, Paco looked at her with longing.

"*Mi amor*, where have you been so long? It has been lonely here without you."

Julie took a vacant seat next to Paco and stretched out in the sun. "I'm sorry, Paco. The pool was so refreshing I just forgot about the time."

Suddenly, without warning, Paco reached over and slid his hand inside her top. Startled, Julie looked around to see if anyone was watching, but they were alone. "Paco, please," she said, removing his hand. "Someone might come by."

Excited now, just at the feel of her firm warm flesh, Paco rose and lifted Julie to her feet. "You're right. Let's go to our cabin."

Julie let herself be led to their stateroom, trying hard not to show the disinterest she felt. Paco opened the door and began feverishly to remove his clothing. As he reached for her, Julie thought sadly, *This is going to be the longest five days of my life.*

"I love Paris in the springtime." Those words from Cole Porter's song, immortalized in the Broadway show *Can Can*, kept running through Julie's head as the limousine made its way up the Champs-Élysée to its final destination—the famous Hotel George V. The *Queen Mary* had docked at Cherbourg early that morning and Julie and Paco had boarded the boat train for Paris. At the station a limousine was awaiting them along with the foreign impresario who would be handling their tour. As the car pulled up in front of the hotel, Julie slipped on the beige kid gloves that matched her new suit, remembering her mother's words. "Julie, no outfit is complete without gloves. They are the signature of a lady." *Well*, Julie thought, *I wish Mom could see me now. I think she would be proud.* The doorman began giving instructions in French to the bellboys as Julie and Paco stepped out of the car. All of a sudden dozens of flashbulbs went off as a barrage of photographers and reporters descended upon them. The impresario tried to clear a path for them to enter the hotel, but the press kept bombarding them with questions, some in French and others in broken English.

"Mees Lauren, thees is your first time in France, no?"

"Mees Lauren, how old are you?"

Paco, who was an old hand in dealing with this kind of situation, just held on tightly to Julie and pushed on ahead into the hotel. At the front desk, the hotel manager proudly introduced himself and showed them to their suite. When Julie saw the rooms she couldn't contain her youthful enthusiasm.

"Oh, Paco, this is the most beautiful place. Everything is so gorgeous." She ran from room to room, marveling at the splendor. It had the kind of old-world charm that Julie had only seen in magazines, and she was totally overwhelmed by her surroundings. Flushed with excitement, she said, "I can't believe it. We'll be staying here for two whole weeks." Throwing open the terrace doors, Julie called for Paco to come join her.

As he stepped out on the terrace, Julie threw her arms around his neck. Her eyes were glowing with happiness. "Oh, Paco, it's so beautiful. I can't stand it. You can see practically all of Paris from here. Look at the Eiffel Tower."

Paco beamed at his beautiful young wife's enthusiasm. It was a delight to show her new places and watch her face light up as she experienced new things. Her happiness was contagious. Putting his arm around her, he said, "It is beautiful, my angel, and we shall explore all of it together."

Julie had never been so happy. She hadn't expected the impact Paris would have on her, and she hoped that the French audiences would love her as much as she already loved their city.

Opening night turned out to be one of the major events of the Paris season. Paco Castell had been a huge star in France for many years. Because of the enormous impact of his records and films, people were anxious to see him in person. Julie was slightly apprehensive about her appearance at the famous Olympia in Paris, a theater that was home to many great international stars. She was afraid she lacked the sophistication needed for that kind of audience.

Adding to her anxiety was the knowledge that out front were the best people in Paris. She was told that among the luminaries was the sad little singer from the Left Bank, Edith Piaf, who had become an idol adored by all classes. Also present was Josephine Baker, the American star who had caused such a sensation in Paris during the thirties, and the legendary Maurice Chevalier. Not speaking the language, Julie was naturally nervous about being able to communicate. But her fears soon vanished when she heard the warm applause that greeted her. She had practiced saying her greeting in French and just enough words to introduce her songs, but because of her nervousness, she stumbled a few times. But instead of resorting to English, she excused herself in Spanish and made a little joke about her terrible accent and disarmed the audience.

The entire show that Paco had assembled with great care was enthusiastically received, and he beamed when he received a standing ovation after the show. After that night, there was no doubt in anyone's mind that Paco Castell had suddenly become the toast of Paris, and that he and Julie Lauren had captivated the public and the press. The days that followed were unforgettable, for Paco could now relax and show Julie the Paris he remembered, but had not seen, for many years.

They visited the Louvre, where Julie stood in awe before the *Mona Lisa* and the Cathedral of Notre Dame. They even rode the elevator up to the top of the Eiffel Tower, but Julie was afraid to look down because of her fear of heights. Julie was captivated by the City of Lights and could understand the fascination it held for tourists the world over. Paco was a marvelous guide, and as they toured the art galleries and museums, he thoroughly enjoyed sharing his vast knowledge of art with such an eager pupil. It was during those hours that they spent together that Julie felt closest to him. She listened attentively as he described Picasso's "blue period" and explained what made an artist great. He expressed a desire to paint himself, but he had never taken enough time off to give it a try. He took Julie to the salons of France's most famous couturiers and bought her little gifts—gloves at Christian Dior, perfume at Guerlain, and a small but charming hat at Patou. Julie wished that she had more spending money of her own so that she could buy gifts for her parents, but she had only a small amount of cash. Still, she managed to get her mother perfume and gloves and her father and brother some ties at Hermès.

The climax of her stay in Paris came the night they visited the famous Maxims. As the rather stern and proper-looking maître d' led them through the crowded tables to the booth Paco had reserved, Julie looked around and was rendered speechless by what she saw. Never had she seen such elegantly dressed women, or such incredible jewels. They were so staggering in their size and beauty, it was hard to believe they were real. She felt slightly uncomfortable in her simple black dress. It had looked perfectly appropriate back at the hotel, but now, amidst all this opulence, it seemed rather plain.

As Paco watched Julie steal nervous glances at the chic Parisian women, he put his hand over hers. "Darling, are you upset about something?"

"No, Paco, of course not. This place is just incredible. I just wish I would have worn something different, that's all."

He cupped her chin in his hand. "Listen to me. You are the most beautiful woman here tonight. You're fresh and vital, not like most of these women, who may be rich, but terribly jaded. The dress you're wearing may not be expensive and your jewelry is relatively unimportant compared to theirs, but it doesn't matter. I watched them look at you when we walked in. They would give anything to look like you, including some of their precious jewels. Besides that, my dear, remember you are an artist, something they can never be. So relax and enjoy this evening. Better still," he said, taking her hand and lifting her to her feet, "let's dance. They're playing a rhumba. When they see you on the dance floor they'll really eat their hearts out."

Following Paco's advice and with slightly more confidence now, she stepped out onto the dance floor and into his waiting arms. As Julie danced, she could sense the admiring glances cast her way. *Can Italy and Spain be even more wonderful than these past few weeks we've spent in Paris? If so, then I may never want to go home.*

CHAPTER
37

The crowds at Ciampino Airport had been awaiting the arrival of Paco Castell under the hot sun for hours. Rome was experiencing its first heat wave of the season, but that didn't seem to deter the hundreds of admirers who were lined up behind the barriers. For weeks, publicity heralding his arrival had been intense, and the Italians, who like the French loved his movies and music, were anxious to give him a warm welcome. As the plane made its final approach, Paco fidgeted in his seat, unable to concentrate on anything but his own thoughts. Julie had her face practically glued to the window, trying to catch a glimpse of Rome, but Paco was still reliving the last conversation with Lew Wallace that had taken place earlier in the week. His agent had reached him by telephone at the Hotel George V in Paris just before they left for the theater. Julie had been busy in the bedroom dressing when Paco answered.

"Paco, it's Lew. Yes, I'm in California and I'm glad I reached you before you left."

"What is it, Lew?" Paco asked excitedly, thinking that perhaps there might be something brewing for him in Hollywood.

"Paco, Universal has another movie for Julie. This is with Rock Hudson, but they would like to test her first."

Paco's mood instantly changed on hearing the news. "Christ, Lew. We've just started the tour. Are you guys out of your fucking minds?"

"Wait, Paco, hold it. I know she's on tour and we won't disturb that. I just thought if she has a few days off between engagements, she could fly home, make the test, and then go back and finish out the tour. The picture doesn't start until the end of August. You will already be back by then, and it would be a great opportunity for Julie."

Conscious of the fact that Julie was within earshot, Paco tried to contain the rage he was feeling. His face, which minutes before had been serene, had changed into an angry mask as he cupped his hand over the receiver.

"Listen to me, Lew," he hissed into the phone. "She is not flying back for any goddamn test and that is final. We are having a huge success over here, and I don't intend to lose my star attraction now or at any other time. This is not like the last time in the Orient when I allowed you to pull her away for a movie. Do I make myself clear?"

"Perfectly," Lew answered coldly. "But if we keep turning down picture opportunities and the studio sees that she's not even available for promotion on the film she's just made, they might get pissed and drop her."

"Then let them drop her. The success she's making with me is far more important to her career than making a low-budget piece of shit in Hollywood."

"Paco," Lew said, the irritation he was feeling now clearly audible in his voice, "a picture with Rock Hudson can hardly be called a piece of shit. He's one of the studio's hottest properties, and they're choosing his movies very carefully."

"Well, let them get someone else. My wife is not available." Without waiting for a reply, Paco slammed down the receiver and started pacing the floor. *What in the hell am I going to do?* he wondered. *If I tell her, she'll want to go. If I don't tell her and she eventually finds out*—Paco paused as he pondered the possible outcome of keeping this news from her. Shaking his head determinedly, he decided to say nothing. *I can't let anything interfere with the tour. I'll just have to chance it that she won't find out.* Now, days later as they were about to land in Rome, Paco was still certain that he had been right in his handling of the situation. There hadn't been any further communications from Hollywood, and Paco assumed that the question of Julie returning home had been put to bed.

A week had gone by since their arrival in the Eternal City, and it had been exhilarating, though somewhat tiring. There had been interviews and photo sessions from morning until evening, and in just a few days Julie's picture appeared on the cover of practically every Italian magazine, making her an instant celebrity. Now, opening night was finally here. The spotlight blazed a trail above the heads of the audience seated in the packed stadium as the wildly enthusiastic Italian men shouted to Julie from their seats, "*la mossa, la mossa.*" The Foro Italico, normally home to sporting events and the summer Olympics, had been temporarily converted into an outdoor auditorium suitable for the show, and as Julie stood there trembling with excitement, she heard the thunderous roar of voices calling out to her again.

"*Bella Julie, fa la mossa.*"

Julie had no idea what they were saying. They had been yelling the same thing from practically the first moment she had started to sing and dance. Every audience she had ever performed for, from Ciro's in Hollywood to the exuberant carnival crowds in Rio, paled in compari-son to the volatile Italians. They screamed and carried on so that it was almost impossible for her to hear her own voice. From the moment she had appeared onstage dressed in her skin-tight gold lamé gown, they had gone wild. There were fifty thousand people out there, and half of them were hot-blooded Italian men who loved to show their appreciation of beautiful women. As the cries of "*la mossa*" grew stronger, Julie turned around questioningly to Paco, who was standing behind her with a broad grin on his face.

"Paco," she whispered. "Do you know what they're saying? Is *la mossa* the name of some song they want? What should I do?"

Paco put his arm around Julie's waist and approached the micro-phone. In half-Spanish and half-Italian he asked them, "*Mia signora, no intiende ustedes. Cosa vuol dire, la mossa?*"

The audience began to applaud and scream with laughter at his question. Seconds later, out of nowhere, a young man jumped onstage, and before the policemen could reach him, he grabbed Julie. She was so startled that she didn't know how to react. Judging by his appear-ance, the boy had to be sitting in the cheaper seats.

In broken English he said, "*Signorina*, look at me. *Guarda*. Signor Paco asked public what is *mossa*? You watch."

Crouching down slightly, with his knees bent and his arms stretched out wide in front of him, he gave a provocative wiggling movement that sent the audience into an uproar. "You see, *signorina* Julie, that is *la mossa*. Now you do it, *cosi.*"

Julie laughed at him. She had learned all kinds of Latin movements and various wiggles but had never seen anything like that. *Well*, she thought, *if that's what they want then that's what I'll give them.*

Crouching in the same position, her tight gown exposing every curve of her body, Julie took a deep breath and imitated the movement perfectly. There were such screams of delight from both men and women that Julie had to repeat it several times. Finally, when they had calmed down enough to let her continue her songs, Julie had a fleeting thought. *How ironic it is that I've accomplished more with a wiggle in one night than with all my years of vocal training.*

After the show, the makeshift dressing room that the Italians had constructed in back of the stage threatened to come apart as the throngs of people tried to get inside. Paco had already removed his tuxedo jacket, which was drenched with perspiration, but Julie didn't dare change. Not with all those people standing outside. She tried fanning herself with one of the programs, but it was useless. The night air was just oppressively hot, and she was still too excited to cool down. The first person to reach them was Franco, their Italian impresario.

His face was glowing as he embraced them. "Paco, Julie, *che successo*. What a triumph. Rome may never be the same. Every important actor and actress in Italy is out there tonight. Lollobrigida, Silvana Mangano, Anna Magnani, Vittorio Gassman, everyone. All the nobility, too— the Crespis, Torlonia, Borghese, *tutti*."

The short balding Italian whose blue suit looked as if it had been slept in, continued on while mentally estimating the millions of lire he would be making from this engagement. "Paco, Vittorio De Sica and Pepe Amato would like to invite you and Julie to a late supper at Giggi Fazi, a restaurant near the hotel. There will be many interesting people there that I think you should meet. What do you say?"

Paco knew of course who De Sica was—one of Italy's most important directors and actors—famous for his films with the French actor Fernandel and even more famous for having discovered Gina Lollobrigida and making her a star.

"Of course, Franco," Paco answered as Julie looked on. "That would be nice. Who is the other man, Amato?"

"Another very important producer, maestro. He just finished making a film with your American actress Linda Darnell." Winking at Paco he added, "He was also, how do you say, involved with her romantically."

Paco glanced over at Julie, who had been listening attentively. "*Querida*, would you like to go? Are you hungry?"

"Oh yes, Paco. I'd love it. I was too nervous to eat lunch. But first, I have to go back to the hotel and change. I can't wash up here."

"Of course, my dear. I too need to get some fresh clothes. Franco, please tell the driver to come here and pick us up and also, on the way out, please see if you can get rid of the crowds outside the door. We'll meet you back at the Hotel Excelsior in about an hour."

When they were escorted into the lovely outdoor restaurant they found the usually crowded room empty except for the table of celebrities waiting for Paco and Julie to arrive. They applauded their entrance and congratulated them on their triumph. As dinner was being served, Vittorio De Sica rose and raised his glass of wine.

"A toast, *signori*, to Maestro Paco Castell and his *bellisima signora*, Julie."

Everyone lifted a glass and with great warmth said, *"chin, chin"*.

Vittorio De Sica smiled as he took his place once again next to Julie. He had been watching her intently ever since she had joined them. Unlike most of the other men seated there, especially Guiseppe Amato, who had difficulty concealing his lust for any young girl, De Sica saw not only her beauty, but sensed a quality in her that interested him professionally. He was experienced enough to realize the minute he saw her perform that she was obviously being groomed as a sex symbol by her older husband. But that was all right. He had nothing against sexy women. But he intuitively guessed that underneath the outer trappings, there was a sensitive young woman who, in the right hands, could come across the screen like a million dollars. *And whose hands,* he thought, *are more capable than mine? Sì carina,* he thought as he studied her intently. *There is much more to you than meets the eye.*

At the opposite end of the long table, now littered with empty bottles of wine and half-eaten dishes of pasta, sat Guiseppe Amato, whose dark eyes were also watching Julie's every move. But his thoughts were far from professional. From the moment he saw her he had been contemplating how he could get rid of her husband for a little while and lure her into bed. *Dìo mio,* he thought as he watched her laugh and fling her long red hair back from her shining face. *She reminds me of a golden fawn with those slender arms and long and shapely legs. She looks like a typical Americana, but yet, there is something Latin about her.* Leaning across the table he studied her face. *Sì,* he kept on thinking. *She could easily play an Italian with her ample breasts and beautiful curves. Her almond-shaped eyes are almost the same color as Carlo Ponti's new discovery, Sophia Loren.* He suddenly felt an overwhelming heat rising up from his loins that began to take control of his body. He wanted to go over to her and ask her something, anything, just to be near her. But he dared not move. Everyone at the table would notice the effect her beauty had made on him, especially her husband. Reaching for his napkin he wiped his moist brow. *I don't know what I want more—to make her a star or fuck her. Maybe I'll do both.*

Paco smiled at Julie as he poured himself a glass of wine, but his mood was anything but gay. *That son of a bitch Amato has been watching her like a hawk all evening,* he thought angrily. *Who the hell does he think he is, David Selznick? It's bad enough,* he thought, trying hard not to show his displeasure, *that De Sica has monopolized her since the moment we walked in. But at least he acts like a gentleman, not like that greaseball with the beady eyes. Well, tough shit, amigo, if you think you've got a chance with her. I've handled situations like this before and, if need be, I will again.*

Julie's mood was exuberant as she basked in the glow of all the attention she was receiving. Unlike the scared kid at Alberto Dodero's home in Uruguay who didn't even know which fork to use, she had acquired enough sophistication to hold her own with even an international crowd like the one assembled tonight. Since arriving in Europe, she had learned to use her knowledge of Spanish to help her communicate with those French and Italians who did not speak English. In Rome, she had picked up a lot of phrases in Italian and tonight was enjoying trying them out. Paco began to feel uneasy as he watched Julie's charm and newfound sophistication take its effect. It had happened so suddenly that, until now, even he hadn't been aware of it. Julie seemed much more at home in Europe than she had ever been in the States. It was as if she belonged here. Paco tried to sort out his emotions as he sat there and listened to the chatter surrounding him. Part of him was happy that Julie was having a love affair with Rome and it with her. The other part was concerned that she might fall under the spell of some good-looking Latin, closer to her own age, who would spirit her away. *I must be on my guard constantly,* he thought as he put his arm around her. *I can't lose her.*

The next few weeks seemed to fly as Julie and Paco became the toast of Italy. *OGGI,* one of Italy's leading magazines, dubbed Julie the Queen of the Cha Cha Cha, and the title stuck. The crowds kept filling the stadium to capcacity every evening, and Franco was thinking of booking them back for a return engagement after they toured Spain.

But the biggest surprise of all was the amazing interest in Julie by Italy's most prominent movie producers. After that first evening, De Sica had promised her that he would soon find something in one of his films that would suit her talents. Guiseppe Amato had been calling them constantly with invitations for lunch and dinner. He too was staying at the Hotel Excelsior on the Via Condotti. He had given up his former apartment in the Piazza di Spagna and had rented a large apartment at the hotel. He was trying to be very discreet about his attentions to Julie, for he had seen that familiar flicker of jealousy in Paco's eyes. Being a Latin, he understood all too well. After their first meeting and a sleepless night spent thinking about her, he decided the following morning to find the perfect vehicle for her beauty and talent. Realizing that it wouldn't be long before other producers would also be after her, especially De Sica, Amato planned how he would beat them to the punch by offering her a long-term contract. He figured that once she was his professionally, then all the rest would fall into place.

With only one performance a night, Julie's stay in Rome seemed like almost a holiday, for she had become accustomed to two or three performances a day. Accompanied always by a horde of photographers, she and Paco toured the city. This was also Paco's first visit to Rome, and he too became enchanted with its ancient beauty. Paco engaged a guide, who pointed out the famous sights that attracted hundreds of thousands of tourists each year. But their real insight into the splendor of Rome came from their newfound friends—members of the Roman aristocracy who brought them into their homes and entertained them. The time was coming soon when their engagement would be over, and Julie was not eager to leave, even though their next stop would be Spain, a country she had always longed to visit. She was acutely aware that Paco was receiving offers for her to appear in various films and she also was aware that he kept putting them off with the excuse "we have to finish the tour first, then we'll see." What she didn't expect was the sudden arrival in Rome of Lew Wallace's right-hand man, Howard Dugan. He called at Paco and Julie's suite shortly after arriving at the hotel and asked if he could come upstairs immediately.

Paco replaced the receiver on the telephone quietly, grateful that Julie was occupied in the other room. He needed time to think. *What in God's name is Howard Dugan doing in Rome and what is the urgency to see both of us immediately? There could be only one answer*, Paco thought as he fixed himself a drink. *Lew Wallace has sent him here to speak to Julie.* Paco gulped the brandy. He desperately needed to steady his nerves before Dugan got there. *I must think of how I'm going to handle this,* he thought frantically. *If Julie finds out that I prevented her from going back to Hollywood to test for the Rock Hudson movie, she will not only be hurt and upset, but eventually she will blame me for ruining her chances in Hollywood.* Before he could decide on what strategy he would employ, there was a knock on the door. Paco quickly rushed to open it.

The tall, slender, gray-haired man, who was probably destined to replace Lew Wallace as head of the agency, was standing there.

"Paco, it's good to see you. You're looking well." After an awkward pause, he asked. "May I come in?"

Paco stepped aside and motioned for him to come in. Dugan looked around the elegantly decorated suite and decided to take a chair near the French doors, which had been left open to allow the summer breeze in.

"God, it's hot out there," he said, fingering his starched white collar, hoping to let some air penetrate his skin. "I wish this place was air-conditioned."

Paco pulled up a chair and sat down facing him. "Howard, you haven't traveled halfway around the world to discuss the weather with me. Why are you here?"

"Well," Dugan said, trying to choose his words carefully so as not to infuriate Paco, "after Lew's conversation with you a few weeks ago in Paris, he relayed your message to the studio and we thought that would end any further discussions regarding Julie. But we were wrong. Since then, the studio has previewed her picture in several cities and the response has been terrific. Universal is convinced they have a potential star on their hands and they want to know when they can have her back."

Paco glanced nervously over at the door leading to the bedroom. *Julie must be in the shower,* he thought. *She hasn't made a sound and obviously doesn't know Howard is here.*

Howard Dugan continued. "Look, Paco. We understand how you feel about having your plans disrupted, and we respect that. Therefore, we have convinced the studio to forgo the test and wait until Julie finishes her commitment. Surely you can't have any objections to that."

Paco rose and pushed the French doors open even wider. "Howard, let's talk out here on the terrace."

"For Christ's sake, Paco, the sun's too hot. Why don't we stay inside?"

Desperate to get him out of Julie's hearing range, Paco walked quickly over to the bar. "I'll get you a drink," Paco said as he opened the refrigerator. "What do you want, scotch or mineral water?"

"Mineral water, thanks. But Paco, I would like to continue our conversation and I'd also like to include Julie. By the way, where is she?"

"She's busy right now," Paco said as he brought him the drink and led him out to the terrace. "Why don't we talk first, then I'll call Julie."

"Very well, Paco. As I was saying. Your wife has the chance of a lifetime staring her in the face. But we have to strike while the iron is hot."

"A lot has happened here in Italy," Paco said, "since I last spoke to Lew. We've had a tremendous success and she has had a lot of picture offers. In fact," he added sarcastically, "they're interested in having me appear in some movies with her. That's a hell of a lot better than what you guys have come up with."

"Paco, I'm delighted for both of you. But Hollywood still is the place where the big-budget films are being made, and American films are what will make her an international star."

Paco looked out over the city, which was teeming with midday traffic and tried to gather his thoughts. He knew that he had to resolve this problem once and for all and at the same time not jeopardize his relationship with Julie.

"Look, I'll make you a proposition. Forget my conversation with Lew and don't mention the Rock Hudson picture. Just tell Julie you're here to discuss her next film *after* the tour is over and nothing else. I'll agree to come home after we finish, but only for one picture. After that we're both coming back to Europe, perhaps indefinitely. She can work here just as well as the United States, and as far as my career is concerned, I can just about write my own ticket."

Howard realized he was dealing with a selfish son of a bitch who was planning on using Julie to open doors that would otherwise be closed to him. Paco's film career was over and he knew it. Now his last hope was Julie. Howard was tempted to tell him what a bona fide prick he was, but he controlled himself. There was nothing more he could do at this time. To try and speak to Julie alone would be fruitless and possibly destructive. Paco could be very vindictive, and if crossed, he would undoubtedly make a big stink and fire the agency.

"All right, Paco," he said reluctantly. "I'll do as you ask. But please make sure she's back in California by September. Now, would you call her please? I'd like to say hello."

"Sure, Howard," Paco said jovially, his mood suddenly brightened by the outcome of his conversation. "Come inside and I'll make you a real drink. By the way, you must see the show tonight. It's sensational."

Paco quickly fixed him a drink and went to fetch Julie. Minutes later she appeared, slightly embarrassed by her appearance, because she had just emerged from the shower and her hair was still wrapped in a towel.

"Mr. Dugan, it's so nice to see you. Paco tells me you're going to see the show tonight. Will you be able to have dinner with us?"

God, she's lovely, Howard thought, his eyes appraising her beauty, which even devoid of makeup was still clearly evident.

"Yes, Julie. I am going to see the show tonight, but I must try and get to bed early so, unfortunately, I won't be able to have dinner with you. I've just arrived from New York and I have to be in Paris tomorrow morning for an important meeting."

"Oh, I'm sorry you can't make it."

"I am too. Maybe another time." Dugan started to say something else, but he caught a warning look on Paco's face and decided against it. *I'll wait until she's back in the States,* he thought. *Then Lew and I will talk to her alone.* As he neared the door, he said, "Julie, I've filled Paco in on basically what's happening over at Universal. We've agreed that it would be wise for you to return to California after the tour is over. By then the studio will have a picture for you. There isn't too much to tell you except that they're very pleased with your performance in *The Pancho Villa Story.* The previews have been great. Paco can fill you in on the rest of our conversation." Looking at his watch, he said, "Now, I think I'll grab a nap before the show. I'm just about done in. I'll see you both later."

As soon as he was gone, Julie turned to Paco. "Isn't that wonderful, Paco? Universal has another movie for me in Hollywood and you have offers from producers here. I can't believe all of this is happening to me."

"Just relax, *querida,* and let me handle everything. After we go back to Hollywood and you make your movie, I think we should seriously consider returning to Italy and establishing a permanent base here in Rome. You and I could make films together, and when we're free, tour all of Europe in personal appearances."

Julie nodded, and removing the towel from her damp hair, she shook her head from side to side, allowing her hair to cascade down around her shoulders in shiny red curls. Standing there in the middle of the room, her tiny body enveloped in the hotel robe, she looked like a little girl. Suddenly, Paco could envision her naked body underneath the robe and that thought impassioned him. Taking her hand, he led her to the couch and pulled her down next to him. Reaching for the belt of her robe, he whispered, "Mi *amor*, no one has your best interests at heart more than your Paco. You just listen to me, my darling, and you won't go wrong."

Julie closed her eyes and surrendered to Paco's urgency. She tried not to think of what was happening to her now, but only of the wonderful things that lay ahead of her. She had vowed to be a good wife and she had kept that promise. She prayed she would find in her work the fulfillment that she had yet to find in her marriage.

CHAPTER
38

Barcelona, August 1st

Dear Mom and Dad,

I hope this letter finds you both well. I'm feeling great and I'm really excited because the trip so far has been fantastic and the show is a huge success. It's hard to decide whether I like Rome more than Paris, because both cities are so beautiful, but I guess I'm a little more partial to the Italian people. They're so friendly and demonstrative, especially when they like you. As I wrote in my last letter, I've received quite a few offers to do movies in Italy, but I won't be able to make any decisions until we finish the tour. I have some other good news. Universal wants me back in California by September for another picture, so any projects over here will have to be put on hold until then. So much is happening. I wish you were here to see all of this. But I promise you that one day I will send you to Europe in style; maybe even on the Queen Mary. Remember when I was a little girl and, as we drove along the West Side Highway, we

*used to see the big ships tied up in the harbor? Remember how
I swore that someday, when I was famous, I would send you to
Europe? Well, that day is not too far away.*

*I haven't had a chance to see much of Barcelona yet because
we arrived only two days ago and have been rehearsing constantly. We'll be performing in the Plaza de Toros (the bull
ring), which is huge, and Paco is terribly concerned about the
sound system and lighting. But the impresario told us not to
worry. They're bringing in the best technicians and the place
is practically sold out for the entire engagement.*

*How are Marshall and Marsha? Send them my love and also
thank them for the picture of my little nephew, Michael. How
are you coping with the weather? The papers over here reported
that New York is having a terrible heat wave and I know how
hot the apartment can get. I hope you are both well and keeping
cool. I miss you so much. That's the only thing that prevents
this from being a perfect trip. But I hope to see you soon. I will
keep you posted about when I expect to be back in New York.
We'll be there for at least two weeks before returning to California. I'm really eager to see everyone when I get home, especially
Grandma Esther. Is she feeling any better? Please give her a
kiss for me. Well, I've got to run now. We're having a press
conference in half an hour and I'm not even dressed. Take care
of yourselves and please write often.*

Love and a million kisses,

Julie

Julie sealed the envelope and placed it next to her purse. She would
drop it off at the concierge's desk on the way out. The press conference
was being held in a famous seaside restaurant that was known for its
paella. Besides the usual array of photographers and reporters, the
impresario had invited some special guests. Paco was already downstairs in the lobby going over last-minute details with Luis. He had
been in an especially good humor since arriving in Barcelona, his
birthplace. He barely remembered the city. When Paco was three, they
had migrated to Mexico, and Paco's father, a music teacher, had found
work teaching the piano to young students. Paco's mother hated leav-

ing her country and family, but his father, Enrique, insisted that he could make a better life for all of them in another country. The family remained in Mexico until Paco was fifteen and then, anxious to be reunited with other members of their family who had settled in New York, they left to join them. Paco had been reluctant to return to his native country until he was a big star. He still remembered the poverty his family had suffered and was determined to return in triumph. When he finally achieved fame, he could never find the time to schedule a tour. But now the moment had finally come and he was enjoying it. Tomorrow he would be presenting his show to over sixty thousand people, and judging from the lines that stretched from the box office all around the block, he could play there indefinitely.

Julie went to the dressing table and studied herself in the mirror. She decided she needed something more colorful and photogenic for the press conference. The majority of the women that she had seen so far in the restaurants and on the streets all seemed terribly exotic to her and she admired the way they carried themselves, with such great assurance. Julie chose a burnt orange silk dress that complemented her hair and cast a coppery glow to her skin. She brushed her hair until it shone and then swept it all to one side of her face, where she secured it with a tortoiseshell comb she had purchased in Rome. She placed the tiniest dab of bronze eyeshadow above her lids, which further heightened the color of her eyes. Stepping back from the mirror, she surveyed the effect she made. Then, reaching into her dressing table drawer, she pulled out a pair of large gold hoop earrings and fastened them to her ears. *There*, she thought, stepping back to see the finished product. *That's better*. She was now ready to face the press, and she hoped that she wouldn't disappoint them.

When Paco and Julie reached the restaurant, they were besieged by photographers and journalists, who asked Julie dozens of questions, some quite personal, regarding her life with Paco. But despite the pressure, she handled herself with her usual charm and dignity. Paco spoke to them in the language of the region, Catalan, which delighted them. They were proud to see that after all those years he had not forgotten his native tongue. After a while Julie began to feel the effect of the summer heat and the strain of answering so many questions. Fortunately, the restaurant had a huge awning, shielding everyone from the blazing sun. Otherwise, it would have been intolerable. Excus-ing themselves from the press, Julie and Paco made their way through the huge crowd and headed for the long table that was set up especially for them. Julie looked at her watch. It was nearly three o'clock and they hadn't even started lunch. Julie had thought the dining hours in France and Italy rather strange, but nothing compared to Spain. Lunch at four, cocktails at nine, and dinner at ten-thirty or eleven. It would take some time to get used to that schedule. As the photographers stood by the door, waiting patiently for the other guests to arrive, Paco took a seat next to Julie.

"Are you tired, *mi amor?*"

"No, not really, Paco. Just hot and very hungry."

"Well, they are going to start serving now. I see that the others have arrived."

Julie looked up and saw several people coming toward them. One of them she recognized instantly as their impresario, Pedro Balaña, who also owned the Plaza de Toros. Accompanying him were two very pretty young women. When they reached the table where Paco and Julie were seated, Señor Balana introduced them.

"Paco, Julie, I would like you to meet two of our leading flamenco dancers—Maria Flores and Conchita Muñoz. They are currently appearing in one of our best flamenco clubs. After the opening I will arrange for you to see the show."

Paco immediately rose, kissed their hands, and invited them to sit down. Julie greeted them and was about to reach for a glass of water when suddenly she felt a tap on her shoulder. Looking up she saw two of the most attractive men she had ever seen. One had jet black hair that was slicked back from his deeply bronzed skin almost like a helmet. His heavy black eyebrows cast a dark shadow over intensely penetrating eyes that right now were appraising Julie.

Bowing slightly, he reached for her hand, which he brushed lightly with his lips.

"*Encantado, señora, mi nombre es Chamaco.*"

Julie smiled and returned the greeting. She then turned her attention to the other young man, who had been standing by patiently waiting to introduce himself. He had dark blond hair, rather fair skin, and eyes the color of the sea. He didn't look at all like the other Latin men Julie had met, but rather like any typical American boy. He too reached to kiss her hand, but there was a shyness about him that instantly appealed to Julie and she smiled warmly at him. Once again the heavyset impresario stepped forward and with great pride in his voice introduced them.

"Paco, Julie, I would like to present two of my greatest young novilleros—Chamaco and Antonio Rivera. Sunday, in the Plaza de Toros, they will be taking their *alternativa*, which means they will then become full-fledged *toreros*. I hope you will honor us then with your presence. I am sure you will find it very exciting."

Paco greeted the novilleros enthusiastically and asked them to join the table. Ever since they had arrived in Spain, he had been telling Julie what an aficionado he was of bullfighting. In Mexico he had watched the greatest *toreros* of all time, including the incomparable Manolete, and now, he was looking forward to seeing his first corrida in Spain. The fair-haired young man, Antonio, took a seat next to Julie while Paco beckoned Chamaco to sit next to him, as he wanted to discuss the forthcoming corrida.

Almost immediately the waiters began to place huge plates of food on the table, and each dish looked and smelled delectable. There was seafood of every variety—from shrimps and baby prawns covered in a spicy brown sauce to lobster and mussels served over a bed of yellow rice. A flamenco guitarist began playing a haunting melody, and the cool wine with fruit the Spaniards called sangría helped to refresh everyone. Julie knew that Paco was enjoying himself immensely. He was being treated like a king in his native Catalonia and basking in adoration. Julie had also been receiving her share of admiration from the Spaniards. Like the Italians, they admired beautiful women, but were slightly more reserved in demonstrating their feelings, especially to a married woman. As the lunch progressed, Julie found herself very taken with the young man seated next to her. Although he was only twenty-three, he explained to her in rather good English that he had already studied law in one of Spain's best universities. He had abandoned his studies only at the request of his father, who had been a famous bullfighter. Unlike most parents, who would have been thrilled to see their only son become a lawyer, Antonio, Sr., had only one ambition—to have his son follow in his footsteps and carry the name "El Rubio" to fame and glory.

Julie listened intently to Antonio as he described his career as a bullfighter. Absorbed in what he was saying, she became almost oblivious to the others around her. From the moment she met him she had felt an almost instantaneous attraction, and she was sure by the way he looked at her that he felt the same way. Flustered all at once by the strange way she was feeling, Julie turned her attention back to Paco, but he was busily engaged in a conversation with Chamaco.

Intuitively sensing Julie's sudden nervousness, Antonio, tried to ease the tension by saying, "I have been so busy telling you all about my life I haven't had a chance to ask you anything about yourself. Do you like Spain? Will you be here long?"

Antonio was still virtually a stranger, and yet she felt comfortable enough to confide some of her hopes and dreams for the future. Antonio listened to her describe her travels to South America and her subse-quent marriage to Paco. Privately, he could not understand how a beautiful young woman could be married to a man so much older—even a famous one, such as Paco Castell. As Julie spoke, he drank in her fresh young beauty, and that intoxicated him more than the wine.

When lunch was finally over, Paco indicated it was time to go, but before Julie could rise, Antonio leaned over to her and whispered, "Julie, you are going to the corrida on Sunday, no?"

"I don't know, Antonio. It all depends on Paco."

"Please try to come. It will be the most important day of my life. I will take my *alternativa* and I would like to dedicate the bull to you."

Julie's heart started to do a flip-flop. His face was only a breath away and his nearness caused her to feel faint. Frightened by what she was feeling, Julie rose suddenly and went over to Paco.

"I've been having an interesting conversation with Antonio. He would like to know if we're going to the bullfights on Sunday?"

"*Como no*, of course. I wouldn't miss it."

Circling her waist possessively, he said with a laugh, "We will watch the bulls being fought in the afternoon and then at night we will perform in the same arena—but with far less danger involved I would imagine. Now I see that some of our guests are leaving and I must say good-bye. Are you coming, Julie?"

"In a minute, Paco. I have to get my purse."

Before Julie could join Paco, Antonio stopped her, and with a burn-ing intensity in his eyes, he told her, "Julie, from this moment on I will be thinking only of Sunday, when once again I will see your beautiful face. Until then, *adiós*."

Julie watched him depart, stopping only briefly at the door to shake Paco's hand. She was feeling confused by these new sensations she was experiencing and she wasn't quite sure if it was the wine or the heady effect Antonio had made on her. But all she knew was that for the first time in a long, long while she felt terribly young and alive. But she also felt ashamed, because she realized that she would have liked to have been kissed. *Stop it*, she told herself. *You're married and you can't allow yourself to think like that. You're just being carried away because it's Spain and he's a handsome toreador and everything here is so romantic. You'll feel differently tomorrow when you're back on the stage where you belong performing with Paco.* But somewhere in the back of her mind, she wasn't quite convinced.

As everyone who had watched the rehearsals had predicted, Paco Castell's return to Barcelona was indeed a triumph. The cheering Catalans, who for years had admired him from afar, showed their approval with one standing ovation after another. The weather on opening night couldn't have been more perfect. The sky was ablaze with millions of stars, and the summer breeze that drifted into the arena from the sea helped to cool the thousands of people gathered there for the concert. Paco had prepared a special program that he knew would appeal to Spanish tastes, and as he stood there conducting his opening number, Julie watched him from a dark corner near the stage. His face was flushed with enthusiasm as he put the orchestra through their paces, and they never played better, for they too were caught up in the excitement. This was the Paco Castell that Julie had admired ever since she was a little girl and she felt proud to be a part of his show. If only the excitement that she felt as she watched him perform on a night like this could have carried over into their marriage, she would have been the happiest girl in the world. But unfortunately that had not happened, and Julie was afraid it never would. *It's strange,* Julie thought as she waited to go on. *I respect him, admire him, and when he isn't flying into an unwarranted jealous rage, I sincerely care for him.* But the feeling that Antonio had evoked when he looked at her so longingly the other day had never happened with Paco. *Antonio,* Julie suddenly thought. *I wonder if he's here tonight. Probably not. Tomorrow he will be fighting two bulls, and from what I've learned, bullfighters, like all other athletes, must get their rest. A mistake for them could mean their lives.* Nevertheless, Julie wished that Antonio could have been there to see her perform. She had worked hard to prepare herself for this evening, and in a short while she would be joining Paco up onstage and singing and dancing for sixty thousand people. And that was what she loved.

She decided to put all thoughts of Antonio out of her mind. She would have to continue to suppress any secret longings that she might have. She had made her choice and she would honor her commitment to Paco as long as she was his wife.

Sunday morning Julie was awakened from a deep sleep by church bells announcing the time. Glancing over at the bedside clock, she was surprised to see that it was already eleven o'clock. Paco was still sound asleep so, quietly, she slid out of bed and tiptoed into the living room. Julie opened the French doors leading to the terrace and allowed the glorious sunshine to pour into the room. Julie felt a sudden rush of excitement as she remembered what was in store for her that afternoon. *My first bullfight*, she thought happily, and what was even more important, her chance to see Antonio again.

The next few hours seemed to drag interminably as Julie waited for Paco to dress, have lunch, and leave for the Plaza de Toros. She had chosen her outfit carefully that afternoon, and as they made their way to their seats, all eyes were focused on the beautiful redheaded wife of Paco Castell.

They were barely seated when a loud trumpet playing "La Virgen de la Macarena" announced the arrival of Antonio and Chamaco. Slowly and elegantly the *toreros* and their *cuadrillas*, the men who composed their entourage, made their way across the sunlit arena, and the sight of them in their dazzling, embroidered *traje de luces* could only be described as spectacular. Respectfully, they bowed their heads to the officials in the boxes above, who would judge their performances. Flinging off their beautifully embroidered capes, both bullfighters approached Julie and Paco and presented them with their capes, which Paco proudly draped on the railing in front of them. The *toreros* then took their places behind the wooden barriers to await the arrival of the first bull.

Paco told Julie that today they would be fighting Miura bulls, the most costly and dangerous bulls in all of Spain. It was a Miura that had fatally gored the famed Manolete in Linares, a small town in Spain, in 1947. There was an air of expectancy stirring through the arena, and when the gate opened and the first bull charged into the center, the crowd let out a cheer. Julie had never seen an animal as ferocious as the beast that rammed the barriers, trying to reach human flesh. After a few preliminary passes by Antonio, who was slated to fight the first bull, the picadors arrived and methodically began to jab at the bull's neck in order to force the animal to lower its enormous head.

Julie closed her eyes because she could not bear to watch any animal being hurt. Paco tried to ease her discomfort by explaining the entire procedure to her, and he reassured her that these bulls had been bred for only one thing—to fight. Julie tried to accept his explanation, and she listened attentively as he described the beauty and artistry of the spectacle. Her understanding of what he was saying grew as she watched Antonio, a solitary figure, alone in the arena, with only a small red cape covering his sword, pitted against a menacing black bull intent on killing him. His grace in handling the cape as the bull passed inches away from his exposed body was as beautiful as any dancer she had ever seen. At each breathtaking pass the thousands of aficionados, who were braving the summer heat to watch the corrida, shouted *olé*. They seemed to know exactly what every movement meant and were not hesitant in showing their approval of the *torero*'s artistry as he brought the bull under control.

Julie, too, was swept away by the dominance and courage that Antonio displayed, and she found herself joining the others who were applauding wildly. Circling the arena, Antonio proudly accepted the applause as the bull stood to one side scraping his hoofs in the dust, menacingly studying his adversary. The sounding of the trumpet announced that the moment of truth had come. It was time for the kill. Antonio approached Julie, and raising his hat in a solemn salute, he looked into her eyes. Julie rose, her body trembling not only with excitement but also with fear for his safety, and accepted his tribute.

"*Señora*, I dedicate the killing of this bull to you. May the Blessed Virgin guide my hand so that I may bring honor to you and to my beloved teacher and father."

Suddenly, Antonio tossed his hat to Julie, which she caught and placed on her lap. The audience enthusiastically applauded his choice. As Antonio walked to the center of the arena, they suddenly became ominously still. In the next few minutes Antonio would have to prove his mettle as a bullfighter. Without any help from his *cuadrilla*, he would be expected to execute a series of dangerous ritualistic passes and finally, with a thrust of his sword, find the exact entry spot behind the bull's head for the kill.

Julie held her breath as Antonio began. His artistry was so pure that, for weeks to come, aficionados would be discussing the corrida and the bravery of this young *torero*. When Antonio sensed that the bull was in exactly the right position, he raised his right arm and, with his cape held low in his other hand to keep the bull's head down, he thrust his sword swiftly into the animal. The bull sank on its knees to the ground, and suddenly, it was all over. The crowd went wild. The women threw flowers and their fans into the arena as Antonio paraded in front of them, smiling at their unbridled enthusiasm. When Antonio came toward Julie to retrieve his hat, Pedro Balana, who was sitting beside her, pressed a bouquet of flowers into her hand. Julie stood and tossed Antonio's hat back to him, but instead of throwing the entire bouquet, she carefully chose one perfect red rose and flung it to the *torero*, who, looking up at her tenderly, touched it to his lips and placed it inside his jacket, close to his heart.

If Paco sensed the electricity that passed between Antonio and his wife, he didn't dwell on it. He couldn't help but notice the way that Antonio had caressed the rose Julie had thrown him, but he decided to say nothing. Paco had begun to realize from the moment they played their first engagement in Europe that Latin men would find Julie very desirable, but he never doubted for a moment that he would be able to keep the situation under control.

The days that followed seemed to pass quickly. *Too quickly*, Julie thought as she applied her makeup before the show. Soon they would be on their way to Madrid—their last stop before returning home. She had hoped to see Antonio one more time before leaving for Madrid, but so far he had not shown up to see her perform. *Perhaps it's just as well*, she thought as she slipped into her gold-colored shoes. *I don't know why he has such an effect on me, but when I see him my heart starts to palpitate and my throat gets dry. God knows I've met many attractive men since we arrived in Europe. Why does Antonio make me feel this way?* Once she was dressed, Julie slipped outside her makeshift dressing room and waited in the dusty hall of the bullfight arena for her cue to go on. The other entertainers were sharing the only other available dressing room, which was the *sanitorio*, the infirmary, where they brought the *toreros* who had been gored. Ever since she saw the bullfight, she could not bring herself to dress there, since the thought of Antonio being carried there, bleeding and hurt, upset her more than she would have believed possible.

Julie felt especially fidgety tonight. She was impatient to get onstage. To her, waiting was always the most difficult thing. Once she was onstage she felt right at home, but standing in the wings, or as she stood now, in the bullfighter's entrance to the arena, unnerved her. As she listened to the music, she noticed that Paco was deviating from his carefully prepared show. His Catalonian fans wanted him to play melodies from the past, and he tried to oblige them whenever possible. Julie tried to decide if she should go back to her dressing room and wait. It was obvious that it would be at least ten minutes more before Paco introduced her. She turned and lifted her gown carefully to avoid the sawdust on the floor when suddenly she saw a tall slender figure approach her from the shadows. She knew instantly that it was Antonio. Before she could gather her thoughts he was beside her, and reaching for her hand, he kissed it tenderly and held it tightly to his chest.

"Julie, forgive me for not coming to see you sooner. To tell you the truth, for the past few days I have been going crazy trying to decide what is the proper thing to do. No, don't speak, not yet. Let me tell you what is in my heart. I am a Spaniard and above all else we respect another man's *novia*, his beloved. But from the moment I saw you in the restaurant I have been obsessed by you. It is not only your beauty, though that would be enough to inflame any man. It is something else. Something in your eyes that lets me look deep into your soul. And what I see there is even more beautiful than your face. Oh, Julie, please forgive me for speaking like this. I know that it is wrong. You are another man's wife. But somehow I feel as if I have known you for many years. You and I are from different worlds and yet, I believe we are much alike. I can sense that when I speak to you. If only we had met before . . ."

Antonio knew that if he continued, he would be dishonoring everything he believed in. Anguished, he suddenly turned away from Julie. Her heart was beating so wildly in her chest she was afraid it would burst. Antonio's face looked so tormented that she longed to take him in her arms to try and comfort him, but she was helpless. Touching his sleeve tentatively, she spoke softly.

"Antonio, please don't turn away. There is nothing to forgive. If anyone is to blame it is me. I am the one who is married, and even though I didn't realize it at the time, I guess I encouraged you. I'm sorry." Antonio turned to face her, and she could make out the strong, clean lines of his face in the half-darkness that surrounded them. Her breath quickened when she saw the tenderness in his eyes, and she knew she must speak quickly and then leave.

"Antonio, I must go. Any moment Paco will be announcing my name and I have to be ready. I can't explain what's happened to us any more than you can. All I know is that I feel the same way about you and it is wrong. I am married and I must respect that, no matter how I feel."

Seeing the pain that clearly marked his face, she realized she must flee quickly or she would lose her resolve. "Antonio, we must say goodbye now."

Julie reached out her hand to touch his cheek as a farewell gesture, but Antonio grasped it tightly and kissed her palm with his lips. A surge of passion, unlike anything she had ever experienced coursed through her body, and she involuntarily felt herself straining toward him.

The feel of her warm skin, which was barely concealed by the thin material of her evening gown, made Antonio forget everything except the softness of her body and his own desire. "Please kiss me, Julie, my dearest. Just one time and I swear on the Holy Madonna that I will never ask you again."

Julie did not have the strength to refuse something that she herself desired with all her heart. Lifting her face up to his she softly touched his lips with her own trembling mouth. Antonio reached for her, and encircling her body with his powerful arms—arms that were strong enough to kill a bull—he kissed her. Softly at first, as if she were a piece of fragile porcelain that might easily break. Then, as the excitement of her body and sweet mouth heated his loins, his mouth covered hers with a passion that swept them both away and made them forget everything except their desire.

"Julie, Julie," he breathed into the fragrance of her hair. "*Mi amor*, let me kiss you just one more time. I cannot let you go."

"Antonio, you must. You swore. Please, let me go."

Julie pulled herself out of the warmth of his embrace and ran blindly toward the safety of the stage, her legs trembling so badly she could easily have fallen. But she had to get away from Antonio or she would be lost. Suddenly, she heard Paco's voice and she knew she had broken away just in time.

"*Señora y señores, tengo el placer de presentar para ustedes mi señora, la guapísima cantante,* Julie Lauren."

Julie half-stumbled up the short staircase that led from the arena up to the stage. Suddenly, the spotlight hit her and she forced herself to smile. As the warm sound of applause greeted her appearance, she carefully walked to the center of the stage, where the microphone awaited her. She knew that Antonio was still out there, somewhere in the darkness watching her, and turning to the direction she had just left, she began to sing, "Amor mio, I just yearn for your kiss. Amor mio, loving you is such bliss."

CHAPTER 39

Lew Wallace strode angrily around his luxurious antique-filled office in Beverly Hills. He was feeling frustrated that his attempts to intervene with Paco on Julie's behalf had been thwarted. Lew had been through some difficult times with Paco during the many years since he had graduated from the mail room and moved up to become head of the agency. But never anything like this. Since Paco's return from Europe and all during the filming of Julie's picture *Wings of the Eagle*, Paco had been making everyone's life miserable, especially Julie's. Just yesterday, when Lew had paid a call to her on the set, on her last day of shooting, she had greeted him with red-rimmed eyes.

"Mr. Wallace," she asked, when she noticed him talking to the director. "Did you want to see Paco? He must be in my dressing room. He was there a minute ago."

"Don't look so frightened and forget Paco for a minute. I came here to see you. How are things going?"

"Fine, I guess. You know I finish today. They've been trying to condense my scenes so Paco and I can return to Europe."

"I know, honey, and I don't think that's a very good idea. Paco talked to the producer and director without my knowledge and somehow arranged for you to finish early. I must tell you that big motion picture careers are not built that way. You should be here doing as much publicity as possible and also being seen around town when you're not working so we can get you loan outs to other studios for better deals. What in the hell is the rush to get back to Europe? You've only been home a few months?"

Julie had to bite her lip to keep from blurting out the truth. She couldn't betray Paco and tell Lew that the real reason they were going back to Italy so soon was because Guiseppe Amato had called and offered a part for Paco. She knew it was an enticement to get her. On hearing this, Paco had immediately accepted and lined up some personal appearances as well. Once she finished shooting the picture in California, he intended to put the house in Bel Air on the market, fulfill some previous engagements in the United States, and then move to Italy indefinitely. As much as Julie loved Europe and as hopeful as she was that she could have a film career there, she still hated the thought of burning all her bridges behind her. And that was exactly what Paco was doing.

"Julie, dear, I've got to talk some sense into that husband of yours. I know that you're going to be eighteen next month, but you're still a baby in many ways. You need guidance and you've got to listen to us. We think you have a big future in American films. Forget Italy. The only American actors working there are unknowns who are making cheap spaghetti westerns. You belong here, where the studio can groom you for big things. Paco has already had his chance. Now you deserve yours."

"I agree with you but I can't seem to convince Paco. He thinks the studio will keep me in small roles indefinitely and that it will eventually ruin my career. He also believes that by combining personal appearances with European films, I can become a big international star. I'm so confused I don't know what to believe. I hate to disagree with Paco. It just causes an argument and I dislike fights."

Lew Wallace nodded in understanding. She was right of course. She was no match for a man like Paco Castell. He was intelligent enough to realize that his career in Hollywood was at an end. The days of big Hollywood musicals were over, and there was no place for a Latin bandleader, even one as famous as Paco Castell. On the other hand, Julie had her whole life ahead of her, and she was already proving that she was a damn good actress. In time she could conceivably fill the spots that would soon be vacated by Rita Hayworth or Ava Gardner, who were older and demanding too much money.

"Listen, Julie. I don't want you to have to argue with Paco. Let me talk to him. We go back many years together. Let's see if I can convince him to put this Italian idea on hold."

Twenty-four hours later, back in his office, Lew was furious with himself for not having been successful. He should have confronted Paco with the threat that he would reveal to Julie his conversation with Howard Dugan in Rome and tell her how he had manipulated every turn in her career. But he had been reluctant to go that far because he realized that it would definitely rupture their relationship. He had done everything in his power to make him see reason, but Paco would not budge.

"I've told you before, Lew, and I'll say it again for the last time. I don't care if the studio drops her. She'll wind up a bigger star in the end by listening to me."

There was no doubt in Lew's mind that the studio would not pick up her option if she went back to Europe. Disgusted by Paco's selfishness, he recognized that, for the moment, he would have to sit back and wait to see what happened to Julie's career once she returned to Europe. As he made his way back to the office he thought, *I may have lost the first battle but the war isn't over. At least, not yet.*

As Paco happily prepared for their departure, Julie roamed wistfully around her beautiful home. *I may never return to this house again*, she thought sadly. If Paco's plans went through, the property would be sold shortly. Even though Julie had not spent too much time there and little in the house belonged to her, it was still her first home, and for the first time in her life she had experienced the luxury of having her own private space. Now, because of Paco's decision, she was faced with the unhappy prospect of having to give it all up and move to a foreign country. During her brief stopover in New York on her way to California, she had discussed with her parents the possibility of her relocating to Italy. As she had expected, they reacted angrily. But Julie eventually quieted them down by insisting that those plans were only tentative. She reminded them that first she had a new picture to make and only after that would she and Paco examine their options.

Now that the film was completed and there was a firm offer from Amato on the table, Paco had set the wheels in motion for their move to Italy. Julie knew full well that once she told her parents of her decision it would trigger an explosive reaction. She decided to delay breaking the news until the very last moment. Paco had booked an engagement for them in Palm Beach over Christmas and New Year's, and Julie had invited her parents to join them.

Reluctantly, they had accepted. They were anxious to see their daughter and at the same time they were also looking forward to a vacation. Her father had begun to speak with increasing frequency of wanting to relocate to a warmer climate. At first, Julie had suspected they might be thinking of Florida. But that was not the case. Her Uncle Edward, her father's youngest brother, had recently opened a restaurant in Phoenix, Arizona, after being forced to move there with his asthmatic wife and two children. The thought of getting out of New York City, which was steadily becoming more congested, greatly appealed to Sam. Even though Rose had strong family ties and had always rejected leaving them, with Julie gone and Marshall becoming increasingly disenchanted with his job and the City, the possibility of Arizona was not as disturbing now as it once might have been.

Thanks to Julie's movie contract and the percentage Sam received as her manager, they had been able to save more money in the past year than in their entire married life. With a little additional help they might be able to invest in Edward's restaurant, which was doing quite well, and have a business of their own. This would free Sam from the shackles of a job that he had grown to hate and finally allow him to be his own boss. Although they would be loathe to admit it, Julie was responsible for their new thinking, and it would be her to whom they would eventually turn for help, once they had made their final decision.

It was with a heavy heart that Julie left California, for she had no idea when she would be returning. She knew that she had turned in a good performance in the picture and that they were pleased with her. Everyone from the director on down had told her so. Rock Hudson couldn't have been more charming, and he had graciously offered to help her in every way he could. But nothing anyone could do could help ease the tension Julie had experienced during the past three months. With nothing to occupy his time except his daily visits to Julie on the set, Paco complained endlessly about what he was giving up for her. Furthermore, she could never relax around her co-workers when he was around. Because of his jealousy, Julie had to suppress her inherent friendliness and sense of humor and retire to the privacy of her dressing room, since even the most innocent encounters could set Paco off. Even Rock, who as everyone knew was partial to his own sex and therefore not a threat, fell under Paco's scrutiny. As she had so often found in the past, Julie was isolated from the friendships she so longed for.

The arrival of Sam and Rose in Palm Beach two days before Christmas helped to lift Julie's spirits, which had been at a low ebb ever since her departure from California. Once she got her parents settled in their room, she arranged to meet them later on at the Palm Beach Country Club, where she and Paco were appearing. She hastily returned to her hotel suite and found Paco was waiting for her impatiently.

"Julie, what took you so long? I've been waiting for hours to tell you the good news." Paco's face was flushed with enthusiasm as he drew her over to the couch. "I've just received a fantastic offer for the house in California and I intend to accept it. That means we can leave for Europe by the end of next month. I'm going to wire Amato that we're available and the broker in Rome to start looking for an apartment immediately."

Julie received the news with certain misgivings. Things were moving too fast, and she was unhappy that she had no control over her destiny. Paco made plans without even consulting her, and like her parents, he expected her to abide by his decisions. It was true that she had enjoyed every minute of her European tour and had been thrilled that the Italian movie producers felt she had such a big future there. Still, moving to Italy was an enormous step, and she dreaded having to break the news to her parents, for she knew full well what their reaction would be. *No use in spoiling the holidays,* Julie thought as she retired to the bedroom, leaving Paco alone to make his calls. *It's hard enough just to keep them acting civilly to each other, and if there's a blowup I'll be the one who suffers.*

Julie was growing increasingly tired of always being placed in the middle of her parents' squabbles with Paco. *Maybe distance is not such a bad idea,* she thought wearily as she drew her bath. Julie removed her clothes and stepped into the steaming tub, hoping to relax before the evening's performance. She lay her head back and let her body soak in the perfumed bubbles. *Italy,* she dreamed. *I guess I'll have to learn how to speak Italian if I'm going to make films,* she thought, her mind now rushing ahead to the future. *Paco will probably want to make another tour in Spain. We were such a hit last summer.* All at once Julie sat up with a start. *Spain,* she thought, as a delightful twinge of excitement rushed through her veins. Antonio would be there. Closing her eyes she allowed herself to think back and remember the burning desire she had felt when he had kissed her, and how she had wished he would never stop. But that was all in the past, she reminded herself, and she could never allow it to happen again. She would throw herself into her work and pray that in doing so she would find an outlet for her pent-up emotions. There was no other way.

CHAPTER 40

The next several months in Italy proved to be a difficult transitional period for Julie. After spending several weeks in the Hotel Excelsior in Rome, Paco and Julie moved into a penthouse apartment in one of the city's most beautiful residential neighborhoods. Their flat, as the Italians referred to it, overlooked all of Rome, and Julie was thrilled to once again have a home of her own, albeit a rented one.

Before leaving New York there had been harsh words and dire warnings from her parents about "being alone with that monster thousands of miles away from your family." The scene that had taken place at the Waldorf Towers a few days before they left still made Julie tremble. She had insisted that Sam and Rose meet them for dinner at Le Pavillon, one of New York's finest French restaurants. The conversation during dinner was strained. As usual, Julie overcompensated for the lack of communication by chatting constantly about her future in Italy, all the films she would be making, and the tours Paco had planned. Her parents were stony-faced, barely picking at their food, while Paco, seemingly oblivious to their hostility, consumed a great deal of wine along with an enormous amount of food. Julie's nerves became so frazzled that, by the time they all returned to the apartment, her hands were shaking. The only reason her parents agreed to come back to the apartment with them was to pick up some presents that Julie had for them. As Julie gathered up the boxes in the bedroom, Rose and Sam took seats on the sofa in the living room. Paco, uncomfortable about being alone with them, poured himself a brandy from the decanter on the bar. Sam Lehman had been wrestling with some questions that he felt had been left unanswered during the evening. Now that they were alone in the apartment he decided to use the opportunity to clarify them.

As Paco took a seat on the club chair opposite them and picked up the newspaper, Sam rose and faced him. "There's something that's been bothering me for quite some time, and before you leave for Europe I'd like to straighten it out."

Paco put down the paper and looked at Sam suspiciously. "What is the problem?"

"Well, the way I see it is in the last few months Julie has become a major attraction in Europe. Am I right?"

Paco took a sip of his brandy and placed it carefully on the coffee table in front of him. "You're right. What about it?"

"Well, my wife and I feel she's entitled to more money when she's out on the road with you. She's not just a band singer anymore. She's become a star."

"You're right. She has become a star, and she owes all of her success to me."

"To you?" Sam asked, his voice rising. "Why you? She would have made it on her own. She's already completed two pictures in Hollywood. She can be a big star without you."

Now, it was Paco's turn to rise. "Is that so? Where the hell would she be if I hadn't hired her? Singing in the chorus with a bunch of other girls. I have showcased her here, in South America, and in Europe. Those audiences are *my* audiences, my fans. That exposure is what helped launch your daughter's career. You should be grateful to me instead of complaining all the time."

Paco reached down and finished off his brandy in one gulp. "The trouble with you people is that you're greedy. You don't care about your daughter's happiness. All you want is her money."

Sam's face turned beet red and Rose, sensing that her husband was about to do something that might endanger his health, jumped up. "Sam, for God's sake take it easy. I don't want that bastard to give you a heart attack."

Hearing the ruckus in the next room, Julie came rushing in. "What's the matter?"

Rose reached for her coat, which was lying on the couch. "What's the use? You never listen to us. The only one you listen to is that man you're married to. *He's* your boss. Well, listen to him. Go back to Europe. Sleep with him, slave for him. Do whatever you want. I'm taking your father home before he has a stroke."

Julie began to cry in despair. Before the evening began she had prayed it would turn out differently, but she should have known better! There could be no peace and harmony between Paco and her parents. It was useless! Nonetheless Julie begged them not to leave like that. She would be going to Italy in just a few days, and she didn't want to part under such bad circumstances. Her pleas were to no avail. When they stood at the door, tearfully saying good-bye, her mother embraced her.

"Don't cry, Julie. We still love you, even though my heart is breaking because we won't see you for such a long time."

Julie kissed them both and promised that as soon as she was settled and financially able, she would send for them for a visit. When Julie returned to the living room, Paco refused to discuss what had brought on the outburst, but he warned her, "If you want to see your parents. Fine. But don't expect me to be in their company again."

Julie completed her picture with Amato in a relatively short time, compared to Hollywood standards, and she now waited for her next offer to materialize. As before, Julie's picture adorned the covers of virtually every magazine in Italy, and the public began to mob her whenever she appeared in public. Determined to master the Italian language, she tried to limit her use of English to her conversations with Paco. She was convinced that once she achieved fluency in Italian she would be offered roles that were more demanding.

Peppino Amato had been wonderful to her during the filming of their picture together. But Julie could not help but be aware of his personal interest in her. He reminded her of a tiger stalking his prey, only waiting for an opportunity to make his move. That move occurred one morning while Paco was in makeup and Julie was alone in her dressing room. When a knock sounded on her door, she called *avanti*, and Peppino walked in. He immediately came over to Julie and kissed her cheek, and she could smell the strong scent of the cologne that he always used.

"*Allora,* Julie. Are you ready for today? We have an important scene to shoot."

"Oh, yes, Pepe," she answered happily. "I've been going over my lines all morning."

"Good. I want to try and get the scene with Maurizio done quickly. That fool may be good-looking and have a big name in pictures, but he is no actor. I should never have listened to my distributor and used him. *Peccato,*" he said, dropping down on the sofa. "It's a pity, but it's too late now to replace him."

Julie put down the hairbrush she had been holding and waited for Peppino to continue. She was nervous being there alone with him, and she hoped that he would get to his business quickly and leave before Paco returned.

Patting the couch, Peppino said to her, "Come, *bella,* sit beside me. I would like to discuss the scene."

Julie hesitated for a moment and then sat down as far away from him as possible. "Julie, I cannot speak to you when you are over there. Come closer."

Julie inched closer, realizing that discussing the scene was the furthest thing from his mind.

Suddenly, Peppino leaned over and pulled her to him. "*Cara,*" he said, caressing her neck. "You are so lovely. Like a fragile flower. Don't you like Peppino just a little bit?"

Julie jumped up like a frightened animal and backed away from the couch. "Please, Peppino. You musn't talk like that. I do like you very much, and I admire you enormously, but my husband is a very jealous man, and I think it would be better if you left immediately."

Peppino Amato stared at her incredulously. *Most Italian girls would give their eyeteeth to win my favor,* he thought. *If not for my appeal, then certainly for my position as a filmmaker and what I could do for them. But this Americana is rejecting my advances and for such a stupid reason. Because she is married. And to an old goat, to boot. Well, I have never before in my life forced a woman and I have no intention of starting now. Eventually, when she tires of Paco, she'll come around. I can wait.*

Fortunately, Paco's constant presence made Peppino's objectives virtually impossible, and for that Julie was grateful. She certainly wasn't interested in any romances. She had all she could do just to handle Paco.

Professionally, Julie was delighted with her role in Amato's picture.

She played a South American girl who comes to Rome to seek fortune and adventure and winds up marrying an Italian nobleman who turns out to be a scoundrel. Peppino spent long hours conferring with his staff on Julie's makeup and hair, insisting that they achieve the look he visualized, and the daily rushes reflected this involvement. She had never been photographed so magnificently. Paco portrayed himself in the picture—a famous bandleader visiting Rome. At first he was upset at the brevity of his appearance, but the amount he was being paid and the fact that Amato agreed to have him write the theme for the movie and give him star billing, placated him somewhat. The hours Julie spent at the studio had been hard and long. The Italians did not have unions that protected the actors or crew, and Julie learned that it was not unusual to be called upon to work way past midnight and not always under the best conditions. But she never complained, and because of her remarkable professionalism, she was admired by one and all. She was a rarity, they all agreed, because other than a handful of seasoned actors, most of the newer Italian "divas" quickly began to believe their own publicity, and temperamental outbursts on the set were not uncommon.

During filming, the Italian press had a field day comparing her to their own voluptuous beauties, Sophia Loren and Gina Lollobrigida, and Julie was honored to be in such illustrious company. Eventually word got out that Amato had captured a bright new star in Julie, and other film offers came pouring in.

As Julie's fame in Italy grew, so did Paco's restlessness, and once he realized that her career was starting to overshadow his, he began to search for something or someone to reaffirm his status as a star. That someone appeared one day while they were at the studio and Julie was busy doing a makeup test for an upcoming picture. Fearing that leaving her alone at the studio with all the handsome Italians might be danger-ous, and bored because he had to wait for her to finish, Paco went into the commissary for a coffee. While waiting for his cappuccino, he couldn't help noticing a voluptuous dark-haired girl staring at him. Returning her glance, he asked her, "Can I buy you a coffee, *signorina?*"

"Oh, *maestro, scusi.* I am sorry I was staring, but I am such a big admirer of yours. Ever since I am little girl I watch you on the screen. Your music is *fantastico.*"

Well, Paco thought. *That's what I like to hear, except maybe the part about a little girl.*

Inviting her to sit down, he watched her walk to the table. She was a large, big-boned girl who might have been considered almost fat by American standards. But in Italy she was just right. *Besides*, he thought as he studied her bosom prominently on display in front of him, *we Latins don't like skinny women. Of course*, he thought as the girl began to redo her lipstick, *Julie is not skinny. She is perfect. Like a doll.* Suddenly, Paco didn't want to think of Julie. He wanted to concentrate on the woman seated next to him, who admired him and still considered him a big star.

"*Signorina,* it is not fair. You know my name but I do not know yours."

The girl laughed, her huge breasts bobbing up and down in her low-cut blouse. "Rossana, *maestro,*" she said as she leaned forward. "Rossana Pampanini. One day my name will be famous like your wife's. Maybe even more because I am Italian."

Paco wasn't interested in her hopes and dreams. He was only interested in watching that inviting flesh she seemed so determined to show him, and he wondered what it would be like to touch her.

"Rossana, I have some free time right now. Would you like to take a drive? My car is right outside."

The girl nodded enthusiastically, unable to believe her good luck. For weeks she had been accepting whatever job she could as an extra, hoping to meet someone famous who could further her career. Who could be better than Paco Castell? Look what he had done for that *Americanita*, Julie Lauren.

They went outside and got into the car. She had no idea where he would be taking her, but it wasn't sightseeing, that was for sure. As they left the studio and the car headed back to Rome, Paco leaned over and put his hand on her thigh. Instantly, her legs caught his hand there, and Paco could feel his body respond as he stroked her warm flesh.

When Paco and the girl entered the darkened apartment, he knew there was no one there. Their cook, Anna, was spending the day at her sister's, and their houseman, Octavio, was busy running errands for him. Paco hesitated for a moment before entering their bedroom. Should he take her into the room he shared with Julie, or into one of the guest rooms? *Mierda*, he thought. *I will take this woman here in my own bed. I am king in my own home.* As soon as Rosanna saw the luxurious surroundings, she began to undress, first removing her skirt and then pulling off her tight blouse, which released her voluminous breasts. Excited and anxious to take her, Paco ripped off his clothes and pulled back the satin bedspread. The girl jumped on the bed and stretched out invitingly in front of him.

Paco knelt beside her and began to tug at her last remaining garment—lavender panties trimmed in lace.

Rossana reached over and grabbed his hands. "Not so quick, *amore*. Before we make love you must promise Rossana something."

Paco suddenly felt irritated. Why was she talking so much when he was so anxious to get at her? "What do you want?"

"I would like you to speak to the director of your wife's new movie. Maybe, Rossana could have a little part? Nothing too big, *caro*. Just some lines."

Paco, whose body was ready to explode, buried his face between her breasts and murmured, "Yes, yes, anything. Now please stop talking and let me fuck you."

His lust spent, Paco rolled off her and went into the bathroom to get a towel. The girl, who had moaned just the right things at the right time, leaned over and retrieved her panties. He had entered her quickly and come to an orgasm almost immediately, something the other men she knew never did. It didn't bother her. She wasn't there for her own gratification. She had her boyfriend, Nino, for that.

Paco stared at himself in the bathroom mirror. Reaching for a towel to wipe his wet face, he noticed Julie's lipstick standing on the sink where she had left it early that morning. Suddenly, he felt a pain in his stomach, as if someone had hit him. *Julie,* he thought, remembering her beauty and gentleness. *This has nothing to do with you or with us. There is no one as lovely as you, my precious beauty, and no one I desire more. But you seem to be growing distant from me and becoming too independent. I want you near me all the time, but if I can't have that, then I will have to amuse myself the best way I can.*

Paco's affair with Rossana continued on for the next few weeks, but as soon as she realized that Paco would not be her stepping-stone to success she began to lose interest. One day, she called him and told him that she would not be able to see him again.

"*Caro*," she said soothingly. "I am so sorry, but I meet this great director at Cinecittà last week and he gives me great part in his new film. But he says Rossana must not go with other men so, *amore*, I must say *ciao*."

Paco was not upset by the news. He had grown tired of her very quickly and had become fearful that Julie might find out. Soon he began to make other plans for their future. He decided to return to public appearances, where he was a star and could still command a great deal of money. Julie had already received several offers for future films with some very prominent actors and directors. Dino De Laurentiis, who had helped launch his wife, Silvana Mangano, to stardom, mentioned at dinner one night that he had a property he felt was tailor-made for Julie. But the offer that interested her most was a film with Vittorio De Sica. Julie could not believe what was happening. It was much more than she could have hoped for, and she felt strongly that to interrupt her film career now with a personal appearance tour would be unwise. She had made that mistake once before by leaving Holly-wood just when she had started to make headway. Frustrated, she tried reasoning with Paco, but he refused to listen. He could become impossible to live with when he didn't get his way, and the thing he hated most was to be denied the opportunity of earning money.

One evening in their apartment in Rome he told her, "We must have an understanding. You expect me to put my work aside and stay in Rome so you can make films. That's all well and good as far as you're concerned, but where does that leave me? I can't just sit around doing nothing. Now I've given the matter considerable thought and I've come up with a plan. If you agree to travel with me, perform whenever and wherever I say and don't complain about the work schedule, then I, in turn, will allow you to pursue your career in pictures."

Julie looked at him in amazement. Paco had been the one urging her to leave Hollywood and pursue a film career in Europe. Over and over again he had assured her that their life in Italy would be gratifying for both of them. Now he was laying down new, unexpected conditions, and he insisted she comply. He left her no choice. She had to agree. Finally she secured a promise from him that they would return from the tour in time for her to begin her film with De Sica. Thus began a pattern for their future—a series of trade-offs. She had made a bargain with the devil that one day she would live to regret.

The publicity that Julie had attracted in Italy followed her to Spain, where she soon became equally famous. Now at last, after weeks on the road, the tour with Paco was finally winding down, and Julie was looking forward with great anticipation to returning to Rome and her film with De Sica. Paco had booked them into all the major cities in Spain with barely a day off to catch their breath. But true to her word, Julie had performed unquestioningly. *I've kept my part of the bargain,*

Julie thought, as she rested in their hotel suite in Madrid. *Now, I hope he keeps his.*

Paco had left earlier that day to rehearse the musicians he had hired to play for them at the Pavilion. The Pavilion was easily the most popular and elegant club in Madrid. Before leaving the States, Paco had disbanded the large orchestra he had been associated with for so many years and retained only a few key men for future engagements. He had shrewdly anticipated during the previous summer's tour of Europe that within a short time Julie would wind up being his star attraction. And now she was proving him right. The audiences that flocked there night after night came to see Paco Castell, the Hollywood movie star, and to watch his beautiful wife sing and dance. They didn't care what kind of orchestra he had, just as long as they played rhumbas and the hot new dance that Julie had introduced, the cha cha cha.

Now, several hours before the show, Julie turned over on her side in the hotel bedroom and closed her eyes. She needed to get some sleep to compensate for the late hours they had been keeping. Nearly every night, after the show, they would join a group of wealthy Madrileños who would cart them off to flamenco clubs that stayed open until the wee hours of the morning. Then, undaunted by the lack of sleep, they would convince Paco and a tired Julie to have coffee and fresh doughnuts in the Puerta del Sol—the old part of the city. With a cool September breeze coming through the open window, Julie fell into a deep sleep. It must have been hours later when she awoke, because the room was dark and she could hear the sound of traffic, indicating the city was coming alive after siesta. Julie sat up in her bed and reached for the light on the nightstand. "Seven o'clock," she said aloud. *My God, I've been asleep since four.* Suddenly, she could hear voices in the next room, and she knew that Paco was back. She slipped out of bed and wrapping a kimono around her, went into the bathroom, splashed some cold water on her face, and went out to greet Paco.

"*Ay querida,*" Paco said, arising from the couch and slipping his arm around her. "I see you are awake. You were sleeping so soundly when I returned I hated to wake you. I have ordered some dinner for us. It should be here shortly."

While Paco was speaking, a distinguished gray-haired man sat watching Julie. *Madre de Dios,* he thought as he appraised her fresh young beauty. *She is even lovelier up close than her photographs. She is perfect for the role of Susana.*

Paco realized he hadn't introduced his guest and he quickly apologized. "Jaime, *perdóname*. I want you to meet my wife, Julie. Sweetheart, say hello to Jaime Rodriguez."

Julie greeted him as he took her hand and kissed it.

"*Mucho gusto, señora*. Paco has been raving about you for the past two hours and now I see what he means. You are charming."

Julie smiled and thanked him for the compliment. She had no idea who he was, but she hoped to excuse herself quickly. She was hungry, and she needed to bathe and prepare for the show.

"*Señora*," their guest continued, "unfortunately, I was out of the country last summer when you performed in the bull rings, so I missed your show. But I hear it was sensational."

"Thank you, Señor Rodriguez," Julie said, smiling at Paco. "But it was really more Paco's success than mine. The audiences went wild when they saw him and heard his music."

"Well, what do we have here? Beauty and modesty, too. You have her well trained Paco."

Julie laughed at his remark. "No, no, it's all true."

"Well, *no importa*. The reason I am here is to offer you and Paco a film here in Spain. With all the publicity you have both been receiving I think the time is right to cash in on some of it. I have a property in mind that would suit both of you, and Paco tells me you will be available after your picture with De Sica."

Julie nodded, aware that Paco was watching her. Obviously this was something that had been brewing without her knowledge for some time. Rather than ask any more questions that might indicate some reluctance on her part, Julie just smiled and said, "If Paco thinks it's right, then, it's fine with me."

"Good, then it's settled. After De Sica, you will return to Madrid and we will begin."

With the deal now wrapped up, Jaime Rodriguez departed and Julie turned to Paco.

"He never even mentioned what kind of role it is, who else is going to be in the film, or even the salary."

Exasperation turned Paco's face into an angry mask. "Please don't interfere with the business. I'll handle that just the way I have in the past. Money should not be important to you. Your career must come first. You'll be compensated enough to be able to continue to send money home to your parents, which," he added sarcastically, "should satisfy them. Don't I take care of all your other needs?"

Julie didn't answer. She found it extremely unpleasant to discuss money with Paco. He made her feel so guilty. The money she had received from Amato had gone into a newly formed corporation called Castle Productions, a combination of their two names. Paco had urged her to sign the papers, making him president before leaving New York. She hadn't even informed her father, who continued to receive a percentage of her earnings as her manager, although he was in no way involved in any aspect of her career. Paco explained that they would both benefit by having a corporation because of taxes. Julie didn't understand anything about finances, and she trusted Paco completely. After all, he was her husband. He would never do anything to hurt her.

CHAPTER 41

Steve Burton sat in his hand-somely appointed office on Madison Avenue and looked at the mound of work on his desk. He realized that he should tackle it before his next scheduled meeting with a client, but he found it hard to concentrate this morning. He needed time to think. Matters at home had not improved, and for the past few months he had been struggling to keep his marriage alive. The arrival of his son, Michael, who was now almost three months old, and a source of great joy, had not accomplished what Steve had hoped for—the revitalization of his marriage. Instead, it had just reinforced his earlier misgivings that he and Sharon were badly suited and shouldn't have married. Sharon's pregnancy had not been easy, and Steve had done everything in his power to be supportive. He had cut down on the amount of time he spent at the office, and when a healthy baby was born, he had demonstrated his unbridled joy. But after the birth, Sharon became even more withdrawn, focusing all her attention on the baby and leaving Steve with an empty feeling of rejection.

But if Steve's home life was less than he had bargained for, it was compensated for by the steady progress he was making professionally. After spending more than a year with the law offices of Reinheimer and Cohen, where he learned a great deal about entertainment law, Steve began to realize that the firm did not offer a great opportunity for advancement, and he began to seriously consider an offer to join a theatrical agency as general counsel. International Artists was not as big an agency as MCA or William Morris, the two giants of the entertainment industry, but they represented many important actors, writers, and directors. In discussing the possible move with Sharon, Steve tried to explain his reasons.

"Look, Sharon. For the past year I've been doing a lot of legal work with various agents and, to tell you the truth, the prospect of moving over to an agency excites me. As general counsel, I would become even more involved with my clients, and who knows, I might even decide eventually to become an agent myself. The thought has crossed my mind."

Sharon, who had strongly preferred that Steve pursue a career in politics and who considered even the practice of law a compromise, was in complete shock.

"Are you crazy?" she asked, her dark eyes registering her displeasure. "First, you reject the DA's office and go into entertainment law. Now, you're talking about moving to a theatrical agency as counsel and, maybe, eventually becoming an agent." She practically spat the word *agent* at him, as if it was a dirty word.

"Sharon, you're not being reasonable. Besides making more money at International, which wouldn't hurt with a new baby to take care of, I'd be doing work that I enjoy more. What's wrong with that? The world doesn't begin and end with being a lawyer. There are thousands like me out there struggling to get ahead. As an agent I would get a chance to not only utilize my legal experience, but also be involved with the creative aspect of show business, which is something I may have a talent for."

Sharon's lips narrowed into a thin line, and her face took on an icy expression as she looked at Steve. "I suppose you have your mind made up."

"No, Sharon. If I did, I wouldn't be sitting here explaining all of this to you."

"Steve," she said rising from her chair. "I've got to go. I think I hear the baby. I've given you my opinion. I think you're making a big mistake, but if that's what you want, then do it."

Sharon started out the door when, suddenly, a thought occurred to her. She stopped and looked back at him. "Have you informed your parents yet?" she asked. "I'm sure your mother will be delighted," she added sarcastically. "After all the sacrifices they made to put you through law school."

Steve felt anger churning in the pit of his stomach, but he restrained himself from answering sharply. "My mother only wants my happiness, Sharon. You, better than anyone, should realize that."

He picked up his briefcase and went to the baby's room, where Michael lay gurgling in his crib. Leaning over, he kissed his tiny son and smoothed the baby's fine dark hair away from his forehead. He loved Michael and would do anything to keep him from being hurt.

A few weeks later, Steve joined International Artists as general counsel, and after a few months he felt certain that he had finally found the right niche for himself. In addition to working on contracts, he began advising agents in the office on how to structure important deals. It soon became apparent that he was exceptionally creative in conceptualizing network deals for clients, and before long, Steve began to develop a name for himself in the television industry.

Conditions at home had not worsened perceptibly since Steve had joined the agency. But because of a growing awareness that his marriage would never offer him the fulfillment he so desired, Steve began to spend more and more time at the office and with his clients. Because he adored his baby boy, he would put everything aside on weekends and take him on outings to the park and the zoo. Sharon would always accompany them, but they usually found little to say to each other. They had become strangers. At home, more often than not, Steve would immerse himself in his work until very late. Because of his new status and recognition as a "deal maker," Steve began to associate more and more with network executives and stars, and it soon became obvious that because of his deal-making ability and "people talent" he was destined to become an agent.

Once Steve had reached his decision to become an agent, he embarked on a diligent search for his replacement as general counsel. When he found the right man for the job, he began to fill him in on all pending matters, while he himself gradually assumed responsibilities in his new capacity. Concentrating on television packaging turned out to be a fortuitous decision, for Steve proved to be not only creative and extremely able, he also thoroughly enjoyed the challenges. With things going so well in his career, he should have been on cloud nine, but he wasn't. The additional money that he was now earning enabled him to move Sharon and the baby into a larger and more comfortable apartment on Central Park West and to engage a steady maid. Sharon was pleased with their new surroundings, but there still existed a barrier between them that neither one of them seemed inclined to tear down. Not having found the happiness he had dreamed of in his marriage, Steve began to search, subconsciously at first, then consciously, for the companionship he was lacking. Initially, it was just a harmless flirtation with a young actress that he met at an audition. Steve had no intention of dishonoring his vows, and when he sensed that things might be getting out of hand, he quickly nipped it in the bud. As time passed, however, the emptiness of his existence, made bearable only by his devotion to his son and the satisfaction he found in his work, made Steve vulnerable to other women. And eventually he succumbed.

Steve had been over at ABC's executive offices working out a series deal for one of his clients, when he suddenly realized it was past seven and he hadn't called Sharon. Excusing himself, he rushed into the outer office and called home. He let the phone ring for what seemed like an interminable time, but no one answered. Frightened at first that something was wrong, he was about to run out the door to find a taxi, when suddenly he remembered that Sharon had mentioned something about taking the baby to her parents' home for the day. He immediately dialed their number, and in a few seconds Sharon came on the line.

"I called the apartment and was worried when no one answered," Steve said, relieved that she was there. "Then I realized that you told me you were going to your folks. How is everything? Are you and the baby okay?"

There was a familiar sound of exasperation in Sharon's voice as she answered. "If you listened to me more often you would have remembered that I said I would be having dinner over here tonight."

"Sharon, I do listen to you. That's why I'm calling you there. What time will you be home? I don't want you traveling late at night in a taxi."

"Don't worry. My father will drive me home. I'll probably get there before you. You're always so busy with your famous clients."

Steve decided to ignore the sarcasm in her voice. He was tired of fighting with her. "All right, Sharon. I'll grab a bite to eat outside. I'll probably be here for another half hour or so."

Steve hung up the phone, and suddenly he felt at loose ends. Even if Sharon *had* been at home, he still wouldn't have looked forward to returning there. Except for Michael, there was nothing there that beckoned him. It was in this frame of mind that Steve finished his conference and decided to walk to one of his favorite Italian restaurants on the East Side. As he strode briskly along Central Park South toward Fifth Avenue, his mind was on his upcoming trip to California. He was about to step off the curb when a car came careening around the corner, and if it hadn't been for someone tugging at his sleeve frantically, he might have been hit. Turning to see who his rescuer was, he shouted in delight, "Carla!"

"Steve," the girl answered breathlessly. "I didn't know it was you. I just saw this tall fellow, who looked like he was daydreaming, about to get himself killed, and I decided to save his life. Seeing that it was you, I'm especially glad I was here."

Steve looked at her appraisingly. She was a spectacular-looking brunette, with creamy skin and a gorgeous figure who worked at CBS as a production assistant. Steve had met her there a few months earlier, and they had struck up a conversation. She was extremely bright and, as he remembered, had a great sense of humor. At that time he had not permitted himself to think of her as anything more than an acquaintance. But now, as she stood there smiling at him provocatively, he felt drawn to her.

"Carla, it's so good to see you again. You look wonderful. And thank you for saving my life. But you must save me from a fate worse than death—having dinner alone. Won't you please join me?"

Carla looked at him rapturously. She had often thought about the good-looking young man she had met briefly and had hoped to see him again.

"I'd love to. I wasn't looking forward to going back to my apartment. The only thing I've got there is some peanut butter and jelly and some stale bread."

Steve took her arm and they walked to Peppinos, where they consumed a huge salad, delicious spaghetti à la puttanesca, and a bottle of white wine. During dinner, Steve found himself relaxing and truly enjoying himself for the first time in many months. Carla was a delightful conversationalist, and she made him laugh as she recounted her experiences on various shows. Steve was sorry when the check was placed before him. The time had passed very quickly and he regretted the evening was at an end.

Carla sensed his mood because, as they reached for their coats, she said. "I lied before. I told you I only have peanut butter and jelly. But I also have a bottle of brandy that would make a lovely nightcap."

He hesitated for a moment. He knew that she found him attractive and that her invitation meant more than just a nightcap. If he went home with her, something might happen. After all, she was a beautiful and desirable woman, and he was a man who desperately needed the passion and fulfillment that for so long had been denied him.

"Steve," she said, touching his arm. "I'm not asking you to marry me. Just to have a drink before we say good night."

Hours later, as he stroked the gentle curve of her back, he knew that he had committed an unspeakable act, but he had been unable to restrain himself. Steve realized that the guilt would come later, but for now, he wanted the pleasure this woman could offer him. Turning her around to face him, he began to caress the silkiness of her thighs, and gradually his hands reached her large breasts now straining up to him. Rubbing her nipples under his fingers he could feel excitement coursing once again through his body as she moaned with pleasure.

"Steve, oh, God, that feels so good. Don't stop."

He gently parted her moist thighs with his leg and began to press down against her. His maleness was so fully aroused that he thought he would burst, but he wanted to wait until he could bear it no longer. Carla reached out and grasped his buttocks and pulled him inside her like a savage animal. He began rhythmically to push deeper and deeper inside of her until they were both moving as one person. Carla cried out as her body arched to envelop him, and together they reached their final orgasm.

Totally spent, Steve looked at Carla, lying next to him peacefully. She was truly a beautiful woman. Feminine, yet lustful in her lovemaking. He thoroughly enjoyed making love to her and knew that he would want to see her again. But something was missing. Carla satisfied his physical needs, and he was grateful that she had been there for him, but she hadn't touched his heart. That still remained intact and untouched, waiting for the right woman.

Steve continued to see Carla until eventually she realized that he would never commit to anything more than an affair, and tearfully she broke it off. When that particular episode ended, Steve felt great remorse that he had betrayed his marriage vows, and he promised himself it wouldn't happen again. But inevitably it did. Steve was searching for the happiness that so far had eluded him. He desperately craved the warmth and tenderness that he had been denied, but unfortunately the women that began to pass through his life could not fill that void. His brief affairs proved nothing more than meaningless encounters, and he began to despair as to whether the woman of his dreams really existed. *If she does,* he wondered, *will I ever find her?*

CHAPTER
42

If she doesn't stop talking pretty soon I'm going to scream, Julie thought as she helped her maid unpack her suitcases. *Maybe I'll scream anyway even if she does stop her stupid prattling. It might do me good to yell once in a while.* These kinds of thoughts were unusual for a girl like Julie, who seldom lost her temper and was always sensitive to other people's feelings. But the last two years of constant traveling and an almost nonstop schedule had started to take their toll. Julie and Paco had returned to Rome early that morning after fulfilling various engagements in the States, which included Las Vegas, New York, and just last Sunday night, "The Ed Sullivan Show." Now awaiting her on her return to Italy was a picture to be filmed on location in Sicily with Peter Ustinov, plus several appearances in the south of France, culminating with the Princess Grace Red Cross gala in Monte Carlo.

The engagements in the States had gone very well, especially one appearance at the Hotel Riviera in Las Vegas. Even though Paco continued to receive top billing, Julie was now undeniably the star of the show. Paco enjoyed conducting the house orchestra and cracking a few jokes to the audience before introducing Julie. He even made a joke out of the fact that his wife had become the star by saying, "Ladies and gentlemen, when I first hired Julie to work for me, the billing was—The Paco Castell Show, featuring, in small letters, Julie Lauren. Then later on it became The Paco Castell Show starring Julie Lauren. Last time we were in Vegas it was The Paco Castell and Julie Lauren Show." With a helpless shrug of his shoulders, Paco then asked the audience. "Did you notice the marquee outside? It now says, Julie Lauren and friend."

Of course the audience laughed at this, thinking that it was only a joke. But in reality, it was Julie's singing and dancing and enormous sex appeal that were responsible for bringing in the customers. Her Italian pictures had not even been shown yet in the United States, but her television and personal appearances had made her a star, and Paco now seemed content with that arrangement. He was doing what he loved, taking it comparatively easy up on the stage, performing to sold-out crowds, and, best of all, collecting a lot of money, which went directly into the corporation. Now, after many months, she was finally back in her bedroom in Rome and feeling very weary.

This trip had been particularly tiring for Julie because of her quick side trip to Phoenix to see her parents and brother. They had been living there for nearly two years, and though they professed to love it, Julie knew that her mother still missed New York and her family. Grandmother Esther had died six months earlier, and Julie still grieved for her and bemoaned the fact that she had been so far away when it had happened. Before leaving for Arizona, Sam Lehman had taken the money that Julie had sent him steadily and invested it in his brother's restaurant. A year later, when it became apparent that more capital would be needed in order to make a go of it, her father turned to Julie for additional help. Reaching her by telephone in Madrid, where she and Paco were appearing, Sam came right to the point.

"Sweetheart, listen. We have a problem here. I need twenty thousand dollars immediately for the restaurant. My brother Edward is putting in the same amount and I can't let him down."

"Dad," Julie cried out, not believing her ears. "What are you saying? I don't have twenty thousand dollars. You know that. Where would I get that kind of money? Paco and I only receive a small salary from the corporation. What happened to the money you have been receiving?"

"I used that for the initial investment, Julie," her father answered, his voice starting to express anger. "Listen, you tell that son of a bitch you're married to that your parents need some money. He's rich. He can afford it. It's the least he can do for the privilege of living with my daughter." Her mother then got on the phone and echoed her father's demands.

Julie hung up the receiver and dropped her head into her hands. This unexpected ultimatum from her father had left her shattered, and she didn't know where to turn. Even her mother, who had always been her ally, seemed unmoved by Julie's tears and had sided with her husband when Julie had appealed to her. *Where in God's name am I going to find twenty thousand dollars?* Julie asked herself. *Paco. He's my only chance.*

That evening, as they were preparing for bed, Julie timidly approached him. "Paco, please don't say no before you hear me out. My parents are in serious trouble with the restaurant and they need money right away. Can you help me?"

Paco stared at her in disbelief. "What the hell did they do with the money you've been sending all along? Don't they appreciate the gifts you sent them and the trips to Europe you've paid for?"

"Please, Paco. This is different. Can't you advance me or lend me the money. I wouldn't ask you if it wasn't an emergency."

"How much do they need?" Paco asked, looking at Julie suspiciously.

Julie took a deep breath and, trying to avoid his eyes, answered, "Twenty thousand dollars."

Paco took the newspaper he was holding and slammed it down on the table, causing Julie to back up against the wall. "*Hijo de puta,*" he shouted. "Son of a bitch. He hates my guts and yet he asks me for money. No, dammit. I won't do it."

"Paco," Julie pleaded frantically. "Don't use that kind of language about my parents." Taking his arm, she begged him. "Please, please won't you lend it to me. They'll lose everything if they don't get it."

"This thing you have with your parents has got to stop. You've got to grow up and stop worrying about them."

Julie looked stricken. Paco had been her only hope, and he was turning her down.

Looking at her face, Paco thought about her request for a minute and then reconsidered. "Look, if it means that much to you, I'll have the corporation lend you the money and you can pay me back personally out of your salary, a little at a time."

Relieved that she could accommodate her parents, Julie ran to Paco and threw her arms around him. "Thank you, Paco. I can't tell you how grateful I am. I must call my parents right away and tell them the good news. It's still early in the States."

Later that night, when she was in bed, Julie had time to think about the day's events. *It's incredible. I've been working like a dog for four and a half years, traveling all over the world, playing in towns that are not even on the map, making movies, doing television, and I don't even have twenty thousand dollars that I can lay my hands on when I need it. Something has got to be wrong. But what? And what can I do?*

Julie questions continued to remain unanswered as they departed by plane for Catania, Sicily, and her new film. Upon arrival a Mercedes sedan would take them to Taormina, an ancient city set like a jewel high in the mountains above the sea. Peter Ustinov, Julie's enormously talented co-star in this, her tenth film in Italy, was already there with his wife. Julie was told that location on their film would probably take about four weeks, and the remainder would be shot back in Rome at Cinecittà Studios. Julie was terribly excited about her part in the film because it would not only give her the opportunity to co-star with a brilliant actor, but also allow her to sink her teeth into a more demanding role and one that many other actresses had coveted. In anticipation of a long stay, Paco had taken a tape recorder along on the trip, intending to make notes for an autobiography he had been planning. Long a frustrated artist, he also planned to try his hand at painting to while away the hours. As the car approached the Hotel San Domenico, which at one time had been a convent, Julie couldn't keep from admiring the quaint and beautiful little streets and shops that were clustered together. It was May and still too early in the season for tourists, which made the town even more charming.

For the next few weeks Julie forgot how tired she had felt before starting the picture and about all her other responsibilities to her family back home. Peter Ustinov was not only an accomplished actor, director, and writer, but also a witty raconteur who delighted everyone with his fabulous anecdotes and stories about his career. Julie immersed herself completely in her role, and she felt that finally all her hard work would not be in vain. *This picture might give me the recognition as an actress that I've been striving for,* she thought as she studied her lines for the next day's shooting. *Peter has been so encouraging, helping me with my characterization and showing me little tricks of the trade. I can never thank him enough for his help.* Blessedly, there were no love scenes in the picture, for that undoubtedly would have been a source of irritation to Paco. *Even Paco,* Julie thought, putting down her script, *has been feeling mellow since we arrived here. He appears quite content sketching away during the day while we work outdoors. This is the happiest I've been in a long time.*

Unfortunately, Julie's happiness was short-lived. A few days later she received a disturbing telephone call from Rome. It was her Italian agent, Franco.

"Julie, *cara.* How are you?"

"Fine, Franco. We've been working very hard, but we're all excited about the picture."

"Well, you should be. I've seen some of the rushes that were sent back to Rome and you and Peter are sensational. But, that's not why I called. We seem to have a problem collecting the money due to you at this point in the film. You know of course I collected an advance when you signed your contract. I also received a second payment two weeks ago. Now, it seems the producer, that *mascalzone,* son of a bitch, claims he has run out of funds and cannot make the next payments. By the way, I talked to Peter's agent and the director, and they are both in the same boat."

Julie motioned to Paco to get on the phone, for when he heard her talking to the agent his ears had perked up. He took the receiver and listened while Franco explained the problem to him. After he had finished, Paco gave him instructions.

"Tell that lying bastard that unless he comes up with the money we're leaving here and he can take his uncompleted picture and shove it. He'll come around fast when he hears that. He can't afford to lose the money he's already invested."

Franco agreed on the strategy and promised to advise the other agents to do the same. That night the entire cast sat around various tables in their favorite restaurant in the center of town and discussed the problem. Julie felt badly, not only for herself but for the rest of the crew, whose salaries had also stopped. Most of them had families back in Rome and could not afford to sit out a long dispute while new financing was being sought. Suddenly, after several carafes of wine had been consumed and many ideas had been tossed around, Peter came up with a plan.

With a devilish gleam in his eye, he said, "Let's confiscate all the equipment while they search for a new producer. That way we can be sure that at least the crew will be paid if the picture is shelved."

Julie and the director agreed that it was a marvelous idea, and with the help of some local townspeople, they hid the equipment in an old building. Days later, when it was evident that they would be returning to Rome to finish the picture under new auspices, they knew that they had made the right decision. The new producer insisted that in order to complete the film everyone would have to work for half of their designated salary. Ordinarily the actors would have refused, but they were so eager to complete the picture that they reluctantly agreed— but on one condition: The rest of the crew had to be paid all that was owed to them and the balance in advance. If not, then the cameras, sound equipment, and even the typewriters would mysteriously disap' pear, which would not be hard to accomplish in Sicily. Months later, at the Venice Film Festival, where the picture received second prize, Julie and Peter sat over a glass of wine in Piazza San Marco and had a good laugh over the episode.

"My dear," Peter said with a laugh, "our picture, as good as it is, didn't deserve the prize. The story of how it got made, did."

Julie laughed with him, and she hoped their deep friendship would remain steadfast throughout the years.

Princess Grace had married Prince Rainier the summer of 1956, and the following year she inaugurated the ball that became the social event of the season. Paco was thrilled that he and Julie had been personally chosen by the princess to entertain on this occasion. In honor of the event and hoping to make a great impact on the jaded audience that usually frequented the galas, Paco went to great lengths to prepare the show. Leaving Julie alone in Monte Carlo for two days, something he would never have done before, he flew to London to round up some Latin musicians who were performing in a nightclub there. Paco then had his brother, Luis, join them in Monte Carlo to handle all the arrangements. Luis hadn't seen Paco and Julie since their last visit to New York, and he was happy to be back on the payroll again.

During the days, Julie toured the quaint streets lined with boutiques representing France's finest couturiers. But as the night of the gala drew closer, so did Julie's nervousness. Other famous celebrities who had entertained there before had warned them, "The audience at the Sporting Club is the pits. Half of the broads there look like they've been embalmed. They never smile and never applaud. They think it's beneath them. They just sit there like fucking statues and watch us sweat."

The night of the show finally arrived and Julie found it hard to keep her composure. When she peeked out from behind the bandstand and looked at the elegantly dressed men and women, she began experiencing a mixture of fear and anticipation. It was the same kind of nervousness she had felt when she played her first engagement at Ciro's in Hollywood.

Presently, the master of ceremonies announced that the show was about to begin, and Paco made his entrance on the bandstand. He was greeted by polite applause, and picking up his baton, he led the orchestra into a medley of some of his greatest hits. When he finished, the audience responded warmly but hardly with the fervor that he was accustomed to. As Paco reached the microphone, he looked around and thought, *I'll get you yet, you arrogant shits.* Going into his usual patter of jokes, he gradually began to feel them unbend. Then noticing a countryman of his sitting ringside, he introduced Salvador Dalí and proceeded to make a few jokes about his famous mustache and strange attire. The audience laughed and Paco sensed he was home free. It was now time to introduce Julie. When she heard her name being announced, she took a deep breath and walked out onto the stage. The evening air was balmy, and as Julie walked to the microphone she flashed her most dazzling smile to cover the apprehension she was feeling. If there was any applause at her entrance, she wasn't aware of it because her heart was beating so wildly. Picking up the microphone she started to sing, moving her hips ever so slightly to the music. Sighs could be heard in the audience as the men drank in her beauty. The women, however, leaned their heads together as they dissected her. They speculated on everything, from her age to her marriage to where she came from. But one thing they all grudgingly agreed upon—she was an undeniable beauty. Julie remembered every lesson she had learned in the past few years and she used them all to impress the audience. By the time she had finished, she had won them over completely, even the women. Watching Julie intently at a table down front was an olive-skinned man wearing very dark glasses. Seated next to him was an attractive blond attired in a beautiful Dior gown and covered in incredible jewels. The moment Julie had appeared onstage he lost his usual bored expression, and leaning back on his chair, he studied her every movement.

As Julie took her final bow, Paco descended from the bandstand and joined her at the microphone to share the applause. Dozens of roses taken from the tables had been tossed on the stage, a traditional sign of approval from an enthusiastic audience. Suddenly, the tall figure of a beautiful woman, elegantly dressed in a pale blue chiffon gown, approached them. In her arms she carried a large bouquet of ruby red roses wrapped carefully in cellophane. Julie's heart started to beat rapidly when she saw Grace Kelly approaching. As she drew nearer, Julie stepped aside to allow the princess access to the microphone. With a warm smile that illuminated her exquisite face, the Hollywood star who had become a fairy-tale princess presented Julie with the flowers and kissed her on the cheek. Then, in a beautifully cultivated voice that matched her regal appearance, she thanked Paco and Julie for their performance and for donating their services to such a worthy cause. Julie stood there, admiring her chiseled beauty and simple elegance. Suddenly, her own gold lamé gown seemed much too obvious and theatrical, and she wished that she were dressed differently. But now was not the time to dwell on that. The audience had risen to its feet, giving Paco, Julie, and the princess a standing ovation. As she prepared to return to her seat, Princess Grace leaned over and whispered to Julie, "My dear, you were lovely. Won't you and Paco join us for a drink after you've changed?"

Julie's eyes sparkled as she nodded yes, and taking Paco's hand they bid the audience good night and left the stage.

Julie was euphoric. She had been prepared for the worst and it had turned out magnificently. When they were both ready, they made their way through a crowd of admirers to the table where their hosts were seated. When she spied them, Princess Grace held out her hand and beckoned Julie to her side.

"Julie, there's someone here who's just dying to meet you." Addressing the somber-faced man who had been waiting impatiently, she said, "Ari, I would like to present Julie Lauren, or should I say, Señora Castell? Julie, this is Aristotle Onassis."

The world-renowned Greek tycoon rose to his feet and kissed Julie's hand. His lips lingered for a moment.

"Señora, you were enchanting this evening. I would love to join you, but unfortunately, I must leave now. But my wife, Tina, and I would like to invite you and your husband for a cruise on our yacht. We leave in two days for Greece. Please think about it. You don't have to give me your answer now. My aide, Mr. Pliahas, will call you at the hotel tomorrow."

Bowing to Paco, who was watching him warily out of the corner of his eye, he and his wife bid their farewells. Julie was speechless. She, like everyone else, was awed by the charismatic Onassis. But what she couldn't understand was why he would invite them on his yacht when they didn't even know him? As fate, and Onassis, would have it, she would soon find out.

CHAPTER 43

Madam, please be careful of the last step. The light is out and I have called someone to fix it, but it is dangerous."

Julie and Paco followed the steward down the hall and stopped as he opened the door and waited for them to enter. Julie tried hard to maintain her composure as she looked around the lavishly decorated suite that had been assigned to them.

"Will madam and the gentleman require anything else?" the steward asked politely as he showed them around. "The refrigerator under the bar is stocked with champagne and wine. There is also a breakfast menu next to your beds. You can tell the night steward what time you would like your trays in the morning."

Turning to leave, he paused for a moment and turned back. "Sir, I neglected to mention that Mr. and Mrs. Onassis would like to have you and madam join them in the lounge for cocktails at eight."

The minute they were alone Julie grabbed Paco's hand in delight. "Paco, can you believe this fantastic yacht? I had no idea it would be this big." Running her hand over the silkiness of the lavender bed-spread, with its huge pillows plumped to perfection, Julie exclaimed,

"Everything is so beautiful—the rugs, the paintings, the furniture. It's hard to believe we're on a boat."

Leaving Paco to admire the paintings, Julie went to inspect the lavender marble bathroom. On the counter were several bottles of unopened French perfume and jars of creams for every purpose. There were flowers everywhere and enough magazines and books to keep a person occupied for a month.

Paco had been apprehensive about accepting this invitation. Onassis had quite a reputation as a ladies man, almost as bad as his own. Just recently he had made the headlines again with a story about his relationship with a famous American society matron who lived in France. The thought of exposing Julie to this kind of man, rich as Croesus and powerful enough to influence governments, disturbed him. But he could not bring himself to turn down a once-in-a-lifetime opportunity to cruise the Greek Islands aboard a yacht like the *Christina*. Still, he was concerned about what was ahead . . .

At precisely eight o'clock, Paco escorted Julie to the lounge, where their hosts were already seated. Julie had taken great pains in selecting something appropriate to wear. In spite of the fact that she was a star and married to a wealthy man, her choice was somewhat limited. Paco didn't mind spending money on her "working clothes," but when it came to her personal wardrobe he was not overly generous. As Onassis rose to greet them, Julie had an opportunity to get a closer look at his Greek wife, Tina. Tina Livanos Onassis was not only the wife of a multimillion-aire who controlled one of the world's largest shipping lines, but also the daughter of one of Europe's richest men. Julie was immediately impressed by the elegance of her understated but exquisitely designed cocktail dress and the magnificent pearls that circled her neck. Tina Onassis cordially extended her hand in greeting, but Julie could not help but notice the distant and guarded expression in her eyes. If she could have read Tina's thoughts at that moment she would have been surprised.

I knew, Tina thought, *what he had in mind when Ari prevailed upon Grace to introduce him to that singer and her husband—to add another trophy to his collection. He has always been drawn to celebrities and especially to beautiful women. Doesn't he know that I have often heard him brag that he approaches every woman as a potential mistress? I barely know these people and yet Ari has acted impulsively and asked them to join us on our cruise. It will be interesting to watch him juggle that bitch Maria Callas while he fawns over his latest interest.*

Onassis was aware of his wife's every mood and therefore was careful not to arouse her suspicions. Putting his arm around Paco, he asked, "Paco, are your accommodations satisfactory? Is there enough champagne and caviar? Please let the steward know if there is anything that you or your wife need. We will be leaving Monte Carlo at mid-night for Portofino. From there we intend to spend a few days in Capri and then on to Greece."

Onassis's description of their itinerary was abruptly interrupted by the arrival of the opera star Maria Callas and her husband, Giovanni Meneghini.

As Julie watched the diva approach Onassis, her arms outstretched and her face flushed with excitement, she could only liken it to the smoldering fires of Mount Etna that she had watched from her window in Taormina. The American-born diva, who was of Greek origin, strode into the room like Diana the huntress, and paying no heed to anyone else, threw her arms around Onassis and kissed him passionately on the lips. As she proceeded to speak to him in Greek, Julie had time to observe the woman everyone was talking about as being seriously involved with Onassis. The prima donna who had captured the musical world with her voice and great dramatic ability was a large woman, with eyes so dark they seemed almost black. Her thick black hair that evening was pulled back in a chignon, allowing her to display a pair of extraordinary ruby earrings. When Julie's eyes traveled down to the rest of her figure, she could see that Maria's legs were definitely not her best asset. They were unbelievably thick, with hardly any delineation between her calves and her ankles, which made the singer seem much heavier than she actually was.

Julie glanced over to where Tina sat with her hands tightly clenched to see what her reaction would be. There was none. After years of repeated infidelities and long absences where both parties had taken other bed partners, Tina had forsaken her right to protest.

But recently Tina Onassis had become increasingly aware that, for the first time, she might be facing a serious rival for her husband's affection. Maria Callas was not like the rest of Ari's women. Both having struggled to achieve their success, they were close in many ways that Tina, who had been born rich, could never understand. And when they were together she felt like an outsider. As the other distinguished guests started to arrive, Paco took Julie aside to point out some of the paintings that decorated the walls. Onassis's collection was formidable, but Paco was amazed that he would subject such works of art to the sea air. When the steward announced that dinner was about to be served, Julie found Ari standing by her side, waiting to escort her into the dining room. Julie looked around for Paco, who during cocktails had struck up a conversation with the wife of a British diplomat. When he caught Julie's eye he indicated that he would see her inside.

Julie was seated on Onassis's left, while on his right sat an irritated Maria, who resented the presence of this new woman. Earlier, the steward had informed them that there were nine guest suites on board ship and glancing around the table, Julie guessed that some of Onassis's guests had not yet arrived. Tina was seated at the opposite end of the oval table and was busily engaged in conversation with a French actor. Julie reached for her napkin and found nestling under its folds a red box with the name Cartier inscribed in gold letters. She looked around to see if there was a mistake of some sort. *Maybe it's someone's birthday and they've put this in the wrong place*, she thought. But at that very moment everyone was discovering a package at their plate. Looking up at her host, Julie asked him politely, "Mr. Onassis, is this some sort of Greek holiday? Are these gifts for us?"

He laughed and patted her arm. "My dear, every day is a holiday on the *Christina*. This is just a little welcome gift for my guests." Gesturing to the others, who were watching, he added, "Please, my friends, open your gifts—a small token of my esteem for each of you."

Julie hurriedly opened the box and gasped when she saw the contents. An exquisite gold compact with her initials set in emeralds. Inspecting it, she noticed that when she flipped the lid open there was a concealed slot that housed a lipstick. The other guests were equally busy opening their gifts and admiring them. The men had received cuff links—some set with diamonds, others in rubies and sapphires. Only Tina had received a different present, and when she opened the Cartier box it revealed a magnificent emerald and diamond bracelet. Carefully, she lifted the bracelet out of its case, and smiling warmly at Onassis she blew him a kiss across the table. It would be their last exchange of endearments for the remainder of the trip.

As the *Christina* cruised through the Mediterranean toward the Aegean, Julie slowly began to unwind after so many months of hard work. The other passengers—an Italian nobleman and his German wife, the British diplomat Lord Taversham and his wife, Lady Taversham, Gerard Marchand, the new hot French sex symbol and his girlfriend, and finally Maria and Giovanni were the only other guests.

The expected arrival of Princess Grace and Prince Rainier had not occurred. The prince, who had succeeded to the throne of Monaco in 1949, was a well-educated man who had at one time considered aligning himself with Onassis to turn Monte Carlo into a Las Vegas-type of operation. But his initial enthusiasm for Ari had waned, and there now existed a coolness between the men. The newspaper's occasional references to Onassis as the unofficial king of Monte Carlo no doubt irritated the prince, and he understandably declined Onassis's invitation to join the cruise. This decision was probably very fortuitous because there was already enough intrigue on board ship without this further complication. Maria Callas had not anticipated having to compete with a younger and more glamorous woman on the cruise, and she greatly resented Julie's presence. Ari liked nothing better than to watch Maria's reactions when he made a fuss over Julie. He wasn't bothered at all by the fact that not only his wife but also both husbands were on board—all extremely jealous. It excited him to instigate an undercurrent of jealousy. Thus far he had not attempted to make any overtures to Julie for one simple reason—he sensed that she would not be responsive. She was not only quite young and innocent but also, from what he had been observing, totally dominated by her husband. *But*, he thought, as he watched her one afternoon sunbathing on deck, *she's so beautiful. It would be a pity not to try.*

The days had more or less settled down into a routine. When in port, most of the guests would depart by motorboat to shop or sightsee while Onassis would retire to his office to direct his multimillion-dollar empire, having installed a forty-two-line telephone and telex system so he could keep in touch with his various offices around the world.

At lunchtime the group would return to the *Christina*, where they would be joined by Ari and Tina for an informal lunch on the open deck. Afternoons were spent either swimming in the pool, which could be covered over for dancing in the evening, or engaging in whatever activities the guests desired. Since leaving port, the dress requirements had been black tie every night. Each evening as Julie sat in front of her makeup mirror, she tried to imagine what splendid new creations Tina Onassis and Maria Callas would wear. Not only were their gowns spectacular, but their jewels as well, although Tina far outdistanced Maria in that arena. Tina had coordinated her clothes to match her jewels, and so far, she had not repeated any color. Green chiffon Jean Dessès gown, emeralds. Red silk Dior, her famous rubies. The blue jersey Grecian-style tunic she had worn only last evening, sapphires, the most beautiful Julie had ever seen. The array of spectacular jewels seemed inexhaustible. Fastening her tiny diamond earrings to her ears, Julie thought, *Paco keeps reminding me that besides having youth and beauty, I am an artist and therefore I don't need all the extra adornments that other women require. Maybe he's right, but it sure would be nice to have something special. My engagement ring looks so yellow that it could almost pass as a canary diamond.* Julie smiled at her reflection in the mirror as she thought back to how her mother had carried on when Paco had given her the ring. *Well, Mom, you were right. But I mustn't let those things bother me. Not when I have more important problems to deal with.*

Julie's face suddenly became pensive as she thought about her situation. The trip so far had been beautiful and exciting beyond her wildest imagination. Onassis had provided every comfort, and they were mingling with elegant people who not only had accepted her, but who she felt genuinely liked her. *Then what is troubling me?* Julie wondered as she walked over to the window to gaze out at the sea. *I have achieved most of my goals. I'm famous on two continents and I'm married to a rich and successful man. I've traveled all over the world and have performed before royalty. I have everything I've ever wanted. But where is love?* Julie opened the window and felt the cool ocean breeze touch her face, and when she looked up she could see millions of stars illuminating the sky. Suddenly, she shivered—not with cold, but with another sensation that inflamed her whole being. *If only I could share this special night with someone I was madly in love with,* she thought sadly. *Someone who would sweep me off my feet and lift me in his strong arms and carry me to the bed, where he would kiss me and caress me until I ached with desire.* The throbbing in her body intensified, and Julie felt weak with longing for someone to unleash the passion she had kept bottled up for so long. Wistfully, she thought, *If only Antonio . . .* Julie closed her eyes for a moment and let her imagination run wild. She could see Antonio, dressed in a tuxedo, dancing with his body pressed tightly against hers while the music on deck played a love song. Antonio, lifting her out of the pool and lying beside her, his lean young body close to hers. Antonio, here in the room, with the moonlight streaming through the window making passionate love to her . . .

"Julie, are you ready yet? We have to be on deck in ten minutes."

Embarrassed by her thoughts and afraid that somehow Paco could read her mind, she quickly tried to recover her composure. "I just have to slip on my gown and I'll be ready."

Julie went to the closet and removed her gown and shoes. She could still feel her face burning, and she prayed Paco wouldn't notice and comment. He might associate her nervousness with Onassis and he would be dead wrong. She was thrilled to be on his yacht and part of her was intrigued by his wealth and power. But as far as being physically attracted to him, that just wasn't the case. What she fantasized about and yearned for was someone else. As Julie started to dress, she was struck with the realization that not even Antonio, as handsome and appealing as he was, could ever be her knight in shining armor. *Is that special man out there for me? But even if he is, what good would it be? I'll never be free to find him.*

The tension aboard the *Christina* intensified as the ship toured the Greek Islands. Maria Callas, ignoring her husband completely, clung to Onassis's arm whenever possible and flirted outrageously with him. Tina grew even more distant, bored now with her guests and furious with her husband for his behavior. Paco quickly grew tired of climbing over rocks to explore the beauty and treasures of Delos and Mykonos and only at Julie's insistence did he agree to ride the donkey trail to the top of Santorini. Onassis never joined his guests on any of the daytime excursions, but he did provide an English-speaking guide to explain the history of each island. When in port at night, he preferred to dine at local restaurants where his small group would be the only occupants, for Ari would take over the entire establishment. It was on their last night, on the island of Hydra, that things finally came to a head.

After a glorious dinner of couscous and roast lamb accompanied by wine that had been delivered from the yacht, local musicians and singers arrived to serenade the guests. When the music started, Maria immediately jumped to her feet and pulling playfully at Ari's sleeve asked him to join her. After ten days on board ship, her already olive skin was deeply tanned to a rich bronze, and instead of pulling her hair back as she usually did, she let it hang loose. She was dressed in a peasant blouse and a skirt that reached practically to her ankles, thus concealing her least attractive feature. Onassis joined her on the dance floor, and he was followed by other members of the party, who were celebrating the last evening of the cruise. Tomorrow the *Christina* would head for Athens, the last stop for most of the guests except for Callas and her husband, who planned to return to Monte Carlo with Tina and Ari.

Julie watched the group, arms entwined, dancing in a circle and was anxious to join them. Tina did not get up to dance, preferring to sulk quietly at the table with Gerard attentively at her side. She had become quite close to the French actor, Julie noted, but she suspected that might be just a ploy to make Ari jealous. At Onassis's insistence that everyone dance, Julie stood and took Paco's hand. They were instantly pulled into the center of the floor by the others. The waiters had stopped clearing the tables and were clapping their hands to the rhythm and yelling *"opa, opa."* Suddenly, the music changed and the tempo slowed to a more sensuous beat. The rest of the group, fairly out of breath and a trifle exhausted by their exercise and the wine they had consumed, returned to their seats. Only Ari remained standing. Taking his handkerchief out of his jacket pocket, he gracefully started to dance to the music with a great deal of expertise. Maria, realizing that he needed a partner, started to return to the floor but stopped dead in her tracks as she saw Onassis approaching Julie. His eyes never leaving Julie's face, he reached down and pulled his handkerchief around her neck, beckoning her to rise. With the others, save Paco, urging her on, Julie rose and, twining her arm around his, as she had seen done, followed his every step. The night air was hot and the music made the atmosphere even more electric. Julie's simple white cotton halter dress whirled about her shapely legs as she forgot everything except the thrill she felt to be dancing again. She had tied her hair back earlier with a ribbon to keep it off her face, but as she and Onassis moved to the music that had now begun to gain momentum, the ribbon came undone and her glorious mane of red hair whirled about her face. Everyone was still clapping as the music grew faster and faster, and when it finally stopped Onassis swung her off her feet and gave her a kiss on the mouth as they all applauded. A flushed Julie returned to her seat and Onassis quickly followed her.

"Paco, please forgive me for monopolizing your beautiful wife. I have been dying to dance with her ever since I saw her in Monte Carlo."

Paco managed to contain the anger he was feeling by reminding himself that tomorrow they would be in Athens and soon after that on their way back to Rome and safety.

"That's quite all right, Ari. Everyone always wants to dance with my Julie, but only I get to go home with her."

Paco's remark embarrassed Julie. If Paco was jealous that Onassis seemed so taken with Julie, it was nothing compared to the rage Maria

Callas was experiencing. When Ari turned to speak to her she furiously unleashed an angry barrage at him that one did not have to be Greek to understand. Pulling her dull and melancholy husband to his feet, she stormed out of the restaurant and into the night. Only Tina Onassis, who understood every word of Maria's outburst, seemed to be enjoying the scene, for she said triumphantly and loud enough for everyone to hear, "This was worth waiting for—to see that fat bitch get her comeuppance."

Ari must somehow have managed to make peace with the temperamental diva because the next afternoon in Athens, as the rest of the party dispersed for their various destinations, the *Christina* set forth for Monte Carlo with Maria and her husband on board. Missing, however, was his wife, Tina, who remained at her family's home in Athens. As Alitalia flew Julie and Paco back to the Eternal City, Julie wondered what the next months would bring. One thing was sure, she thought as she glanced over at Paco, who was sleeping. *That trip will be my last vacation for a long time. Paco has already made that quite clear.*

CHAPTER 44

The torrential rains that had begun more than a week ago continued to beat down on the windows outside Julie's dressing room in Milano. Although it was only three o'clock in the afternoon the sky was ominously dark and Julie couldn't shake off her feelings of despair. Today was her twenty-third birthday, and she couldn't think of a worse way to spend it than to be cooped up all day rehearsing in a television studio. Paco and Julie had been in Milano for the past three months doing a weekly television show that from the very beginning had taken off and had become a huge success. Because of the unprecedented acceptance by Italian audiences, it now seemed likely that they would be there the rest of the winter. The prospect of spending all that time in a city where Julie had no friends and where the sun rarely shone only heightened her depression.

On the rare occasions when they weren't filming or rehearsing, Paco and Julie had explored the city, which with all its beautiful shops and great restaurants, she found to be exciting. They also found the Milanese to be very friendly and extremely cultured, taking great pride in their famous bastion of opera—La Scala. But Julie's discontent stemmed from the fact that she not only was working very hard but, because of her schedule, was forced to spend every waking moment with only Paco for company. She was gradually suffocating. When they first received the offer of a television series, Julie had had certain reservations about accepting. Her motion picture career was now in high gear, with one film currently in release and doing phenomenal business and another being readied for a spring premiere. There wasn't a week that went by when her face wasn't on the cover of a European magazine. Her fame had spread to France, Spain, and England, and undeniably, she was now considered a major star. Although she had a dozen film offers to choose from, Julie felt an obligation to Paco to accept the television offer. The show, which would be built around them, was to be the most expensive production the government-controlled RAI-TV had ever produced. It would undoubtedly give Paco's sagging career a much-needed shot in the arm since it offered him the opportunity to star in a musical variety show with Julie, who was then enjoying such great popularity. Once the deal was set, Paco, who had been feeling morose and irritable because of his idleness for the past few months, became more cheerful as they prepared for their departure for Milano.

"*Signora,* Julie," the stage manager called. "*Cinque minuti, per favore.*"

Five minutes, Julie thought, reaching for her costume. *I'd better move. If we're lucky we might get through early tonight. I'd love to go somewhere for dinner instead of having room service again. Nearly every night it's been the same routine. We return to the hotel, shower, have dinner, Paco reads, and we go to bed. It's my birthday and I would love to do something different, like maybe go dancing. Anything, except go back to that damn hotel with Paco.*

The difference in their ages and vitality was becoming increasingly apparent. There was also a growing difference in their professional thinking. One afternoon during rehearsal with Paco, what had started out as a simple disagreement over Julie's song selection developed into a major issue that culminated in a bitter argument in their dressing room. It was one of the rare times that Julie spoke up and defended her ideas, and Paco characteristically reacted angrily.

"For God's sake, Julie. Haven't I always chosen your music? What is this crap you're giving me about wanting to sing these romantic ballads and not something rhythmic where you can dance? I know my audience."

It was the same story he had given her over and over again, but Julie continued to argue her point. "Paco, I realize you know your audience, but now they're my audience too, and frankly I think they're getting tired of seeing me do the same kind of songs show after show. It's either 'Que Rico Cha Cha Cha,' or 'Cuban Mambo,' or 'Chiu Chiu.' They're all the same. Even the producer and director agree with me. They'd like me to sing some romantic Italian songs without even moving a muscle. They think I have a good voice and don't have to shake my hips all the time."

"Tell them to mind their own damn business. I'm your husband and you'll do as I say."

Julie whirled away from him, her eyes flashing, and for the first time in her life, she reacted temperamentally. Zipping her gown down savagely she stepped out of it and threw it on the couch, barely missing Paco's head. Pulling on her robe she turned back to him and said defiantly, "I will not do as you say when it comes to my work. I've always listened to you and respected your opinion, but you never respect mine. Did you read the reviews of last week's show? Well, I know it by heart. 'Julie Lauren looks ravishing and sings and dances beautifully, but her songs are getting tired. The Queen of the Cha Cha Cha had better expand her repertoire before she is dethroned.' "

Glaring at him with all the frustration and pent-up emotion that she was feeling, she tried reasoning with him again. "Paco, why can't you understand my viewpoint. I'm not saying I shouldn't do some of our old stuff. But there's a whole new audience out there watching television and some of them are quite young and don't remember your pictures."

Paco turned away from her and slammed the music he was holding down on the table. His expression was rigid, and by now Julie knew what that meant. Obey or be prepared to fight.

Julie was getting sick and tired of constantly being dictated to. Didn't he realize that she had taste and very definite opinions of her own, and that what she was telling him might be valid? Hadn't the critics already attacked his old-fashioned jokes and music? The only reason the show was enjoying such a huge success was because of her. But she couldn't bring herself to remind him of that. She still felt too much in his debt.

Straightening his tie, Paco said coldly, "I'm going out on the set, Julie, and you'd better come too. They're waiting for us."

Dammit and damn him, Julie thought disgustedly. *As far as he's concerned that's the end of the discussion. I'm so sick and tired of him and his domineering ways that I'd like to slap his smug face, walk out of here, and never come back again. If only I had the guts to do it.* Julie let him walk to the door before she moved reluctantly to follow him.

They finished the day in silence. It was especially difficult for Julie to pretend in front of the camera that they were lovey-dovey and laugh at all his stale jokes. Paco was much better at that kind of deception than she. He could fake a smile even if he was seething inside.

Now, back in the hotel hours later, she could barely pick at her dinner. *What a birthday,* she thought unhappily. *Paco hasn't even mentioned it.* Shoving the room service cart to one side, she got up and started for the bedroom.

Paco rose from the table and came over to her. Cupping her face in his powerful hands, he told her, "Julie, I know you're upset, but I can't help it. You were wrong and I had to make you see that. Now, cheer up. I have a surprise for you. In two weeks it will be Christmas and we have a three-week vacation before we continue the show. I have rented a villa in the Costa Brava in Spain where we can relax and not think about work. You will love the Costa Brava. It is very beautiful there even at this time of year. Now, put a smile on your face and give your Paco a kiss. Happy Birthday, *querida.*"

Noticing her surprised expression, he added, "You see, my angel, I didn't forget. Monday we will go shopping on the Via Montenapoleone and pick out a wonderful gift for you."

Julie tried to respond graciously, but all she could think of was the news he had just told her about Spain. *Great,* she thought. *A country house in Spain, in the middle of winter, cooped up with only Paco for company. That really cheers me up.* But she did manage a weak smile and trying to keep the sarcasm out of her voice, replied. "That sounds marvelous, Paco. I can hardly wait." Feigning sleepiness, she yawned, then indicated she was going to turn in.

Paco patted her cheek and went back to his dinner. Nothing ever disturbed his appetite, and his waistline was beginning to show the effects of eating pasta with rich sauces twice a day.

A week later, the plane touched down at Barcelona airport. Julie had hoped to sneak into the country unnoticed, but somehow the press had gotten wind of her arrival and there was a mob of photographers waiting for her at the airport. Paco received his share of attention, for he was still beloved by his countrymen, but it was obvious that Julie had become the star attraction, and it was she who was bombarded with questions.

"Señorita Lauren, oh, *perdoname*, Señora Castell, is it true you are coming to the Costa Brava to settle down permanently and have a baby?"

Julie almost burst out laughing. She had only come to Spain for a brief vacation and as far as a baby was concerned, that couldn't be further from the truth. Even if their sex life had been better, Paco, for some unexplained reason, had been unable to father a child with his ex-wives. And, even if he could, she doubted whether he would have wanted one. Not tolerating any intrusion in his relationship with Julie by her family or even allowing her to cultivate close friendships, it was obvious to Julie that a baby would be out of the question. Paco was impatient to get started on their trip to the Costa Brava, and he was also becoming irritated about the fuss the press was making over Julie. Taking her arm, he pulled her away and led her out of the airport, where a car and driver were waiting. Julie settled down and tried to relax during the drive to S'Agaró. As Paco chatted with the chauffeur, Julie looked out of the window at the small picturesque villages that boarded the sea. Even though it was late December, the weather was mild and she opened the car window so that she could smell the fresh sea air. Paco hadn't told her too much about the house he had rented, but that wasn't unusual. He rarely consulted her when making decisions of nay kind. She only hoped that somehow she would find a way to escape her loneliness. In the past year, Paco had become more and more withdrawn from even the few friends they had made in Italy. With his ever-increasing jealousy and constant fear of having Julie exposed to any outside influences, he had created a fortress around them, and Julie felt trapped.

As dusk settled over the mountains the car made its way over the winding road that led to S'Agaró and the Hostal de la Gavina. It was a truly splendid hotel built on top of a cliff overlooking the sea. The hotel and the entire village of S'Agaró had been developed by one man, who owned all the land. To protect his little community he sold parcels for future homes only to people who agreed to build in a style that conformed to the architecture of the existing hotel. The houses already built were close to the hotel and owned by Spaniards and wealthy foreigners who had discovered this beautiful and secluded part of Spain. Señor Encesa was determined that this area not be turned into another French Riviera. The car carrying Paco and Julie arrived at the front of the hotel and they got out to stretch their legs. As Paco picked up the keys to their rented villa from the concierge, Julie wandered through the magnificent entry, getting her first glimpse of the hotel that many considered the finest in Europe.

There were a few couples seated around a roaring fire having cock-tails as Julie entered the loggia of the hotel, and now, even with evening approaching, it was still bright and cheery. Peeking into the small writing room, she paused to admire the exquisite furniture and old tapestries when suddenly Paco appeared at her side.

"Julie, before we go up to the house, would you like to have a glass of vermouth?"

Julie nodded and followed Paco out of the room and back into the foyer. As they neared the bar, Julie could hear the sound of raucous laughter, and somehow it seemed totally out of place given the quiet decorum of the hotel. Entering, Julie saw three people there—two men, who were standing at the bar with drinks in their hands, laughing uproariously at a woman seated with her back to Julie. Paco took Julie's arm and led her to the bar. He was about to order when the woman turned around on her stool to glare at the intruders, a slight frown marring her otherwise beautiful face. Suddenly, she let out a whoop of delight when she recognized Paco.

"Paco," she said, embracing him warmly. "You old son of a bitch. What are you doing here in no-man's-land?"

Paco gave her a kiss and drew Julie close to him. "Ava, I'd like you to meet my wife, Julie. Sweetheart, this is the notorious Ava Gardner, an old friend from my Hollywood days. Be careful of her. She drinks and swears like a man but, believe me, she's all woman."

Julie smiled, unable to tear her eyes away from the awesome beauty of a woman she had only read about for so many years.

Ava leaned over and tweaked Paco on the cheek. "Paco, why the fuck are you making up lies about my drinking and swearing? You know that I'm just a sweet little southern girl who drinks nothing but a glass of sherry now and then. Right fellas?"

The two men who had been watching their companion tease Paco, joined in. "Yes, sir," the taller of the two said. "Our Ava barely touches the stuff."

The actress stepped down and put her arms around the two hand-some men. "I want you to meet my drinking companions. This big ugly fella with the mustache is Bob Ruark. I'm sure you've read some of his books. The son of a bitch spends a lot of time in Africa writing about the Mau Mau's and that kind of crap." Ava glanced up at the writer fondly, her beautiful green eyes sparkling with pride and delight.

Turning to her other companion, she said, "This skinny guy with the patent leather hair and big cock is my latest discovery, Manolo Pedroza, Spain's newest and bravest matador. He's leaving me next month to go fight in Mexico, the rotten shit, but I just may decide to go with him. Now, don't look so shocked, Julie. The boy doesn't understand much English. Just the dirty words I've taught him. Right, sweetheart?"

The handsome bullfighter embraced her possessively and bent over to murmur something in her ear. Ava looked up and smiled, winking her eye at him.

"Later, *mi amor*. Now Paco, Julie, why don't we get down to some serious drinking. Then you can come back with us to Ruark's place in Palamos. It's not far from here. I've got some Gypsies coming by later for flamenco."

Julie was at a loss for words. She had never heard a woman use that kind of language before, and even though she was somewhat shocked and surprised by her bawdy behavior, she couldn't help but like this exquisite creature who stood there smiling impishly at her.

Robert Ruark, who had been listening to his good pal, Ava, dominate the conversation spoke up. "Mr. Castell, I certainly would like to have you and your wife join us at my house for dinner and whatever else my friend Ava has cooked up. My wife, Virginia, is in Barcelona, but she should be back in an hour or so. I'd like you to meet her."

Before Paco could answer, Ava jumped in. "By the way, Paco, where are you and Julie staying? Not at the hotel, I hope. Right now it's about as exciting as my first husband, and you know how exciting he was."

"We've rented a house right up the road here for three weeks, Ava. Julie and I have been working hard and she wants to rest."

"Rest, my ass. She's just a baby. There's time enough to rest when you're dead. Paco, you're probably the one who wants to rest." Turning to Julie, she asked, "How old are you, honey, twenty, twenty-one?"

"I'm twenty-three, Miss Gardner. My birthday was last week."

"Ava, honey. Well, that's all the more reason to celebrate. Now you go get yourself settled and do whatever we girls do. We'll expect you by ten. Ginny is bringing a few other people down from Barcelona for the holidays."

Ava turned and beckoned to Manolo, who was watching her, and circling her arm around his waist, the three of them departed. Julie watched them leave. Even though the actress was dressed in a simple cashmere sweater and skirt with low-heeled shoes, she still was more beautiful than any other actress she had ever seen. Her luminous skin had been practically devoid of any makeup and her dark hair combed simply and held back with a pin. *Still,* Julie thought, *there is something about her that is animalistic. She reminds me of a panther in the jungle— wild and free-spirited. I wish I were more like her—uninhibited and unafraid.* Julie could not dwell any longer on the famous actress because Paco was anxious to get to the house. Minutes later, they arrived at the villa, which was set on a hill overlooking the sea. Julie was pleasantly surprised. The house, which was owned by a wealthy Englishman, was incredibly beautiful.

She had not anticipated the grandeur of the house, expecting it to be merely a country cottage. All of the main rooms overlooked the terrace and beautifully manicured lawn. The house itself sat on a bluff only a half mile up from the hotel and facing the sea. There were a series of steps that led down from the house to a private beach just below, and Julie wished that she could have been there in the summer to enjoy swimming in the aquamarine Mediterranean sea. As Julie began to put her things away in the airy bedroom with its thick walls to keep it cool in the summer and warm in the winter, she began to plan her days ahead. She would take long walks on the beach, read some books that she had brought with her, and try not to think of anything that would spoil her vacation—not her mother and father, who were in one of their "we're not talking to Julie" phases; not Paco, who had been impossible to please and live with the past months; and not even her future. *Thank God,* she thought happily, *that we bumped into Ava and her friends right off the bat. I hope she remains here during our vacation even though I'm sure she'll be busy with her bullfighter.* Suddenly, Julie stopped what she was doing and sat down on the bed. *Bullfighter,* she thought pensively. *Antonio. I wonder if I'll ever see him again? But what if I did? It wouldn't matter. I'm married, and even if I weren't, he's Spanish and very Catholic and I'm a Jewish girl from Manhattan. But it would be exciting just to be in his company again.*

In the living room Paco sighed contentedly. He was happy. He was in his beloved Spain—in a beautiful house in the Costa Brava, all alone with his Julie. What could be better? No flirtatious young actors or aggressive producers and directors to worry about. None of her family to put ideas in her head—just peace and quiet and Julie. *Yes*, he told himself. *These next few weeks are going to be perfect.*

And they would have been *if* Ava Gardner had gone off to Mexico with her new boyfriend as she had originally planned. And *if* she hadn't convinced her friend Bob Ruark to give a big New Year's Eve party at his home. Until then, things had been idyllic in the peace and quiet of the beautiful countryside—for Paco, at least. Julie spent her days walking the beach and reading while Paco dabbled at some sketching. Some days he would take her to the surrounding villages, where they would walk over the cobblestones exploring quaint little shops that opened on the weekends for the occasional tourist. Julie enjoyed those excursions, for it was during those hours alone with Paco when he was describing his early recollections of Spain and his youth that he was the easiest to be with. But the nights, when they were alone, were something else, and Julie began dreading them. His desire for her was insatiable and his demands made Julie recoil because she felt nothing except repulsion whenever he touched her now.

One night, after a huge dinner in a restaurant in the little village of San Feliú, Julie and Paco returned to the villa. It was almost midnight when they turned on the lights, and the house was quiet, as all of the servants were asleep. Julie had enjoyed the delicacies the restaurant had offered. The fresh prawns, the delectable chicken simmering in a spicy brown sauce, and her favorite dessert, Crema Catalana. But, as was her custom, she ate sparingly. She had never felt the need to diet because her weight always remained the same. Nevertheless, too much food and wine upset her stomach and she knew when to stop. Such was not the case with Paco, whose weight had been ballooning since they arrived in Europe. Tonight he had again overeaten and had finished two carafes of wine all by himself.

After entering the bedroom, Julie began to remove her makeup and brush her hair while Paco went into the bathroom. She was feeling a little apprehensive. During the short drive home, Paco had begun to stroke her bare leg and murmur words of endearment. The wine had started to take effect and Julie hoped that by the time they reached the house his passion would have subsided as he grew sleepy.

Julie finished cleansing her face and was about to slip on her nightgown when she felt Paco's arms around her.

"*Mi amor.* You look delicious. Just like a piece of ripe fruit. I think I will eat you."

Julie tried to free herself, but he was holding her too tightly. When she turned she could smell the combination of alcohol and garlic on his breath and it made her sick. She had to get away or she would throw up.

"Paco, please. It's very late. Why don't you go to bed now."

"I don't want to go to bed now," he said, pushing her down on the bed. "I want to eat you."

"Paco, stop it. You're drunk."

"I'm not drunk, *querida*. I know exactly what I'm doing."

But as he said this, he suddenly slipped off her body and rolled over on his side, where he instantly fell asleep. Julie looked at this man who was her husband and shuddered. Tonight she had been spared. But what about tomorrow and the day after tomorrow? How long could she go on like this, fighting off his advances and pretending she was happy?

A few nights later, Julie and Paco accepted Bob Ruark's invitation and joined him and his wife in welcoming in 1959. The writer's house, which sat on the beach in a quaint little town called Palamos, was brightly lit as Paco and Julie drove up. The front door was open, and when they walked in, the party was already in progress. There were a few people there whom Julie had already met during their brief stay in S'Agaró: two prominent society friends of Ruark's who were spending the holidays at their villas in S'Agaró and some of his friends from London, where the Ruarks' had a town house. Ava was standing off in a corner, surrounded by her entourage. As Julie approached her she could see her friend's animated face engaged in conversation with Manolo and another man, whose face was hidden from view. Paco had left Julie's side for a moment to greet a friend of his from Barcelona, and when Ava saw Julie making her way across the room, she interrupted her companion and extended her arms in welcome.

"Julie, you doll. Come over here. I want you to meet someone."

Julie gave her a quick kiss on the cheek and turned, only to face Antonio, who was standing there smiling tenderly at her. Julie felt the blood rush to her face and her knees go weak. Her first instinct was to run—to get out of there before Paco came back and saw the two of them together. For surely he would notice how unnerved she was by Antonio's presence and guess what was going through her mind.

"Julie, for Christ's sake, say something. This young man has been waiting all evening to say hello to you."

Julie regained her composure and extended her hand to Antonio, who raised it gently to his lips and kissed it.

"Antonio and I have already met, Ava. It was a few years ago in Barcelona when Paco and I played our first concert there."

"Why, you sly *pendejo*," Ava said to Antonio, who was now anxious to pull Julie aside so he could speak to her alone. "You didn't say you knew this little gal. You just let me go on and rave about her beauty and sweetness when all the time you already knew her."

"I just wanted to hear you reconfirm what I already knew—that Julie is a most exceptional girl."

"Well, *torero*. Don't turn around now but her most exceptional husband is on his way over here, and if it's the same old Paco from Hollywood days, he'll probably blow a fuse when he sees her talking to a handsome young guy."

Julie's back immediately stiffened in fear. Before she could move away, Paco was at her side. "*Querida*, where were you? I wanted you to meet Salvador Oller, a good friend of mine." Suddenly, he stopped when he realized that he had come face-to-face with Antonio. Suspicion immediately clouded his face, and as he usually did when he felt threatened, he lashed out at Julie.

"Well, my dear. I see you've been too busy with your friend, the famous bullfighter, to look for your husband. I have to admit, he *is* young and good-looking. And so romantic when he fights the bulls with his tight pants and colorful jackets. No wonder all the American girls have hot pants for *toreros*. Right, Ava?"

"Stop being such a son of a bitch. The poor girl was only saying hello. As for American girls and bullfighters. Well, you know that's all bullshit. We don't care what guys do for a living as long as they're a good fuck."

Julie, who was horribly embarrassed by Paco's outburst and Ava's vulgar response, quickly excused herself and went in search of her hosts. She would have liked to have gone back to her house to spare herself any further humiliation, but she knew that would be impossible. After what seemed like an eternity, dinner was finally served, and the countdown to midnight began. Julie had been avoiding Paco's eyes all evening, and she dared not look around to see where Antonio was. At last it was midnight and when the musicians began to play the equivalent of "Auld Lang Syne" the couples embraced each other and lifted their champagne to toast in the new year. Paco gave Julie a perfunctory kiss on the cheek and proceeded to drink more heavily than ever. *It's as if he can read my mind,* Julie thought as she watched his strange behavior. *He must sense the attraction that Antonio and I feel, and he's reacting accordingly. But he should realize that I know my responsibilities and that I will never dishonor him. Haven't I proven that over the years? Despite all the temptations that have been thrown in my path, I have never done anything that I am ashamed of, except maybe that one night at the Plaza de Toros, when Antonio kissed me.*

All at once, Paco got up, and after murmuring something about getting some air, he abruptly left. Julie looked around and saw that most of the guests had gone out to the terrace and were dancing. A few minutes went by, and feeling terribly lonely, Julie strolled out to the garden to watch the waves pound the shore. She turned to look for Ava, and when she couldn't find her she figured that the actress must be off somewhere with her boyfriend, welcoming in the new year in her own way. She was about to go inside to look for Paco when she felt someone touch her arm. She turned. She couldn't see Antonio in the darkness, but she could feel his presence and the beating of her own heart.

"Julie, I have been waiting for a chance to talk to you, but you have been avoiding me all evening."

"Antonio, please. Paco is terribly jealous of you and if he sees me out here he'll have a fit. I must go."

"My beautiful Julie, why are you so afraid of him? You and I have done nothing to make him angry."

Julie looked around anxiously, expecting to see her husband at any moment. "I don't know. He's just very suspicious whenever you're around."

"Then he is a smart man, Julie, because he must sense what is in my heart. Oh, Julie, I have thought of you so often. I read about you all the time and have seen all your movies, sometimes twice. You are more beautiful and desirable than ever. Are you happy?"

Julie turned her head away. "Antonio, please don't ask me that. I really don't know what I am anymore. I'm so confused I can't think. Now, seeing you again has only confused me more. I wish I could straighten out my life, but I can't seem to find the way. I guess that's the price I'm paying for success."

"Julie, don't you realize you could have success and happiness too? Why do you feel you have to pay? What foolish fears has that man put in your mind?"

"Antonio, my life is too complicated. How can I expect you to understand when I don't understand myself."

Julie's eyes filled with tears as she spoke. She could feel Antonio's genuine concern. Suddenly, she couldn't bear the pain alone any longer and putting her cheek against his chest, she started to cry. Antonio lost all his resolve not to add to her burden and took her in his arms.

"Please, Julie, do not cry. You are so lovely and good. You do not deserve this unhappiness."

Lifting her wet face to his, he kissed her, tenderly at first. Then, with a mounting passion, his lips became more demanding, until they both were fighting for breath. She could feel his body hardening against her, and instead of pulling away, she pressed herself against him, never wanting to let him go. He was kissing her eyelids, the hollow of her throat, and finally once again bruising her mouth, hungry with desire.

"Julie, Julie," he murmured as he caressed her. "I love you."

"No, Antonio. Please, don't say that. You can't. You mustn't."

Pushing at his chest with all the strength she could muster, Julie pulled out of his arms and ran into the house. Every part of her body was tingling with emotion and passion and she knew that if she had not pulled away she would have been lost. Distractedly, she ran into the driveway, looking for their car, and found Paco standing there.

"I was just about to come and get you," he said. "I was feeling lousy so I went to the bathroom to throw some water on my face. I guess I drank too much. Are you ready to go home?"

"Yes, Paco, I'm ready. Let's get out of here."

Julie spent the rest of her vacation in total solitude, afraid of seeing people. All she looked forward to was returning to work. To her, work represented her only salvation, the only escape from her terrible unhappiness. Paco never mentioned that night at the Ruark's and Julie was grateful for that. She was determined to put Antonio out of her mind forever. She was intelligent enough to realize that what she felt for him was not love, but only a fierce passion. Knowing that, she resolved never to let it happen again. At least she was comforted by the knowledge that she was indeed capable of great passion when aroused by the right person.

Two days before leaving, Paco decided to buy the house they were renting so they could spend their free time there. Julie didn't protest because in her state of mind one place was as good as another. She loved the Catalonian people, and under the right circumstances would have welcomed a home there with great enthusiasm. But now it just didn't matter. When they reached their apartment at the Hotel Principe di Savoia in Milano to resume their television series, they found four urgent telephone messages and two telegrams from Freddie Barnett in New York. Walking to their rooms, Paco hastily ripped open the telegrams and, after glancing at them, handed them over to Julie without comment. Her heart pounding wildly, Julie read the contents.

> *Been trying to reach you by phone. Urgent you call me immediately. Have offer for Julie to star in Broadway show. Rehearsals start April first. Important Hollywood director already set. Lew suggests Julie accept part. Film version likely to be sold. Call me immediately at the office or my home. Regards, Freddie.*

Julie didn't dare glance at Paco to see his reaction, because she was afraid of what it might be. When they reached their apartment, Paco opened up his briefcase and handed her his telephone book. "You'd better call him right away. He must still be at the office."

Julie couldn't believe her ears. Paco was actually urging her to make the call. What Julie didn't realize then was that Paco was happy that they would be returning to the States. He realized that European men had started to become a serious threat to their marriage. It would be better to remove her from such a romantic environment.

What *Paco* didn't realize was that Julie was also eager to go home. After the incident with Antonio, she didn't trust herself anymore. Throwing off her coat, Julie reached for the telephone and asked the operator to get her the number in New York. As she waited for the connection, all she could think of was *Broadway—I may be going back to Broadway. And this time as a star.*

CHAPTER
45

Steve hurried through the TWA terminal, anxious not to miss his plane. Wrapping up loose ends at his New York office had taken longer than expected, and if he was to get to the gate on time he'd have to run. *Dammit*, he thought as he darted through the crowds, *I always get the very last gate no matter where I'm going.* Just as he was about to reach the tunnel leading to Gate 22, he dropped the newspapers he was carrying and quickly bent down to retrieve them. When he straightened up, he bumped headlong into one of the most beautiful girls he had ever seen. She was momentarily startled by the jolt, and for a minute he thought she would fall. Reaching his arm out to steady her, he grabbed her around the shoulders, and the full impact of her beauty made him catch his breath.

"Please, forgive me, miss. I just wasn't looking where I was going. Are you okay?"

She flung her long red hair away from her face and smiled at him reassuringly. "Yes, I'm fine, but you sure pack a wallop."

"I'm so sorry. I dropped the papers and didn't see you coming. I've been rushing around like this all day."

Looking at his watch, he realized he would have to really dash to get to the gate before it closed. But he was reluctant to leave her. She was not only extraordinarily lovely, but seemed vaguely familiar to him.

"If you're sure you're all right then I'll be on my way. I'm terribly late."

"Please, go ahead. I have to get to the baggage claim area. My husband must be wondering where I am."

Strangely, Steve felt a sense of great disappointment when he heard that she was married. *But what the hell*, he thought sadly. *So am I.*

Bidding her good-bye, he ran the entire way to the gate and reached it just in time before the door closed. When he finally settled down in his seat for the long trip to California, he put aside his briefcase with all the work he had intended to concentrate on during the flight and took out his newspapers. Being an avid baseball and football fan, Steve usually turned to the sports section first. But something on the second page of the *New York Post* caught his eye. Staring at him was a photograph of a beautiful young woman. With a flash he recognized her as the girl in the terminal. Quickly, he read the caption.

> *Julie Lauren heads back to Broadway. The famous actress and singer, who is married to Latin bandleader Paco Castell and who has been living in Italy, is heading back to New York to star in a Broadway show,* The Captain's Wives. *Welcome home, Julie.*

He stared at her picture. *Julie Lauren, Julie Lauren*, he thought. *Of course, I should have recognized her.* But Steve rarely got to nightclubs. Most of his clients were involved in motion pictures and TV, and even though Julie had done guest shots on important variety shows, he had never seen her perform. While admiring her striking image in the photograph, Steve began to think, *There's something else about her that strikes a bell.* Steve leaned back in his seat and tried to place where else he might have seen her. Suddenly, it dawned on him. *Jesus, she was married at the Waldorf-Astoria the night before I was. Freddie Barnett told me about it at my wedding. She looks like she's just a kid. She can't be more than twenty-two or three. Now what in the hell is a beautiful, successful young girl doing married to a guy like Paco Castell? I've heard only bad things about him.*

Folding the newspaper, he placed it in the seat pocket in front of him and pulled out his briefcase. He began to go over some scripts he was bringing back to California with him, but occasionally a vision of

Julie would pass in front of his eyes, and he couldn't help but remember the softness of her body when he had held her briefly and the fragrance of her hair. Annoyed with himself for fantasizing about a girl he barely met, Steve decided to concentrate on his work and put her out of his mind. *God knows*, he thought, *my life is complicated enough without dwelling on a girl I'll probably never see again.* But his concentration was gone, and instead of focusing his attention on the papers in his lap, Steve leaned his head back and began to reflect on the events that had taken place in his life these past few months.

At his insistence, he and Sharon and their six-year-old son, Michael, had moved to California six months earlier. The move had not been a particularly happy one, at least not as far as Sharon was concerned. Since joining International Artists, Steve's career had been making incredible strides—so much so that they soon offered him a partnership and a huge increase in salary. Just a year ago, he alone had been responsible for selling two television pilots to the networks that had gone on to become hit series. When he was approached about relocating to the West Coast in order to head up the television department, Steve jumped at the opportunity. He had gradually become disenchanted with New York, and the idea of raising his son in a better climate and a more suburban environment greatly appealed to him. Unfortunately, Sharon was of a different mind.

"Give up New York and all my friends? You must be joking. There's nothing out there that would interest me—no theater to speak of, no art galleries, nothing—only movie and television people, who are consumed with one topic of conversation—their careers. I just couldn't take it, Steve."

He tried to convince her that her attitude was typical of many snobbish New Yorkers and not based on fact. He knew that if only she made half an effort, she would find that California had a lot to offer. The schools, he was told, were excellent, and during one of his business trips, he had already started to scout out different residential areas in the eventuality that Sharon would agree to move.

When the moment arrived for a decision, Steve used the only argument he thought might have any impact on Sharon's determination not to leave New York—Michael's well-being and future.

"Just think of how wonderful it would be to have a swimming pool and a big yard for Michael to play in. You said that you couldn't stand another winter of snow and sleet. Do you remember how many colds Michael had last year?"

Sharon had remained silent. Somewhere along the way they had stopped communicating with each other and had drifted further and further apart. Now, their only bond was their son. He was, in fact, the only reason that Steve had remained in a loveless marriage this long.

At first, Sharon remained steadfast in her decision not to move. But eventually, impressed by photographs of several houses that were within their budget, and by Steve's description of places they could take Michael for short vacations, she began to relent. She finally agreed to fly to California to join in the search for a home. Almost immediately they found the perfect place and made an offer. After the price was settled on and a brief period of escrow, Steve moved Sharon and his son out to California and their new home.

Once they were settled in, Steve gave her free rein to hire a decorator and furnish the house as she saw fit. Relaxed in his new surroundings, Steve started to concentrate on making the television department of his agency the biggest and best in the business. He began to package deals that brought the agency significant revenue, and in a very short time, he became one of the hottest young executives in town. Soon, Steve and Sharon were invited to the best parties, and their circle of friends began to include not only famous actors, but prominent writers and directors. All of this should have made Sharon very happy, but it didn't, and their already fragile relationship continued to disintegrate. She gradually began to pull away from Steve's friends, preferring to surround herself with a few girlfriends who, like she, were displaced New Yorkers and unhappily married. Whenever they argued, which was happening with increasing frequency, Sharon would threaten to go back to New York and take Michael with her. In order to protect his little boy from seeing his mother and father fighting all the time, Steve began to spend more and more time away from home. His business required him to make frequent trips to New York, which was a welcome respite from the turmoil at home. It also gave him the opportunity to visit his parents, who missed their son and grandchild terribly. Through the years they had never been able to form a bond with Sharon, and eventually, Steve had given up trying to make it happen.

Suddenly, the stewardess's voice came over the loudspeaker, jolting him back to the present. "Please fasten your seat belts. We are approaching Los Angeles and will be landing in fifteen minutes."

Gathering up his papers, he started to put them away when the seat in front of him popped back up and the newspaper he had saved fell into his lap. Steve looked at the picture of Julie once again, but this time he allowed himself the pleasure of thinking about her.

She's so lovely, he thought, *and so much prettier in person than this photograph. I wonder what she's really like once you get to know her?* He found actresses vain and terribly self-centered, certainly not the kind of woman he would be attracted to. But somehow, in that brief moment when he'd looked into Julie's eyes, he'd seen a sweetness and vulnerability that seemed incongruous with her image. Waiting for the wheels of the plane to touch down, Steve tried to dismiss her from his thoughts. But the memory of her lingered.

CHAPTER 46

*I*t's amazing, Julie thought as she unpacked the trunks that had just arrived from Rome. *Just a few short months ago I was so firmly entrenched in Italy that the very thought of leaving there would have been unsettling. But now, as I'm about to begin rehearsals for the show, I couldn't be happier.* It was still hard to believe she was returning to Broadway. As a star. The only sad note was that her staunch supporter and singing teacher, Esther Lieber, would not be there to cheer her on and encourage her on opening night. Esther had died quietly in her sleep the year before, but Julie knew how proud she would have been to see her pupil once again onstage in a starring role.

There was a great deal to do before rehearsals began. The furnished apartment that Paco had rented on Park Avenue was really lovely, and now with her own things scattered about, it would seem more like home—or at least the semblance of one. In the eight years she had been married to Paco, she had never had a real home. Only rented apartments and hotel rooms. *Maybe,* she thought, *if the show is a big success, we can settle down in one place for a while. It would be nice to live a normal life and not have to travel so much.* Even though she had not spent as much time in their apartment in Rome as she would have liked, Julie was going to miss it. As soon as the decision was made to return to New York, Paco immediately called the owner of their apartment in Rome and terminated the lease. He assured Julie that if and when they returned to Europe to work, they could use their newly acquired home in the Costa Brava as their home base. Julie was sad to leave Rome—a city that she had grown to love. The Italians held a special place in her heart and she hoped they wouldn't forget her. She was comforted by the fact that she still had a commitment for a picture to be shot in Spain with Vittorio De Sica. Before leaving Italy, De Sica had assured her that she was so perfect for the starring role that he would wait for her, no matter how long it took.

When Freddie Barnett sent her the script of *The Captain's Wives* Julie was still in Milano working in their television show. After reading the script, which she found to be tailor-made for her, Julie turned it over to Paco for his opinion. He agreed that it was an outstanding role and urged her to accept it. Julie was amazed that Paco had not voiced any opposition. It was so unlike him not to object to a project that would prevent her from performing with him. But his motives soon became quite clear. Besides wanting to get her away from European men who constantly fawned over her, he also felt he could use her offer as a way to further his own career. As soon as he read the script he called his agents in New York and informed them that he wanted to play one of the leads in the show. Furthermore, he told them he would make that a condition if they expected to have Julie. Unlike the many other instances when he had employed devious schemes in order to achieve his goals, this time he made his demands very clear right from the beginning.

"Either they use me, or they can't have you."

Julie knew that Paco was perfectly capable of pressuring her until she gave in. He didn't care if he jeopardized this great opportunity by attempting to force them to accept someone they didn't want. That was his condition, and the producers would have to live with it. Against their better judgment, they agreed. They were determined to have Julie, and if Paco had to be part of the deal, then so be it.

Now, with rehearsals only a few days away, Julie concentrated on what lay ahead of her. Her costar, Tony Adams, would be flying in from California the following day to meet with her and the rest of the cast. He had abandoned Broadway two years earlier, after having achieved phenomenal success in several shows and went on to even greater heights in motion pictures. He appeared in many Rock Hudson comedies, usually cast as the nervous and downtrodden "best friend" and had recently been nominated for an Oscar for best supporting role. He and Tony Randall, another Broadway alumnus, were two of the busiest actors in Hollywood, and Julie was thrilled at the prospect of working with him.

Privately, Paco was having his own fears about the show. He was not particularly adept at memorizing lines and it worried him. In movies, his dialogue had been kept to a minimum, and even then, he had found it difficult. Additionally, in Hollywood he had the luxury of working in front of a camera where they could do as many takes as necessary in order to get a shot.

What in hell am I going to do out on the stage if I forget the lines? he wondered nervously as he sat alone in the bedroom of their apartment. *I can't even remember the first page and I have a whole damn script to memorize.*

Paco's dilemma soon became everyone's problem, and the tension during rehearsals became excruciating. The director, who at one time had been an actor himself, tried to be patient. But as the time drew closer to their departure for Boston, where tryouts were scheduled to begin, even he began to despair. Taking Julie aside one afternoon, he gently tried to express his reservations about Paco's performance.

"We know you're in a terrible situation and don't want to hurt Paco. But this is just not working out. Paco is a bandleader, not an actor, and this role calls for a strong second banana, someone who Tony can play off of."

Julie stood there quietly, fearful of what was coming.

"It's not only his performance, dear. If it were, I would devote myself to working with him to bring him into shape. It's his memory. He just can't remember his lines, and he's throwing everyone's timing off. We've already cut his part to the bone and eliminated two of his songs. But, Julie, he *has* to sing somewhere in the show. This is a musical comedy."

Joe Evans, who had directed many actors during his career in Hollywood and on Broadway, had never come across a problem more frustrating or insolvable. He had tried every device he knew to help Paco, but nothing worked, and he just couldn't sacrifice the show because of one man, especially someone who had used his wife as leverage to get the part in the first place.

Julie started to tremble when she realized what her options were. If they fired Paco he would undoubtedly insist that she quit. "Joe, isn't there anything else we can do? Paco has his heart set on doing this show."

"Julie, I've discussed this with the producers, and to be frank, they're justifiably concerned about the backers' investment. You're coming off like a dream in the show. A lot of people are going to be surprised by your great singing voice and flair for comedy. We can't afford to let one person bring down an entire show."

"Can't you give him a little more time? I'm working with him at home every night, cueing him on his lines."

The director looked at her troubled face and felt great compassion for her predicament. "Be honest with me. Are you afraid that if he leaves he'll insist that you quit too? I know that was his ultimatum at the beginning. But surely now that he sees how great you are and what a success you're going to make in this show, he must feel differently."

"I swear I don't know. But I'm being torn to pieces and I just can't take the pressure. Please, talk to Tony and the producers. At least wait until we open in Boston. If Paco still can't come up to the part, then do what you have to do. It will make things easier for me if you wait."

Joe Evans did not want to risk losing his star, and he knew that by dumping Paco he would be running that risk. He finally convinced the producers to wait until the tryouts in Boston before making any decision. In desperation, they fitted Paco with a wireless receiver that would enable him to have his lines fed to him by a prompter offstage. They tried to keep this ridiculous charade from the other actors, but it was impossible to hide something so obvious. Pretty soon, Paco became the butt of nasty jokes among the cast, and when Julie learned of it, she was mortified. Although she didn't like seeing her husband ridiculed in that fashion, she understood their scorn. She was surrounded by talented working actors who had struggled for years to achieve recognition. They resented Paco for taking the part away from a qualified actor more deserving of the chance.

With all the stress that Julie was undergoing, her energy started to wane, and when she arrived in Boston, she began to battle a sore throat. The transmitter device had not been functioning properly and Paco was becoming increasingly more irritable. On their way to the Schubert Theater the night before opening, Paco once again started to complain bitterly.

"It's all your fault I'm in this show. Who needed this shit? Memorizing lines, being concerned about speaking loud enough. Those bastards are driving me crazy. And those songs. They keep telling me not to

worry about singing the melody. Just talk it like Rex Harrison or Yul
Brynner. When I do that they say they can't hear me."

Kicking his foot against the cab door, he shouted, "*Cabrones,* I
should have stayed in Europe."

Since leaving the Costa Brava, Paco had become meaner and more
demanding. Unable to cope with his own deterioration, which was
not helped by his drinking, Paco took out all his frustrations on Julie.
Even though he felt her slipping away from him, he continued to abuse
her, thus pushing her even further away.

Julie looked out the window and had to bite her tongue to keep from
spitting out what she was thinking. *Who the hell asked you to be in
the show in the first place? You pushed yourself in the minute you heard
they wanted me. It's not their fault that you can't remember lines and
can't act.* Allowing Paco to ramble on, Julie fought not to let his
tirade upset her. She was still on antibiotics and desperately needed to
conserve every bit of energy for the next day's opening. Paco's future
in the show would be decided at that evening's dress rehearsal, and
Julie was almost certain that he would be replaced. Unbeknownst to
anyone in the cast, except Julie, Ed Harrison, an accomplished Broadway actor with great credentials, had been contacted as a possible
replacement for Paco. He was already prepared for the part and standing by in New York, awaiting a call after the dress rehearsal. That
night, when the curtain finally came down at the end of the show,
Julie knew for sure that Paco's future in the show was doomed. Even
with his lines being prompted to him, his performance could only be
described as pitiful. He was awkward, unamusing, and terribly self-
conscious. The debonair bandleader who for years had enchanted audiences with his charm and showmanship, had exposed himself to ridi-
cule, and the decision was quickly made to replace him.

"Who the fuck do they think they are?" Paco shouted at the top of
his voice, after being told.

Julie quickly shut the dressing room door so that the cast wouldn't
hear his screaming.

"Telling me, Paco Castell, who has performed all over the world in
front of royalty and heads of state, that it's just not working out and,
for the good of the show, it would be better for me to step down."

Paco ripped his jacket off and slammed it down on the table, sending
some bottles of cologne that were sitting there crashing to the floor.

"I'll step down all right, but I'm going to take someone with me—
their star."

Julie, who had been standing near the door, afraid to even breathe, asked Paco in a hoarse whisper, "Paco, what do you mean?"

"Just what it sounds like. Go outside and tell those bastards to come in." Julie's face was stricken as she opened the door and beckoned the two producers and Joe Evans inside. Once they were there, Paco lost no time in seeking his vengeance.

"If I'm not good enough for your lousy show, then neither is my wife. She is giving you two weeks' notice." Julie gasped and her face went white. She had to hold on to the chair to keep from falling.

Ned Blackman, one of the producers, spoke up. "Paco, you're not being reasonable. Our decision has nothing to do with your talent as an artist. The stage is a different medium that's all. You haven't had the training to be a musical comedy performer. But you've been a big star for many years in other areas. Why should you be concerned about doing a Broadway show? You don't need the publicity and God knows, you can make a helluva lot more money doing other things. But Julie is different. She is going to become a major Broadway star after this show. You wouldn't want to see her give that up just because you're angry and upset with us?"

"She doesn't need this show to be a big star," Paco answered angrily. "Don't you read the papers? She's already a major star in Europe and in nightclubs and television here. And speaking of money, what you're paying her is crap compared to what she's giving up."

Joe Evans, who had been quiet until now, said, "I understand that your feelings are hurt and I'm sorry about that. If you remember, though, we were against you doing this part from the very beginning. But you said that you wanted the chance and we gave it to you. Now, we are only four weeks away from opening in New York, and we have got to use this time out of town to perfect the show. We have a chance of bringing in a major hit. And to do that, we need Julie."

"Well, that's too damned bad because she's leaving too."

Suddenly, Julie felt outraged that everyone was discussing her as if she were a child incapable of making her own decisions. It was probably her own fault for always deferring to Paco whenever anything important came up. But now, with her future at stake, she had to speak her mind. "Please, Paco, Joe, everyone. Why don't you ask me what I want?"

"What is it that the famous Julie Lauren wants?" Paco asked sarcastically.

Julie looked her husband in the eye and said simply, "I want to stay in the show. I'm terribly sorry that you've been hurt, Paco, but I can't do anything about it. You must realize what this means to me. My career *began* on the stage when I was only thirteen. For me, to return to Broadway as a star is a dream come true—something I've wanted ever since I was a kid. Please, don't deny me this chance."

"But what about me? What am I supposed to do?"

"Paco, you can record and do a million things," Julie answered. "This is terribly important to me. Please, try and understand what I'm saying."

Paco looked at her, his blue eyes still throwing off sparks of anger. "Get them out of here, Julie. I want to speak to you alone."

Julie ushered them out of the room. When she turned back to Paco she saw his arms were folded across his chest and he was glaring furiously at her.

"How dare you contradict me in front of those bastards. You cut off my *cojones* right in front of them."

"Paco, I had to speak up. I have a run-of-the-show contract and they could sue me. But, more important, I *want* to do the show. Can't you understand that?"

"Now I can see what an ungrateful bitch you are. Do the damned show and I'll do what I have to do." Practically shoving her out the room, he added, "Get out of here before I really lose my temper."

Julie left, but she did not feel victorious. However, she had managed to remain in the show.

Despite a sore throat and a high fever, Julie Lauren proved to the Boston audiences that she was much more than a band singer who could shake her hips. After a grueling day of rehearsal, with Paco not speaking to her and refusing to come to the opening that night, Julie still managed to carry off a performance that the critics the next day would term "magical."

The next few weeks flew by as the director finely honed the actors and play to perfection. When they left New Haven, where they had been appearing for two weeks, to return to New York, everyone was convinced that the show was destined for a long run on Broadway. The chorus kids were especially delighted, for a hit show would mean no cattle calls for a while. They would have enough money to pay their rent and still attend singing and dancing classes during the day. Most of the "gypsies" were terribly ambitious and hoped to one day become stars. Julie felt a tremendous bond with those young kids, for she remembered herself at that age, and she knew all too well the feelings of drive and ambition. Sometimes, when one of the young girls would express her admiration and desire that one day she would end up in Julie's position, she was tempted to warn her, *Be careful. Don't sacrifice your whole life for your career. Sometimes we have to pay too dear a price to achieve stardom.*

Throughout the out-of-town tryouts, Paco continued to sulk and Julie prayed that eventually he would get sufficiently bored and return to New York. But he stayed on, taking out his hostility on Julie. She could only hope that, once they were back in New York, he would resume some kind of activity and things might return to normal.

After six days of previews to a select group of invited guests, opening night in New York finally arrived. Julie sat in her dressing room and waited for the stage manager to call half an hour. Tony Adams's dressing room was right next to hers, and she could hear him gargling for the fourth time in the last half hour. He had been throwing up since noon, and Julie felt pangs of compassion. She was not feeling too steady herself. *It's incredible*, she thought as she listened to her friend next door, *he's a seasoned Broadway actor who has never had a bad review and he's so nervous he can't keep his food down. How should I feel?*

She paced the floor, anxious for the show to begin. Her mother and father were seated out front, thrilled that their daughter was the star of a Broadway show. They had flown in from Phoenix the day before, and Julie had arranged for them to stay at the Plaza Hotel. Mercifully, Julie had managed to trade two of her house seats with Tony so that her parents would not be seated next to Paco. *That's all I need*, she thought as perspiration began to trickle down her back, *a fight between Paco and my parents on opening night.* Suddenly, there was a knock on the door and Julie practically jumped.

"Five minutes, Miss Lauren."

Julie opened the door and found Tony standing there, totally composed and handsome in his captain's uniform

"Tony, you look great. How are you feeling?"

"Perfect, my love, and why not? I never get nervous on opening nights. Now, give me a hug and go out there and kill them. I'll see you onstage."

Julie had to laugh at his remark. *He never gets nervous*, she thought. *Just like I never get nervous.* During rehearsals, he had sometimes acted like a pain in the ass, giving her directions contrary to the director's. But he was a superb actor and a consummate professional. She couldn't have hoped for a better costar.

Suddenly, the house lights dimmed and the orchestra started the overture. Julie could feel her heart beating right through her costume and her mouth suddenly went dry. Taking her place behind the set, she waited for the overture to finish and the curtain to rise. Her entrance would come almost immediately after that. The music ended to thunderous applause and she heard the stage manager say, "Places, please." Panic overtook Julie, as her mind suddenly went blank. There was a burst of applause as Tony entered the stage and spoke his opening lines. *Oh God*, she prayed, *please don't do this to me. I can't remember my first line.* Then she heard her cue and there was nothing to do but enter.

"Rosita, I see you have been waiting for me. Come to me my darling."

Julie walked out into the bright spotlight, and as if in a far distance, she could hear people applauding. Standing there, with her arms outstretched to embrace her costar, she spoke her first line.

"*Mi amor*, you have been away so long. Come give your Rosita a kiss."

The fear had evaporated and Julie was home free.

Although *The Captain's Wives* did not win the critical acclaim that everyone had anticipated, for Julie and Tony Adams it still represented a personal triumph. The morning newspapers had almost unanimously decreed that because of the outstanding performances turned in by a first-rate cast headed by two extraordinarily gifted stars, *The Captain's Wives* would probably have a long run. They singled out Julie's performance, praising her vocal range and great stage presence. They couldn't ignore her physical attributes, and one critic called her, "the most beautiful and exciting woman to hit Broadway since Gertrude Lawrence."

Professionally the months that followed were the most exhilarating time of Julie's life. She had now achieved stardom on the Broadway stage. Personally, however, her life was a disaster. Paco bitterly begrudged her success and their life had become unbearable because of their constant fights.

Paco's jealousy continued to mount, and for no reason he would burst into a rage that frightened her. She often found him waiting outside restaurants where he knew she had luncheon interviews, scowling at her because she had left him alone. His visits to the theater were always unpredictable. Sometimes Julie would catch him watching her from the wings or he would unexpectedly visit her dressing room in between acts, glancing around suspiciously, as if he were expecting to find a secret lover. Paco insisted that Julie return home immediately after the performance, and sometimes, in her haste to leave, she would find herself apologizing to guests who had visited her backstage and wanted to chat. She wasn't sure how much longer she could live like that. And yet she could not find a way of leaving him. Because she was such a private person and such a good actress, no one suspected how unhappy she really was. After Paco's hasty and noisy withdrawal from the show, there had been rumors and speculation among the cast that all was not well in their marriage. But Julie had quickly squelched those rumors by demonstrating affection whenever Paco was around and praising him when he was absent. Although her unhappiness was steadily increasing, she was too insecure of her future alone, and in her mind, their lives and finances were too heavily entwined for Julie to consider leaving.

Now, as she hurried along Fifth Avenue on her way back to the apartment, Julie wondered what Paco's urgent telephone message was all about. She had been having her hair done at Kenneth, her favorite hairdresser in New York, when she had received a call from Luis. He asked her to return as soon as she was finished. Paco wanted to speak to her. The brisk autumn weather was so invigorating that Julie decided to walk rather than take a cab. She loved New York at this time of year. The red and gold leaves had already started to cover the streets, and she liked hearing them scrunch under her high heels as she walked briskly past the Plaza Hotel and over to Madison Avenue. People walking by recognized Julie and smiled admiringly at the beautiful woman dressed so smartly in her navy blue wool suit. Even though the major portion of Julie's salary from the show went into their corporation, with some of that siphoned off to her parents, she had managed to save enough to dress elegantly. Paco had opened charge accounts at various department stores, but he grumbled so much about bills that Julie preferred to pay for certain things herself. As she turned up Park Avenue and headed toward their apartment building, she wondered what Paco was up to.

"Julie," he said as she came rushing into the living room, "come over here and sit down. I have some great news for you."

Julie hadn't seen Paco in such a good mood for months. Whatever was making him so happy she was all for it.

"Julie, I've just signed to play the Waldorf-Astoria again for four weeks with options to stay on indefinitely. Isn't that exciting?"

"That's wonderful. I'm so happy you're going to be doing something you enjoy again. I know that this inactivity has been driving you crazy."

"Well it has, but that's over. We open in two weeks. But you haven't heard the best part. At my insistence, they've agreed that you have to do only the midnight show instead of both. I explained to them how important your Broadway show is to you and that you can't leave because of your contract. They agreed. In fact, they're delighted. Your publicity will keep the room packed. Now, I have to figure out who I'm going to get for the dinner show. Maybe I'll talk to Belafonte. But I don't have to worry about that. My agents will come up with someone."

Julie stared at him in disbelief. Not even Paco could expect her to do eight shows a week at the theater and then rush over to do a midnight show at the Waldorf. Carefully choosing her words so as not to upset him, Julie said, "I'm really thrilled for you, but I just don't know how I'm physically going to be able to handle it. You know how taxing my performances are. I'm on the stage practically all the time. Only last week the house doctor had to be called because I felt faint before the show. He told me my blood pressure is terribly low and that I should take it easy during the day. How can I possibly run off the stage at eleven, change out of my costume, put on fresh makeup, and then dash over to the Waldorf for another show? It's too much work."

Paco began to seethe the minute Julie started explaining, and by the time she had finished he was fuming. "Don't you understand that you are part of the deal? Without you there *is* no deal. They bought the orchestra with the condition that you appear at least once a night. You see, my dear, I've created a Frankenstein by making you famous and now you are turning on me."

Luis and Julie stood by helplessly as they listened to Paco rave on. "If it weren't for me where the hell would you be today? I taught you. I groomed you. You were a stupid, awkward child when I met you, and I made you into an international star. This is the thanks I get. I sacrificed my career for you so you could live in Italy and make pictures. Then when you decided you wanted to become a 'big Broadway star,' stupid, obliging Paco accompanied you back to America and got you a beautiful apartment with every luxury. And this is how you repay him? I thought my ex-wife was selfish, but you could give her lessons."

It was now Julie's turn to explode, and for the first time in her life, she lashed back at him. "How dare you speak to me like that? I wasn't stupid and awkward. I was already on the stage when I met you and

I would have probably gone on to do other shows. As for my career in Europe, *you* had nothing to do with it. Every single picture I made was because they wanted me. If you must know the truth, they didn't even want you on our television series, but I insisted that we do it as a team." Unleashing the rage she had controlled for so many years she shouted, "How dare you call me selfish? You're the one who's selfish. Pushing yourself into the show when you knew you couldn't hack it and they didn't even want you. Insisting that I quit just when I was ready to achieve a goal I had dreamed about for years. Do you think the past few months have been pleasant for me with you sulking around and making me miserable? Following me wherever I go. Watching every man who talks to me as if he were my lover. It's humiliating to be treated like a whore when I've always been a devoted wife."

Spent, Julie sat down and tried to keep her hands from trembling. She had confronted him at last, but the things she had told him were only the tip of the iceberg. The rest—their miserable sex life together, his constant abuse—were still festering.

"Julie," Paco said sarcastically. "I had no idea you considered me such a prick and I must apologize. But, despite what you think we *are* considered a team, and as long as you are my wife, that team will continue. Without me you are nothing. Do you hear me?" he screamed. "Nothing. Therefore, I expect you to fulfill your obligation to me and perform when I ask you to. I promise that I will look around for a replacement for you as soon as possible. I'm sure there are a lot of pretty young girls out there who would just die for a chance to sing with my orchestra. Until I can groom one of them, however, I expect you to open with me at the Waldorf as planned and do the midnight show." Turning on his heels, he stormed out of the room with Luis following meekly behind him.

Julie sat there stunned. She would either have to get out or continue to be enslaved by him. *But get out where?* she wondered. No matter how much happiness might lay elsewhere, the thought of abandoning a safe harbor for unknown waters was terrifying. This was not some-thing she could discuss with her parents. With their dependence on her for support, they were very much part of the problem. If she could have confronted these problems logically, she would have realized that as a star, she was in a position to do many things alone. But for years Paco had played on her insecurities, and now she was too afraid of the unknown to risk losing everything she had achieved. With a heavy sigh of resignation, Julie realized that she would have to agree to Paco's demands. But she hated him for bullying her and she hated herself even more for accepting it.

The strain that Paco had placed on Julie's health by insisting that she appear with him eventually took its toll, and one night, barely into the first act, Julie fainted onstage. To the dismay of the audience, her understudy was rushed on to replace her. Although Julie was able to return two nights later, the doctor warned her that to continue on at such a pace might seriously endanger her health. The four weeks that she had originally agreed to with Paco had stretched into six, and Julie knew she could not continue on much longer. Her producers finally put their foot down and protested her nightly appearances with Paco. They felt it detrimental to the show to have their star appearing in another engagement in the same city while she was under contract to them. Their opposition gave Julie the out she had been praying for, and right after New Year's Eve, she sang her last performance at the Waldorf. Paco continued on for a while, constantly trying out new singers, but despite his boasts, he never found anyone to replace her. The strain of having to smile at Paco every night onstage and joke with him was finally over, and for that, too, Julie was grateful.

But the tension between them only intensified, and Julie constantly felt herself on the verge of tears. Even a Tony nomination for best female performance in a musical comedy could not erase her depression. At the end of a year she found herself emotionally and physically unable to continue with the show, and she requested that they replace her. Reluctantly, the producers agreed. Tony Adams was also anxious to leave. The show had served its purpose, and he was now ready to pick up where he had left off in Hollywood.

Paco was delighted to have Julie back for himself, and he eagerly began talking about their future plans. "Julie, we have been receiving offers from all over the world—the Orient, South America, Vegas. We can pick and choose whatever we want."

She cringed when she heard this. "I've barely been out of the show for two weeks. Don't you think it's a little early for me to return to work? I'm exhausted."

"I don't mean right now, *querida*. Take all the time you want—a month or two. We could go to the Costa Brava and relax. But we must make plans for the future. As the saying goes 'you must strike when the iron is hot.' "

"You seem to forget that I promised Vittorio De Sica I would make a picture with him as soon as I was free. He's waited a year for me. I think I owe him the courtesy of letting him know that I am available."

Paco grimaced at the mention of De Sica's name. His plan was to get Julie back on tour with him as quickly as possible. But he realized that he would have to be cautious. Their relationship had been rocky, and to push her right now might prove dangerous.

"Let's call him or wire him. First, we can go to the Costa Brava. You can relax for a while, then when he's ready, you can make the picture. It's perfect. Meanwhile, I will prepare a nice little itinerary for us after the film is completed. Nothing too taxing, of course."

Smiling at her benevolently, he said, "You see, Julie, I have everything under control just like before."

Under control, Julie thought as she listened to his plans. *Under your control you mean. Paco, if you only knew what was in my heart. Whatever affection I felt for you is dead. Whatever admiration and respect I had for you has vanished. I can't bear to have you touch me. When you're near me I want to run and hide. It's over, Paco, and there's nothing you can ever say or do that will make me feel differently.* These thoughts were bursting to escape, but she still couldn't bring herself to say them aloud.

CHAPTER
47

Julie placed the script she had been studying on the night table next to her bed and reached for the light. She had been so engrossed she hadn't realized the sun had set, casting the room into darkness. She had no idea where Paco was, but knowing him, he couldn't be far. Although the producers had provided them with a sumptuous suite at the Hotel Castellana Hilton in Madrid for the duration of the picture, Julie missed the apartment in New York. Before leaving for Spain, Paco had renewed their lease, and now, with the prospects of a tour looming in the near future, he was talking about buying it.

They had been in Madrid for nearly ten weeks and the film was nearing completion. In De Sica's film *La Gitana*, Julie portrayed a Gypsy flamenco dancer who leaves her village in Andalucia to seek a career in Madrid. The part was very demanding, and De Sica, a perfectionist, had arranged to have Julie coached in flamenco dancing. Her two leading men, one a Spaniard, the other Italian, were also staying at the hotel, but knowing Paco's jealousy, Julie had avoided any contact with them except when absolutely necessary. Her role called for passionate love scenes with both the handsome young actors and whenever the cameras started rolling, the air became charged with electricity. Paco visited the set constantly and his jealous barbs directed at Julie and her co-stars had become increasingly more frequent and more petulant. There was no way to keep him off the set, short of an ultimatum from De Sica, and she requested that the director not do it. In the long run, it would only cause more trouble.

Julie slipped out of bed and opened the terrace doors facing the wide tree-lined boulevard—the Paseo de Castellana. She breathed in the heady scent of gardenias that were planted outside and watched some young couples strolling hand in hand, seemingly without a care in the world. It was June and she was in a city that was incredibly romantic, but she felt terribly alone. At that moment, Julie would have traded places with any one of the young girls who was walking down the street gazing lovingly into her sweetheart's eyes. Julie's unhappiness had reached such a pitch that if it weren't for the distraction of working in the film, she often felt that she would have gone stark raving mad. Returning to the quiet of her bedroom, Julie sat down at the dressing table and studied her reflection in the mirror. *No lines, no wrinkles*, she reassured herself as she turned her head from side to side. *I guess twenty-five would be a trifle young to start showing signs of age. But, after all I've been through in the past year, it wouldn't surprise me.*

If Julie could have heard the comments being made about her by the crew, some of whom she had worked with before, and from De Sica himself, she would have felt comforted and not too concerned about her looks.

"*Dìo mio*," the director had remarked after seeing her for the first time in more than a year. "She is more beautiful than ever. Her face has lost its fullness, which makes those incredible cheekbones even more prominent. In fact, there is a new womanliness about her and an even greater sensuality than when she first arrived in Italy."

Julie rose from the table and put on a record of flamenco music that she had purchased the day before. Removing her robe, she slipped on the dress she would be wearing for her big dance scene. Raising her arms high above her head, she started to practice her motions in front of the mirror. Arching her back as far as it would go, she gracefully turned and twisted her hands in exactly the position she had been taught. The music grew steadily more exciting, and Julie could feel herself caught up in its spell. Posing provocatively, she imagined herself dancing in a taverna with young Gypsies behind her, chanting and clapping to the passionate music. Suddenly, she knew where she wanted to be. *Out there*, she thought. *Away from Paco and with some young man who would take me in his arms and make me feel like a woman.* The music grew faster and faster as Julie twirled around and around until, finally, she was breathless. Suddenly, she stopped and with a plaintive cry she flung herself on the bed. Beating the pillows with her hands, she sobbed uncontrollably. "I can't go on like this any longer. I want to be free."

With only a week to go before winding up the film, De Sica invited the cast to join him on Sunday for lunch and the bullfights. Julie prevailed upon Paco to attend, explaining that it would be an insult for her to refuse. After a sumptuous lunch of paella at La Riscal, a quaint restaurant near the hotel, the party left for the Plaza de Toros. Julie had no idea who would be fighting that afternoon. If she had known ahead of time that Antonio was to be one of the matadors, she would have refused to go. Since their last meeting at Ruark's house in the Costa Brava, Julie had not seen or even heard of him again. In fact, she had promised herself at that time to forget about him. Their attraction for each other ran deep, but she knew that he could never be anything more than a friend.

When they arrived, the arena was crowded with aficionados anxious to see three of their favorite *toreros* vie for the title of *numero uno*. De Sica sat down next to Julie and Paco and waited for the trumpet to herald the entrance of the *toreros*. He planned on asking one of them to appear in a short scene in the movie, and after the corrida, he would make his choice.

The first two fights were relatively uneventful. The bulls were good and the crowd was pleased by the performances of the two matadors. Julie fidgeted constantly in her seat, anticipating Antonio's entrance. The air was very still, and even in the shade, the heat was intense. She took out her fan and began to fan herself vigorously. Paco had been quiet ever since arriving at the plaza, and although Julie tried to engage him in conversation, he had very little to say. Julie watched Antonio intently as he came into the arena, and she breathed a sigh of relief when one of his *cuadrilla* gave his cape to De Sica. As Antonio neared the place where they were sitting, he glanced up briefly at Julie and nodded his head in recognition. But his attention remained focused on the bulls.

When the third bull stormed out into the bright sunshine, rearing his enormous head in the direction of the red cape, Julie suddenly experienced a wave of apprehension. The animal looked much fiercer than the others and turned with incredible speed. Antonio was brilliant in his opening passes, and the audience began shouting in unison, "*olé, olé, matador.*" When the moment arrived for Antonio to change his large cape for the smaller muleta, the noise died down as the crowd waited for that eventful moment when the matador would display his dominance over the beast. Antonio executed the first few faenas magnificently, and Julie started to breathe easier. But there was some-thing about that bull that worried her and she wished the corrida was over. Suddenly, Antonio walked into the center of the arena, too far away from his *cuadrilla* if he were to run into trouble, and as he turned, he smiled at Julie. Her heart started to pump wildly as she felt Paco's eyes sear into her face. Keeping her eyes fixed ahead of her, she kept watching Antonio. For a moment, the matador remained motionless. Then calling to the bull, "*ahe toro, ahe toro*", he placed the muleta in front of his body and firmly stood his ground. At first the huge animal just stood there, shrewdly eyeing his opponent. Antonio repeated his challenge, "*ahe toro.*" Without warning, the bull charged, coming at the almost defenseless man with the speed of a locomotive. Antonio lowered his cape in preparation for executing a pass when, unexpect-edly, the bull, ignoring the muleta, reared his massive head and pressed his horns into the groin of the torero, sending him flying into the air. Julie screamed as members of his *cuadrilla* frantically rushed in to lure the bull away from his prey. The animal dropped Antonio to the ground, and as the wounded bullfighter tried valiantly to roll to safety, the bull repeatedly dug his horns into his battered body. Julie felt as if she were about to faint. De Sica placed his arms around her and she was grateful for someone to lean on. As the crowd continued to scream, she burrowed her head into his shoulder. Part of her wanted to see if Antonio was still alive, but the other part couldn't bear to watch him being carried out of the arena. Still holding on to her to keep her from trembling, De Sica told Julie, "*Cara,* I think we should leave."

She nodded, her voice too choked with emotion to speak. The gray-haired director stood up and said to Paco, "Your wife is terribly upset. Don't you think we should take her back to the hotel?"

"What in hell is she upset about? That *pendejo* had it coming to him. Let's watch the rest of the fight."

Julie whirled about and turned on him. "How can you be so hateful? What has that poor boy ever done to you?"

"Keep your voice down, my lovely, or I will embarrass you right here and now. If you want to leave, then go. I will be back later."

Julie took Vittorio's hand, and with tears streaming down her face, she left the Plaza de Toros not knowing whether the young man who had briefly touched her life was alive or dead.

Julie entered the darkened living room of her hotel suite and made her way to the bedroom. She hadn't spoken a word during her ride back from the bull ring and De Sica hadn't pressed her, for he, too, had been shaken by the day's events.

Tossing her purse down on the bed, Julie sat down in an easy chair near the window and folded her hands in her lap. The room was eerily still. Even though it was almost six, many people were still enjoying their afternoon siesta. The heavy wooden venetian blinds that kept out the bright afternoon sun were open just enough to allow a flicker of light to filter through. Julie sat there without moving and watched the shadows dance on the bedroom wall. She felt numb—emotionally drained. She could not even feel sorrow for Antonio, who, for all she knew, might be dead.

Suddenly she heard the door open in the next room. Paco came in, and her body immediately stiffened in anticipation and fear. She had no desire to see him and no strength to endure another confrontation. Her wish was not to be granted, however, for in a few moments the door flew open and Paco walked in. Switching on the lights, he noticed Julie sitting there.

"Why in hell are you sitting in the dark? Are you grieving for your boyfriend? Well, don't be upset. The son of a bitch is going to live."

Julie valiantly tried not to show any emotion, but a tear escaped and fell on her already tear-streaked face.

Paco watched her, his face an ugly mask of jealousy and spite. "What are you crying about? Were you afraid you were never going to see him again? Well, my darling wife, you're not. This time I'll make sure of it."

Julie started to say something, but stopped.

"What were you going to say, Julie? Were you going to tell me you don't have the hots for that little prick? Do you think I'm a fool and that I don't have eyes? I've seen the way he looks at you, and the way you become all starry-eyed when he's in the same room. Well, you'll have to forget about your darling bullfighter, my dear, because if you don't, I'll make him wish he'd never been born."

As Paco continued his tirade, it was as if a rocket had suddenly gone off in Julie's brain, jolting her into action. Her face deathly white, she rose from the chair and went over to Paco. Grasping his arms, she cried, "Paco, I can't go on like this any longer. I'm sick and tired of your jealousy and your possessiveness. It's driving me mad. You have no idea what you're doing to me. You've taken something innocent and blown it out of all proportion. I won't put up with it anymore."

Paco pulled himself free and backed away, still looking at her with scornful eyes. "Okay, you say you're not going to take it anymore. What do you propose to do about it?"

Julie sat down on the bed and lowered her eyes as she stared at her trembling hands. In a hushed voice, she said, "I'm sure you've been aware for some time that something is terribly wrong with our marriage. Things are just not working out and I think we should separate. I'm not happy and I guess I'm making you unhappy, too. I'm sorry, but I can't go on like this."

As the words began to spill out, all the pent-up emotions that Julie had suppressed for so many years suddenly were released, and she began to heave deep sobs.

"I've got to have time alone so I can sort out my life. I can't function anymore with you hovering over me and flying into jealous rages whenever a man talks to me. I swear to God I don't want to live anymore if I have to live like this." She flung herself on the bed and tried to stifle her sobs in the pillow. Somehow she had found the strength to tell him and now all she wanted was for him to leave.

Suddenly, Julie felt herself being pulled by her hair from the bed and dragged to her feet. She screamed out in pain as she desperately tried to get him to release her.

"Paco, stop. You're hurting me."

With a face so contorted with rage that he was practically unrecognizable, Paco flung her against the wall and swung his powerful hand across her cheek. Julie's head snapped at the force of the blow, and for a moment she didn't know where she was. When her head cleared, she pushed at him with all her might as she tried to escape into the living room. But, Paco caught her and slapped her again, this time with even greater force. Julie was momentarily stunned, and as she sunk to her knees she could taste the blood in her mouth. *He's going to kill me,* she thought. *Oh, my God. He's going to kill me.*

Once again, Paco pulled her to her feet and clutching her throat with a murderous rage, he screamed, "You're going to leave me? Oh no, you're not going anywhere because if you try, I will kill you."

Julie tried to pry his massive fingers away from her throat, but the more she pulled the more insane he became. "You will never speak of leaving me or divorcing me again. Do you understand that?" Julie tried to nod that she understood, but she could barely move her head. "Good," he said, suddenly releasing her.

The minute she was free Julie ran for the door, but Paco was too quick for her, and he caught her before she could open it. Throwing her against the door with an impact that rattled her teeth, he began hitting her head against the door. She started screaming with all her might.

"Help me," she shouted at the top of her voice. "Somebody help me." Paco had lost all control, and the more she screamed the more enraged he became hitting her over and over again.

"You'll never get away from me. Do you hear? I have your passport and your money. There's no place you could hide where I wouldn't find you."

Julie was about to black out, when she faintly heard someone pounding at the door.

"*Señora*, are you all right? It's Mr. Juarez, the manager. Please, open the door."

Suddenly, Paco stopped. His eyes were glazed as if he were sleep-walking. The pounding grew more insistent.

"Señora Castell, please open the door. Señor Castell, *por favor, abra la puerta.*"

Paco leaned close to Julie's battered face and whispered into her ear, "Tell him to go away—that you're fine."

Julie could barely speak. The cuts on her mouth were bleeding badly, and she could feel her face starting to swell.

"*Señor*, if you don't open the door we will have to come in."

"Everything is fine," Paco answered. "Why are you disturbing me?"

"*Señor*, we heard a woman screaming in there, and we just wanted to make sure everything was all right."

"I told you. We are fine. Now, go away."

"*Señor, perdoname*. But if you could just have the *señora* speak to us for a moment, then we will leave."

Paco twisted Julie's arm so tightly she thought it would break. "Tell him you're all right, *hija de puta madre*. Tell him."

Gasping for breath, Julie whispered in a hoarse voice, "I'm fine, thank you."

"*De nada, señora*," the manager said, not convinced that she was telling him the truth, but realizing that he was unable to intervene. "Just ring if you should need anything."

The footsteps down the marble hall assured Paco that the danger was over and he released Julie, who sank to the floor. As rapidly as the anger had possessed him, it suddenly had abated the same way. He seemed not even to notice Julie's condition or the pain he had inflicted on her. Sinking down on the couch, he started whimpering in a strange voice, "*Mi amor*, you cannot leave me. I would not want to live without you."

Julie dragged herself to the bedroom and painfully pulled herself on the bed. She dared not look in the mirror because she was afraid of what she'd see. It was fortunate that she didn't, because she was unrecognizable. Her face, which had already started to turn black and blue, had started to swell and her lips were badly cut. Angry red welts were visible on her throat where Paco's fingers had clutched her, and a huge bump on her head was bleeding profusely. Curling herself up into a tiny ball, Julie lay there, afraid to move. She knew that she should try to get up and attend to her injuries, but she was in too much pain to move. Then suddenly she remembered. The picture—she still had a week to go before finishing. But there was no way that she would be able to face the cameras. Paco had seen to that. *I don't care anymore*, she thought. *I don't care about anything. He might as well have killed me because I'm already dead inside.* The only emotions she was capable of feeling were hate and revenge.

Julie stayed that way for what seemed hours. Occasionally, she could hear Paco walking around the living room. She must have finally fallen asleep because when she awoke she could see Paco through the open door, having his dinner. Painfully, she tried to get up, but all her limbs ached, and when she touched her face she could feel dried blood at the corners of her mouth. Slowly, she raised herself up slightly and tried to pour herself some water from the carafe on the nightstand. She was too weak and the glass crashed to the floor. Suddenly, Paco was in the room and standing by her side. Julie cowered for a moment, desperately afraid that he would hurt her again, but he seemed perfectly in control.

"Oh, Julie. I see you are awake. Would you like some dinner?"

Julie looked at him through her swollen eyes and turned her face back into the pillow. Sitting down next to her, Paco took her hand in his.

"I'm sorry, *querida*, that we had that fight. I know you were upset about the corrida and you didn't realize what you were saying. But you upset me very much by telling me you want to leave me. Now, let's forget all about what happened today. I'll call De Sica tomorrow and tell him you have the flu. You can rest for a few days."

Paco began to stroke her lifeless arm, which Julie did not have the energy to pull away. A few seconds later, she could hear him tearing at his clothes, and before she could move he had crept into bed beside her and begun to caress her body. With a look of pure hate and revulsion, Julie summoned all of her remaining strength and pushed him away from her. Paco hesitated for a moment and then rose to this feet. There was no mistaking the look in her eyes and he decided it would be unwise to push her too far. Not after what had happened. Putting on his robe, he said, "*Querida*, you should have something. Maybe a little wine?"

Barely able to speak through swollen lips, Julie muttered, "I don't want anything, Paco. Just order some ice for my face and leave me alone."

When Paco left the room to call for the hall porter, Julie stumbled to the bathroom and locked the door behind her. *You son of a bitch, she thought. Is that all we had—a fight? You almost killed me, you bastard. You let me lie there for hours without even coming in to see whether I needed help. Then, you dared to come near me and touch me with your slimy hands. The same hands that were around my throat almost choking me to death. Did beating me turn you on, you sick bastard? Was that to be my final humiliation? Sex with a man I loathe.* Julie was afraid to look in the mirror, afraid of what she'd find there. Holding on to the sink to steady her, she finally raised her head. Her eyes could not believe what they saw. It was much worse than she had expected, a nightmare come true. *Look at my face, Paco, and tell me now how much you love me. Well, I hate you. I hate you enough to kill you.* Suddenly, her parched lips started to tremble and she began to cry like a little girl.

She was afraid. Afraid of him but also afraid of the future without him. Afraid of what he had instilled in her all these years: that she could never succeed alone. But most of all afraid of what he would do to her if she left.

Julie sank down on the marble floor, tears racking her frail body. Hugging herself tightly, she made herself a vow. *I don't know how and I don't know when, but one day, as sure as there's a God, I will make you pay for what you've done to me. I will find a way to leave you, Paco. I swear it.*

CHAPTER
48

The persistent ringing of the telephone in their apartment startled Julie back to the present. It had grown late and she had spent the whole day thinking back over her life and the years she had spent with Paco. *If only I had never met him,* she thought. *How different my life might have been.* But it was too late now to dwell on the past. If she were to act, it would have to be done quickly, before Luis arrived to take her to the airport. Picking up the phone, she heard Paco's voice. "Julie, are you almost ready? Luis will be there any minute."

"Yes, Paco. I'm ready."

"Good. I'll see you in Chicago."

She replaced the receiver and jumped off the bed. There was a fierce, new determination in her heart, and she could feel a surge of strength forging up inside of her that she hoped would give her the courage that she would need in the next few hours. In reviewing her life, a heavy veil had finally been lifted, and now Julie was able to see her mistakes. She had spent ten years with a selfish, vindictive man who had exploited her, abused her, and nearly destroyed her life. She had been blind and foolish not to have tried to leave before. Stupidly, she had allowed her parents' needs and her own weakness and dependence to chain her to a man she didn't love. Perhaps it wasn't too late. But she would have to hurry. There would be no time to take anything but her makeup case, which was already packed. Luis could walk in at any minute. Grabbing a coat, Julie slipped it over her nightgown. She had no idea where she was going or how she was going to manage. All she knew was she had to get away. Taking one final look around her bedroom, her eyes filled with tears because she knew that she would probably never see it again. Lifting her head high, she picked up her case and ran out the door. As she raced toward the elevator, she heard the door slam on her past life.

The next few weeks became a living nightmare for Julie, and sometimes, when things became too difficult, she wondered whether she had made a mistake. But when she thought back over the past, over the physical and mental abuse she had endured, she knew that she had done the right thing.

When Paco realized that she had left him and he could not obtain any information on her whereabouts, he became frantic. After completing his week-long engagement in Chicago, Paco returned to New York and hired private detectives to try and locate her. The first place he called when Luis discovered her gone was her parents' home in Phoenix. In the most cordial voice he had used in ten years, he questioned them about Julie's whereabouts.

"Sam," he pleaded. "You must know where she is. You've got to tell me. I'm going crazy trying to find her."

"Of course I know where she is, but hell could freeze over and I wouldn't tell you anything. We just thank God she's finally free of you."

Paco then tried her brother, Marshall, and even went so far as to offer him money. But Marshall hung up on him after explaining that his sister was not for sale.

When Julie fled the apartment that momentous day, she had gone to a small hotel in the East Fifties that was managed by a friend of her parents. Fortunately Neal Hopkins was in when she arrived by taxi, distraught and without any suitcases. Sensing her despair, and without asking any questions, he personally escorted her to a small suite and told her she could stay there as long as she needed. Julie was grateful to have found a temporary sanctuary, but she was concerned about finances. She did not have a lot of money in her personal checking account, and there was no way that she would be able to call the accountant to release funds from the corporation. But, at least for the time being, she was safe. She immediately called her parents, and without going into much detail, she told them what had happened and where she was staying. Her mother quickly offered to come to New York to be with her, but Julie refused.

"Mom, I appreciate it, but I'd rather you didn't. I have to sort out my life and I must do it alone."

For the first few days, Julie slept practically around the clock. It was as if her body were trying to refuel itself for what lay ahead. Finally, she realized that she would have to find a way to get some clothes from the apartment and begin to make plans. But how could she accomplish that without bumping into Luis or, even worse, Paco? Finally, Julie hit upon a plan. She would call their part-time maid, Leola, who adored Julie, and ask her to sneak some clothes and personal belongings out of the apartment when no one was there. With her help, Julie would have enough to get by with for a little while. All her evening gowns and many of her good clothes had gone on to Chicago with Paco, but she was hopeful that once their differences were resolved, he would return her all personal belongings.

The minute Paco arrived back in New York he devoted his every waking moment to finding Julie. He instructed his brother to call everyone he knew and every hotel in town. The detectives questioned personnel in the apartment building and other leads that Paco had given them. But they could not uncover any trace. With the hotel manager's cooperation, Julie had registered under a false name, and for two weeks, she managed to maintain her anonymity. But unfortunately the doorman, innocently trying to help an obviously distraught husband, remembered hearing Julie give an address to the taxi driver and passed this information on to Paco, who immediately went into action.

The days that followed became a living hell for Julie. Paco lost no time in informing the press that he and his wife had a "little spat," but that it was nothing serious and he was sure that she'd be home in a few days.

"Julie is just overtired," he told them, "and needs a rest. But, I can assure you, our marriage has never been better."

He also purposely let it be known where she was staying, and from then on, Julie never found a minute's peace. The press waited for her in the lobby, and when the manager complained that they were disturbing the guests, they found a way through the service elevator to get up to her floor, where they camped outside her suite, pleading with her to give them an interview.

Julie thought she would lose her mind. She was a prisoner again. Finally, in desperation, she called Freddie Barnett and told him of her plight. He immediately came to the hotel, and suddenly the press was gone. Julie never knew what means he used to get rid of them, but she was grateful for his intervention. Explaining that she would soon run out of money, she asked Freddie what she should do.

"First thing you must do, Julie, is to ask yourself whether your marriage is really over? If the answer is yes, then you must get a lawyer immediately."

"I guess you're right. But I don't know anyone."

"Julie, you understand that I can't get personally involved with this. Paco is still a client. But let me make some inquiries, and perhaps without compromising myself, I can get some recommendations."

When Freddie left, Julie tried her best to relax, but she was still too apprehensive. The picture that Paco had painted in the newspapers about their split bothered her. He obviously did not believe that their separation was permanent, and she was worried about what he might do.

She had every reason to worry. Paco soon began bombarding her with letters. At first, they were loving and repentant. "I'm sorry I worked you so hard," he wrote. "I promise if you come back we will take a year off and just relax."

The letters went on and on about how much he needed her and loved her and how desperately he wanted her back. But after a while his letters took on a new and much more familiar tone.

"Julie, I'm warning you. Don't do this to me. I've told you before. I can't live without you and I won't let you live without me." Julie couldn't ignore the threats. She still remembered only too vividly the beating she had suffered in Madrid when she told him she was leaving.

With Freddie's help, Julie obtained the name of a prominent attorney and she quickly made an appointment to meet with him. Slipping out a side door of the hotel, she went to his office late one evening and painfully told him the whole story. Disgusted by what he heard, he readily agreed to represent her.

The weeks that followed were filled with anguish as Julie began to learn of Paco's dishonesty and deception. When her attorney summoned Julie to his office one rainy afternoon in April, Julie knew by the expression on his face that there was trouble.

"Prepare yourself for a terrible shock. I have been reviewing the corporation's financial statements submitted by Paco's lawyers and his accountant. I'm not going to go into all the gory details, but the bottom line is—according to the corporate records, you're not entitled to any money from the corporation."

Julie sat there frozen. *There must be some mistake,* she thought. *He can't be right. I've been working like a dog for all these years and, aside from what I send my parents, all of my earnings went directly into the corporation. What has he done with it?*

Her lawyer, Paul Basinger, explained as simply as he could to the young woman seated in front of him what had happened. Paco, in collusion with their business manager and accountant, had devised schemes that would insure that Julie would be forever financially dependent on Paco. She owned nothing. Not the apartment in New York or the house in the Costa Brava. Not even her tenth wedding anniversary present from Paco—the Rolls-Royce. Everything was in the corporation's name, and Paco alone totally controlled the corporation. Furthermore, her lawyer informed her that if she wanted to get a quick divorce, she would need Paco's consent to obtain a Mexican decree. To get that consent, Julie would have to agree to forfeit everything—all rights to the furniture in their homes, all the great paintings that Paco had acquired during their marriage, even the wedding gifts they had received. Only then would Paco consider consenting to a divorce and agree to return her music and personal belongings. Furthermore, she was told, her things would have to be removed in front of Paco's brother, who had a complete inventory of everything they owned.

Julie couldn't bear for him to continue. She broke down and placed her head on his desk and cried as if her heart would break. Paul came over to her and put his hand on her shoulders, but there was nothing he could say to comfort her. *This poor girl has been royally screwed,* he thought, *and she never knew what was happening to her.*

"Julie," he said after a few minutes. "Please, look up."

With tear-stained eyes, she looked at him.

"You have your whole life ahead of you. You're only twenty-six, and you're a famous star. You can work anywhere in the world and make more money than you've ever dreamed possible. You've got to put this behind you and get on with your life. Let Paco take what he wants. Not that I won't fight those guys tooth and nail all the way. But if we're unsuccessful, then take the Mexican divorce and get rid of him once and for all. If you go to court he'll fight you for years because he doesn't want the divorce—you do."

"But I have to fight. How can I allow him to get away with what he's done to me—the money he's taken from me, the beating in Spain? It's not fair."

"Do you really want to expose yourself to the kind of publicity a court fight would bring you? Take the beating, for example. You told me no one else in the world knows about that incident. We don't have pictures of you taken at the time, or any witnesses. There isn't even a police report. He can deny everything, and remember, you did sign papers agreeing to the structure of the corporation."

"I never read the papers I signed. I trusted Paco implicitly. As far as the beating is concerned, the manager of the hotel was outside my door. *He* heard my screams."

"Julie, dear. That man is in Spain and Paco is Spanish. Furthermore, you say he never saw you. We wouldn't have a leg to stand on."

She was defeated. It was no use. Paco would have his way until the very end. Thanking her attorney, Julie told him to proceed and make arrangements for her to go to Juarez as soon as possible. She didn't want her name to be Mrs. Castell one minute longer than necessary. As she walked dejectedly back to her hotel, Julie thought, *Maybe I could win if I decided to fight him. But I don't want to prolong this any more. Let him have the damn house and apartment and everything else. I hope he rots in it. I just pray that I never ever have to see his face again as long as I live.*

Julie had serious concerns about how she was going to live for the next few weeks until she could get some bookings. There was also her parents to think about and their monthly checks. Naturally they would expect that to continue. When she reached the hotel, she immediately called Freddie. Explaining her predicament, she asked for his advice and help.

"Get your divorce as quickly as possible. If you need money, we can get you an advance on a Las Vegas engagement. The Riviera wants you to open in June as their headliner. In the meantime, as soon as you've settled your personal affairs, we want you to go to California and do the 'Jack Benny Show.' The offer just came in today."

Julie began to cry in relief. She *could* work after all. People did want to see her onstage, and without Paco. All these years he had been drilling into her mind that she would be nothing without him. Well, she would show him. The lawyer was right. She *did* have her whole life ahead of her and she was ready.

EPILOGUE

Julie was escorted to her table at Chasen's by Julius, the maître d', and as she walked through the crowded restaurant, all heads turned to watch her and, more important, to see who she was meeting. As she approached the table, Marvin Siegal, who had been eagerly awaiting her arrival, stood up to greet her.

Marvin was a highly regarded personal manager who had recently come to California for the sole purpose of convincing Julie to sign a management contract with him. When he had seen her onstage in *The Captain's Wives*, he was impressed. Recently, he had heard her sing at a charity benefit in New York. He had walked away convinced that with the proper guidance Julie's career could skyrocket. Now, he was determined to sign her.

Taking a seat, Julie ordered a glass of wine and tried to relax. She had been rehearsing all day at NBC for the next night's taping of the "Jack Benny Show," and she had left the studio quite late. Rushing back to her suite at the Beverly Hills Hotel, she had showered, changed into a black lace dress that showed off her figure beautifully, and taken a cab over to Chasen's. Now, breathing a sigh of contentment, she sipped the wine and listened intently to what Marvin was saying.

"Julie, you're drop-dead gorgeous and sexy as all get out. I'm telling you, you could have as big a film career here as you have in Europe—maybe bigger."

"I appreciate your kind words, but everything is happening too fast. I've just been divorced a week, and after this show I have to begin working on a new act for Vegas. But before I even tackle that, I must return to Italy to film a commercial that I signed to do last year."

"That's exactly what I mean. You need someone to put your life in order."

"I understand that, but right now it's hard for me to commit to anything. Paco dictated my every move for so many years, that somehow I like the idea of making my own decisions."

"Well, honey, that man you were married to almost ruined your career. You made a lot of mistakes because of him. But it's not too late to rectify that and put your career back on course."

"Marvin, just give me a little time. I want to go to Europe and do some thinking. I promise I'll make a decision by the time I return to New York."

"Wonderful," he said, patting her hand. "Now, if you'll excuse me a second, I have to make a quick call, but I'll be right back."

Julie was happy to have a moment alone. Marvin was pushing too hard for her to sign with him—she had been through too much in the past few months to allow anyone to rush her into anything. Since their acrimonious separation and subsequent divorce, Julie and Paco had been front-page news. Paco had seen to that by calling the tabloids and giving them heart-wrenching stories of how much he loved his beautiful wife and how he couldn't understand why she had left him. He portrayed himself not only as a discarded husband, dumped by an ungrateful wife whom he had made famous, but as an extremely generous man. He claimed that during the course of their marriage he had lavished his wife with homes, furs, and expensive jewels that added up to millions of dollars.

At first, Julie wept after reading the lies that were printed about her. But then, as the stories grew even more ludicrous, she began to see what a publicity-mad, ridiculous figure her soon-to-be ex-husband had become, and she had to laugh. Not to be laughed at, however, were the threats Paco continued to make, even after the divorce settlement was signed. She was also terrified of the way he'd follow her whenever she left the hotel. She had discussed it several times with her attorney and he advised Paco's lawyers that he would go to court and seek a restraining order if Paco continued to harass his client.

Despite his threats, Julie proceeded with her plans, and a few weeks later, in a dingy office in Juarez, a judge pronounced her a free woman. She had acquiesced to all of Paco's demands and she was leaving the ten-year marriage with nothing except the thing she valued most—her peace of mind.

When Marvin returned to the table he told Julie, "I hope you don't mind, but I've invited a friend of mine to join us for coffee. He's a partner at International Artists and I have to discuss something with him before I leave for New York tomorrow. He's a terrific guy who is kind of in the same boat as you. He and his wife just got divorced and she took their kid back to New York. The poor guy is just devastated. He adores that little boy."

They were still discussing her career when a tall, handsome man approached their table and extended his hand in greeting to Marvin.

"Thanks for meeting me here, Steve. I'm leaving early tomorrow morning, and I needed to speak to you about that television special we've got going."

Steve Burton could scarcely be polite to Marvin. His attention had been diverted the minute he saw Julie sitting there. She was exactly the way he had remembered her—only much more beautiful. Taking a seat next to her, he waited for Marvin to introduce them.

"Julie, I'd like you to meet Steve Burton, a great guy and one of the few agents I trust."

Julie smiled at him. "How do you do, Mr. Burton. I wonder why Marvin has such a low opinion of agents?"

"I could answer you, Miss Lauren, but I don't use that kind of language in front of ladies, especially when I'm hoping to make a good impression."

"What a line this guy has," Marvin said, laughing. "No wonder all the girls are nuts about him."

"Don't pay any attention to him, Miss Lauren. My line, as Marvin so crudely puts it, is only for women who expect flattery. Whatever I say to you tonight and in the future, I assure you, will be sincere."

Julie had found Steve wildly attractive the moment she saw him— with his green eyes and dark hair. But his manner and the way he looked at her made her heart skip a beat. For some strange reason, she believed every word he said.

Steve found it extremely difficult to concentrate on business with this beautiful and desirable woman sitting next to him. But he did need to clarify some things with Marvin before he returned to New York. For the next few minutes, Julie listened attentively as Steve outlined his plans for the television special. As soon as he had finished, he quickly turned, focusing all his attention back on Julie. "How long do you intend to remain in Los Angeles?"

"Just a few days. I tape the 'Jack Benny Show' tomorrow and the next day I thought I'd do some shopping. I haven't been to L.A. for a long time."

Just then, Marvin interrupted them. "I can see that as far as you two are concerned, I might as well be in China, but Julie, if I'm to drive you home we'll have to leave shortly. You have an early call and I have a plane to catch."

"Marvin, why don't you let me drive Miss Lauren home. It's on my way, and even if it weren't, I'd love the opportunity of telling her what a great manager you are."

"You are really one smooth character. How about it, Julie? Is that okay with you?"

"That will be fine, but on one condition. That Mr. Burton call me Julie instead of Miss Lauren."

"You have a deal," he said, mesmerized by her haunting eyes.

When they were alone, Steve turned to her and asked, "Are you terribly tired? Because if you're not, I was thinking you might want to hear some fantastic jazz at a local spot called Shelly's Manne Hole? I promise I won't get you home late."

"Actually, I'd love it. I'm not at all sleepy and I don't have to be at NBC until ten."

Steve escorted Julie out of Chasen's and when his car was brought around helped her to get in. His eyes could not help glancing at her long and incredibly shapely legs as she gracefully swung them into the car. She was not only the personification of femininity, but from what he was able to observe so far, she was unbelievably sweet and unassuming.

As they sat in the intimate club, talking and listening to the music, Julie felt as if she'd been given a present. *It's amazing how much we have in common,* she thought. *I feel so comfortable with Steve and I've only known him a few hours.*

Steve suddenly glanced at his watch and groaned. "Julie, I'm sorry.

I had no idea it was so late. I'd better get you back to the hotel right away."

Steve had totally lost track of time, for he had been fascinated listening to Julie describe bits and pieces of her life on the road and living in Europe. She hadn't spoken much about her ex-husband, but that was understandable. Steve had read about their divorce, and although he wasn't aware of the details, he could see flashes of pain in her eyes whenever she mentioned Paco's name. Wisely, he surmised that she must still be suffering. Julie was different than he had always imagined her. So real and unaffected.

After paying the check, he escorted her to his car, and as they drove back to the hotel, each was unaware that the other was wishing the same thing: that the evening was not coming to an end. Steve insisted on walking Julie to her suite. It was late, and even though he knew that the hotel was safe, there was something about her that seemed so terribly vulnerable that he felt the urge to protect her.

Reaching the door, he took her key and opened it before saying good night.

"Steve, thank you for a lovely evening. I really enjoyed talking to you, although I'm a little embarrassed that I did all the talking and I didn't give you an opportunity to tell me about yourself."

"My life is not nearly as interesting as yours, Julie. And, besides, that will give me an excuse to see you again."

Julie stood there, her eyes shimmering in the dimly lit hallway, looking as fresh and beautiful as she had early in the evening. Steve felt a sudden overwhelming urge to touch her translucent skin to see if she was real.

"Well, you haven't answered me. Do I get to see you again before you leave? Now before you answer, I must warn you. I'm a very persistent guy."

Julie looked at Steve standing there, tall and so impeccably dressed, with an impish twinkle in his incredibly kind eyes as he waited for her answer. She knew then that she wanted to see him again—soon. "I'll be at NBC all day tomorrow until we finish taping. We should be through by nine. I've been invited to a party at Jack Benny's house after the show. Perhaps you would like to join me? I don't have an escort."

"I'd love to, Julie. But I'll come by the studio earlier in the day. I have a client shooting a TV pilot there."

Julie extended her hand to say good night and Steve took it in his own and kissed it gently. She felt a wave of excitement pulsate throughout her body as his warm lips touched her hand. Steve could feel her tremble, and suddenly, reaching over, he lifted her chin and kissed her mouth.

Julie responded tentatively at first. It had been so long since any man had kissed her. She was almost afraid of her own response. But as the pressure of his mouth became more demanding, she was suddenly swept away by desire and returned his kiss with a mounting passion.

Suddenly, Steve backed away, shaken by what he was feeling. "Julie, do you have any idea of what you do to me?"

She smiled, for she was feeling the same way and she wasn't sure if she was ready for it. "I think we should say good night, Steve. It really *is* getting late. Thank you again for a wonderful night. I hope to see you tomorrow."

"You mean today. Yes, beautiful Julie. I'll be there and until I see you again, I'll be thinking of you."

Julie closed the door and leaned her head back against it. *This is silly,* she thought. *I can't be falling in love. It isn't possible. Not with the first man I meet. No, it's probably just a sexual attraction because he's so terribly good-looking and so nice to be with.* But Julie remembered the feeling of his lips on hers and his strong arms embracing her. In her heart she felt it was more than just a passing attraction, but she would have to give herself time. She was twenty-six years old, but she had never been sixteen. In many ways she was like a teenager out on a first date. *I can't let myself be swept away,* she thought. *Not yet. Not until I'm sure.*

The next day, Steve watched Julie's dress rehearsal and spent whatever free time she had with her in her dressing room. Since saying good night to her at her hotel, she had not left his thoughts, and he was confused by his emotions. During his unhappy marriage to Sharon and since his divorce, there had been many women, but none of them had been able to fill that void in his heart. Now all of a sudden, this redheaded beauty had walked into his life, complicating matters completely. Before meeting Julie, Steve had been perfectly happy to concentrate on his work and his son. Not having found the right woman, his frequent affairs were casual and brief. But he sensed that Julie would be different, and he wondered if he was ready for it. *Time will tell,* he thought as he watched her rehearse her sketch with Jack Benny. But one thing was certain. He had to see her as much as possible and really get to know her. She was special, and he didn't want to lose her.

Steve was soon at her dressing room door. "I hope I'm not rushing you, Julie, but I was anxious to tell you how great you were."

Julie was terribly pleased and proud that she had impressed him. He had never seen her perform in person before and his presence there had made her a little nervous. "I'm all ready. I'm happy you liked the show. Jack Benny was marvelous to work with. His timing is perfection, and I learned a great deal from him."

"Jack was wonderful, but you were pretty funny yourself. Fortunately you've got a great sense of humor, because you're not particularly attractive. At least you have one thing going for you."

"Funny," she shot back, "I was thinking the same thing about you last night, but I didn't want to hurt your feelings. I know how sensitive men are about their looks."

Laughing, Steve put his arm around her and said, "Okay, you win. You're not really *that* unattractive. In fact," he said, bending over to whisper in her ear, "you happen to be one of the most beautiful and desirable women I've ever seen, and if we don't leave now we'll both be in big trouble."

On their way back to Beverly Hills and the Benny house, Steve suddenly turned to her. "Julie, are you really committed to going to this party?"

"Why do you ask?"

"Because, if you think Jack wouldn't be offended, I'd just as soon not share you with a mob of people. There's a little Italian restaurant in Beverly Hills that is very quiet and secluded. We could have some pasta there while I tell you all about *my* life. What do you say?"

Julie thought for a moment and answered, "Well, I guess I wouldn't be missed that much. I know there will be lots of people there tonight, and tomorrow I *could* send the Bennys flowers with a note of apology."

Looking at Steve's handsome profile, Julie made her decision. "Let's go have pasta."

The next few hours seemed to fly as Julie and Steve sat and talked. They were amazed to find they had such similar backgrounds. They were both New Yorkers and both Jewish. They had been married only a day apart at the same hotel and had both suffered unhappy marriages. Steve didn't divulge too much about his divorce except to say how miserable he was that his son lived three thousand miles away. There was nothing, short of a court battle, that could have prevented Sharon from moving back to New York. Steve was reluctant to fight, even though their decree had clearly spelled out that she could not take their son out of the state. Steve felt that if she was that unhappy it would gradually affect their son's happiness, and he therefore reluctantly consented. Julie listened attentively as Steve described his work and his goals. They were so similar to what she wanted out of life. Naturally, he told her, he hoped to continue making strides in his career. But most of all he wanted someone to share his life with. Someone who would love him and he could love in return. Julie could sense, by the way Steve talked about his son, Michael, that he eventually wanted to have more children, and this thought warmed her heart.

Their hands touching across the table, gazing into each other's eyes, Julie and Steve forgot the world around them. Finally, when it was time to leave, they walked slowly to the car. As Steve reached down to open the door, Julie touched his arm, and when he looked up, he saw her smiling at him, as if she intended to speak. Before she could say anything, his mouth swooped down and covered hers with a fierce intensity that startled them both. Running his fingers through her hair, his tongue parted her lips to taste the sweetness of her mouth as his arms tightened around her body. Julie could feel his desire and her own. Straining their bodies together, they continued to kiss passionately until Julie, breathless, pushed him gently away.

"Steve, we mustn't. People might see us."

"Julie," he murmured into her hair. "I want you so."

"Oh, Steve. I want you, too. But not this way."

"You're right. I'm acting like a schoolboy with his first crush. But I've been dreaming about kissing you all night."

Julie smiled at him and touched his face tenderly.

"Let's go back to the hotel."

Steve drove back quickly and once again escorted Julie to her suite. But this time she asked him in. Now that they were finally alone, Steve's mouth once again sought hers in an electrifying kiss that sent shivers of delight through her body. Julie had never been kissed like this before, and she responded to it by molding her body to his. Steve traced his tongue across her lips, urging them to part. When his tongue plunged into her mouth, their kiss set him on fire and he pulled her hard against him. Tenderly, his hands traced the contours of her body. When his exploring fingers reached the zipper of her dress, he began tugging at it with an urgency that frightened Julie.

"Steve," she said, stepping away from him abruptly. "I can't do this. I'm not ready."

Steve saw the panic in her eyes and he immediately became contrite. "Julie, dearest one, I'm sorry. I didn't mean to frighten you. It's just that you're so beautiful and I want you so much. I'm afraid I got carried away."

"Oh, Steve," Julie cried, angry at herself for pulling away. "I'm the one who should be sorry. *You* didn't frighten me. I'm frightened of my own feelings. No man has ever made me feel the way you do."

He took her delicate hands in his as he tried to reassure her. "Julie, please don't be upset. This is only our first date. There is plenty of time ahead of us. You know how I feel about you and how much I want to make love to you. But I care too much to want to rush you into anything before you're ready to give yourself to me freely. You'll *know* when the time is right and I can be patient until then."

Kissing her gently on the lips, Steve bid her good night. But before closing the door, he said, "Tomorrow is your last day here. I would like to plan something special for tomorrow evening. Do we have a date?"

Julie looked at him, happiness glowing in her eyes. "Yes, Steve, we do. Thank you for being so understanding. You are very special, you know?"

"Yes," he answered, grinning. "My mother tells me that all the time."

After Steve had gone, Julie sat down at her dressing table and looked at herself in the mirror. "You silly fool," she told her image. "Why couldn't you have acted like a grown-up woman instead of a frightened baby? It's a wonder he wants to see you again."

But he *did* want to see her again, and she hoped the next time she would be capable of giving herself to him completely, without fear or reservations. Because that was what she wanted, more than anything else in the world.

Julie awakened the next morning feeling exhilarated. It had been so many years since she had felt that way, it was almost a new experience for her. The radiance on her face reflected her newfound happiness and she knew the only reason for that was Steve.

"Steve," she murmured to herself, remembering last night.

Even the sound of his name could make her body tingle with delight. *How strange and wonderful life is,* she thought. *A few months ago I didn't care whether I lived or died, and now I'm acting like a schoolgirl just waiting for the stores to open so that I can buy a new dress for tonight.* Jumping out of bed, Julie ordered her breakfast and planned her shopping spree in Beverly Hills. She would buy some clothes, have her hair done, and maybe even treat herself to a massage. Even though she was on a fairly tight budget, she decided to splurge a little. She had to look her best tonight, for it would be her last evening with Steve.

Hours later, when Steve picked her up at the hotel, she saw the admiring look in his eyes and Julie knew her efforts were not in vain.

As his black convertible pulled away from the entry, Julie sat back and watched Steve out of the corner of her eye as he drove to their destination. She loved to look at the back of his neck, where his dark hair lay smoothly against his perfectly shaped head. She wished she could run her hands through his hair and see what he looked like all messed up. He looked so meticulously groomed—perfect suit and tie— just the right subtle touch of cologne—his hair neatly combed and in place. She wondered how he'd look dressed in just a pair of jeans and a casual shirt, riding with her in an open convertible. Probably like a kid, she thought, for he was only six years older than she, and for all his outward sophistication, he still retained a boyish look.

Minutes later, Steve pulled up in front of the Beverly Hilton Hotel and helped Julie out. Steering her toward the elevator, they got in, and Steve pushed the button that would take them up to the roof and the famous Escoffier Room. While the maître d' checked their table, Julie looked around. The room was incredibly beautiful. A small orchestra was playing as they followed the captain to their table. When they sat down, Julie looked out the large picture windows that lined the room, and she could see the twinkling lights of the city. In the center of the table, there were white carnations and one single yellow rose. There was a little card hung on the rose with her name on it, and Julie picked it up and read it.

"Julie, thank you for three wonderful days. I will miss you. Steve."

Steve had a mischievous look on his face. "Julie, I don't know how those flowers got here. They must be for another table."

"Oh, and I suppose there are two other people here tonight named Julie and Steve?"

"I guess so," he said, his eyes sparkling. "What an amazing coinci-dence."

Reaching her hand across the table to touch him, Julie said, "You are so incredibly thoughtful and sweet. I'm going to miss you, too, terribly."

These last words were spoken in a voice choked with emotion. Steve held her hand tightly, not wanting to let her go. She looked so beautiful sitting there, her hair piled high on her head with soft tendrils framing her luminous face. His gaze wandered down briefly to her gleaming skin partially exposed by the deep bodice of her dress. *How I'd love to caress that skin*, he thought longingly as desire began to stir inside of him. *She is a woman just made for love, but I must wait until she's ready. I mustn't frighten her again.*

After ordering dinner, Steve asked Julie to dance, and as they approached the dance floor and the bandleader recognized Julie, the music suddenly stopped and the vocalist began to sing "The Second Time Around."

Julie looked up at Steve with deep emotion in her eyes and said, "Is that just another coincidence or did you arrange for the band to play that?"

"Julie," Steve answered teasingly. "You must think I have great pull around here. They must be playing that for that other Steve and Julie, but it *is* a lovely song and it *does* happen to apply to us."

Julie moved closer to Steve into the protective wonder of his arms. She wished that she could stay like this forever and never have this evening end.

Hours later, when they were back at Julie's suite, she reached to turn on the light, but Steve stopped her before her hand could touch the switch.

"No, Julie. Don't. I want to look at you in the moonlight."

Taking her hand, he led her to the French doors where light was filtering in through the open shutters. Cupping her face in his hands, he began to kiss her very gently at first, as if they had all the time in the world and she didn't have to make an early plane. The moonlight cast tiny shadows on her face, but he could still see those incredible eyes that were looking at him between kisses, adoringly. Slowly, meticulously, he undid the pins in her hair, which released her mane of glorious hair and made her seem even more sensual. Running his hands through its silkiness, he began to kiss her neck, slowly running his tongue up to the tip of her ear, and then turning he sought her mouth, which was now trembling with desire. Steve continued kissing her, long and hard kisses that inflamed his body so that he was afraid if he didn't stop now, he would be unable to control himself. Briefly, he thought of pulling away, but Julie was responding passionately, and when she slipped her arms around his waist, drawing herself even closer, he knew he was lost. Steve didn't realize what was happening until Julie's dress was in a heap on the floor. Stepping back, Steve drew his breath in sharply as he looked at the perfection of her body, bare except for her bra and panties. She was more exquisite than he had ever imagined, and standing there in the moonlight, she looked like a goddess, except that she was real. With a groan of passion, he reached for her and undid her bra, releasing her firm breasts from their lacy confines. Steve ripped off his jacket and shirt and pulled her to him. The feel of her nipples against his chest drove him wild, and he was afraid his body would explode with desire.

Julie kicked off her last vestige of clothing as Steve lifted her up in his arms and carried her to the bedroom. The sight of her lying there, her arms opened wide to receive him and her eyes glowing with a passion that equaled his own, drove him wild. Furiously, he tore at the rest of his clothes, and desperate to feel every inch of her flesh, he covered her body with his own. He longed to enter her and feel her wetness, but he wanted to prolong the delicious ecstasy as long as possible. Placing his hands under her rounded buttocks, he began kissing her mouth again, gradually letting his lips travel down over the incredible smoothness of her skin until they reached her rounded breasts. Julie flung her arms out as she began to writhe in passion. Steve reached out and pinned her there as his tongue circled her hardened nipples and tenderly sucked their sweetness. His tongue continued to skim the flat plane of her beautifully molded torso, and when he reached the moistness of her pubic hair, he buried his face in its curly tendrils and tasted the sweetness inside.

Julie could not bear the agony of waiting any longer and arching her body toward him, she cried out, "Steve, now. Take me now."

Steve lifted himself up and with a single thrust entered her, feeling her soft wetness envelop his body like a cocoon. Julie moaned his name over and over again as Steve continued to thrust himself deep inside of her. He had never felt such passion before and he could not get enough of her. The delicious torment of their lovemaking continued until Steve felt he could bear it no longer. As Julie shifted her position to accommodate his throbbing body, he plunged into her again and again, until, wild with desire, they exploded together, their limbs entwined, their hearts beating as one. Steve brushed Julie's damp hair back from her forehead. She looked so beautiful lying there, her face still flushed from their lovemaking. *She's more than just beautiful,* he thought as he continued to stroke her tenderly. *There is a sweetness and gentleness about her that makes me want to take care of her always and protect her.* No woman had ever been able to arouse the emotion that Steve felt about Julie. She was not just a conquest to him. He had fallen in love with her, and that realization suddenly overwhelmed him. He knew, just as surely as if he had known her for years, that this was the woman he had been searching for and had almost given up hope of finding. But did she feel the same? Her marriage to Paco had been a disaster, and she had no experience with men at all. By all rights she should spend the next six months or even a year as a free woman, perhaps even date other men. *But,* Steve thought, with a pang of jealousy, *I don't want that. I want to take her in my arms and tell her that I love her and ask her never to leave me.*

But Steve couldn't do that. It was too soon, and he couldn't rush her into making a commitment to a man she had just met, even though they were passionately drawn to each other. *I must give her time to make up her mind,* he thought. *She's leaving tomorrow and will then go back to Italy for a few weeks. I won't press her now, but I intend to see her as often as possible. If what we have is real, it will stand the test of time.*

Julie had dropped off to sleep in Steve's arms, and when she awoke, she could feel his body curled up around hers. Turning slightly so she could see him, she looked at his peaceful face as he slept.

Well, I finally know how he looks with his hair messed up. Like a little boy, she thought as a wave of tenderness engulfed her. *Oh, Steve, you've shown me what love and passion are really like. What a fool I've been to have accepted a poor substitute all those years. You've taken me to heights I never dreamed existed, but with a gentleness and caring that has shown me what kind of man you are. Now that I've found you I don't want to leave you. But I can't fling myself at you just because I've fallen in love.*

Julie remained in that position until the bedside clock told her she must awaken Steve so she could get ready for her departure. Trying desperately not to be sad, she watched him dress, knowing that in a few minutes he would be gone. When he was ready, Steve took her in his arms and held her tightly.

"Are you sure that you don't want me to drive you to the airport?"

Steve whispered against her hair. "I hate the thought of you going alone."

"No, Steve. I'll be fine. The studio is sending a car. Anyway, I'd rather say good-bye here."

"Not good-bye, darling. That sounds too final. We'll be together soon."

"Will you call me in New York?" Julie asked as she looked into his eyes for the last time.

"I think I'll find time to call the most beautiful, wonderful, sweetest girl in the world."

"Yes, I know. But will you call *me*?"

"Julie, Julie," Steve said holding her close and laughing. "You are incredible and I adore you."

Kissing her one more time, Steve left her suite, and with an aching heart, Julie returned to her packing. *Three weeks is a long time*, she thought as she closed her suitcases. *Will he still feel the same when I return?*

Julie walked into her hotel suite in New York hoping to find a message from Steve, but there was none. Her plane had been late and it was already nine P.M. *Only six o'clock in L.A.*, Julie thought. *I wonder what Steve is doing? No use starting that*, she told herself. *He has a business to run and other things to think about besides me.*

After taking a hot bath, Julie watched some television, and by eleven o'clock she found herself drifting off. She was awakened abruptly by the telephone ringing in her bedroom. Glancing at the clock, she saw that it was only six o'clock in the morning. *Who in God's name could be calling me at this hour?* she wondered.

Picking it up, she said in a sleepy voice, "Who is this?"

"My, my, what a way to greet someone who cares for you."

"Steve," Julie gasped, instantly awake. "Why are you calling so early? It's only three in the morning where you are. Is everything all right?"

"Yes, my darling Julie. I just wanted to tell you I miss you."

"Well, I miss you, too. When am I going to see you?"

"Soon, sweetheart, very soon."

"How soon is soon?"

"Don't be impatient. Just be a good girl and one day I'll just surprise you and show up. Now please, go back to sleep."

"Hm-m. I will go back to sleep and dream about you."

"That's a great idea. Just dream that I'm knocking at the door and when you let me in, well—you know the rest."

"You're bad, but I love it. Good night, darling. I mean good morning."

"Good-bye, sweetheart."

Julie pulled the covers back over her body and snuggled down into the softness of her bed. Steve's call had relieved some of her sadness and she would try to sleep another few hours. She was just about to drift off again when she heard someone knocking at the living room door. Thinking that it must be a mistake, she turned over, but the knocking became more insistent. Julie sat up and wondered who it could be at that ungodly hour. Grabbing her robe, she went to the door.

"Who's there?"

"A delivery, Miss Lauren."

"A delivery at this hour? Where is it from?"

"California, Miss."

"California?" *Maybe it's something from Steve.* Opening the door a fraction, she peeked outside and gasped with delight. "Steve. Oh, my God. What are you doing here? I just spoke to you on the phone."

"Are you going to ask me in or do I have to break down the door?"

Julie pulled open the door and flew into his arms. As he began to cover her face with kisses, she asked, "But you said on the phone that you were in California."

"No, my darling. *You* said I was in California. I was calling you from the lobby. I flew in on the red-eye this morning and came right here. Now, young lady, if you're through with all your questions, I have something else in mind for us."

"And what could that be, pray tell?" she asked as they walked arms entwined into the bedroom.

"Something I've flown three thousand miles for and I've dreamed about ever since you left."

The next few days, with Steve at her side, were the happiest days of her life. While he visited with his son, Julie kept herself busy preparing for her trip to Italy. They spent the rest of the time together, taking long walks up Madison Avenue and stopping at street corners to kiss as they waited for the light to change. Everything that Julie had seen hundreds of times before took on a new and special meaning now that she had found him. The more time Steve spent with Julie, the more he found himself falling under her spell.

Their nights together became even more rapturous than their last night in California as they found new and exciting ways to please each other. Finally, on their last night before Julie was to leave for Rome, they drove up to a country inn in Connecticut where they would dine and spend the night. After dinner, they took a walk through the beautiful gardens before returning to their suite. Even though it was June, Steve lit a fire, and wrapped in his arms, Julie watched the burning embers. Steve noticed how silent she had become and he turned to face her.

"Julie, my darling. What's wrong? You look so unhappy?"

"Oh, Steve, I don't want to leave tomorrow. I hate going away for so long. Please, tell me not to go."

He took her face in his hands and looking deep into her eyes said tenderly, "I can't tell you not to go. It isn't fair to you. I know I've kind of swept you off your feet, but I couldn't help it. I had to be with you these past few days. But darling, you have a commitment in Italy that you must honor. Besides," he said thoughtfully, "I want you to have time to think clearly, without me around to influence you. Don't look so stricken, sweetheart. I'm sure of my feelings and I want you to be sure of yours."

Julie knew that he was right, but the next few weeks were going to be hell without him.

Julie left New York the next afternoon for Rome and began work almost immediately on the commercials. As they had mutually agreed before she left, Steve did not call Julie. Irritable and anxious to finish, Julie worked long hours at the studio, returning to the Excelsior Hotel exhausted and depressed. *I should never have left him,* Julie thought one night, as she prepared herself for bed. *I didn't need time to think. I already know my feelings. I'm in love with him.*

Suddenly, the doorbell interrupted her thoughts and Julie called out, "*Avanti.*"

A bellman walked in holding a silver tray in his hand. "*Signorina,* a telegram for you."

Julie's heart started to race. Telegrams made her nervous. It was a throwback to when she was a kid. Ripping it open quickly, she scanned the message.

> *Having a wonderful wish. Time you were here. Come home quickly, my darling, and be my wife. I love you with all my heart. Steve.*

Julie clutched the telegram to her breast as tears of joy filled her eyes. "Oh, yes," she cried. "I love you, too, my darling. I'm coming home. I'm finally coming home."